Preface to the Second Edition

inues to make incisive suggestions, and that over the years her
ural charm has tempered my natural irritability. So once again, this
k is dedicated to her, to Michael, and this time to Alexander as

Jerome H. Skolnick

keley, California
uary, 1975

JUSTICE WITHOUT TRIAL:

Law Enforcement in Democratic Society

SECOND EDITION

JEROME H. SKOLNICK

University of California,
Berkeley

From the Research Program of
THE CENTER FOR THE STUDY OF LAW AND SOCIETY

John Wiley & Sons, Inc.   *New York   London   Sydney   Toronto*

11.50

For Arlene, Michael, and Alexander

Library of Congress Cataloging in Publication Data:

Skolnick, Jerome H
 Justice without trial.

 "From the research program of the Center for the
Study of Law and Society."
 Includes index.
 1. Criminal justice, Administration of—United States.
2. Police—United States. 3. Law enforcement—United States.
I. California University Center for the Study of Law and
Society. II. Title.

KF9223.S54 1975   336   74-34145
ISBN 0-471-79539-9
ISBN 0-471-79542-9 (pbk)

Printed in the United States of America

10 9 8 7 6 5 4 3 2 1

iv

con
natu
boo
well

Ber
Jan

Preface to the Second Edi

It is a pleasure to be permitted the luxury of r
work and commenting on it from the perspective
are no major changes in the original eleven chapte
anticipate themes that I continue to explore. Beside
changes would impair the integrity of a younger m;
changes I perceive in substantive areas are discuss
chapter, the Epilogue.

As I concluded this Epilogue, and the brief exerc
on which it was based, I was impressed once again
of an operating system of criminal law. The legal
envisioned as the most formally normative of all s
because it contains a codified and carefully interpre
But, in practice, it continues to be a highly discretio
level, mediated by subtle, sometimes unarticulate(
norms held by actors in the system. Consequently, t
of criminal justice in America is still best understo
phenomenon expressed in the contradiction between a
written rules, interpretations, and practices mediat(
values, perceived organizational needs, and a continui
man personalities and aspirations.

Once again, I thank the so-called "subjects" of r
people who teach me about the reality of the administr:
justice. They know who they are and they have my sin
 The Center for the Study of Law and Society at th
California at Berkeley, continues to be my intellectual
my colleagues and students there are still a source of
knowledge. For this edition, I am especially indebted to
and Mark Morris for their advice and criticism, to Da
his research assistance, and to Carol Morra for her secre
friendship. Larry Maltz did the indexing for the Epilogu
 As continuity seems to be the theme of this new Pr
add that Dr. Arlene Skolnick and I continue to reside tog

Preface to the First Edition

Criminal or related proceedings in which an individual may lose his liberty, his reputation, or his property constitute the principal indicator of the character of a society. More than that, the very idea of *process* —of a disinterested, fair, and intelligent hearing when claims of right are presented—constitutes the underlying idea of a society that subscribes to governance by rule of law. This book is a sociologist's attempt, through the use of a variety of observational techniques, to understand how such governance may be enhanced or impeded. By examining the day-to-day behavior of police and other legal actors, I have tried to learn how those who are charged with enforcing criminal law in a constitutional democracy come to interpret rules of constraint—thereby giving these life and meaning—and to analyze the practical dilemmas they face. I have tried to be as impartial and objective as possible in analyzing the structure and dynamics of police behavior, but I make no claim to having been "value-free." Indeed, the study will hopefully contribute to a growing body of literature attempting to understand, as a general matter, the social foundations of the rule of law.

It is an author's pleasure to have the opportunity of acknowledging long-held debts, and his fear that some of these will also have been forgotten. The idea for the study began when I was teaching at Yale Law School and was especially encouraged by Professor Abraham S. Goldstein. My "behavioral science" colleagues there, Professors Harold D. Lasswell and Richard D. Schwartz, were always a source of guidance and friendship.

Empirical study commenced at the Center for the Study of Law and Society, Berkeley, and the book was completed there. Philip Selznick, Chairman, and Sheldon Messinger, Vice-Chairman, created an intellectual environment for the pursuit of empirical research. They and other colleagues at the University of California were both encouraging and constructively critical. Professor Edward L. Barrett, Jr. was especially helpful, as was Law Professor Sanford Kadish at a later period. Professors Herbert Blumer, Erving Goffman, David Matza, S. M. Lipset, and Neil Smelser, Department of Sociology, made pointed and useful criticisms, as did Dr. Leonard S. Cottrell, Jr. of the Russell Sage

Foundation, and M. Phillipe Nonet, of the Center for the Study of Law and Society. J. Richard Woodworth and Forrest D. Dill were research assistants. Woodworth collected and analyzed data and wrote first drafts of the appendixes. Dill edited, proofread, constructed the index, and made numerous useful suggestions regarding the final draft.

I am very grateful to the three foundations that provided funds for relief from teaching duties and for secretarial and research assistance: the Social Science Research Council (Committee on Governmental and Legal Processes), the Russell Sage Foundation, and the Walter E. Meyer Research Institute of Law.

My greatest debt is to my "teachers"—those policemen and lawyers in the cities studied who took the time and interest to "show the ropes" to a novice. Without their cooperation, the study could not have been completed. I should also like to thank the two men who were my first teachers of criminal law, in the order that they taught me: my father, William Skolnick of the New York Bar, and Professor Richard C. Donnelly of Yale Law School. My wife, Dr. Arlene S. Skolnick, heard out my ideas, commented on rough drafts, offered intelligent criticism, assumed the anxieties of a "policeman's" wife, and tolerated my irritability. This book is dedicated to her and to our son, Michael.

Jerome H. Skolnick

Cambridge, Massachusetts
October, 1965

Contents

Chapter 1

Democratic Order and the Rule of Law

For what social purpose do police exist? What values do the police serve in a democratic society? Are the police to be principally an agency of social control, with their chief value the efficient enforcement of the prohibitive norms of substantive criminal law? Or are the police to be an institution falling under the hegemony of the legal system, with a basic commitment to the rule of law, even if this obligation may result in a reduction of social order? How does this dilemma of democratic society hamper the capacity of the police, institutionally and individually, to respond to legal standards of law enforcement?

Such questions have posed a predicament since the introduction of the London metropolitan police in 1829. Charles Reith, in his book *The Police Idea*,[1] describes the hostility of early nineteenth-century England even to the idea of developing a metropolitan police force out of fear that the notorious activities of the pre-Revolutionary French police would be duplicated. He cites a parliamentary report of 1818 which considered the police idea and recommended against the establishment of a police force:

> The police of a free country is to be found in rational and humane laws—in an effective and enlightened magistracy—and in the judicious and proper selection of those officers of justice, in whose hands, as conservators of the peace, executive duties are legally placed, but above all, in the moral habits and opinions of the people; and in proportion as these approximate towards a state of perfection, so that people may rest in security; and though their property may occasionally be invaded or their lives endangered by the hands of wicked and desperate individuals, yet the institutions of the country being sound, its laws well adjusted, and justice executed against offenders, no greater safeguard can be obtained without sacrificing all those rights which society was instituted to preserve.[2]

[1] Charles Reith, *The Police Idea: Its History and Evolution in England in the Eighteenth Century and After* (London: Oxford University Press, 1938).
[2] *Ibid.*, p. 188.

1

Reith, who is pro-police and pro-Peel, may exaggerate somewhat the degree of opposition to the police. Other authors also interpret the period as one of considerable hostility to a formal institutionalization of police. Mather, for example, points out that historians, like Whigs, are fundamentally antipolice.[3] Given such opposition, therefore, before introducing his "Bill for Improving Police in and near the Metropolis" in 1829, Peel laid a formidable groundwork. A. A. W. Ramsay describes it as follows:

Peel, with his usual caution, brooded for years over the problem before he undertook to solve it. In 1826 he began to collect evidence for the purpose of comparing crime with population. In 1828 he secured the appointment of a Parliamentary Committee to investigate the subject—the last of four successive Committees in the past twenty-five years, but the first to do valuable work. He had at first intended a measure which should create a police force throughout the kingdom: he ended with a modest scheme, whose operation was confined to London, and at first to a limited number of parishes.[4]

To buttress his argument for the necessity of a police force, Peel based his claims on the need for public order. Citing population statistics from London and Middlesex, he argued that crime was dramatically increasing in this early period of industrial revolution, and increasing at a faster rate than population. In the period of 1821 to 1828, population had increased 15½ per cent, while criminal committals had risen by 41 per cent. Deploring the existence of an army of "trained and hardened criminals" in London and Middlesex, Peel announced that "not less than one person in every three hundred and eighty-three had been convicted for some crime or other in 1828,"[5] without mentioning, although he was fully aware of the fact, that the number of acts considered criminal was so large, and the conditions of the working classes so onerous, that the figures he cited were hardly shocking.

In making this appeal for more efficient controls over crime, Peel was quick to add that he was "confident they would be able to dispense with the necessity of a military force in London for the preservation of the tranquility of the metropolis,"[6] an assurance he could hardly dispense with considering the strength of his opposition. The early conception of police accountability to the rule of law is a tradition which has contin-

---

[3] F. C. Mather, *Public Order in the Age of the Chartists* (Manchester: The University Press, 1959), p. v.

[4] A. A. W. Ramsay, *Sir Robert Peel* (New York: Dodd, Mead and Company, 1938), p. 88.

[5] *Op. cit.*, p. 250.

[6] *Ibid.*

ued to the present day. Maitland reaffirmed it in 1885 when he wrote in a book entitled *Justice and Police:*

There is a large body of rules defining crimes and the punishment of those who commit them, rights and the remedies of those who are wronged, but there is also a body of rules defining how and by whom, and when and where, rules of the former kind can be put in force. . . . It will little avail us that our law about rights and remedies, crimes and punishments, is as good as may be, if the law of civil and criminal procedure is clumsy and inefficient.[7]

This same tradition of the hegemony of the rule of law is eloquently stated in the 1962 Royal Commission Report in a refutation of the argument that a national police force would lead to the development of a "police state" in Great Britain. The commission argues:

British liberty does not depend, and never has depended, upon any particular form of police organization. It depends upon the supremacy of Parliament and on the rule of law. We do not accept that the criterion of a police state is whether a country's police force is national rather than local—if that were the test, Belgium, Denmark and Sweden should be described as police states. The proper criterion is whether the police are answerable to the law and, ultimately, to a democratically elected Parliament. It is here, in our view, that the distinction is to be found between a free and a totalitarian state. In the countries to which the term police state is applied opprobriously, police power is controlled by the government; but they are so called not because the police are nationally organized, but because the government acknowledges no accountability to a democratically elected parliament, and the citizen cannot rely on the courts to protect him. Thus in such countries the foundations upon which British liberty rests do not exist.[8]

The theory of the police in the United States mirrors the conflict between order and legality found in English conceptions of the police, but characteristically American features add complexity. In reading about the American police, especially through the period of the 1930s, one feels that constitutional issues of legality have been almost too remote to be of immediate concern. Not that American police conformed to the rule of law. Rather, they seemed so far out of line that a writer summarizing a major American study of police practices entitled his book *Our Lawless Police.* The study, completed in 1931 by the National Committee of Law Observance and Enforcement (the Wickersham Commission), found practices so appalling and sadistic as to pose no intellectual issue

---

[7] F. W. Maitland, *Justice and Police* (London: Macmillan and Company, 1885), pp. 1–2.

[8] Royal Commission on the Police Cmnd. 1728. (London: Her Majesty's Stationary Office, 1962), p. 45.

for civilized men.[9] It is one thing to talk quietly to a suspect without his counsel and artfully, perhaps by deceit, persuade him to incriminate himself; it is quite another to hang a suspect out of a window by his heels from a great height, or to beat a con'fession out of him by putting a telephone book on his head and pounding the book with a blackjack so it does not leave marks. Both techniques may be illegal, but responsible police officials would not publicly support blackjack interrogation. On the other hand, interrogation of suspects without the presence of counsel and even deceptive interrogation are standard "professional" police techniques.[10]

For many municipal police forces in the United States, the observer's question is, therefore, not whether police operate under the constraints of due process of law, but whether they operate within bounds of civilized conduct. In the old-fashioned police department, riddled with political appointees and working hand in hand with the rackets, a reformer is not concerned primarily with the niceties of constitutional rights. When the citizenry is facing the arbitrary use of "club, blackjack, and gun," [11] the police reformer's problem is to reduce gross brutality, which seems traditionally to have been associated with corruption. Given this situation, it is not surprising that the solution to the "police problem" in America has been frequently conceived as changing the quality of people, rather than the philosophies of policing. Fosdick wrote in 1920, in a characteristically American passage on police reform:

We are concerned with facts and conditions and not with theories or labels. It is not a matter of democracy, of caste, or birth, or position, or anything else. It is solely a matter of finding the best possible brains to handle a most difficult public task.[12]

Police reform means finding a new source of police, and police control is a matter of having the "right" sort of people in control. "Reform" of police means increasing the efficiency of police personnel. It is rarely recog-

[9] National Commission on Law Observance and Enforcement (Washington, D.C.: U.S. Government Printing Office, 1930–1931), Publications, No. 1–14.

[10] See Fred E. Inbau and John E. Reid, *Criminal Interrogation and Confessions* (Baltimore: The Williams and Wilkins Company, 1962), pp. 20–115; Charles E. O'Hara, *Fundamentals of Criminal Investigation* (Springfield, Illinois: Charles C Thomas, 1956), pp. 95–114; and Worth R. Kidd, *Police Interrogation* (New York: R. V. Basuino, 1940), pp. 124–125, pp. 133–186.

[11] For a summarization of the Wickersham Commission Report, see Ernest Jerome Hopkins, *Our Lawless Police* (New York: The Viking Press, 1931), index reference to "National Commission on Law Observance and Enforcement."

[12] Raymond Fosdick, *American Police Systems* (New York: The Century Company, 1920), p. 221. (Fosdick's italics.)

nized that the conduct of police may be related in a fundamental way to the character and goals of the institution itself—the duties police are called upon to perform, associated with the assumptions of the system of legal justice—and that it may not be men who are good or bad, so much as the premises and design of the system in which they find themselves. For example, V. A. Leonard, a specialist in police administration, indicates how the conception of punishment as the basis of order invites objectionable side effects:

A system of legal justice based upon the thesis of punishment has exerted a tremendously negative effect on the professionalization of police service. As a corollary the low quality of personnel required to exercise the police power under these conditions was not conducive to good public relations, with the result that a negative public opinion had been created. The withdrawal of public interest and support, together with public apathy and indifference, has further served to retard the advance toward professionalization. No less important has been the fact that a substandard personnel became easy prey for corrupt political figures and others in the community who profit when the risks associated with vice operations are reduced. The highly lucrative enterprises of prostitution, gambling, and narcotics enjoyed a field day during this period of American police history.[13]

Leonard, however, does not raise the basic issue of the meaning of the "professionalization of police service." Clearly such a notion suggests that police must be honest and capable. But is this enough? The question is what the concept of "professionalization" suggests to police in a society committed to the rule of law.

With the concern for reform of police practices in America, a growing and responsible debate over the theory of the police in America may be anticipated. There are those police officials and other spokesmen for law enforcement who emphasize the importance of social order. They are not unconcerned about the arbitrary use of police authority, but feel that that answer lies in the continued improvement of internal police administration. By raising the standards for admission to the police force and by making efficiency a goal and personal honesty a requisite, the quality of police work will be raised and police work will become akin to a "science." [14]

At the same time, there has always been a considerable body of opin-

---

[13] V. A. Leonard, *Police Organization and Management* (Brooklyn: The Foundation Press, 1951), p. 6.

[14] Cf. William H. Parker, *Parker on Police*, ed. O. W. Wilson (Springfield, Illinois: Charles C Thomas, 1957); O. W. Wilson, *Police Planning* (Springfield, Illinois: Charles C Thomas, 1962); also see two police journals, *The Police Chief* (pub. Chicago) and *Police* (pub. Springfield, Illinois).

ion, usually outside police circles—among defense attorneys, law professors, and judges—demanding that police adhere strictly to the rules governing the legal system, that they ultimately be accountable to the legal order irrespective of their "practical" needs as law enforcement officials. This position was summarized in the landmark case of *Escobedo* v. *Illinois*,[15] the United States Supreme Court overturning a conviction when the police refused to honor the request of a suspect to have a lawyer present at his interrogation. Justice Goldberg, for the majority, wrote:

We have . . . learned the . . . lesson of history that no system of criminal justice can, or should, survive if it comes to depend for its continued effectiveness on the citizens' abdication through unawareness of their constitutional rights. No system worth preserving should have to *fear* that if an accused is permitted to consult with a lawyer, he will become aware of, and exercise, these rights. If the exercise of constitutional rights will thwart the effectiveness of a system of law enforcement, then there is something very wrong with that system.[16]

The purpose of this study is to show, through empirical investigation of police, how value conflicts of democratic society create conditions undermining the capacity of police to respond to the rule of law. Its chief conclusion (and orienting hypothesis), elaborated in the closing chapter, may be summarized: *The police in democratic society are required to maintain order and to do so under the rule of law. As functionaries charged with maintaining order, they are part of the bureaucracy. The ideology of democratic bureaucracy emphasizes initiative rather than disciplined adherence to rules and regulations. By contrast, the rule of law emphasizes the rights of individual citizens and constraints upon the initiative of legal officials. This tension between the operational consequences of ideas of order, efficiency, and initiative, on the one hand, and legality, on the other, consititutes the principle problem of police as a democratic legal organization.* The work attempts to analyze, through empirical investigation of police, how conceptions associated with order and interpretations regarding legality develop within a professionalized police department, and to study the processes through which these conceptions and interpretations come to be associated with certain patterns and practices of policing.

LAW AND ORDER: THE SOURCE OF THE DILEMMA

If the police could maintain order without regard to legality, their short-run difficulties would be considerably diminished. However, they

---

[15] 378 U.S. 478 (1964).
[16] 378 U.S. 478, 490.

are inevitably concerned with interpreting legality because of their use of *law* as an instrument of order. The criminal law contains a set of rules for the maintenance of social order. This arsenal comprises the *substantive* part of the criminal law, that is, the elements of crime, the principles under which the accused is to be held accountable for alleged crime, the principles justifying the enactment of specific prohibitions, and the crimes themselves. Sociologists usually concentrate here, asking how well this control system operates, analyzing the conditions under which it achieves intended goals, and the circumstances rendering it least efficient.[17]

Another part of the criminal law, however, regulates the conduct of state officials charged with processing citizens who are suspected, accused, or found guilty of crime.[18] Involved here are such matters as the law of search, the law of arrest, the elements and degree of proof, the right to counsel, the nature of a lawful accusation of crime, and the fairness of trial. The procedures of the criminal law, therefore, stress protection of individual liberties *within* a system of social order.[19]

This dichotomy suggests that the common juxtaposition of "law and order" is an oversimplification. Law is not merely an instrument of order, but may frequently be its adversary.[20] There are communities that appear disorderly to some (such as bohemian communities valuing

[17] See, for example: Harry Elmer Barnes and Negley K. Teeters, *New Horizons in Criminology* (New York: Prentice-Hall, 1951); Sheldon Glueck, *Crime and Correction: Selected Papers* (Cambridge: Addison-Wesley Press, 1952); Richard R. Korn and Lloyd W. McCorkle, *Criminology and Penology* (New York: Holt, 1959); Norval Morris, *The Habitual Criminal* (Cambridge: Harvard University Press, 1951); Joseph Slabey Roucek, *Sociology of Crime* (New York: Philosophical Library, 1961); Walter Cade Reckless, *The Crime Problem* (New York: Appleton-Century-Crofts, 1961); and Edwin Hardin Sutherland and Donald R. Cressey, *Principles of Criminology*, 6th ed. (Philadelphia: Lippincott, 1960).

One exception is the text of Paul W. Tappan, which emphasizes criminal procedure in great detail. Tappan, it should be noted, however, was also trained as a lawyer. See *Crime, Justice and Correction* (New York: McGraw-Hill, 1960).

[18] Thus, a current leading casebook in criminal law devotes its final sections to problems in the administration of criminal law. See Monrad G. Paulsen and Sanford H. Kadish, *Criminal Law and Its Processes* (Boston: Little, Brown and Company, 1962).

[19] See Sol Rubin, Henry Wiehofen, George Edwards, and Simon Rosenzweig, *The Law of Criminal Correction* (St. Paul: West Publishing Co., 1963); Paul W. Tappan, *op. cit.*; and Lester B. Orfield, *Criminal Procedure from Arrest to Appeal* (New York: New York University Press, 1947). An excellent discussion of problems of criminal procedure is found in Abraham S. Goldstein, "The State and the Accused: Balance of Advantage in Criminal Procedure," *Yale Law Journal*, **69** (June, 1960), 1149–1199.

[20] See Alan Barth, *Law Enforcement Versus the Law* (New York: Collier Books, 1963).

diversity), but which nevertheless maintain a substantial degree of legality. The contrary may also be found: a situation where order is well maintained, but where the policy and practice of legality is not evident. The totalitarian social system, whether in a nation or an institution, is a situation of order without rule of law. Such a situation is probably best illustrated by martial rule, where military authority may claim and exercise the power of amnesty and detention without warrant. If, in addition, the writ of habeas corpus, the right to inquire into these acts, is suspended, as it typically is under martial rule, the executive can exercise arbitrary powers.[21] Such a system of social control is efficient, but does not conform to generally held notions about the "rule of law." [22]

Although there is no precise definition of the rule of law, or its synonym, the principle of legality, its essential element is the reduction of arbitrariness by officials—for example, constraints on the activities of the police—and of arbitrariness in positive law by the application of "rational principles of civic order." [23] A statement expressive of the rule of law is found in a report on police arrests for "investigations." The authors, who are lawyers, write, "Anglo-American law has a tradition of antipathy to the imprisonment of a citizen at the will of executive officers." [24] A more explicit definition of the rule of law in the administration of criminal law has been presented as follows:

> The principle of *nulla poena sine lege* imposes formidable restraints upon the definition of criminal conduct. Standards of conduct must meet stringent tests of specificity and clarity, may act only prospectively, and must be strictly construed in favor of the accused. Further, the definition of criminal conduct has largely come to be regarded as a legislative function, thereby precluding the judiciary from devising new crimes. The public-mischief doctrine and the sometimes over-generalized "ends" of criminal conspiracy are usually regarded as anomalous departures from this main stream. The cognate principle of procedural regularity and fairness, in short, due process of law, commands that the legal standard be applied to the individual with scrupulous fairness in order to minimize the chances of convicting the innocent, protect against abuse of official power, and generate an atmosphere of impartial justice. As a consequence, a complex network of procedural requirements embodied variously in constitutional, statutory, or judge-made law is imposed upon the criminal adjudicatory process—public trial, unbiased

---

[21] See Charles Fairman, *The Law of Martial Rule* (Chicago: Callaghan and Company, 1943), especially Chapter 3, "The Nature of Martial Rule," pp. 28–49.

[22] See Notes 23, 24, and 33, *infra*.

[23] Philip Selznick, "Sociology and Natural Law," *Natural Law Forum*, 6 (1961), 95.

[24] *Report and Recommendations of the Commissioners' Committee on Police Arrests for Investigation* (District of Columbia, July, 1962), 42.

tribunal, legal representation, open hearing, confrontation, and related con-
comitants of procedural justice.[25]

Thus, when law is used as the instrument of social order, it necessarily
poses a dilemma. The phrase "law and order" is misleading because it
draws attention away from the substantial incompatibilities existing between the two ideas. Order under law suggests procedures different from
achievement of "social control" through threat of coercion and summary judgment. Order under law is concerned not merely with the
achievement of regularized social activity but with the means used to
come by peaceable behavior, certainly with procedure, but also with
positive law. It would surely be a violation of the rule of law for a legislature to make epilepsy a crime, even though a public "seizure" typically
disturbs order in the community. While most law enforcement officials
regard drug addicts as menacing to the community, a law making it a
crime to *be* an addict has been declared unconstitutional.[26] This example, purposely selected from substantive criminal law, indicates that
conceptions of legality apply here as well as in the more traditional
realm of criminal procedure. In short, "law" and "order" are frequently
found to be in opposition, because law implies rational restraint upon
the rules and procedures utilized to achieve order. Order under law,
therefore, subordinates the ideal of conformity to the ideal of legality.

CONCEPTIONS AND APPLICATIONS:
THE DILEMMA COMPLICATED

The actual requirement of maintaining social order under the principle of legality places an unceasing burden upon the police as a social institution. Indeed, the police is *the* institution best exemplifying the
strain between the two ideas. The 1962 Royal Commission on the Police states the law enforcement dilemma as follows:

[25] Sanford H. Kadish, "Legal Norm and Discretion in the Police and Sentencing
Processes," *Harvard Law Review*, **75** (1962), 904–905.
[26] *United States* v. *Robinson*, 361 U.S. 220 (1959). Lon Fuller criticizes the
grounds of the decision. The court held in this case that the statute violated the
Eighth Amendment by imposing a "cruel and unusual punishment" for an "illness."
Professor Fuller argues that the statute should have been overturned on grounds that
it is both *ex post facto* and vague in *The Morality of Law* (New Haven: Yale University Press, 1964), pp. 105–106. My own position is in between, since I do not
conceive of an addict as one who necessarily had the intent of becoming one when
he began using drugs. Therefore, I find the *ex post facto* objection less than compelling. On whatever grounds, however, the case stands as a good example of positive
law in violation of the rule of law.

The police systems in England, Scotland and Wales are the products of a series of compromises between conflicting principles or ideas. Consequently, in contrast to other public services such as health and education, the rationale of the police service does not rest upon any single and definite concept of the public good. Thus, it is to the public good that the police should be strong and effective in preserving law and order and preventing crime; but is equally to the public good that police power should be controlled and confined so as not to interfere arbitrarily with personal freedom. The result is compromise. The police should be powerful but not oppressive; they should be efficient but not officious; they should form an impartial force in the body politic, and yet be subject to a degree of control by persons who are not required to be impartial and who are themselves liable to police supervision.[27]

The law enforcement dilemma, however, is more complex than suggested by the Royal Commission. Not only are the police in a democracy the product of a series of compromises between conflicting principles or ideas, but the ideas themselves are not as clear as they (and we) have so far suggested. If "law and order" is a misleading cliché, then a gross conception of order may be even more misleading. Depending on the institution or community, there may be quite different conceptions of order, some more permissive, others less. A traditional martial conception of order, for example, abhors individual differences. The soldier whose bearing or uniform sets him off from his comrades in arms is an abomination to his commanding officer. Even the slightest deviation, such as wearing gloves on a cold day, is forbidden as an expression of differences in individual feelings. In any given military unit, either all the soldiers wear gloves, or none do. The hands of some soldiers will perspire, others will be numb with cold, but all soldiers *will* act alike.

Other institutions or portions of society are traditionally more yielding. The area surrounding the University of Paris is noted for its emphasis upon individuality. Students, artists, writers may be dressed elegantly or poorly, raffishly or provocatively, the mode being considered an extension of the ego, an expression of personality, or perhaps merely an attempt to experiment with novelty. The idea of order in this setting is surely a more permissive conception than the standard military notion. Our conclusion is that conceptions of order seem to be variable and tend to correspond to the requirements of different communities or institutions.

Conceptions of order also seem to be associated with conceptions of appropriate modes of achieving it. The response of a soldier needs to be quick and unquestioning, since failure to respond instantaneously may result in severe damage to himself and to his comrades-in-arms. The so-

---

[27] Royal Commision on the Police, *op. cit.*, p. 9.

cialization of the soldier therefore emphasizes unquestioning *obedience*. A trained soldier is a man who responds unthinkingly to command, and the norm of command is *sharp* command. Failure to respond is met with punishment, seemingly severe to those who receive it. Its justification, however, is located not in the precipitating act itself, but in the implications of nonobedience for the combat situation. The basic trainee whose inspected boot has been found to have a relatively low gloss may lose a weekend's liberty not because a less than sparkling boot is intrinsically important, but because it presumably signifies future sloth.

By contrast, an institution expressive of liberal and humanistic values, such as a university, will usually emphasize persuasion through reason as the instrument for the achievement of order. Since its institutional goal is scholarship, it is traditionally tolerant of behavioral and attitudinal variations, stressing contemplation and dialogue over obedience to rules, and persuasion rather than force as the instrument of an order predicated upon diversity. University police, for example, are far more permissive than local urban police forces. Later on, some of the reasons for such a difference are discussed, notably the relative absence of danger within the university community. Here it is enough to state as an hypothesis of the study that varying social conditions—the nature of the criminal law, the presence of danger in the community, the political complexion of the community, the social dissimilarity of the population being policed —all contribute to the conception of order held by the police.

The organizational model of the police also influences their conception of order. To the degree that police are organized on a military model, there is also likely to be generated a martial conception of order. Internal regulations based on martial principles suggest external cognitions based on similar principles. The presence of an explicit hierarchy, with an associated chain of command and a strong sense of obedience, is therefore likely to induce an attachment to social uniformity and routine and a somewhat rigid conception of order. Such a conception of order is probably increasingly at variance with segments of the community where police, perceiving themselves as "workers" who should exercise initiative, are coming to be concentrated. As this process occurs, police are more likely to lean toward the arbitrary invocation of authority to achieve what they perceive to be the aims of substantive criminal law. Along with these effects is an elevation of crime control to a position where it is valued more than the principle of accountability to the rule of law.

Aiding this process is ambiguity about the application of the rule of law. In the abstract, the rule of law embodies rational restraints upon authority as it defines criminal conduct. There must be specificity, clarity, prospectivity, and strict construction in favor of the accused. There must be procedural regularity and fairness, and so forth. In practice, however, such standards may not be clear. The principle of procedural regularity and fairness commanding that the legal standards be applied so as to "minimize the chances of convicting the innocent, protect against the abuse of official power, and generate an atmosphere of impartial justice" [28] is, for example, subject to varying interpretation by the police and the courts. One year illegally seized evidence may be admitted into evidence under a legal system subscribing to the rule of law, and the next year it may not. A confession may be admitted into evidence at one time whether or not the suspect was informed of his right to counsel; at a slightly later time such a confession is found to violate constitutional protections. Thus, although certain fundamental and relatively changeless principles of the rule of law are specifiable, the practical constraints on official conduct derived from these principles are always in a degree of flux. A legal order is never a fixed body of rules, but, as Fuller suggests, an "enterprise" of governance by rule.

It may also be suggested, as some of the following materials will show, that whenever rules of constraint are ambiguous, they strengthen the very conduct they are intended to restrain. Thus the policeman already committed to a conception of law as an instrument of order rather than as an end in itself is likely to utilize the ambiguity of the rules of restraint as a justification for testing or even violating them. By such a process, the practical ambiguity of the rule of law may serve to undermine its salience as a value. In sum, the actual enterprise of maintaining order by rule of law serves to complicate the conflict of these principles inherent in a democratic society.

THE SECLUSION OF ADMINISTRATION: THE DILEMMA'S SETTING

Perhaps if the administration of criminal law conformed to its popular image, study of the police would be less important. Popularly, even though the police are an object of much romanticized attention, the trial is perceived as the *culmination* of the process of administering criminal law.[29] Trials are dramatic spectacles, and folklore surrounding prominent criminal trial attorneys has had a profound impact on the

---

[28] Kadish, *op. cit.*

[29] Thus, a television program called "Arrest and Trial" implied by its title that the latter inevitably follows upon the former. The tendency to make the implication is understandable.

general public. In fact, the typical method of conviction is by the accused's plea of guilty, with no trial required. In the federal courts, the guilty plea receives the heaviest use, 86 per cent in the fiscal years 1960 through 1963, while in the state courts, the use of the plea trails by 5 to 10 per cent.[30] (The county under study in this report was about average, with 82 per cent of convictions obtained by plea of guilty in 1961.) Mostly, therefore, the system of administering criminal justice in the United States is a system of justice *without* trial.[31]

The plea of guilty is often seen by criminal law personnel as a means of coping with the problem of limited court facilities. In partial justification for a heavier sentence on the one of five defendants who refused to plead guilty, a federal judge opined: ". . . if in one year, 248 judges are to deal with 35,517 defendants, the district courts must encourage pleas of guilty. One way to encourage pleas of guilty is to establish or announce a policy that, in the ordinary case, leniency will not be granted to a defendant who stands trial." [32] Not only is the plea of guilty recognized as playing an integral role in the criminal process, it is also evident that the necessity for frequent invocation of the plea is a key institutional factor in shaping the position of the defendant vis-à-vis the State.

The statistical pattern of guilty pleas and the reasons for this pattern are interesting themselves, but not so interesting as their implication that routine decision-making in the administration of criminal justice is hidden from public view. When a plea of guilty is entered, encounters between prosecutor and defense attorney, defense attorney and client, prosecutor and policeman, policeman and suspect, are never brought to public attention, and in the nature of the situation cannot be. The case is often "tried" in an informal setting, perhaps over a cup of coffee or in the corridor behind the courtroom.

[30] United States, Administrative Office of United States Courts, Annual Report of the Director, 1963, p. 132.

[31] Some important work on the plea of guilty has been conducted by Donald J. Newman. See his "Pleading Guilty for Considerations: A Study of Bargain Justice," in Norman Johnston, Leonard Savitz, and Marvin E. Wolfgang (eds.), *The Sociology of Punishment and Correction* (New York: John Wiley and Sons, Inc., 1962), pp. 24–32; and his *The Decision as to Guilt or Innocence* (Chicago: American Bar Foundation, 1962). An able review of the subject is to be found in a paper prepared by Dominick R. Vetri, "Note: Guilty Plea Bargaining: Compromises by Prosecutors to Secure Guilty Pleas," *University of Pennsylvania Law Review*, 112 (April, 1964), 865–895. Also, some interesting materials on the guilty plea are to be found in Arnold S. Trebach, *The Rationing of Justice: Constitutional Rights and the Criminal Process* (New Brunswick: Rutgers University Press, 1964).

[32] *United States* v. *Wiley*, 184 F. Supp. 679 (N.D. Ill., 1960). See also, Vetri, *ibid.*

The frequency and seclusion of the plea of guilty raise far-reaching questions in legal theory: (1) To the extent that courts seek to control the behavior of police in such areas as searches and seizures, eavesdropping, and confessions, does the frequent invocation of the plea of guilty serve to shield from public view the patterned occurrence of violations of criminal law by police? (2) At every other level of the system are there systematic practices which rarely or never come to light because the guilty plea "covers up" whatever took place before it occurred? (3) What factors influence agreement to a plea of guilty, and what is the relationship of these factors to what would be countenanced in the formal system of appellate decisions? (4) Finally, how does heavy dependence on the plea of guilty affect the accomplishment of the goals of the legal system? [33]

Police work constitutes the most secluded part of an already secluded system and therefore offers the greatest opportunity for arbitrary behavior. As invokers of the criminal law, the police frequently act in practice as its chief interpreter. Thus, they are necessarily called upon to test the limits of their legal authority. In so doing, they also define the operative legality of the system of administering criminal law. That is, if the criminal law is especially salient to a population which has more or less recurrent interactions with the police, it is the police who define the system of order to this population. This work of interpretation, this "notice-giving" function of police, is a crucial consideration in assessing the degree to which legality penetrates a system of criminal justice.

Whenever a system of justice takes on an *insular* character, a question is raised as to the degree of *justice* such a system is capable of generating. Lon L. Fuller, a legal philosopher, has suggested the broadest significance of the seclusion of criminal law administration when he discusses the affinity between legality and justice. He asserts that both share a common quality, since they act by known rule. Fuller discusses the significance of public scrutiny as follows:

The internal morality of the law demands that there be rules, that they be made known, and that they be observed in practice by those charged with their administration. These demands may seem ethically neutral so far as the external aims of law are concerned. Yet, just as law is a precondition for good law, so acting by known rule is a precondition for any meaningful appraisal of the justice of law. "A lawless unlimited power" expressing itself

[33] Donald J. Newman points out that the effect of informal conviction methods ("bargain justice") on selection for probation is to make placement on probation dependent on the skill of the defendant or his lawyer rather than on factors thought to have relevance for rehabilitation through probationary treatment. See his "Pleading Guilty for Considerations. . . ," *op. cit.*

solely in unpredictable and patternless interventions in human affairs could be said to be unjust only in the sense that it does not act by known rule. *It would be hard to call it unjust in any more specific sense until one discovered what hidden principle, if any, guided its interventions.* It is the virtue of a legal order conscientiously constructed and administered that it exposes to public scrutiny the rules by which it acts.[34]

The system of justice without trial is not a system of "unpredictable and patternless interventions." Rather, it is one which operates against a background of known rules, but which also, especially in the instance of the police, develops a set of informal norms or "hidden principles" in response to the formal rules. These, in turn, are influential in determining how the formal rules actually operate.

LAW AS AN ENTERPRISE

That law is an enterprise summons us to its empirical study. It reminds us that highly general propositions about law may be either circular or premature. Consider the following propositions: the economic structure of the society affects law; the power structure affects law; public opinion affects law; the Protestant ethic affects law; and so on. All such statements are but a beginning, as is a statement that law is "integrative," or that law affects the economy. Whether law is seen as an independent or dependent variable, the important work is the specification of those processes intervening between the two. Thus, from the perspective of law as an enterprise, what needs to be specified is how economy affects law, politics affects law, and the kind of legal order enhancing types of social integration. The development of a sociology of law depends upon detailed analysis of the social foundations of legality and of empirical elaborations of processes through which relations among variables result in determinate outcomes.[35]

[34] Fuller, *op. cit.*, pp. 157–158. (Italics added.)

[35] Although the subjects of this research are primarily policemen, and police mirror the conflict between legality and order, the theoretical concern is with the phenomenon of law and its enforcement, rather than with the police as an occupational category. It is, therefore, to be interpreted as a study in the sociology of law, rather than as one concerned with issues found in the sociology of work. The fundamental concern of the sociology of work is with the division of labor in society and how the nature and conditions of work affect society and are affected by it. The sociologist of work is, for example, interested in such issues as the sources of recruitment into an occupation, the conditions under which occupations rise and fall or achieve a status in society and how working conditions influence men's feelings regarding the meaningfulness of labor. These important concerns may be more or less related to the issues of the sociology of law. In studying law enforcement, for example, the question of

It may be instructive to draw an analogy to the sociology of bureaucracy, where scholars have taken a similar view. They have not tried to spell out the "functions" of bureaucracy in society, but rather have concentrated on case studies investigating problems associated with certain forms of organized cooperation. Neither have they primarily attempted to be managerial experts who would improve the efficiency of this system. They have been concerned, to be sure, with the effects of different forms of organized cooperation on the satisfactions of human existence; but as scholars, they have sought first of all to understand the conditions under which these forms result in varying outcomes. Their approach has been to consider what Crozier has termed "the bureaucratic phenomenon." [36]

Crozier sees this as the indispensable "exploratory" phase of scientific development, a phase which elaborates the problem by the generation of descriptive hypotheses. Such hypotheses serve only as examples, to be sure, and are valid only for the case at hand. Crozier adds, however, that, limited as such examples may seem initially, they are capable of yielding more information about the functioning of social systems of the same order, and even of larger systems, than studies insisting upon a "premature rigor." He concludes:

> To resolve upon a clinical approach may seem regressive after certain earlier ambitions of the social sciences. However, this seems to us indispensable for all those problems which touch upon the sociology of institutions and the sociology of action. There are no shortcuts possible. General statistical relations, which can be perceived at the opinion level, are fragmentary and undifferentiated; they can testify to accomplished changes, but not to the process of change, nor to the laws of action, nor even to the general direction of the evolution. Only models of functioning at an operational level can help us progress. This is what a clinical approach can offer us.[37]

Crozier's examination of French bureaucracy also indicated to him that understanding the dynamics of bureaucracy is not possible unless its operation is examined within the setting of a culture. Although there are similarities, under close empirical examination the dynamics of bureaucracy in France and in Germany are distinguishable. Crozier asserts that the "study of the bureaucratic phenomenon permits a new break-

---

the social status of police work is significant to the extent that it affects the policeman's working manner. Analysis of the latter is the distinctive concern of the legal sociologist.

[36] Michel Crozier, *The Bureaucratic Phenomenon* (Chicago: University of Chicago Press, 1964).

[37] *Ibid.*, pp. 4–5.

through at this more 'operational' level." [38] Similarly, Blau found that certain features of the bureaucratic model were not equally applicable in different cultures. He argues that in the Germany of Max Weber strict hierarchical control may have constituted the most efficient method of management, but that in an American culture valuing social equality "permitting junior officials considerable discretion in discharging their responsibilities may be a more efficient system of administration." [39] Such findings, and others as well,[40] suggest that the operation of social organizations always reflects cultural, political, social, and economic contexts. The important task is to *specify* the role of culture and ideology in determining the conduct of men and their social organizations.

LAW ENFORCEMENT IN DEMOCRATIC SOCIETY

The police in this study are considered as a class of authorities facing the problem of managing divergent expectations of conduct. Democracy's ideological conflict between the norms governing the work of maintaining order and the principle of accountability to the rule of law provides the justification for various demands upon the policeman. He may be expected to be rule enforcer, father, friend, social servant, moralist, streetfighter, marksman, and officer of the law. The problem of organizing and defining such demands furnishes the basis for the institutional analysis of police. The problem itself suggests the situational difficulties affecting the policeman's capacity to be a responsible law enforcement official who enforces order under the rule of law.

The dilemma of the police is further complicated. It is possible in practice for applications of the rule of law as well as conceptions of order to vary. Standards for applying the rule of law are developed by the courts in the setting of specific police practices. Standards governing search and seizure practices, for example, are usually developed in narcotics cases, while standards of the legality of procedures for obtaining confessions typically arise in cases where there is an element of assault. Similarly, conceptions of order are subject to varying interpretations and

[38] *Ibid.*, p. 8.
[39] Peter Blau, *The Dynamics of Bureaucracy* (Chicago: University of Chicago Press, 1955), pp. 202–203.
[40] Reinhard Bendix, *Work and Authority in Industry* (New York: Harper and Row, 1963); Burton R. Clark, *The Open Door College* (New York: McGraw-Hill, 1960); Alvin Gouldner, *Patterns of Industrial Bureaucracy* (Glencoe, Ill.: The Free Press, 1954); and Philip Selznick, *TVA and the Grass Roots* (Berkeley: University of California Press, 1949).

tend to influence and be influenced by conditions prevailing in police work. General statements about the police conception of order and its sources can be made (as attempted in Chapter 3), but it is also possible to show how the generalized conception is modified by the perceived requirements of various police assignments. When the informer system is discussed, for example, it becomes clear that the meaning of criminal conduct is differently evaluated depending on how the perceived criminality fits in with procedures characteristically used to enforce specific categories of the law.

The division of labor within the police department (burglary, vice control, traffic control, patrol) supplies a methodological framework for observing and comparing the assumptions and outcomes of police practices in democratic society. Policing specialties generate distinctive patterns for the invocation and enforcement of the law of crimes: who first sees a criminal act, how it is reported, how apprehension takes place. In gathering participant-observational data, then, the division of police labor set the background for the working hypothesis of the study: *the characteristic pattern of enforcement, with its special arrangements for gathering information, processing offenders, and evaluating the competence of personnel, all under rule of law, determines operational law enforcement.* The idea of operational law enforcement should suggest both the attitudes and behavior of policemen responding to judicial rulings, and interpersonal relations with the accused, the prosecutor, defense attorney, judge, and whenever applicable, with the general public.

Underlying this working question is a more general and fundamental issue growing out of the concept of law enforcement. This issue is the meaning and purpose of law in democratic society. The idea of law enforcement in such a society, taken seriously, suggests that legally constituted institutions such as the police exist not only to preserve order, but to serve the rule of law as an end in itself. On the other hand, the circumstances of the occupational environment, with its associated requirements that the police maintain order, might develop a very different conception of law in police, a conception without articulation or explicit philosophical justification, but existing nevertheless. Such a conception might perceive law not primarily as an instrument for guaranteeing individual freedom, but, as in the Soviet Union, an instrument of education, as a father is a teacher of children. Harold Berman describes the paternalistic character of Soviet legality and its consequences as follows:

Soviet law cannot be understood unless it is recognized that the whole Soviet society is itself conceived to be a single great family, a gigantic school, a church, a labor union, a business enterprise. The state stands at its head, as the parent, the teacher, the priest, the chairman, the director. As the state, it acts officially through the legal system, but its purpose in so acting is to make its citizens into obedient children, good students, ardent believers, hard workers, successful managers.

This, indeed, is the essential characteristic of the law of a total state.

We have seen that legal consequences follow from this conception of the role of law. Court procedure is informal and speedy; the judge protects the litigants against the consequences of their ignorance, and clarifies to them the nature of their rights and duties; there is elaborate pre-trial procedure directed toward uncovering the whole history of the situation. The rule: "Let the punishment fit the crime" is supplemented (though not supplanted) by the rule: "Let the punishment fit the man." [41]

The conception of law as a teacher is closely connected with the idea that law is primarily an instrument for achieving social order. Thus, the Soviet regime (and the Chinese Communist as well) adopted a secret police almost immediately on coming into existence. The Soviet secret police, the Cheka, was given broad powers, although it was not until 1924 that even a document was published explaining its existence and purposes. Under this statutory authorization, the main task of the secret police was to act as the investigative and punitive arm of the dictatorship, hunting out and liquidiating "counterrevoluntionary . . . attempts and actions throughout Russia, no matter what their origin." [42] The Cheka was answerable only to the top leadership of the Party and government, although experience was to demonstrate that whatever actions the Cheka considered necessary to defend the dictatorship (of the proletariat), including arrest, imprisonment, and even execution, would be approved by the Party leadership, notwithstanding any formal or legal limitations on its power.

As a system based upon law as the instrument for imposing a "necessary" social order, the Cheka became the object of wide-ranging criticism, not only among its opponents, but within the ranks of the Party itself. Its own *Weekly* acknowledged these complaints, noting that "reports are coming in from all sides that not only unworthy but outright criminal individuals are trying to penetrate the . . . Chekas." [43] But in reply to such criticisms, Lenin defended the secret police on grounds that the arbitrary use of authority was permissible in the cause of achieving a society ordered on proletarian principles. He said to a

[41] Harold J. Berman, *Justice in the U.S.S.R.* (New York: Random House, 1963), p. 366.

[42] *Pravda*, Dec. 18, 1927, p. 2, quoted in Simon Wolin and Robert M. Slusser (eds.), *The Soviet Secret Police* (New York: Frederick A. Praeger, 1957), p. 4.

[43] *Yezhenedel'nik* [Cheka Weekly], No. 2, September 29, 1918, p. 11, quoted in Wolin and Slusser (eds.), *op. cit.*, p. 6.

conference of Cheka representatives in November, 1918 that despite the presence of "strange elements" in its ranks, the Cheka was "putting into practice the dictatorship of the proletariat, and in this respect its role is invaluable; there is no other path to the freeing of the masses than the suppression of the exploiters by force. The Cheka is engaged in this, and in this consists its service to the proletariat." [44]

The meaning of law in a society is ultimately dependent upon its political and social philosophy. When law is viewed primarily as an instrument of education or as an instrument of order, rather than as a goal in itself, the society no longer conceives of punishment as a last resort, to be used only reluctantly. Lipson describes Soviet law as the instrument of state morality as follows:

> Coercion to virtue is esteemed not only for virtue's sake but also as a means of reducing the incidence of lawbreaking. The number of violations of public order is swollen by the difficulties of the society and by the broadly inclusive notion of what *amounts* to a violation. The more precarious the equilibrium of the state, the greater the perceived danger of subversion; the narrower the line, the harder it is not to deviate from it. Even short of disorder, subversion, and deviation, the failure to do one's part in raising the wealth of the state is an offence against the presuppositions of the leaders and thus against the laws of the realm. If *homo oeconomicus* is not yet respectable enough to be allowed on the stage, let his lines be given to *homo juridicus*: Soviet morality permits the government to threaten pain in order to push the citizen to many acts to which it cannot yet pull him by hope of reward.[45]

It is not only that the law of a total state has as its essential condition that the society conceive of itself as a single great family. Single great families where the question of values is open to discussion are imaginable. There needs to be also a conception of the inevitability of events, a sense of place in the interpretation of the grand sweep of history, a logical connection, and, ultimately, a belief in the righteousness of killing for the sake of logic. This sort of certainty as to what is right, and the willingness to adopt the most extreme punitive measures in defense of it, is the essence of the conception of law in a total state. Father knows all in such a family, and he may, if he thinks it necessary, rule by the rod. This conception of law necessarily contemplates minimal restraint on authority.

By contrast, a democratic society envisions constraint upon those who are granted the right to invoke the processes of punishment in the name

[44] V. I. Lenin, *Sochineniya* [Works] (Moscow-Leningrad, 1926–1932, 2nd ed.), **23**, pp. 273–274, quoted in Wolin and Slusser (eds.), *op. cit.*, p. 6.

[45] Leon Lipson, "Host and Pests: The Fight against Parasites," *Problems of Communism*, **14**, 2 (March–April, 1965), 72–73.

of the law. They must draw their rules clearly, state them prospectively. The rules themselves must be rational, not whimsically constructed, and carried out with procedural regularity and fairness. Most important of all, rule is from below, not above. Authorities are servants of the people, not a "vanguard" of elites instructing the masses. The overriding value is consent of the governed. From it derives the principle of the accountability of authority, accountability primarily to courts of law and ultimately to a democratically constituted legislature based upon universal suffrage.

It is interesting that while Lenin justified the excesses of the Cheka on ideological grounds, namely, that they were necessary to establish the sort of social order envisioned by the conception of the dictatorship of the proletariat, a more sociological analysis of the excesses was made by a high-ranking Chekist, Martin Latsis, who saw the occupational environment as creating the conditions for Chekist brutality. Latsis asserted that "work in the Cheka, conducted in an atmosphere of physical coercion, attracts corrupt and outright criminal elements which, profiting from their position as Cheka agents, blackmail and extort, filling their own pockets. . . . However honest a man is, however crystal-clear his heart, work in the Cheka, which is carried on with almost unlimited rights and under conditions greatly affecting the nervous system, begins to tell. Few escape the effect of the conditions under which they work." [46]

The Soviet secret police may be taken as an example of law enforcement which, while having administrative accountability, is without serious dilemmas regarding the rule of law.[47] The philosophy of the society does not see legality as an end in itself but as the instrument for the achievement of a political order in which law will ultimately disappear. The theory is that "legal rules will undergo a qualitative transformation into non-juridical moral standards. This in turn will lead to a concomitant expansion of the sphere of behavioral norms and habits identified . . . as 'rules of socialist community life.'" [48] What happens during the period of transformation is, however, open to some question.

[46] M. Ya. Latsis, *Chrezvychainye komissii po bor'be s kontrrevolyutsiyei* [The Extraordinary Commissions for Combating Counterrevolution] (Moscow, 1921), p. 11, quoted in Wolin and Slusser (eds.), *op. cit.*, p. 6.

[47] In the United States, by contrast, the Federal Bureau of Investigation, corresponding roughly to the Cheka as a "national" law enforcement agency, is greatly concerned about responsibilities to obey the rule of law. Most restrictions on police have originated on the federal level, and the states usually have had to be brought into conformity with the more stringent constraints upon authority imposed upon federal law enforcement bodies.

[48] Albert Boiter, "Comradely Justice: How Durable Is It?" *Problems of Communism*, 14, 2 (March–April, 1965), 90.

Latsis' observation that unconstrained authority corrupts suggests one consequence. His conclusion is by no means new, but a sociologist wishes for the opportunity to study the process by which even the honest and well-meaning policeman in a totalitarian society may become corrupted. From the point of view of the social scientist, not only the outcome is important, but also the analytic exploration among variables in the system accounting for the outcome. The nature of a totalitarian society, however, precludes such investigation.

One of the virtues of a society with democratic values is the obligation police themselves may feel for self-analysis and improvement, including even a willingness to have themselves examined on the job by a potentially critical professor. In return, they are entitled to factual accuracy and tenable interpretation in the description and analysis of their work. The emphasis upon the work of police should in this study not be understood as an investigation such as the police themselves might conduct. The purpose is not to reveal that the police violate rules and regulations. That much is assumed. The interest here is analytic description, the understanding of conditions under which rules may be violated with greater or lesser intensity. There is an emphasis on the "action perspective" (elaborated in the next chapter) and on the meaning of his work to the policeman himself, especially as it is derived from and reflects back upon societal ideas regarding worker autonomy, the need for order, and the rule of law. Such an emphasis should provide the basis for conclusions on how the working environment of police influences *law* enforcement, that is, the capacity of police to respond and contribute to the rule of law as a master ideal of governance. Such conclusions should hopefully contribute to the development of a theory of law enforcement in democratic society, and to the role of police within such a system.

Chapter 2

The Setting, Method, and Development of the Research

THE purpose of this chapter is to answer standard methodological questions: the nature of the community being studied, the character of the police department, the time of the study, and the methods used to obtain information. Special emphasis is given to the developmental aspect of the research, in effect, to discussing the question of how a study initially considered as exploratory grows into a variety of research interests and assignments.

One way of presenting a methodological background is to present only results, suggesting, perhaps unintentionally, that topics were worked out systematically beforehand; but it is neither true nor fair to the method used here to suggest a greater degree of initial order than actually existed. A reader who finds this sort of report tiresome may prefer to skip the chapter, especially the section on phases of data collection and those following. On the other hand, the reader interested in questions of how relations with police and others in the criminal law community are developed; of the nature of participant observation in such a setting; of ethical problems in this research stance, should find these sections of the chapter interesting.

THE SETTING OF THE STUDY

Data for this book were drawn from a study of criminal law officials conducted by the author mainly in Westville, a city of approximately four hundred thousand with a nonwhite population of about 30 per cent. For the sake of broad comparison, two weeks were also spent in Eastville, a city of comparable size, nonwhite population, industry, and commerce. I also visited police departments and rode patrol in two other cities. In addition, federal, state, and local law enforcement personnel were interviewed at several lengthy conferences. All this, however, was background material to put Westville in perspective. In the main, therefore, this is a study of the administration of criminal justice in one middle-sized city.

How representative of the United States is Westville and its administration of criminal justice? There are fifty-one separate jurisdictions in the United States, each with a body of statutory and case law, although some, modeled on the Federal Rules of Criminal Procedure, are more alike than others. In addition, there are practical differences in the administration of justice from county to county and city to city in any state, and among federal districts. Furthermore, in assessing the representativeness of a specific jurisdiction, it is difficult to single out with assurance which criteria are most relevant to determining the legal character of a community. Since we do not presently have a theory of the administration of criminal justice, we cannot say whether such variables as community size, rural-urban character, regional characteristics, degree of industrialization, racial and ethnic composition, political links of court and legislature, or history of corruption are to be equally or differentially evaluated. Lacking such a theory, we are in no position to assert which of these "test" variables it is important to control. To point out the difficulty of estimating the representative quality of a criminal courts community, is not the same, however, as to suggest that comparability is not desirable. To be able to draw inferences about the etiology of distinctive patterns, several case studies along the lines of the one that follows would be preferable. Given limited time and resources it was not possible, however, to complete even two intensive case studies.

Theory or no, it may be assumed that the social, economic, and historic facts of the city studied, the general outlines of the environment, are relevant to the operation of the machinery of justice. Such factual background is found in Appendix A. Factual background about the police department is in Appendix B. In addition to these fundamentals, there are several outstanding characteristics of Westville and its administration of criminal law that are important enough to bring to immediate attention.

First, Westville is a "real" city. It is neither a college town where the role of a researcher might be limited by his connection with the university, nor a megalopolis like New York or London that dominates the surrounding country. In New Haven, for instance (where I lived for almost ten years), social research is inevitably affected by the history of town-gown relations. Professional relations with the New Haven police department tend to have a special edge of delicacy, since the university and public institutions in general are interested in improving relations with one another. By contrast, the University of California is not located in Westville, there has consequently been no prolonged history of animosity, and the university is not a major political force in the community. It was realized, of course, that I was a "college professor," but nobody seemed to care which college it was.

Along with being a "real" city, Westville is reputed to have an exemplary machinery for administering criminal justice. The prosecutor's office, the police department, and the office of the public defender are generally of as high quality in facilities, pay, and national renown as those of any middle-sized city in the United States. The city jail is bright and clean. Courtrooms are modern, well-lighted, and air-conditioned. The police are housed in a modern building and are technically well equipped. In testimony before an advisory committee to the U. S. Commission on Civil Rights (1963), the head of the Westville NAACP, while stressing the continuing need for communication and understanding, said, in response to a question concerning rapport between the police department and the NAACP:

> I have the feeling that as a total police organization the Westville Police Department is head and shoulders above any other law enforcement agency in the region. This is not to say that they are perfect, or that they have even begun to approach their responsibility. They have within their Department many individuals who make . . . oppressive actions. But, at the same time, they are also enjoying an influx of new personnel . . . and the people within the Department are taking more of a professional attitude toward their responsibilities to the community.

The salutary reputation of Westville's criminal justice machinery extends throughout the United States and even abroad. During my visit to Eastville, several high-ranking officials of the police department there expressed strong interest in coming to Westville to learn its operating procedures. Consequently, since Westville is generally regarded as a model of efficiency and modernity, its administration of criminal law cannot be claimed to be representative of the United States as a whole. On the contrary, it would be more accurate to consider it as an example of the top stratum of American criminal justice administration.

THE ACTION PERSPECTIVE

To conduct research with any group whose norms and values may not conform with those of the observer, the latter must empathize with the situation of his subjects. In trying to do this, I took William F. Whyte as a model participant-observer.[1] At the time Whyte made his observa-

---

[1] See the Appendix, "Evolution of Street Corner Society," in William Foote Whyte, *Street Corner Society: The Social Structure of An Italian Slum* (Chicago:

tions, his subjects would probably have been considered young hoodlums by the tenets of conventional morality. Whyte did not, however, *judge* his subjects, but rather observed them with the intent of understanding the bases of their behavior. As a result, the corner boy emerges as a complex human being. He appears as an actor responding to a culture in conflict at points with a conventional morality that permits certain kinds of people to be exploited and others to be treated with considerable tenderness and concern. Most importantly, the corner boy is seen by Whyte as a human being trying to work out a life for himself.

Similarly, in studying the policeman the sociologist must not, if he is to develop scientifically useful hypotheses, merely emphasize the extent police behavior varies from legal ideals. Those who are of a liberal or left persuasion may find it easier to identify with the "underdog" than with constituted authority, especially the police. A participant-observer, however, must genuinely be prepared to see the world through the eyes of his subjects. Such a position does not undermine scientific objectivity, unless science is limited to the narrowest sort of positivism. On the contrary, scientific knowledge should be enhanced, provided the participant-observer is neither captured nor repelled by his subjects.

In making this investigation, therefore, I took a cue partly from sociology and partly from legal philosophy. From sociology I borrowed the "action perspective," the idea that the investigator can best perceive the meaning of events through the eyes of the participant. From legal philosophy, I borrowed Fuller's conception of law as an enterprise, a way, not always certain, of trying to reach ideals. Law is not only problematic in that its contours are vague; it is also problem-solving. It is a mechanism through which human beings, officials of varying morality and competence, struggle to solve exceedingly grave and complex problems and to balance such fundamental and conflicting ideals as order and liberty.

The legal world of rules may deceive the fresh observer into an erroneous tendency to overestimate their regularity and to consider the operation of laws as "mechanical" since they are written and need not be inferred. In reality, however, the rules of a legal order are always problematic, since the occasions for and outcomes of invoking them

University of Chicago Press, 1964), pp. 279–358; cf. also Howard S. Becker, "Problems of Inference and Proof in Participant Observation," *American Sociological Review*, **23** (1958), 652–660; and Morris S. Schwartz and Charlotte Green Schwartz, "Problems in Participant Observation," *American Journal of Sociology*, **60** (1955), 343–353.

vary. The legal philosopher H. L. A. Hart has eloquently expressed an underlying assumption used in observing the actors in this study when he speaks, in a somewhat different context, of "the open texture of law." Hart says:

> It is a feature of the human predicament . . . that we labour under two connected handicaps whenever we seek to regulate, unambiguously and in advance, some sphere of conduct by means of general standards to be used without further official direction on particular occasions. The first handicap is our relative ignorance of fact: the second is our relative indeterminancy of aim. If the world in which we live were characterized only by a finite number of features, and these together with all the modes in which they could combine were known to us, then provision could be made in advance for every possibility. We could make rules, the application of which to particular cases never called for a further choice. Everything could be known, and for everything, since it could be known, something could be done and specified in advance by rule. This would be a world fit for "mechanical" jurisprudence.

"Plainly," adds Hart, "this world is not our world." [2]

Once having observed men in a legal setting, an opposing tendency may arise. When it becomes clear that laws are not nearly so certain as was assumed, and that organizational and situational requirements often affect the actor's interpretation of laws, the sociologist may tend to forget about the rules and to interpret behavior almost purely as a response to other situational factors. The proper interpretative path here is tricky but always exciting to traverse: to see rules as a context for the behavior of legal men. As Alexander M. Bickel has stated, we are governed not by laws but by *men* who make laws:

> A government of laws simply means that no capricious commands are issued; that rules which are laid down to govern conduct are of general application; that no one man or one institution has power unchecked by anyone else; and that the lawmakers sometimes surrender immediately desired objectives for the sake of conforming to a superior norm of principle, which is itself, of course, also man-made.[3]

A study of law in action, whether of judges, lawyers, or policemen, is a study of men interpreting and thereby transforming principles and associated rules within legal institutions. Above all, it is a study of men at work. The action perspective is intended to reveal the meaning of the work to the men performing it.

[2] H. L. A. Hart, *The Concept of Law* (Oxford: Oxford University Press, 1961), p. 125.

[3] *The New Republic*, **151** (October 10, 1964), 9.

THE ADVANTAGE OF AN OVERVIEW

Although this book is specifically about police, it is also about other officials, the defense attorney, the prosecutor, the judge, the probation officer, because they too are woven into the system of justice without trial. A methodological conclusion of the present work is that the sociologist gains a more adequate understanding of the police by examining the work of these other officials in the system. For example, to estimate the extent of illegal police activities of various kinds, police reports alone cannot be relied on. All police have enemies, and the natural enemies of the policeman are the defense attorney and his client. Indeed, an important reason for studying a criminal law *community* is that each segment tends to be more critical of the others than of itself. From a methodological point of view it does not matter whether such criticism is justified. What matters is that natural antagonisms provide leads for investigation; more important, the absence of criticism suggests the investigator may take seriously assertions of innocence of the segment being studied. Thus, if police say there is no bookmaking or numbers racket in a city, and this assertion is confirmed by conversations over a period of several years with defense attorneys, clients, police, and court reporters, as well as random citizens in the community (who are critical of the police in other respects), it may be confidently inferred that a large-scale gambling racket does not exist. This is the basis for the conclusion that Westville does not presently have organized graft.[4]

It is, incidentally, not very difficult (as Lincoln Steffens demonstrated) to find out whether police take graft in a city. If the researcher approaches police as someone who, in effect, has worked in another police department, he finds that they, like defendants who "cop out" thinking interrogators know more than they often successfully pretend to know, will reveal themselves. There is, however, *little* revelation actually involved. In Eastville, for example, graft is routine. The police realize that a social researcher or reporter (as contrasted with a *legal* investigator who wants names and dates and places) can easily learn about the general pattern. Awareness of petty graft and corruption is necessarily widespread. If there is bookmaking, at least everybody (and his brother) who bets on horse races knows the bookmaker exists. Similarly, if numbers are being sold, knowledge of this must also be widely distributed.

---

[4] The reasons for absence are complex and deserve a study in themselves. It may be noted in passing, however, that the proximity of Nevada to California draws off much gambling money. Westvillers who might otherwise bet with a bookmaker are attracted to spend their weekends at the neon glitterings of Reno and Las Vagas.

So long as the policeman trusts the reseacher to protect his anonymity, the policeman has little to fear.

Even more important than the tactical advantage of being able to verify claims of participants is the overview an observer gains by having a form of access to the system unavailable to each of the individual participants. Under these conditions, the investigator may participate in events closed to interested actors whom he has been observing in the course of their work. For example, the "dealing out" of cases against prostitutes may take place in the chambers of a judge from which the police are excluded because their conduct is at issue in the bargaining. The researcher's presence in the judge's chambers may be of great advantage for observing how the work of the police comes to be evaluated by other actors in the system of justice without trial.

A broad overview, with access to different parties, cannot but help to aid an observer in making sociological interpretations of informal processes as well as those legally prescribed within the system. A participant-observer constantly finds himself involved in the business of interpreting the meaning of the behavior of the actors whom he is observing, and, as a corollary, the meaning the events they are engaged in present to them. Indeed, success as a sociological investigator may be measured primarily according to how well this is done, since the meaning of legal action is hardly obvious.

For example, the preliminary hearing before a magistrate is ordinarily considered as that point in the criminal procedural process at which the State must show to the satisfaction of a magistrate that there is sufficient evidence against the accused to warrant his standing trial for the crime with which he is being charged. Prosecutors and defense attorneys who were observed and interviewed during the course of preliminary hearings all felt that in *most* cases the real purpose of having a preliminary hearing, which the defendant may waive, was *not* to convince a judge there was sufficient evidence against the accused to warrant that he stand trial. That question has usually been settled to the satisfaction of both parties by the time the preliminary hearing is conducted. The prosecutor tends to find the preliminary hearing useful as an opportunity to observe how well the key State's witnesses hold up under cross-examination. On the other side, the defense attorney frequently uses the preliminary hearing as a "fishing expedition." When a defense attorney uses this expression, he suggests that in part the preliminary hearing allows him to seek actual flaws in the testimony of the State's witnesses. It also enables him to search for any statement by the witness under oath, in hope that it will later be contradicted by the same witness during the trial, thereby impeaching the validity of the witness's trial testimony.

In addition, the preliminary hearing may be used as a device by which the defense attorney controls a client reluctant to enter a guilty plea. Since a good part of the prosecutor's case may be revealed at the preliminary hearing, this step in the legal process, ostensibly designed to enable a magistrate to reach a decision, also serves as a mechanism through which the State can communicate its case to the accused. An actual demonstration of strength compels the defendant to face the reality of his legal situation, which may have been misread and misinterpreted to him by "jailhouse lawyers," and aids the defense attorney in controlling his client's agreement to plead guilty. Thus, to place this event in an "intelligible and more inclusive context of meaning," the sociological interpreter is advantaged by observing both sides of the adversarial structure.

DEVELOPMENT OF DATA COLLECTION

The study began early in the summer of 1962. I saw my task at that time as familiarizing myself with the city, the county, and especially the organization of its criminal courts community. Appendix C deals with this subject in detail. Let it be noted here as an introduction that there are two superior courts at the county level, where felony cases are tried, and that 61 per cent of all felony arrests in 1962 arose out of Westville. The public defender of La Loma County handled about 61 per cent of the 1,893 felony cases in the county. There are also 7 municipal courts which hold preliminary hearings and try misdemeanors. The "hard core" of the criminal courts community in La Loma County consists of about 40 district attorneys of varying rank, some 15 attorneys in the public defender's office, approximately 20 to 25 private defense attorneys of whom no more than 6 make a living primarily from the practice of criminal law, and 15 judges. Thus, in a county of almost one million population, the criminal courts community is very much a face-to-face one. Everybody soon knows everybody else, and most can draw upon a history of mutual relationships to estimate the merit of opinions and contentions.

It is not only size but the need for repeated interaction which makes this a face-to-face community.[5] Most of the time, a practicing attorney

[5] Indeed, during the course of this study, a "Criminal Courts Association" was formed, on grounds that all parties concerned with the administration of criminal law should have a common meeting group. Although the charter members are lawyers, their feeling is that they tend to have more in common with others in the criminal courts community, such as probation officers, than with, for example, corporation lawyers. Probation officers are not permitted to become members but are asked to attend specific meetings.

does not do the same kind of work that a scholar does. He has a case on his hands, and his job is to dispose of it as expeditiously as possible. Since most of his cases are settled without trial, the quality of his "contacts" will to a marked degree determine his behavior and his success as an attorney. For a practicing criminal lawyer, "knowing the ropes" often reduces to knowing people; and since interactions are necessarily frequent, he comes to know many people in a relatively short time. For instance, I found that after several months of participating in the Westville criminal courts community, I knew more people there than in my own department at the University of California; and certainly I knew people in the criminal courts community better than colleagues in such related fields as political science, law, history, anthropology, economics, and psychology. This statement may say something about the impersonality of the University of California, but I believe it reveals more about the difference in occupations. Scholarship is essentially a lonely calling. When scholars talk with one another, it is usually a social matter or results from assignment to a committee. The work of criminal lawyering, by contrast, demands repeated working contacts with others in the criminal courts community. To carry the academic analogy through, the work of criminal lawyering is like repeated assignment to an *ad hoc* committee judging the merits of an issue. The difference is that in the criminal law community, one issue is predictably repetitive: the guilt of a citizen accused of crime.

The study commenced with observation of the work of the public defender in the fall of 1962. Phases of his work which were observed included: initial interviewing of the defendant; his classification as a particular category of offender; processing of the case through several stages of criminal procedure, such as arraignment, preliminary hearing, and so forth; re-evaluation of the relative strength of the defendant's case and the prosecution's on the basis of information related to these stages; communication to the defendant as to what his case is "worth" and advice as to what charge he should plead to; the defendant's reaction; the working out of a "deal" with the prosecutor; and relations between public defender and defendant, probation officer, judge, and prosecutor after the plea has been entered. Approximately two hundred hours were spent in the office of the public defender.

After several months of such observations, I felt that I had not adequately experienced the law enforcement side of the criminal courts system. It became evident that interactions between the defense attorney and the accused, as individuals, were necessarily more infrequent than those between defense attorney and prosecutor. Thus, an appropriate vision of the system of processing of criminal cases places the prosecutor and the defense attorney at the top as spokesmen and interpreters for the real adversaries who are, on the one hand, the complainant, and on the other, the accused. Given this conception, it seemed necessary to see the system of criminal law processing from the law enforcement side.

By this time, I was fairly well known to several of the deputy district attorneys who had met me while I was looking over the shoulders of men on the public defender's staff. I suggested to the head of the public defender's office that I would like to see how "the other half" lived. Through his recommendation, plus an extended interview with the district attorney, I was permitted to become a participant-observer in that office. After several weeks of observation in the office of the Westville district attorney, it seemed important to know more about the work of the police. It turned out, for instance, that policemen were often complainants, as in traffic or narcotics cases, and that even when they were not, they often represented the actual complainant. Thus, if A claimed that B had stolen his watch, a detective, after interrogating B, would talk over the case with a deputy district attorney to decide with what offense B should be charged. It became apparent that the quality of the relations between policeman and suspect influenced the working relations between policeman and prosecutor. With this in mind, I asked my "contacts" in the prosecutor's office if it would be possible to arrange observation of the police carrying out their duties.

The Chief of Police was willing to entertain the idea. It is again important to emphasize that this police department regarded itself as exemplary. It had, about a decade earlier, been a tainted police department, but it was now sure of its honesty and efficiency. The Chief was known as a man who ran a taut ship. Not beloved by either his men or the community, he was generally respected as hard-working, intelligent, and honest, although perhaps a bit cold, aloof, and sensitive to direct criticism. His attitude toward the research was made up partly of cooperation and partly of the defiance of a sensitively placed public official who feels he has done a commendable job and can say, "Go ahead and look at anything you want. Not only do we have nothing to hide in this department, but we are desirous of having our story told. We don't want a whitewash, but we do want you to be objective and truthful." On these terms my observations of the Westville Police Department began.

The Chief assigned his aide, Lieutenant Doyle, to make introductions within the department. The Lieutenant was a genial man who had been on the force for almost twenty years, knew everybody, and was personally liked, as I later learned, throughout the department. We decided that the best place to begin the study was with the patrol division which, in Westville, has one-man vehicles and three ranks: supervising detective, sergeant, and patrolman.

I spent eight nights with these patrolmen, mostly on weekends, on the shift running from 7 P.M. to 3 A.M. All of this time was spent interviewing and observing, talking about the life of the policeman, and the work of the policeman. I understood my job was to gain some insight and understanding of the way the policeman views the world. I found that the most informative method was not to ask predetermined questions, but rather to question actions the policeman had just taken or failed to take, about events or objects just encountered, such as certain categories of people or places of the city.

I soon learned, however, that patrol work is minimally connected with legal processing. To be sure, some street behavior is relevant to the policeman's role as a legal actor. On the street, the policeman has the greatest potential for discretionary judgment not to invoke the criminal law, a decision of major legal consequence for those involved. Nevertheless, I thought that the typical activities of a patrolman were not those of a *law* officer, but rather those of a *peace* officer. This distinction, I later discovered, had already been made separately by Michael Banton [6] and Arthur Stinchcombe.[7] Thus, Banton states:

> A division is becoming apparent between specialist departments within police forces (detectives, traffic officers, vice and fraud squads, etc.) and the ordinary patrolmen. The former are "law officers" whose contacts with the public tend to be of a punitive or inquisitory character, whereas the patrolmen . . . are principally "peace officers" operating within the moral consensus of the community. Whereas the former have occasion to speak chiefly to offenders or to persons who can supply information about an offense, the patrolmen interact with all sorts of people and more of their contacts center upon assisting citizens than upon offenses.[8]

Such a distinction is, of course, preliminary to the notion of an "enforcement pattern" based upon specific police assignment.

With the realization that law enforcement is not to be found in its most significant and interesting forms on the streets, I again consulted with Lieutenant Doyle (who was most helpful and considerate throughout the study). I felt that I ought to begin to study detective work, es-

---

[6] Michael Banton, *The Policeman in the Community* (London: Tavistock Publications, 1964).

[7] Arthur L. Stinchcombe, "Institutions of Privacy in the Determination of Police Administrative Practices," *American Journal of Sociology*, 69 (September, 1963), 150–160.

[8] Banton, *op. cit.*, p. 7.

pecially the work of the vice squad, but I also felt that I wanted to learn more about the policeman's use of legal authority in mundane and routine matters. Lieutenant Doyle suggested observation of the traffic division, and also suggested spending a week or so with the traffic warrant police. As it turned out, this was a useful idea, because it gave me the opportunity, as is described in one of the chapters, to observe policemen under conditions where they have wide discretion.

In line with the more general perspective of law as a problematic phenomenon, I kept in mind that observations should shed light on the policeman as a legal actor. The study of how the work of the policeman affects his family life is a reasonable subject for a sociologist of the family. The policeman's family life, however, should be studied by the legal sociologist only if there is theoretical reason to suspect a strong relation between it and his work as an officer of the law. Family life would seem to affect only shadings of work behavior, not fundamental patterns. Thus, the most important consideration here was the projected level of generalization. I was not, in this study, concerned with *individual* differences among policemen, but rather with the issue of how working conditions associated with varying enforcement specialties give rise to distinctive attitudes and behaviors of police obliged to carry these out.

With such a perspective in mind, and having already had some background in the police department, I decided to attempt to study that portion of it which seemed to me central to an understanding of the police as legal men, and perhaps also the most difficult to study: the working of the vice control squad. From the viewpoint of the sociology of law, my interest in the vice control squad was motivated by several factors.

First, the vice control squad, as a matter of observation, was in closest contact with the district attorney's office. Partly this could be attributed to exceptionally good personal relations between the head of the narcotics squad and the head of the Westville prosecutor's office. It was also dependent, however, upon a feature of vice control enforcement discussed at some length in the text: that in vice control the policeman is typically the sole legal complainant.

Associated with this was an impression, gained from working in the prosecutor's office, that vice control officers seemed in closer contact than other detectives with some of the defense attorneys. Their position as sole complainant seemed to give them a special status as an interested party in the defendant's fate. It was therefore in the interest of the defense attorney to deal with them directly in negotiating a plea of guilty.

In addition, there were some notions about the relations between substantive criminal law and criminal procedure I wished to explore. The underlying idea was that the enforcement of vice laws, especially narcotics laws, created situations inviting policemen to violate search-and-seizure restrictions; and that, as a result, the enforcement of narcotics laws had the unanticipated consequence of calling judicial attention to the behavior of the policeman, thereby restricting his future area of working discretion. But I certainly had no more than a vague idea of how this process actually worked, especially of the differing conditions under which such a generalization might be more or less true. This, then, was the perspective with which investigation of the vice control squad was begun.

Observations were usually made on weekend nights, when most activity occurred. I also spent time during the day with vice control men, especially in court-related duties, but on investigative work as well. It is difficult to state precisely how much time actually was spent with the vice control squad. Some of the most illuminating observations were made observing vice-control police in interaction with the district attorney (at which time I was primarily observing the work of the district attorney) or in interaction with other detectives while the latter provided the base for observation.

I spent six weeks, however, directly observing the vice control squad. In addition, four weeks were spent with the burglary squad and two with robbery and homicide to compare the detective's work where there is typically a citizen complainant. Weeks of intensive observation were spaced over a period of fifteen months, during which time I would drop in at least one or two afternoons a week to keep up acquaintances. I also spent one month in the summer of 1963 studying the La Loma district attorney's office. This is the office to which felony defendants are bound over after a preliminary hearing in Westville. Thus, during three months as participant-observer in the local and county offices of the prosecutor, I frequently came into contact with police.

Under direct observation, detectives were cooperative. They soon gave permission to listen in to telephone calls, allowed me to join in conversations with informants, and to observe interrogations. In addition, they called me at home when an important development in a case was anticipated. Whenever we went out on a raid, I was a detective so far as any outsider could see. Although my appearance does not conform to the stereotype of the policeman, this proved to be an advantage since I could sometimes aid the police in carrying out some of their duties. For example, I could walk into a bar looking for a dangerous armed robber who was reportedly there without undergoing much danger myself, since I would not be recognized as a policeman. Similarly, I could drive a disguised truck up to a building, with a couple of policemen hidden in the rear, without the lookout recognizing me.

At the same time, I looked enough like a policeman when among a group of detectives in a raid for suspects to take me for a detective. (It twice happened that policemen from other local departments, who recognized that I was not a member of the Westville force, assumed I was a federal agent.) Even though I posed as a detective, however, I never carried a gun, although I did take pistol training on the police range. As a matter of achieving rapport with the police, I felt that such participation was required. Since I was not interested in getting standard answers to standard questions, I needed to be on the scene to observe their behavior and attitudes expressed on actual assignments.

One problem that this sort of research approach raises is whether an observer's presence alters the normal behavior of the police. There is no certain control for this problem, but I believe the following assumptions are reasonable. First, the more time the observer spends with subjects, the more used to his presence they become. Second, participant-observation offers the subject less opportunity to dissimulate than he would have in answering a questionnaire, even if he were consciously telling the truth in response to standardized questions. "Arguing some matters," as Whyte put it, is "part of a social pattern . . . one could hardly participate without joining in the argument." [9] The process of "arguing," discussing, especially in the setting of the police work itself, creates an air of informality when opinions seem to be more openly expressed. Third, in many situations involving police, they are hardly free to alter behavior, as, for example, when a policeman kicks in a door on a narcotics raid.

Finally, if an observer's presence does alter police behavior, I believe it can be assumed that it does so only in one direction. I can see no reason why police would, for example, behave *more* harshly to a prisoner in the presence of an observer than in his absence. Nor can I imagine why police would attempt to deceive a prisoner in an interrogation to a greater degree than customary. Thus, a conservative interpretation of the materials that follow would hold that these are based upon observations of a top police department behaving at its best. However, I personally believe that while I was not exposed to the "worst," whatever that may mean, most of what I saw was necessarily typical of the ordinary behavior of patrolmen and detectives, *necessarily*, because over a long period of time, organizational controls are far more pertinent to policemen than the vague presence of an observer whom they have come to know, and who frequently exercises "drop-in" privileges. If a sociologist rides with police for a day or two he may be given what they call the

⁹ Whyte, *op. cit.*, p. 302.

"whitewash tour." As he becomes part of the scene, however, he comes to be seen less as an agent of control than as an accomplice.

ETHICAL ISSUES [10]

This sort of approach raised several ethical issues. The most apparent of these was the effect of my presence on the defendant's fate. Was it justifiable for me to deceive suspects into believing I was a policeman by not identifying myself otherwise? It seemed to me that the ethical justification for such an approach was to be located mainly in its consequences. Certainly, as mentioned above, it is most improbable that police would treat suspects more severely, or with less regard for their constitutional rights, in my presence than out of it. Similarly, it seems hardly reasonable to suppose that police would be more lax, less concerned with the quality of their work, less efficient, under outside observation. It is thus hard to imagine that the presence of a participant-observer interfered with the civil liberties of the suspects or with the efficiency of the policemen studied.

I do, however, feel uneasy with the idea of pretense, since such a charade is necessarily an invasion of privacy. For instance, when a suspect believes you to be a policeman, he may attempt to say things to you which will aid his cause. Since you are not a policeman, it would be unconscionable to permit him to confide in you, when you cannot respond as an authority. Whenever a suspect did try to explain away his evidently culpable actions to me I would say, "Wait a moment, Detective so-and-so is in charge of the case," and call that detective over. Then I would listen to the story, having again assumed the role of observer. Although such behavior also constitutes an invasion of privacy, it does not ordinarily have legal consequences one way or the other for the suspect.

Similarly, in listening to telephone calls on an extension, I felt I was not interfering with outcome, although as a matter of general principle, I do not approve of this invasion of privacy. Here my justifications are two. First, such conduct is commonplace among detectives. If, for in-

---

[10] A number of enlightening discussions of ethical problems in field research are found in the volume edited by Arthur J. Vidich, Joseph Bensman, and Maurice R. Stein, *Reflections on Community Studies* (New York: John Wiley and Sons, Inc., 1964). See especially the following articles there: Howard S. Becker, "Problems in the Publication of Field Studies," pp. 267–284; Art Gallaher, Jr., "Plainsville: The Twice-Studied Town," pp. 285–303; and Arthur J. Vidich and Joseph Bensman, "The Springdale Case: Academic Bureaucrats and Sensitive Townspeople," pp. 313–349. For general problems associated with field research, see also Richard N. Adams and Jack J. Preiss (eds.), *Human Organization Research* (Homewood, Ill.: Dorsey Press, 1960), *passim*.

stance, a detective receives a telephone call relating to a case, he will commonly signal his partner to pick up an extension telephone. The second justification is the legitimacy of the research. I hope that the value of the study affords me certain privileges, as the worth of medical training allows students to observe patients intimately in the name of science.

No matter how scrupulous an observer may attempt to be, however, he must to a small degree influence the fate of his subjects. For instance, suppose that as an observer, I listen to a conversation between detective and suspect or between detective and informer and the detective asks me for an opinion of what he has been told. In such a situation, I might have said "no comment," but I could not divorce myself from the fact that I was there. The detective might try to read an opinion from my facial expressions and possibly come to a conclusion opposite to one that I held. Moreover, I believe that although I may have a fairly good poker face (even when playing poker), to keep it outside that setting destroys rapport.

The ethical line here is hard to place, but I did decide that in most cases it would be permissible for me to give an opinion, if it was solicited, on the following grounds. If I was accompanying a detective, or listening in to a telephone call, I was doing exactly what a partner of a detective might do in a similar situation. Under such circumstances, it would be normal for one detective to solicit the opinion of a colleague as to the truth of a suspect's statement. Therefore, since I was in effect *taking the place of a detective*, it was permissible for me to play the role of consultant, since to have refused to do so would have put the detective at an unfair disadvantage by depriving him of another opinion. I trusted that the opinion I would give would be as responsible as that of a genuine detective and would not adversely affect the suspect's lawful rights.

This position, of course, raises the more general issue of how far a participant-observer should aid the police in carrying out their duties. Once again I offer no simple or general solution to the problem, since the dictates of my conscience might be different from somebody else's and might not be especially persuasive. I found in practice that while no general rule could be formulated, the aid I offered tended to vary with the seriousness of the crime according to *my* personal moral standards. Thus, I would not put myself in a position to be solicited by a prostitute (as suggested half-seriously by a couple of vice control policemen; had I gone along with the suggestion so would they, I am reasonably certain). At the same time, I felt little hesitation in using my civilian appearance, as the reader will by now have concluded, an asset to the police department, to try to apprehend an armed robber or professional counterfeiter. Similarly, I signed my name to several confessions given by suspects in my presence while the suspect was being interrogated by a detective. Here I felt that if I had not accompanied the detective, somebody else would have, and signed the confession in my stead. Fortunately, I was never called upon to testify, but these confessions also raised a problem. To what extent would a lawyer, seeing my name on a confession, choose not to bring the case to trial because a "professor" who witnessed the confession and swore that no intimidation was used, would be an unusually effective witness for the prosecution? Again, I resolved this issue on grounds that I would have testified only as to the truth, and that truthful testimony by an "acting detective" is not unethical.

For those whose conscience is offended by what I have reported, I might add that mine is also troubled, especially at having listened in to telephone conversations. Fortunately, however, most of my "participant-observation" was routine and therefore inconsequential; often merely a matter of courtesy or communication, for instance, passing a flashlight from one detective to another, or delivering a message. Such activities are necessarily involved in the method.

So far, I have expressed concern mainly over the consequences of an observer's presence upon the fate of suspects. I think the most serious ethical issue may be responsibility to the police who cooperated with the project. In the course of this study, I report them as having sometimes engaged in activities for which they might be criticized by superiors, defense attorneys, judges, or members of the community. I should like to remind these others that none of us is perfect. A careful scrutiny of our own professional behavior would normally show some discrepancy from ideals, and policemen are no exception. Thus, in presenting such materials, I was not intending to rake muck, but to show behavior as it actually occurred.

Police do engage in activities that are either illegal or on the border of legality. This can be gleaned from the public statements of leading professional police by reading the least bit between the lines. Even the eminent O. W. Wilson confesses: "If we followed some of our court decisions literally, the public would be demanding my removal as Superintendent of Police and—I might add—with justification." [11]

All the factual materials in this book have been read in one state of draft or another by the law-enforcement personnel involved, and they have generally responded by saying that the portrait is fair and accurate, although they have sometimes disagreed with interpretations. Wherever

[11] O. W. Wilson, "Police Authority in a Free Society," *Journal of Criminal Law, Criminology and Police Science*, **54** (June, 1963), 177.

possible, I have tried to revise the materials to take advantage of their usually perceptive criticism.

I have also kept the names of the communities studied anonymous to underscore the goal of the study. If I were to state, for instance, that this was a study of the "Houston" Police Department or the "New Haven" Police Department, it would appear that I was investigating these cities, when in fact I was analyzing conditions influencing police to act as they do. Thus, it is an underlying assumption of this study that no set of police is morally "better" than another, but rather that each responds to the conditions of his own bailiwick. Carrying this general logic to persons, I also was not interested in the individual behavior of Patrolman A or Sergeant B, but in their conduct as it represented characteristic behavior of police in certain circumstances.

It may be that some of the people whose conduct is reported in this volume will be recognizable to colleagues and others in the criminal-courts community, despite disguised names and the blurring of those identifying facts that do not influence the general points being made. If these persons should be caused embarrassment or discomfort, I hope they will accept the sincere apologies of a troubled author. To the reader I might add that this too is one of the problems of the research method for which the author has found no simple solution.

CONCLUSION

This chapter has tried to answer, first of all, such standard methodological questions as the size of the city studied, its ecology, the character of police organization, the amount of time spent in various aspects of the study, and the methods used to make observations. Additionally, the chapter contains a description of the development of the study from exploration to completion. Thus, the reader has been given the reasons behind decisions to study specialties within the police department. Finally, there was a discussion of the ethical problems involved in this kind of research.

In conclusion, I should like to note that I was painfully aware at the outset of the limitations of basing conclusions on the detailed study of one city, one police department, one prosecutor's office, one criminal court's community. I tried to overcome some of these limitations by examining another police department, and attempting to parallel, through census and other reports, such characteristics as population, industry, and commerce. Eastville and Westville are the two cities most alike in the United States in these factors.

With limitations acknowledged, there are advantages to studying one community, indeed to studying one part of it, and to studying it oneself. Robert Dahl has justified his study of New Haven government on grounds that classical contributions to political theory were made by scholars who witnessed politics on the small scale.[12] Besides Dahl there are numerous outstanding contemporary social science studies with this approach. The underlying reason for employing this research strategy is, I believe, as follows. In attempting to understand a social or political process such as democracy, oligarchy, bureaucracy, or justice, the process itself must be learned in intimate detail. To do that the researcher must immerse himself in it. The larger purpose is, of course, to construct generalizations about the process. That goal, however, cannot be accomplished without first-hand knowledge of the process itself. Surveys and reports of others can usefully supplement notions gained through self-experience, but they cannot substitute for that experience.

It should also be noted that case studies of the kind presented here may meet the scientific demand for replication, while studies appearing more rigorous are frequently not redone. Many of our more rigorous sociological studies are sufficiently time consuming and expensive so that their duplication is unlikely. By contrast, we may confidently predict that this study will by no means be the last word on police.

[12] Robert Dahl, *Who Governs?* (New Haven: Yale University Press, 1961), p. vi.

Chapter 3

A Sketch of the Policeman's
"Working Personality"

A RECURRENT theme of the sociology of occupations is the effect of a man's work on his outlook on the world.[1] Doctors, janitors, lawyers, and industrial workers develop distinctive ways of perceiving and responding to their environment. Here we shall concentrate on analyzing certain outstanding elements in the police milieu, danger, authority, and efficiency, as they combine to generate distinctive cognitive and behavioral responses in police: a "working personality." Such an analysis does not suggest that all police are alike in "working personality," but that there are distinctive cognitive tendencies in police as an occupational grouping. Some of these may be found in other occupations sharing similar problems. So far as exposure to danger is concerned, the policeman may be likened to the soldier. His problems as an authority bear a certain similarity to those of the schoolteacher, and the pressures he feels to prove himself efficient are not unlike those felt by the industrial worker. The combination of these elements, however, is unique to the policeman. Thus, the police, as a result of combined features of their social situation, tend to develop ways of looking at the world distinctive to themselves, cognitive lenses through which to see situations and events. The strength of the lenses may be weaker or stronger depending on certain conditions, but they are ground on a similar axis.

[1] For previous contributions in this area, see the following: Ely Chinoy, *Automobile Workers and the American Dream* (Garden City: Doubleday and Company, Inc., 1955); Charles R. Walker and Robert H. Guest, *The Man on the Assembly Line* (Cambridge: Harvard University Press, 1952); Everett C. Hughes, "Work and the Self," in his *Men and Their Work* (Glencoe, Illinois: The Free Press, 1958), pp. 42–55; Harold L. Wilensky, *Intellectuals in Labor Unions: Organizational Pressures on Professional Roles* (Glencoe, Illinois: The Free Press, 1956); Wilensky, "Varieties of Work Experience," in Henry Borow (ed.), *Man in a World at Work* (Boston: Houghton Mifflin Company, 1964), pp. 125–154; Louis Kriesberg, "The Retail Furrier: Concepts of Security and Success," *American Journal of Sociology,* **57** (March, 1952), 478–485; Waldo Burchard, "Role Conflicts of Military Chaplains," *American Sociological Review,* **19** (October, 1954), 528–535; Howard S. Becker and Blanche Geer, "The Fate of Idealism in Medical School," *American Sociological Review,* **23** (1958), 50–56; and Howard S. Becker and Anselm L. Strauss, "Careers, Personality, and Adult Socialization," *American Journal of Sociology,* **62** (November, 1956), 253–363.

Analysis of the policeman's cognitive propensities is necessary to understand the practical dilemma faced by police required to maintain order under a democratic rule of law. We have discussed earlier how essential a conception of order is to the resolution of this dilemma. It was suggested that the paramilitary character of police organization naturally leads to a high evaluation of similarity, routine, and predictability. Our intention is to emphasize features of the policeman's environment interacting with the paramilitary police organization to generate a "working personality." Such an intervening concept should aid in explaining how the social environment of police affects their capacity to respond to the rule of law.

We also stated earlier that emphasis would be placed on the division of labor in the police department, that "operational law enforcement" could not be understood outside these special work assignments. It is therefore important to explain how the hypothesis emphasizing the generalizability of the policeman's "working personality" is compatible with the idea that police division of labor is an important analytic dimension for understanding "operational law enforcement." Compatibility is evident when one considers the different levels of analysis at which the hypotheses are being developed. Janowitz states, for example, that the military profession is more than an occupation; it is a "style of life" because the occupational claims over one's daily existence extend well beyond official duties. He is quick to point out that any profession performing a crucial "life and death" task, such as medicine, the ministry, or the police, develops such claims.[2] A conception like "working personality" of police should be understood to suggest an analytic breadth similar to that of "style of life." That is, just as the professional behavior of military officers with similar "styles of life" may differ notably depending upon whether they command an infantry battalion or participate in the work of an intelligence unit, so too does the professional behavior of police officers with similar "working personalities" vary with their assignments.

The policeman's "working personality" is most highly developed in his constabulary role of the man on the beat. For analytical purposes that role is sometimes regarded as an enforcement speciality, but in this general discussion of policemen as they comport themselves while working, the uniformed "cop" is seen as the foundation for the policeman's working personality. There is a sound organizational basis for making this assumption. The police, unlike the military, draw no caste distinc-

---

[2] Morris Janowitz, *The Professional Soldier: A Social and Political Portrait* (New York: The Free Press of Glencoe, 1964), p. 175.

tion in socialization, even though their order of ranked titles approximates the military's. Thus, one cannot join a local police department as, for instance, a lieutenant, as a West Point graduate joins the army. Every officer of rank must serve an apprenticeship as a patrolman. This feature of police organization means that the constabulary role is the primary one for all police officers, and that whatever the special requirements of roles in enforcement specialties, they are carried out with a common background of constabulary experience.

The process by which this "personality" is developed may be summarized: the policeman's role contains two principal variables, danger and authority, which should be interpreted in the light of a "constant" pressure to appear efficient.[3] The element of danger seems to make the policeman especially attentive to signs indicating a potential for violence and lawbreaking. As a result, the policeman is generally a "suspicious" person. Furthermore, the character of the policeman's work makes him less desirable as a friend, since norms of friendship implicate others in his work. Accordingly, the element of danger isolates the policeman socially from that segment of the citizenry which he regards as symbolically dangerous and also from the conventional citizenry with whom he identifies.

The element of authority reinforces the element of danger in isolating the policeman. Typically, the policeman is required to enforce laws representing puritanical morality, such as those prohibiting drunkenness, and also laws regulating the flow of public activity, such as traffic laws. In these situations the policeman directs the citizenry, whose typical response denies recognition of his authority, and stresses his obligation to respond to danger. The kind of man who responds well to danger, however, does not normally subscribe to codes of puritanical morality. As a result, the policeman is unusually liable to the charge of hypocrisy. That the whole civilian world is an audience for the policeman further promotes police isolation and, in consequence, solidarity. Finally, danger undermines the judicious use of authority. Where danger, as in Britain, is relatively less, the judicious application of authority is facilitated. Hence, British police may appear to be somewhat more attached to the rule of law, when, in fact, they may appear so because they face less danger, and they are as a rule better skilled than American police in creating the appearance of conformity to procedural regulations.

---

[3] By no means does such an analysis suggest there are no individual or group differences among police. On the contrary, most of this study emphasizes differences, endeavoring to relate these to occupational specialities in police departments. This chapter, however, explores similarities rather than differences, attempting to account for the policeman's general disposition to perceive and to behave in certain ways.

THE SYMBOLIC ASSAILANT AND POLICE CULTURE

In attempting to understand the policeman's view of the world, it is useful to raise a more general question: What are the conditions under which police, as authorities, may be threatened? [4] To answer this, we must look to the situation of the policeman in the community. One attribute of many characterizing the policeman's role stands out: the policeman is required to respond to assaults against persons and property. When a radio call reports an armed robbery and gives a description of the man involved, every policeman, regardless of assignment, is responsible for the criminal's apprehension. The *raison d'être* of the policeman and the criminal law, the underlying collectively held moral sentiments which justify penal sanctions, arises ultimately and most clearly from the threat of violence and the possibility of danger to the community. Police who "lobby" for severe narcotics laws, for instance, justify their position on grounds that the addict is a harbinger of danger since, it is maintained, he requires one hundred dollars a day to support his habit, and he must steal to get it. Even though the addict is not typically a violent criminal, criminal penalties for addiction are supported on grounds that he may become one.

The policeman, because his work requires him to be occupied continually with potential violence, develops a perceptual shorthand to identify certain kinds of people as symbolic assailants, that is, as persons who use gesture, language, and attire that the policeman has come to recognize as a prelude to violence. This does not mean that violence by the symbolic assailant is necessarily predictable. On the contrary, the policeman responds to the vague indication of danger suggested by appearance.[5] Like the animals of the experimental psychologist, the po-

[4] William Westley was the first to raise such questions about the police, when he inquired into the conditions under which police are violent. Whatever merit this analysis has, it owes much to his prior insights, as all subsequent sociological studies of the police must. See his "Violence and the Police," *American Journal of Sociology*, 59 (July, 1953), 34–41; also his unpublished Ph.D. dissertation *The Police: A Sociological Study of Law, Custom, and Morality*, University of Chicago, Department of Sociology, 1951.

[5] Something of the flavor of the policeman's attitude toward the symbolic assailant comes across in a recent article by a police expert. In discussing the problem of selecting subjects for field interrogation, the author writes:

A. Be suspicious. This is a healthy police attitude, but it should be controlled and not too obvious.
B. Look for the unusual.
   1. Persons who do not "belong" where they are observed.

liceman finds the threat of random damage more compelling than a predetermined and inevitable punishment.

Nor, to qualify for the status of symbolic assailant, need an individual ever have used violence. A man backing out of a jewelry store with a gun in one hand and jewelry in the other would qualify even if the gun were a toy and he had never in his life fired a real pistol. To the policeman in the situation, the man's personal history is momentarily immaterial. There is only one relevant sign: a gun signifying danger. Similarly, a young man may suggest the threat of violence to the policeman by his manner of walking or "strutting," the insolence in the demeanor being registered by the policeman as a possible preamble to later attack.[6] Signs vary from area to area, but a youth dressed in a black leather jacket and

2. Automobiles which do not "look right."
3. Businesses opened at odd hours, or not according to routine or custom.
C. Subjects who should be subjected to field interrogations.
  1. Suspicious persons known to the officer from previous arrests, field interrogations, and observations.
  2. Emaciated appearing alcoholics and narcotics users who invariably turn to crime to pay for cost of habit.
  3. Person who fits description of wanted suspect as described by radio, teletype, daily bulletins.
  4. Any person observed in the immediate vicinity of a crime very recently committed or reported as "in progress."
  5. Known trouble-makers near large gatherings.
  6. Persons who attempt to avoid or evade the officer.
  7. Exaggerated unconcern over contact with the officer.
  8. Visibly "rattled" when near the policeman.
  9. Unescorted women or young girls in public places, particularly at night in such places as cafes, bars, bus and train depots, or street corners.
  10. "Lovers" in an industrial area (make good lookouts).
  11. Persons who loiter about places where children play.
  12. Solicitors or peddlers in a residential neighborhood.
  13. Loiterers around public rest rooms.
  14. Lone male sitting in car adjacent to schoolground with newspaper or book in his lap.
  15. Lone male sitting in car near shopping center who pays unusual amount of attention to women, sometimes continuously manipulating rearview mirror to avoid direct eye contact.
  16. Hitchhikers.
  17. Person wearing coat on hot days.
  18. Car with mismatched hub caps, or dirty car with clean license plate (or vice versa).
  19. Uniformed "deliverymen" with no merchandise or truck.
  20. Many others. How about your own personal experiences?

From Thomas F. Adams, "Field Interrogation," *Police*, March–April, 1963, 28.

[6] See Irving Piliavin and Scott Briar, "Police Encounters with Juveniles," *American Journal of Sociology*, 70 (September, 1964), 206–214.

motorcycle boots is sure to draw at least a suspicious glance from a policeman.

Policemen themselves do not necessarily emphasize the peril associated with their work when questioned directly, and may even have well-developed strategies of denial. The element of danger is so integral to the policeman's work that explicit recognition might induce emotional barriers to work performance. Thus, one patrol officer observed that more police have been killed and injured in automobile accidents in the past ten years than from gunfire. Although his assertion is true, he neglected to mention that the police are the only peacetime occupational group with a systematic record of death and injury from gunfire and other weaponry. Along these lines, it is interesting that of the two hundred and twenty-four working Westville policemen (not including the sixteen juvenile policemen) responding to a question about which assignment they would like most to have in the police department, [7] 50 per cent selected the job of detective, an assignment combining elements of apparent danger and initiative. The next category was adult street work, that is, patrol and traffic (37 per cent). Eight per cent selected the juvenile squad, [8] and only 4 per cent selected administrative work. Not a single policeman chose the job of jail guard. Although these findings do not control for such factors as prestige, they suggest that confining and routine jobs are rated low on the hierarchy of police preferences, even though such jobs are least dangerous. Thus, the policeman may well, as a personality, enjoy the possibility of danger, especially its associated excitement, even though he may at the same time be fearful of it. Such "inconsistency" is easily understood. Freud has by now made it an axiom of personality theory that logical and emotional consistency are by no means the same phenomenon.

However complex the motives aroused by the element of danger, its consequences for sustaining police culture are unambiguous. This element requires him, like the combat soldier, the European Jew, the South African (white or black), to live in a world straining toward duality, and suggesting danger when "they" are perceived. Consequently, it is in the nature of the policeman's situation that his concep-

[7] A questionnaire was given to all policemen in operating divisions of the police force: patrol, traffic, vice control, and all detectives. The questionnaire was administered at police line-ups over a period of three days, mainly by the author but also by some of the police personnel themselves. Before the questionnaire was administered, it was circulated to and approved by the policemen's welfare association.

[8] Indeed, the journalist Paul Jacobs, who has ridden with the Westville juvenile police as part of his own work on poverty, observed in a personal communication that juvenile police appear curiously drawn to seek out dangerous situations, as if juvenile work without danger is degrading.

tion of order emphasize regularity and predictability. It is, therefore, a conception shaped by persistent *suspicion*. The English "copper," often portrayed as a courteous, easy-going, rather jolly sort of chap, on the one hand, or as a devil-may-care adventurer, on the other, is differently described by Colin MacInnes:

> The true copper's dominant characteristic, if the truth be known, is neither those daring nor vicious qualities that are sometimes attributed to him by friend or enemy, but an ingrained conservatism, and almost desperate love of the conventional. It is untidiness, disorder, the unusual, that a copper disapproves of most of all: far more, even than of crime which is merely a professional matter. Hence his profound dislike of people loitering in streets, dressing extravagantly, speaking with exotic accents, being strange, weak, eccentric, or simply any rare minority—of their doing, in fact, anything that cannot be safely predicted.[9]

Policemen are indeed specifically *trained* to be suspicious, to perceive events or changes in the physical surroundings that indicate the occurrence or probability of disorder. A former student who worked as a patrolman in a suburban New York police department describes this aspect of the policeman's assessment of the unusual:

> The time spent cruising one's sector or walking one's beat is not wasted time, though it can become quite routine. During this time, the most important thing for the officer to do is notice the *normal*. He must come to know the people in his area, their habits, their automobiles and their friends. He must learn what time the various shops close, how much money is kept on hand on different nights, what lights are usually left on, which houses are vacant . . . only then can he decide what persons or cars under what circumstances warrant the appellation "suspicious."[10]

The individual policeman's "suspiciousness" does not hang on whether he has personally undergone an experience that could objectively be described as hazardous. Personal experience of this sort is not the key to the psychological importance of exceptionality. Each, as he routinely carries out his work, will experience situations that threaten to become dangerous. Like the American Jew who contributes to "defense" organizations such as the Anti-Defamation League in response to Nazi brutalities he has never experienced personally, the policeman identifies with his fellow cop who has been beaten, perhaps fatally, by a gang of young thugs.

[9] Colin McInnes, *Mr. Love and Justice* (London: New English Library, 1962), p. 74.

[10] Peter J. Connell, "Handling of Complaints by Police," unpublished paper for course in Criminal Procedure, Yale Law School, Fall, 1961.

SOCIAL ISOLATION

The patrolman in Westville, and probably in most communities, has come to identify the black man with danger. James Baldwin vividly expresses the isolation of the ghetto policeman:

. . . The only way to police a ghetto is to be oppressive. None of the Police Commissioner's men, even with the best will in the world, have any way of understanding the lives led by the people they swagger about in twos and threes controlling. Their very presence is an insult, and it would be, even if they spent their entire day feeding gumdrops to children. They represent the force of the white world, and that world's criminal profit and ease, to keep the black man corraled up here, in his place. The badge, the gun in the holster, and the swinging club make vivid what will happen should his rebellion become overt . . .

It is hard, on the other hand, to blame the policeman, blank, good-natured, thoughtless, and insuperably innocent, for being such a perfect representative of the people he serves. He, too, believes in good intentions and is astounded and offended when they are not taken for the deed. He has never, himself, done anything for which to be hated—which of us has? and yet he is facing, daily and nightly, people who would gladly see him dead, and he knows it. There is no way for him not to know it: there are few things under heaven more unnerving than the silent, accumulating contempt and hatred of a people. He moves through Harlem, therefore, like an occupying soldier in a bitterly hostile country; which is precisely what, and where he is, and is the reason he walks in twos and threes.[11]

While Baldwin's observations on police-Negro relations cannot be disputed seriously, there is greater social distance between police and "civilians" in general regardless of their color than Baldwin considers. Thus, Colin MacInnes has his English hero, Mr. Justice, explaining:

. . . The story is all coppers are just civilians like anyone else, living among them not in barracks like on the Continent, but you and I know that's just a legend for mugs. We *are* cut off: we're *not* like everyone else. Some civilians fear us and play up to us, some dislike us and keep out of our way but no one —well, very few indeed—accepts us as just ordinary like them. In one sense, dear, we're just like hostile troops occupying an enemy country. And say what you like, at times that makes us lonely.[12]

MacInnes' observation suggests that by not introducing a white control group, Baldwin has failed to see that the policeman may not get on

[11] James Baldwin, *Nobody Knows My Name* (New York: Dell Publishing Company, 1962), pp. 65–67.
[12] McInnes, *op. cit.*, p. 20.

well with anybody regardless (to use the hackneyed phrase) of race, creed, or national origin. Policemen whom one knows well often express their sense of isolation from the public as a whole, not just from those who fail to share their color. Westville police were asked, for example, to rank the most serious problems police have. The category most frequently selected was not racial problems, but some form of public relations: lack of respect for the police, lack of cooperation in enforcement of law, lack of understanding of the requirements of police work.[13] One respondent answered:

As a policeman my most serious problem is impressing on the general public just how difficult and necessary police service is to all. There seems to be an attitude of "law is important, but it applies to my neighbor—not to me."

Of the two hundred and eighty-two Westville policemen who rated the prestige police work receives from others, 70 per cent ranked it as only fair or poor, while less than 2 per cent ranked it as "excellent" and another 29 per cent as "good." Similarly, in Britain, two-thirds of a sample of policemen interviewed by a Royal Commission stated difficulties in making friends outside the force; of those interviewed 58 per cent thought members of the public to be reserved, suspicious, and con-

[13] Respondents were asked "Anybody who knows anything about police work knows that police face a number of problems. Would you please state—in order—what you consider to be the two most serious problems police have." On the basis of a number of answers, the writer and J. Richard Woodworth devised a set of categories. Then Woodworth classified each response into one of the categories (see table below). When a response did not seem clear, he consulted with the writer. No attempt was made to independently check Woodworth's classification because the results are used impressionistically, and do not test a hypothesis. It may be, for instance, that "relations with public" is sometimes used to indicate racial problems, and vice versa. "Racial problems" include only those answers having specific reference to race. The categories and results were as follows:

Westville Police Ranking of Number One Problem Faced by Police

	Number	Per Cent
Relations with public	74	26
Racial problems and demonstrations	66	23
Juvenile delinquents and delinquency	23	8
Unpleasant police tasks	23	8
Lack of cooperation from authorities (D.A., legislature, courts)	20	7
Internal departmental problems	17	6
Irregular life of policeman	5	2
No answer or other answer	56	20
	284	100

strained in conversation; and 12 per cent attributed such difficulties to the requirement that policemen be selective in associations and behave circumspectly.[14]

A Westville policeman related the following incident:

> Several months after I joined the force, my wife and I used to be socially active with a crowd of young people, mostly married, who gave a lot of parties where there was drinking and dancing, and we enjoyed it. I've never forgotten, though, an incident that happened on one Fourth of July party. Everybody had been drinking, there was a lot of talking, people were feeling boisterous, and some kid there—he must have been twenty or twenty-two—threw a firecracker that hit my wife in the leg and burned her. I didn't know exactly what to do—punch the guy in the nose, bawl him out, just forget it. Anyway, I couldn't let it pass, so I walked over to him and told him he ought to be careful. He began to rise up at me, and when he did, somebody yelled, "Better watch out, he's a cop." I saw everybody standing there, and I could feel they were all against me and for the kid, even though he had thrown the firecracker at my wife. I went over to the host and said it was probably better if my wife and I left because a fight would put a damper on the party. Actually, I'd hoped he would ask the kid to leave, since the kid had thrown the firecracker. But he didn't so we left. After that incident, my wife and I stopped going around with that crowd, and decided that if we were going to go to parties where there was to be drinking and boisterousness, we weren't going to be the only police people there.

Another reported that he seeks to overcome his feelings of isolation by concealing his police identity:

> I try not to bring my work home with me, and that includes my social life. I like the men I work with, but I think it's better that my family doesn't become a police family. I try to put my police work into the background, and try not to let people know I'm a policeman. Once you do, you can't have normal relations with them.[15]

Although the policeman serves a people who are, as Baldwin says, the established society, the white society, these people do not make him feel accepted. As a result, he develops resources within his own world to combat social rejection.

---

[14] Royal Commission on the Police, 1962, Appendix IV to *Minutes of Evidence*, cited in Michael Banton, *The Policeman in the Community* (London: Tavistock Publications, 1964), p. 198.

[15] Similarly, Banton found Scottish police officers attempting to conceal their occupation when on holiday. He quotes one as saying: "If someone asks my wife "What does your husband do?", I've told her to say, "He's a clerk," and that's the way it went because she found that being a policeman's wife—well, it wasn't quite a stigma, she didn't feel cut off, but that a sort of invisible wall was up for conversation purposes when a policeman was there" (p. 198).

POLICE SOLIDARITY

All occupational groups share a measure of inclusiveness and identification. People are brought together simply by doing the same work and having similar career and salary problems. As several writers have noted, however, police show an unusually high degree of occupational solidarity.[16] It is true that the police have a common employer and wear a uniform at work, but so do doctors, milkmen, and bus drivers. Yet it is doubtful that these workers have so close knit an occupation or so similar an outlook on the world as do police. Set apart from the conventional world, the policeman experiences an exceptionally strong tendency to find his social identity within his occupational milieu.

Compare the police with another skilled craft. In a study of the International Typographical Union, the authors asked printers the first names and jobs of their three closest friends. Of the 1,236 friends named by the 412 men in their sample, 35 per cent were printers.[17] Similarly, among the Westville police, of 700 friends listed by 250 respondents, 35 per cent were policemen. The policemen, however, were far more active than printers in occupational social activities. Of the printers, more than half (54 per cent) had never participated in any union clubs, benefit societies, teams, or organizations composed mostly of printers, or attended any printers' social affairs in the past 5 years. Of the Westville police, only 16 per cent had failed to attend a single police banquet or dinner in the past *year* (as contrasted with the printers' *5 years*); and of the 234 men answering this question, 54 per cent had attended 3 or more such affairs *during the past year*.

[16] In addition to Banton, William Westley and James Q. Wilson have noted this characteristic of police. See Westley, *op. cit.*, p. 294; Wilson, "The Police and Their Problems: A Theory," *Public Policy*, **12** (1963), 189–216.

[17] S. M. Lipset, Martin H. Trow, and James S. Coleman, *Union Democracy* (New York: Anchor Books, 1962), p. 123. A complete comparison is as follows:

Closest Friends of Printers and Police, by Occupation

	Printers N = 1236 (%)	Police N = 700 (%)
Same occupation	35	35
Professionals, business executives, and independent business owners	21	30
White-collar or sales employees	20	12
Manual workers	25	22

These findings are striking in light of the interpretation made of the data on printers. Lipset, Trow, and Coleman do not, as a result of their findings, see printers as an unintegrated occupational group. On the contrary, they ascribe the democratic character of the union in good part to the active social and political participation of the membership. The point is not to question their interpretation, since it is doubtlessly correct when printers are held up against other manual workers. However, when seen in comparison to police, printers appear a minimally participating group; put positively, police emerge as an exceptionally socially active occupational group.

POLICE SOLIDARITY AND DANGER

There is still a question, however, as to the process through which danger and authority influence police solidarity. The effect of danger on police solidarity is revealed when we examine a chief complaint of police: lack of public support and public apathy. The complaint may have several referents including police pay, police prestige, and support from the legislature. But the repeatedly voiced broader meaning of the complaint is resentment at being taken for granted. The policeman does not believe that his status as civil servant should relieve the public of responsibility for law enforcement. He feels, however, that payment out of public coffers somehow obscures his humanity and, therefore, his need for help.[18] As one put it:

> Jerry, a cop, can get into a fight with three or four tough kids, and there will be citizens passing by, and maybe they'll look, but they'll never lend a hand. It's their country too, but you'd never know it the way some of them act. They forget that we're made of flesh and blood too. They don't care what happens to the cop so long as they don't get a little dirty.

Although the policeman sees himself as a specialist in dealing with violence, he does not want to fight alone. He does not believe that his specialization relieves the general public of citizenship duties. Indeed, if possible, he would prefer to be the foreman rather than the workingman in the battle against criminals.

The general public, of course, does withdraw from the workaday world of the policeman. The policeman's responsibility for controlling dangerous and sometimes violent persons alienates the average citizen perhaps as much as does his authority over the average citizen. If the

---

[18] On this issue there was no variation. The statement "the policeman feels" means that there was no instance of a negative opinion expressed by the police studied.

policeman's job is to insure that public order is maintained, the citizen's inclination is to shrink from the dangers of maintaining it. The citizen prefers to see the policeman as an automaton, because once the policeman's humanity is recognized, the citizen necessarily becomes implicated in the policeman's work, which is, after all, sometimes dirty and dangerous. What the policeman typically fails to realize is the extent he becomes tainted by the character of the work he performs. The dangers of their work not only draws policemen together as a group but separates them from the rest of the population. Banton, for instance, comments:

. . . patrolmen may support their fellows over what they regard as minor infractions in order to demonstrate to them that they will be loyal in situations that make the greatest demands upon their fidelity. . . .

In the American departments I visited it seemed as if the supervisors shared many of the patrolmen's sentiments about solidarity. They too wanted their colleagues to back them up in an emergency, and they shared similar frustrations with the public.[19]

Thus, the element of danger contains seeds of isolation which may grow in two directions. In one, a stereotyping perceptual shorthand is formed through which the police come to see certain signs as symbols of potential violence. The police probably differ in this respect from the general middle-class white population only in degree. This difference, however, may take on enormous significance in practice. Thus, the policeman works at identifying and possibly apprehending the symbolic assailant; the ordinary citizen does not. As a result, the ordinary citizen does not assume the responsibility to implicate himself in the policeman's required response to danger. The element of danger in the policeman's role alienates him not only from populations with a potential for crime but also from the conventionally respectable (white) citizenry, in short, from that segment of the population from which friends would ordinarily be drawn. As Janowitz has noted in a paragraph suggesting similarities between the police and the military, ". . . any profession which is continually preoccupied with the threat of danger requires a strong sense of solidarity if it is to operate effectively. Detailed regulation of the military style of life is expected to enhance group cohesion, professional loyalty, and maintain the martial spirit." [20]

SOCIAL ISOLATION AND AUTHORITY

The element of authority also helps to account for the policeman's social isolation. Policemen themselves are aware of their isolation from

[19] Banton, *op. cit.*, p. 114.
[20] Janowitz, *op. cit.*

the community, and are apt to weight authority heavily as a causal factor. When considering how authority influences rejection, the policeman typically singles out his responsibility for enforcement of traffic violations.[21] Resentment, even hostility, is generated in those receiving citations, in part because such contact is often the only one citizens have with police, and in part because municipal administrations and courts have been known to utilize police authority primarily to meet budgetary requirements, rather than those of public order. Thus, when a municipality engages in "speed trapping" by changing limits so quickly that drivers cannot realistically slow down to the prescribed speed or, while keeping the limits reasonable, charging high fines primarily to generate revenue, the policeman carries the brunt of public resentment.

That the policeman dislikes writing traffic tickets is suggested by the quota system police departments typically employ. In Westville, each traffic policeman has what is euphemistically described as a working "norm." A motorcyclist is supposed to write two tickets an hour for moving violations. It is doubtful that "norms" are needed because policemen are lazy. Rather, employment of quotas most likely springs from the reluctance of policemen to expose themselves to what they know to be public hostility. As a result, as one traffic policeman said:

You learn to sniff out the places where you can catch violators when you're running behind. Of course, the department gets to know that you hang around one place, and they sometimes try to repair the situation there. But a lot of the time it would be too expensive to fix up the engineering fault, so we keep making our norm.

When meeting "production" pressures, the policeman inadvertently gives a false impression of patrolling ability to the average citizen. The traffic cyclist waits in hiding for moving violators near a tricky intersection, and is reasonably sure that such violations will occur with regularity. The violator believes he has observed a policeman displaying exceptional detection capacities and may have two thoughts, each apt to generate hostility toward the policeman: "I have been trapped," or "They can catch me; why can't they catch crooks as easily?" The answer, of course, lies in the different behavior patterns of motorists and "crooks."

[21] O. W. Wilson, for example, mentions this factor as a primary source of antagonism toward police. See his "Police Authority in a Free Society," *Journal of Criminal Law, Criminology and Police Science*, 54 (June, 1964), 175–177. In the current study, in addition to the police themselves, other people interviewed, such as attorneys in the system, also attribute the isolation of police to their authority. Similarly, Arthur L. Stinchcombe, in an as yet unpublished manuscript, "The Control of Citizen Resentment in Police Work," provides a stimulating analysis, to which I am indebted, of the ways police authority generates resentment.

The latter do not act with either the frequency or predictability of motorists at poorly engineered intersections.

While traffic patrol plays a major role in separating the policemen from the respectable community, other of his tasks also have this consequence. Traffic patrol is only the most obvious illustration of the policeman's general responsibility for maintaining public order, which also includes keeping order at public accidents, sporting events, and political rallies. These activities share one feature: the policeman is called upon to *direct* ordinary citizens, and therefore to restrain their freedom of action. Resenting the restraint, the average citizen in such a situation typically thinks something along the lines of "He is supposed to catch crooks; why is he bothering me?" Thus, the citizen stresses the "dangerous" portion of the policeman's role while belittling his authority.

Closely related to the policeman's authority-based problems as *director* of the citizenry are difficulties associated with his injunction to *regulate public morality*. For instance, the policeman is obliged to investigate "lovers' lanes," and to enforce laws pertaining to gambling, prostitution, and drunkenness. His responsibility in these matters allows him much administrative discretion since he may not actually enforce the law by making an arrest, but instead merely interfere with continuation of the objectionable activity.[22] Thus, he may put the drunk in a taxi, tell the lovers to remove themselves from the back seat, and advise a man soliciting a prostitute to leave the area.

Such admonitions are in the interest of maintaining the proprieties of public order. At the same time, the policeman invites the hostility of the citizen so directed in two respects: he is likely to encourage the sort of response mentioned earlier (that is, an antagonistic reformulation of the policeman's role) and the policeman is apt to cause resentment because of the suspicion that policemen do not themselves strictly conform to the moral norms they are enforcing. Thus, the policeman, faced with enforcing a law against fornication, drunkenness, or gambling, is easily liable to a charge of hypocrisy. Even when the policeman is called on to enforce the laws relating to overt homosexuality, a form of sexual activity for which police are not especially noted, he may encounter the charge of hypocrisy on grounds that he does not adhere strictly to prescribed heterosexual codes. The policeman's difficulty in this respect is shared by all authorities responsible for maintenance of disciplined activity, including industrial foremen, political leaders, elementary schoolteachers, and college professors. All are expected to conform rigidly to

[22] See Wayne R. La Fave, "The Police and Nonenforcement of the Law," *Wisconsin Law Review* (1962), 104–137, 179–239.

the entire range of norms they espouse.[23] The policeman, however, as a result of the unique combination of the elements of danger and authority, experiences a special predicament. It is difficult to develop qualities enabling him to stand up to danger, and to conform to standards of puritanical morality. The element of danger demands that the policeman be able to carry out efforts that are in their nature overtly masculine. Police work, like soldiering, requires an exceptional caliber of physical fitness, agility, toughness, and the like. The man who ranks high on these masculine characteristics is, again like the soldier, not usually disposed to be puritanical about sex, drinking, and gambling.

On the basis of observations, policemen do not subscribe to moralistic standards for conduct. For example, the morals squad of the police department, when questioned, was unanimously against the statutory rape age limit, on grounds that as late teen-agers they themselves might not have refused an attractive offer from a seventeen-year-old girl.[24] Neither, from observations, are policemen by any means total abstainers from the use of alcoholic beverages. The policeman who is arresting a drunk has probably been drunk himself; he knows it and the drunk knows it.

More than that, a portion of the social isolation of the policeman can be attributed to the discrepancy between moral regulation and the norms and behavior of policemen in these areas. We have presented data indicating that police engage in a comparatively active occupational social life. One interpretation might attribute this attendance to a basic interest in such affairs; another might explain the policeman's occupational social activity as a measure of restraint in publicly violating norms he enforces. The interest in attending police affairs may grow as much out of security in "letting oneself go" in the presence of police, and a corresponding feeling of insecurity with civilians, as an authentic preference for police social affairs. Much alcohol is usually consumed at police banquets with all the melancholy and boisterousness accompanying such occasions. As Horace Cayton reports on his experience as a policeman:

> Deputy sheriffs and policemen don't know much about organized recreation; all they usually do when celebrating is get drunk and pound each other on the back, exchanging loud insults which under ordinary circumstances would result in a fight.[25]

[23] For a theoretical discussion of the problems of leadership, see George Homans, *The Human Group* (New York: Harcourt, Brace and Company, 1950), especially the chapter on "The Job of the Leader," pp. 415–440.

[24] The work of the Westville morals squad is analyzed in detail in an unpublished master's thesis by J. Richard Woodworth. *The Administration of Statutory Rape Complaints: A Sociological Study* (Berkeley: University of California, 1964).

[25] Horace R. Cayton, *Long Old Road* (New York: Trident Press, 1965), p. 154.

To some degree the reason for the behavior exhibited on these occasions is the company, since the policeman would feel uncomfortable exhibiting insobriety before civilians. The policeman may be likened to other authorities who prefer to violate moralistic norms away from onlookers for whom they are routinely supposed to appear as normative models. College professors, for instance, also get drunk on occasion, but prefer to do so where students are not present. Unfortunately for the policeman, such settings are harder for him to come by than they are for the college professor. The whole civilian world watches the policeman. As a result, he tends to be limited to the company of other policemen for whom his police identity is not a stimulus to carping normative criticism.

CORRELATES OF SOCIAL ISOLATION

The element of authority, like the element of danger, is thus seen to contribute to the solidarity of policemen. To the extent that policemen share the experience of receiving hostility from the public, they are also drawn together and become dependent upon one another. Trends in the degree to which police may exercise authority are also important considerations in understanding the dynamics of the relation between authority and solidarity. It is not simply a question of how much absolute authority police are given, but how much authority they have relative to what they had, or think they had, before. If, as Westley concludes, police violence is frequently a response to a challenge to the policeman's authority, so too may a perceived reduction in authority result in greater solidarity. Whitaker comments on the British police as follows:

As they feel their authority decline, internal solidarity has become increasingly important to the police. Despite the individual responsibility of each police officer to pursue justice, there is sometimes a tendency to close ranks and to form a square when they themselves are concerned.[26]

These inclinations may have positive consequences for the effectiveness of police work, since notions of professional courtesy or colleagueship seem unusually high among police.[27] When the nature of the policing enterprise requires much joint activity, as in robbery and narcotics enforcement, the impression is received that cooperation is

[26] Ben Whitaker, *The Police* (Middlesex, England: Penguin Books, 1964), p. 137.
[27] It would be difficult to compare this factor across occupations, since the indicators could hardly be controlled. Nevertheless, I felt that the sense of responsibility to policemen in other departments was on the whole quite strong.

high and genuine. Policemen do not appear to cooperate with one another merely because such is the policy of the chief, but because they sincerely attach a high value to teamwork. For instance, there is a norm among detectives that two who work together will protect each other when a dangerous situation arises. During one investigation, a detective stepped out of a car to question a suspect who became belligerent. The second detective, who had remained overly long in the back seat of the police car, apologized indirectly to his partner by explaining how wrong it had been of him to permit his partner to encounter a suspect alone on the street. He later repeated this explanation privately, in genuine consternation at having committed the breach (and possibly at having been culpable in the presence of an observer). Strong feelings of empathy and cooperation, indeed almost of "clannishness," a term several policemen themselves used to describe the attitude of police toward one another, may be seen in the daily activities of police. Analytically, these feelings can be traced to the elements of danger and shared experiences of hostility in the policeman's role.

Finally, to round out the sketch, policemen are notably conservative, emotionally and politically. If the element of danger in the policeman's role tends to make the policeman suspicious, and therefore emotionally attached to the status quo, a similar consequence may be attributed to the element of authority. The fact that a man is engaged in enforcing a set of rules implies that he also becomes implicated in *affirming* them. Labor disputes provide the commonest example of conditions inclining the policeman to support the status quo. In these situations, the police are necessarily pushed on the side of the defense of property. Their responsibilities thus lead them to see the striking and sometimes angry workers as their enemy and, therefore, to be cool, if not antagonistic, toward the whole conception of labor militancy.[28] If a policeman did not believe in the system of laws he was responsible for enforcing, he would have to go on living in a state of conflicting cognitions, a condition which a number of social psychologists agree is painful.[29]

---

[28] In light of this, the most carefully drawn lesson plan in the "professionalized" Westville police department, according to the officer in charge of training, is the one dealing with the policeman's demeanor in labor disputes. A comparable concern is now being evidenced in teaching policemen appropriate demeanor in civil rights demonstrations. See, e.g., Juby E. Towler, *The Police Role In Racial Conflicts* (Springfield: Charles C Thomas, 1964).

[29] Indeed, one school of social psychology asserts that there is a basic "drive," a fundamental tendency of human nature, to reduce the degree of discrepancy between conflicting cognitions. For the policeman, this tenet implies that he would have to do something to reduce the discrepancy between his beliefs and his behavior. He would have to modify his behavior, his beliefs, or introduce some outside factor to justify

This hypothetical issue of not believing in the laws they are enforcing simply does not arise for most policemen. In the course of the research, however, there was one example. A Black civil rights advocate (member of CORE) became a policeman with the conviction that by so doing he would be aiding the cause of impartial administration of law for Blacks. For him, however, this outside rationale was not enough to sustain him in administering a system of laws that depends for its impartiality upon a reasonable measure of social and economic equality among the citizenry. This recruit identified with the Black community. He challenged directives of the department; the departments claimed his efficiency was impaired. He resigned under pressure in his rookie year.[29a]

Police are understandably reluctant to appear to be anything but impartial politically. The police are forbidden from publicly campaigning for political candidates. The London police are similarly prohibited, and before 1887 were not allowed to vote in parliamentary elections, or in local ones until 1893.[30] It was not surprising that the Westville Chief of Police forbade questions on the questionnaire that would have measured political attitudes.[31] One policeman, however, explained the chief's refusal on grounds that, "A couple of jerks here would probably cut up, and come out looking like Commies."

During the course of administering the questionnaire over a three-day period, I talked with approximately fifteen officers and sergeants in the Westville department, discussing political attitudes of police. In addition, during the course of the research itself, approximately fifty were interviewed for varying periods of time. Of these, at least twenty were interviewed more than once, some over time periods of several weeks. Furthermore, twenty police were interviewed in Eastville, several for periods ranging from several hours to several days. Most of the

---

the discrepancy. If he modified his behavior, so as not to enforce the law in which he disbelieves, he would not hold his position for long. Practically, then, he may either introduce an outside factor or modify his beliefs. The outside factor would have to be compelling to reduce the pain resulting from the dissonance between his cognitions. For example, he would have to convince himself that the only way he could make a living was by being a policeman, or modify his beliefs. See Leon Festinger, *A Theory of Cognitive Dissonance* (Evanston, Ill.: Row-Peterson, 1957). For a brief explanation of Festinger's theory see Edward E. Sampson (ed.), *Approaches, Contexts, and Problems of Social Psychology* (Englewood Cliffs, N.J.: Prentice-Hall, 1964), pp. 9–15.[29a] I thank Gwynne Pierson for pointing out the inaccuracy of the first edition's report of this incident.

[30] Whitaker, *op cit.*, p. 26.

[31] The questions submitted to the chief of police were directly analogous to those asked of printers in the study of the I.T.U. See Lipset et al., *op. cit.*, "Appendix II–Interview Schedule," 493–503.

time was *not* spent on investigating political attitudes, but I made a point of raising the question, if possible making it part of a discussion centered around the contents of a right-wing newsletter to which one of the detectives subscribed. One discussion included a group of eight detectives. From these observations, interviews, and discussions, it was clear that a Goldwater type of conservatism was the dominant political and emotional persuasion of police. I encountered only three policemen who claimed to be politically "liberal," at the same time asserting that they were decidedly exceptional.

Whether or not the policeman is an "authoritarian personality" is a related issue, beyond the scope of this discussion partly because of the many questions raised about this concept. Thus, in the course of discussing the concept of "normality" in mental health, two psychologists make the point that many conventional people were high scorers on the California F scale and similar tests. The great mass of the people, according to these authors, is not much further along the scale of ego development than the typical adolescent who, as they describe him, is "rigid, prone to think in stereotypes, intolerant of deviations, punitive and anti-psychological—in short, what has been called an authoritarian personality." [32] Therefore it is preferable to call the policeman's a conventional personality.

Writing about the New York police force, Thomas R. Brooks suggests a similar interpretation. He writes:

> Cops are conventional people. . . . All a cop can swing in a milieu of marijuana smokers, interracial dates, and homosexuals is the night stick. A policeman who passed a Lower East Side art gallery filled with paintings of what appeared to be female genitalia could think of doing only one thing—step in and make an arrest.[33]

Despite his fundamental identification with conservative conventionality, however, the policeman may be familiar, unlike most conventional people, with the argot of the deviant and the criminal. (The policeman tends to resent the quietly respectable liberal who comes to the defense of such people on principle but who has rarely met them in practice.) Indeed, the policeman will use his knowledge of the argot to advantage in talking to a suspect. In this manner, the policeman *puts on*

---

[32] Jane Loevinger and Abel Ossorio, "Evaluation of Therapy by Self Report: A Paradox," *Journal of Abnormal and Social Psychology*, **58** (May, 1959), 392; see also Edward A. Shils, "Authoritarianism: 'Right' and 'Left'," in R. Christie and M. Jahoda (ed.), *Studies in Scope and Method of "The Authoritarian Personality,"* (Glencoe, Ill.: The Free Press, 1954), pp. 24–49.

[33] Thomas R. Brooks, "New York's Finest," *Commentary*, **40** (August, 1965), 29–30.

the suspect by pretending to share his moral conception of the world through the use of "hip" expressions. The suspect may put on a parallel show for the policeman by using only conventional language to indicate his respectability. (In my opinion, neither fools the other.)

A COMPARATIVE GLANCE AT POLICE ROLE AND CULTURE

Must this theory of the policeman's working personality be limited to the police under observation, or can it be generalized to a wider police population? Unfortunately, there are few systematic studies of police for comparison. American studies, as well as reports of police chiefs, indicate that the policeman typically perceives the citizenry to be hostile to him.[34] Thus, for example, a recent survey made by James Q. Wilson of an urban American police force concludes:

> Criticisms of the way a big-city police department was run were largely confined to the younger, most recently promoted sergeants, but "alienation" —an acute sense of citizen hostility or contempt toward officers—was found in almost all age groups. Over 70 per cent of the over 800 officers scored high on an index of perceived citizen hostility—more, indeed, than thought the force was poorly run (though these were over half the total).[35]

This finding of Wilson's, so close to those reported here, is not surprising, and therefore not forceful in persuading the reader that the findings are generalizable. The common pattern of activities of American urban police, for instance, their enforcement of traffic laws, suggests that findings in one city would be similar to those in another. Furthermore, since the Westville police are high caliber, greater citizen hostility would be anticipated in other American cities where the enforcing authorities are less respected and therefore more likely to generate citizen hostility. Assuming that hostility is correlated with social isolation, this feature of police life also is likely to be more pronounced in other American urban areas.

Suppose, however, we were to consider the "working personality" of police who constitute part of a relatively homogeneous society, and who also enjoy an international reputation for honesty, efficiency, and legality. A study of such a police force has been completed by Michael Banton, who observed five police departments in Scotland and in the

---

[34] Cf. *Parker on Police*, ed. O. W. Wilson (Springfield: Charles C Thomas, 1957), pp. 135–146; O. W. Wilson, "Police Authority in a Free Society," *Journal of Criminal Law, Criminology and Police Science*, 54 (June, 1963), 175–177; Michael J. Murphy, "Stereocracy v. Democracy," *The Police Chief* (February, 1962), 36, 38.

[35] James Q. Wilson, "Police Attitudes and Citizen Hostility" (unpublished draft, Harvard University, September, 1964), p. 24.

United States.[36] The main object of his inquiry is the urban Scottish constable, roughly the equivalent of the American patrolman or "cop on the beat." Comparing the social isolation of American and British police, Banton writes:

Before my visit to the United States I thought that for a variety of reasons American police officers might well experience more social isolation than their British counterparts. I assumed that the heavier incidence of violent crime, the high proportion of 'cop-haters,' the 'shoot first, ask afterwards' tactics American police have to use on occasion, and the lower prestige of police work, would cause policemen to feel more like outcasts or like troops in occupation of enemy territory. Such an expectation was in accordance with an impression to be gained from a study of Westley's dissertation, where it is said: 'The exigencies of the occupation form the police into a social group which tends to be in conflict with and isolated from the community; and in which the norms are independent of the community' (Westley, 1951, p. 294). The locality in which Westley's research was conducted turns out, however, to be far from representative of the present-day situation, and a reconsideration of his evidence from a comparative rather than a purely American perspective reveals a whole series of influences which operate in a contrary fashion. *American police may seem isolated from the community to an American observer because he compares them with other occupational groups in the same society; they may at the same time seem to an outsider much less isolated than policemen in other societies.*[37]

Banton accounts for the relatively greater isolation of British police by emphasizing the consequences of the exemplary character of the British policeman's role. British police, as portrayed by Banton, are reserved, dignified, impersonal, detached. For them, the role is the man, and the example to be set is taken seriously. He writes:

Most officers with twenty years' service in a county force can remember the days when a policeman who proposed to marry was required first to submit the name of his fiancee to his superiors so that they could ascertain whether she was a fit and proper person for the role of policeman's wife.[38]

Although the element of danger is not so ultimate for the British policeman, it nevertheless exists. "In Edinburgh," writes Banton, "violence means to a policeman, I suspect, either fists or stones, or at the worst, assault with sticks or iron bars. It does not mean guns or knives."[39] Furthermore, the theme of the police being a "race apart" is a recurring one in Scotland, which Banton attributes to the requirement that

[36] Banton, *op. cit.*
[37] *Ibid.*, p. 215 (italics added).
[38] *Ibid.*, p. 195.
[39] Banton, personal communication, 24 August, 1964.

policeman must examine critically every statement made to them.[40] In our interpretation, these reports suggest that the policeman, wherever located, is in a position of vulnerability. Exposure to physical danger represents the height of vulnerability, a situation the British policeman encounters less often than the American. He does, however, experience the possibility of lesser physical danger and of attacks upon his professional competence. The policeman's role is therefore exceptional insofar as he must be so often on the defensive. Banton finds one of his subjects defining "the police mind" as follows: ". . . you suspect your grandmother and that's about the strength of it."

Although the elements of authority and danger have similar consequences for the British and American policeman, the processes bringing about social isolation seem different. British police are inclined to take the initiative in separating themselves from society. They tend to internalize authority, to perform an exemplary role, and thereby are instruments of their own isolation. Even in Great Britain, however, there seem to be differences between the Scottish police studied by Banton and the British police in general. Although the 1962 Royal Commission concluded that a social survey conducted by the Home Office constituted an overwhelming vote of confidence in the police, that interpretation has been widely criticized. For example, the survey disclosed that 42.4 per cent of the public thought policemen took bribes, 34.7 per cent that the police used unfair methods to get information, 32 per cent that they might distort evidence in court and 17.8 per cent that on occasions they used too much force.[41] The Royal Commission, however, felt that since almost half of those interviewed did not believe that the police took bribes, used unnecessary violence, employed unfair means of getting evidence, or gave false evidence in court, it was reasonable to "assert, confidently, on the basis of this survey, that relations between the police and the public are on the whole very good." [42] This interpretation is obviously overoptimistic. Police relations, especially with certain segments of the public, are clearly strained.

In America there has not been a comparable national survey. There have, however, been enough complaints to such groups as the U. S. Civil Rights Commission to suggest that American police are no more beloved or trusted than their English counterparts.[43] The chief difference may be that in America hostile public attitudes isolate policemen

[40] Banton, *op. cit.*, pp. 207–208.
[41] Whitaker, *op. cit.*, p. 15.
[42] *Ibid.*, p. 103.
[43] Commission on Civil Rights Report, Book 5, *Justice* (Washington, D.C.: U.S. Government Printing Office, 1961), pp. 5–44. In New York, a number of civil rights groups have formed an unofficial citizens' board to review charges of police brutality. (*New York Times*, May 23, 1964.)

who would prefer to be more friendly. Although the Westville policeman has been presented as a man who is conservative, suspicious, relatively isolated from the community at large, clannish, and resentful of public apathy, this is only part of the portrait of a complex being. The Westville policeman sees himself as a relatively congenial person, able to make friends. Policemen were asked to rank eight qualities in the order they felt these qualities best described them.[44] Here we find the quality of "congeniality and the ability to make friends" ranking high. In Great Britain also, the social survey finds police rueing their lack of friends, especially the rural police. Of these, 74 per cent thought they would have more friends if they had a different job. On the whole, 66.8 per cent of policemen said that the job adversely affected their outside friendships.[45]

Unfortunately, the nature of his work often inhibits the policeman from indulging his gregariousness in a personally meaningful way. He would like to be friendlier but, of the public over whom he is an authority, he must be suspicious of strangeness, oddity, indeed any sort of *change*. The elements of danger and authority in the policeman's work evidently impede gregarious tendencies and, in general, account for similar cognitive inclinations in American and British police. To be sure, differences exist in the salience and character of these elements and in the processes by which danger and authority affect the policeman's way of looking at the world. Nevertheless, both elements seem to be present, specific outcomes such as social isolation are similar and, most importantly, the British and American police seem to see the world similarly.

COGNITIVE SIMILARITY AND THE RULE OF LAW

If the proposition is largely correct that elements of the policeman's role result in broadly similar "working personalities" in British and American police, is the validity of this conclusion affected by observations that British police conform to rules of legal procedure more closely than American? [46] Should not the similarity of cognitive inclination manifest itself in the behavior of the policeman? Although a number of factors, such as relations of the police organization to the community

---

[44] These categories were taken from an unpublished paper, "Articulated Values of Law Students." The categories were suggested by the eight-value system elaborated by Harold Lasswell. See, e.g., H. D. Lasswell and A. Kaplan, *Power and Society* (New Haven: Yale University Press, 1950).

[45] Whitaker, *op. cit.*, p. 127.

[46] See Bruce Smith, *Police Systems in the United States* (New York: Harper and Brothers, 1960, second rev. ed.), pp. 3, 11, *et. passim*; and Sir Patrick Devlin, *The Criminal Prosecution in England* (New Haven: Yale University Press, 1958), *passim*.

and a less moralistic substantive criminal law, may help to account for such behavioral differences, this final discussion is confined to the effect of the general social environment. The discussion that follows is limited to the question of how differences in general social environment can influence the relation between the elements of danger and authority in the direction of apparently greater compliance with the rule of law.

It is important to note that the *actual* degree of difference often stated is open to serious question. A reader of memoirs of British police is impressed by the extent to which they describe violations of the judges' rules.[47] One officer writes: "You can see that if we worked according to the strict letter of the Rules we would get nowhere. . . . We have to break the law to enforce it. . . ."[48] Evidently, the British policeman does not conform to rules so much as he knows how to present the appearance of conformity. By contrast, when the American policeman varies from canons of procedural regularity, his misbehaviors tend to be more visible. Reared in a society with finer social distinctions, the British policeman is schooled in etiquette to a degree unknown to most Americans. Victor Meek, a former inspector of the Metropolitan Police, describes how an English policeman investigating a burglary manages to "stop" relatively large numbers of people, at the same time avoiding the appearance of procedural irregularity. He writes:

> You see, when a policeman has stopped a hundred people, which number has included perhaps ten proved guilty persons, he has learned the behaviour under these conditions of ninety innocent people and of ten thieves. In the next hundred stopped he will have twenty thieves, in the next perhaps thirty. Not altogether because thieves are thicker but because his "Police here," or "Excuse me a moment, Sir," are enough to satisfy him, by the reaction of the person stopped, whether he is dealing with a sheep or a goat, whether chummy is in the clear or loaded. So to the sheep his next remark is "I am very sorry to bother you but my watch has stopped. Can you please tell me the time?" The answer will naturally be "If you want to know the time I thought you had to ask another policeman," and the mutual appreciation of this witticism sends chummy away chuckling and quite unaware that Section 66 [49] has been tried on him.[50]

[47] See, e.g., Victor Meek, *Cops and Robbers* (London: Gerald Duckworth and Co., Ltd., 1962); William Gosling, *Ghost Squad* (Garden City: Doubleday, 1959); and a "Letter from English policeman on use of judges' rules," in William Thomas Fryer (ed.), *Selected Writings on the Law of Evidence and Trial* (St. Paul: West Publishing Co., 1957), pp. 845–846.

[48] Fryer, *ibid.*

[49] "Any constable may stop, search and detain any vessel, boat, cart or carriage in or upon which there shall be reason to suspect that anything stolen or unlawfully obtained may be found, and also any person who may be reasonably suspected of having or conveying in any manner anything stolen or unlawfully obtained."

[50] Meek, *op. cit.*, p. 86.

The British policeman's ability to make fine social discriminations, plus his training in etiquette, enable him to distinguish not only among those who are more likely to commit crimes but also among those who are more likely to report procedural irregularities. As Meek says, ". . . the names and address of a Section 66 complainer is doubly worth passing on to a good copper of the manor on which chummy lives or works." [51]

Thus, when we envision the "discretion" of the British policeman, we should certainly keep in mind more than the issue of whether he decides to invoke the law. A key distinction between the English and American policeman is that the former tends to be more *discreet* in an interactional sense as well as *discrete* in an administrative one, thereby avoiding the censure that is often the lot of the American policeman. Indeed, as the rest of this study of a "professionalized" American police force is read, the reader may find it interesting to speculate as to what constitutes central elements of professional training. We believe the materials to follow will suggest that the training of etiquette, including the ability to make fine social distinctions, is such an element; more, indeed, than the development of an actual regard for the rule of law.

CONCLUSION

The combination of *danger* and *authority* found in the task of the policeman unavoidably combine to frustrate procedural regularity. If it were possible to structure social roles with specific qualities, it would be wise to propose that these two should never, for the sake of the rule of law, be permitted to coexist. Danger typically yields self-defensive conduct, conduct that must strain to be impulsive because danger arouses fear and anxiety so easily. Authority under such conditions becomes a resource to reduce perceived threats rather than a series of reflective judgments arrived at calmly. The ability to be discreet, in the sense discussed above, is also affected. As a result, procedural requirements take on a "frilly" character, or at least tend to be reduced to a secondary position in the face of circumstances seen as threatening.

If this analysis is correct, it suggests a related explanation drawn from the realm of social environment to account for the apparent paradox that the elements of danger and authority are universally to be found in the policeman's role, yet at the same time fail to yield the same behavior regarding the rule of law. If the element of danger faced by the British policeman is less than that faced by his American counterpart, its ability to undermine the element of authority is proportionately weakened.

[51] *Ibid.*, p. 85.

Bluntly put, the American policeman may have a more difficult job because he is exposed to greater danger. Therefore, we would expect him to be less judicious, indeed less discreet, in the exercise of his authority. Similarly, such an explanation would predict that if the element of actual danger or even the perception of such in the British policeman's job were to increase, complaints regarding the illegal use of his authority would also rise.

There have been spectacular cases supporting this proposition. One of these, resulting in a government inquiry which suspended two top police officers, took place at Sheffield on March 14, 1963. Several detectives brutally assaulted four men in five successive and separate relays with a truncheon, fists, and a rhinoceros whip. The report of the Inquiry concludes that the police were undoubtedly guilty of "maliciously inflicting grievous bodily harm of a serious nature on two prisoners." [52] The assaults were described as "deliberate, unprovoked, brutal and sustained . . . for the purpose of inducing confessions of crime." The detectives had been formed into a "Crime Squad" which felt it had the authority to use "tough methods to deal with tough criminals and take risks to achieve speedy results." The leading offender told the Inquiry "that criminals are treated far too softly by the Courts, that because criminals break rules, police may and most do so to be a jump ahead, that force is justified as a last resort as a method of detection when normal methods fail, and that a beating is the only answer to turn a hardened criminal from a life of crime." [53]

Perhaps the most interesting feature of the report are the mitigating factors the Inquiry took into account. They found that the detectives were overworked (in a city where crime was on the rise); that the detectives were, and felt, under pressure to obtain results; that the use of violence had been encouraged by hints beforehand by senior officers; that senior officers instituted, witnessed, and joined in the violence and were wholly inadequately dealt with by the chief constable; and that the detectives were told to give a false account in court by a senior officer, who concocted it. The entire report suggests that the detectives who engaged in the beatings were not unusual men. There was no evidence of mental instability on their part, neither of psychosis, psychopathy, nor neurosis. Not one man on the force reported the incident, although several had learned of it. The report gives the feeling that while the event itself was exceptional, the conditions leading to it, such as overwork, pressure to produce, and encouragement by superiors,

---

[52] Sheffield Police Appeal Inquiry, Cmnd. 2176, November, 1963.
[53] *Ibid.*, p. 5.

were ordinary. Although the report does not use the language of social science, it strongly suggests that the structural and cultural conditions in the police force supported this sort of response.

Also interesting is the evident racial bias of the Sheffield police. One of them testified he carried his rhinoceros whip to deal with "coloured informants." The racial issue is significant for the British police as a whole. The *New York Times* reported on May 3, 1965 that although the London police force is six thousand men short of full strength, not one colored applicant has been accepted, even though fifteen West Indians, six Pakistanis and six Indians tried to join the force in the preceding three years. The official reason given is that the applicants did not meet the qualifications. Apart from three part-time constables in the Midlands, however, there was, at the time of the report, not one colored policeman in Britain, even though Pakistanis, Indians, and West Indians, all officially classified as colored by the British, account for nearly 2 per cent of the population.

Suggestions have been made to enlist colored policemen for colored neighborhoods, or to bring in trained colored policemen from the Commonwealth. Others have asked for the introduction of colored policemen in white neighborhoods, especially in London. The *New York Times* story closes with a suggestion by one critic, Anthony Lester, that British police chiefs take a trip to New York to see how Negro policemen fit in. "Policemen have a different status here than in the States," he is reported to have said. "They are more a father figure, a symbol of authority with their tall helmets and slow walk. It's difficult to get people to accept colored men in this job. They have had no Negro officers in the Army, no way of getting used to taking orders from colored men."

To complete the analogy of similarity of police action with similarity of social conditions, problems of police behavior also appear to be correlated with the restriction of marihuana use, a recent police phenomenon in England. Colin MacInnes argues, in a letter published in the fall of 1963, that when the London police began vigorously enforcing the marihuana law:

. . . it looks as if the hallowed myth that English coppers never use violence, perjury, framing of suspects—let alone participate in crimes—is at last being shattered in the public mind. Now, what has been foolish about this legend is not that coppers *do* do these things—as all police forces do and must—but that national vanity led many to suppose that our coppers were far nicer men than any others.[54]

[54] "The Silly Season," *Partisan Review*, **30** (Fall, 1963), 430, 432.

Although MacInnes' statement may be overly strong, it does suggest that those who too clearly contrast American and British police in favor of British are probably generally wrong. Of course, there are always individual as well as group differences in police behavior. However, even if conduct varies more than MacInnes indicates, and conduct will vary with relations of the police organization to the community, the character of the substantive criminal law being enforced, and the social conditions of the community, it is nevertheless likely that the variables of danger and authority in the policeman's role, combined with a constant pressure to produce, result in tendencies general enough and similar enough to identify a distinctive "working personality" among police. The question becomes one of understanding what the police do with it. Given this conception of the policeman's "working personality" as background, the chapters that follow analyze the sources of police attitudes and conduct as observed in the setting of specific assignments.

Chapter 4

Operational Environment and Police Discretion

IF the central task of the administration of criminal law is to balance the conflicting principles of order and of legality, the dilemma is epitomized in the question of police discretion. Whether one sees legality as being undermined for the sake of order, or vice versa, the issue reduces to whether there ought to be a loosening or a tightening of restraints on the decisional latitude of police. The issue has recently been given increasing attention by legal scholars concerned primarily with how much discretion police ought to have and how this discretion may be controlled.[1] All conclude that criminal law enforcement can be substantially improved by introducing arrangements to heighten the visibility of police discretion to permit its control by higher authority. Two authors make the general point, while a third specifically advocates the creation of a board to appraise and recommend nonenforcement policies as well as to follow up and review the consequences of implemented proposals.[2]

The sociologist of law, however, is initially more interested in understanding the sociological significance of discretion, as well as its causes and effects, than in suggesting and rationalizing specific reform measures. Such concern invites several analytical distinctions. The most significant contrast is between *delegated* and *unauthorized* discretion, between discretion clearly accorded to the policeman, and discretion which he exercises, but for which he may not have authority. Most of

[1] Thus, Wayne La Fave asks: "Should the police, under any circumstances, be entitled to exercise discretion as to when the criminal law is to be enforced, resulting in their sometimes neither arresting nor reporting an apparent criminal offender?" "The Police and Nonenforcement of the Law—Part II," *Wisconsin Law Review* (1962), 179.

[2] La Fave, *op. cit.*, pp. 104–137, 179–239; Sanford H. Kadish, "Legal Norm and Discretion in the Police and Sentencing Processes," *Harvard Law Review*, 75 (1962), 904–931; Joseph Goldstein, "Police Discretion Not to Invoke the Criminal Process: Low-Visibility Decisions in the Administration of Justice," *Yale Law Journal*, 69 (1960), 543–594.

the problems in the administration of criminal law revolve around un-clarity of authorization, but it is instructive to consider the problems of discretion even when authorization is clear. The latter is the purpose of this chapter.

To understand problems associated with delegated discretion, let us consider as an analogy the admissions officer of a university. Such an official is delegated the authority to make alternative official decisions, such as to select some students for admission, and to reject others. That he is delegated authority, however, also implies that he must carry out his discretionary decisions in line with the *standards* of the institution. Such standards imply both the *principle* or *principles* of the institution and the *criteria* for justifying decisions made on the basis of the principle. An educational institution, for instance, might select students on the basis of a simple principle, such as that students shall be admitted according to scholarly promise. Given the *principle* of scholarly poten-tial, the official must base his decision on relevant *criteria* including grades, admission examination scores, and personal recommendations. Those who have had experience with such criteria know how slippery they are, and how difficult it is for an administrator to give them proper weight under the principle being applied.

Now let us introduce another complication, typically found in institu-tions of higher learning. Most of these colleges and universities are com-mitted to more than one principle. For example, schools depending for survival upon alumni contributions may admit students, especially un-dergraduates, not only on the basis of scholarly promise, but will also consider the applicant as alumnus; here, specific criteria such as wealth, energy, and social standing are needed. In private insti-tutions, admissions officers have customarily been required to strike a balance between these two commitments, one having to do with the essential purpose of the institution and the other with its main-tenance, by admitting scholarship students *and* creating *mimimum* standards for admission. There are also other possible commitments based upon the characteristics of the institution. It may be committed to admitting only men or women students, or it may emphasize the geo-graphical diversity of its student body, admitting students because of lo-cation rather than personal ability, should the two conflict. Similar di-verse commitments may be found in public institutions where such norms as public service prevail.

It is not my intent to analyze the admissions policies of universities, but to suggest some complexities associated with decisions made in the exercise of clearly delegated discretion. Depending upon the principles and criteria utilized, the official will achieve more or less justice, based on the precept that like cases shall be treated alike. Justice depends primarily upon the commitment which the official is attempting to fulfill and the fairness with which he uses the criteria. Some may feel, as I have and do, that there is a fundamental injustice in admissions based on social standing or sex or race, but that geographical diversity may well be a legitimate educational commitment. It is clearly possible for an official to exercise authoritative discretion unjustly, but it is equally possible for honest men to disagree over the nature and ranking of institutional commitments and the appropriate criteria for fulfilling them.

If such problems exist in the exercise of authoritative discretion, they will be intensified under conditions of unauthorized discretion where an official invents, claims, or usurps discretionary authority without it having been specifically delegated. When one discusses the issue of police discretion, therefore, one must distinguish between the problems associated with delegated discretion and those arising out of the creation of discretionary opportunity for the purpose of satisfying personal or institutional motives. The conditions under which questionable discretionary authority comes to be claimed and the problems associated with the exercise of unauthorized discretion are treated in Chapters 5, 6, 7, and 8. The present chapter is an introduction to police discretion, and concentrates upon the simpler, but still complex, area of delegated discretion. The chapter begins with a description of the enforcement of parking meter violations, the most cut-and-dried of field assignments. Next is a description of the automated processing of traffic tickets, which allows no discretion. The automated process, however, may lead to the issuance of traffic warrants of arrest. The decision to arrest when a defendant cannot post bail is completely delegated to the discretion of the warrant officer. His decision depends upon his perception of the principles controlling his work and the interplay of a number of criteria, the most socially significant of which is the defendant's race. Since this chapter deals with the relatively simple issue of delegated discretion, and since race is typically such an important feature of the interaction between policeman and citizen, the relation between race and operational law enforcement is introduced and emphasized.

AUTOMATED JUSTICE: PARKING VIOLATIONS

The processing of a meter violation is doubtless the best illustration of automation in the administration of criminal law. This is so, of course, because in the enforcement of meter violations, the officer's opportunities for the exercise of choice are narrowly circumscribed. His task is simply to read a meter. If the red flag is down, legal requirements have been fulfilled. If it is up, the law has been broken. Even under these simple criteria, however, it sometimes happens that the officer must introduce discretionary judgment. This underscores an extremely important jurisprudential fact: it is impossible to eliminate discretion entirely from the administration of criminal law, even for such a simple and routine operation as the enforcement of parking meter violations. For instance, the driver of a vehicle may return to it when the flag is up and just as the officer is preparing to write out a ticket. If he has not begun to write, the officer usually will ignore the violation. The officer's action here is based upon (1) a private moral conception compatible with institutional goals—a man is entitled to a "break" even though he has committed a crime—and (2) an "institutional principle"—the general goals of the police department are best served if the law is not enforced so strictly as to generate resentment in the ordinary law-abiding citizen. Thus, the officer has not acted arbitrarily, as he would have had he ignored the violation based on his personal feelings toward the motorist. The criteria he employs are compatible with the standards of the police department.

Once the officer has begun to write, he initiates the formal legal process, and it becomes more cumbersome to exercise discretion. Like a judge, he is now responsible to the machinery of the state, since each ticket is numbered and must be accounted for. The city treasurer's office checks to determine whether any of the copies or sets of tickets are missing from the officer's book. The absence of tickets or loss of a book reflects discredit upon his competence. Loss of citations is a more serious infringement than the defacing of a single ticket, requiring the writing of a letter in several copies explaining the loss.

It is still possible, however, even after the officer has begun to write, for the violator to "talk his way out of" the ticket. Generally, he accomplishes this by telling a story indicating intent to comply with the law. Thus, if the officer sees him walking out of a drugstore with small change in his hand, which he claims he was going to use to fill the meter, he may dissuade the officer from issuing the ticket. If this should happen, the officer takes an additional responsibility upon himself. He has committed a significant act by defacing an official form which is consecutively numbered, thereby making his discretionary action public.[3] As a result, the officer must follow through and, like a judge,

---

[3] In any organization, consecutively numbered papers constitute an important means of executive control over the discretionary activities of subordinates. In this respect, the policeman who hands out parking citations, the waitress who dispenses food checks, and the department store clerk who hands out sales slips all share a common characteristic in the way their work is controlled by higher-ups.

present reasons for his action. These will be written on the face of the ticket and evaluated by his superiors in the police department and the municipal court.

Typically, the officer will simply lodge a legal summons under the windshield wiper of the offending vehicle.[4] This action introduces the most rational and efficient process in the administration of criminal law, almost eliminating the defendant's rights. A policeman has made a judgment of guilt, and it rarely happens that this judgment is encumbered by any of the procedural protections accorded the accused by the rule of law. There is customarily no question of right to counsel, venue, jurisdiction, or statutes of limitation. It is the best single example of speedy, massive control of socially undesirable conduct by penal sanctions. Precisely because these sanctions are so relatively slight, the constraints on authority are minimal.

The summons lodged by the officer is one of three copies, known in the traffic bureau as the "soft" or defendant's copy. Behind it is a "pink" copy, forwarded to the municipal court and serving as a complaint. The third, or "hard" copy, is an IBM card. While the soft copy is out in the community, the other two copies are routinely processed. First, the officer transfers the two copies to the traffic division of the police department, where they are dropped in a locked box (along with any other copies he may have filled out). This repository provides the facilities for a control operation. Citations served by each unit, such as a platoon, are counted to determine whether there has been a significant deviation from numerical standards maintained by other units. The work of the individual officer, however, is not counted. When the quantity control operation has been completed, the copies are turned over to the traffic bureau of the municipal court. The traffic bureau divides the copies and sends the pink copy to the statistical section of the police department, from which it is returned within a day; the hard copy is sent to a county data processing facility, which returns it to the traffic bureau.

In the meantime, of course, the owner of the motor vehicle is supposed to follow the instructions on his copy, containing information as to the violation committed and the amount of bail set by the court for the violation. The bail is two dollars for the offense of overtime parking at a meter. The defendant may appear in court and plead not guilty; or he may plead guilty in court; or he may post his bail at the traffic bureau and forfeit. In recent years nobody has pleaded not guilty to a meter violation. Several years ago the constitutionality of "double taxation"

[4] For the year 1961, there were 294,954 traffic citations in Westville, of which 132,033 were meter violations.

was challenged, but came to naught. Occasionally, a plea of guilty is entered, with an explanation of extenuating circumstances. Usually the claim is made that money was placed in a defective meter. Approximately two-thirds of all parking situations are returned within the due date listed on the citation, along with the bail.

Unpaid citations are listed by date in the office of the traffic bureau and are pulled out of the files twenty-eight to thirty days after issuance. All unpaid citations are sent to the state data-processing facility which carries out a critical operation. It alone has the information needed to punch out names and addresses of owners corresponding to license plate numbers. The duplicates containing this information are returned to the municipal traffic bureau, where they are checked against paid citations. Those are shipped back to the county data-processing facility, where notices of illegal parking are automatically filled out on a standardized form. These notices are then routinely returned to the municipal traffic bureau.

TRAFFIC WARRANTS: THE CULMINATION OF MASS PRODUCTION

A notice of illegal parking tells the violator which law he broke, when, and where; the make of his vehicle and license number; the number of his traffic citation and the time it was issued; and finally, the amount of his bail and its due date. The amount of bail on a notice is always twice the amount of the original citation—four dollars for a meter violation. When a notice is mailed five results may follow, depending on the recipient's response. One is posting and forfeiture of bail. This closes the case and occurs approximately 60 per cent of the time. The second possibility is a plea of guilty, with an explanation to reduce the double bail. This is rarely done, since the amount of even double bail is so small.[5] In about 5 per cent of the cases, the notice of illegal parking is returned with its reverse side—a declaration of nonownership—filled out. In this event, the new owner's name and address—listed by the former owner

---

[5] However, there are certain patterns of activity—of an indeterminate frequency—which lead to nonpayment of original citations. Swiping parking tickets has always been a juvenile prank, but adults also play law-evasive games. One is to take your own citation and slip it under the windshield wiper of a neighboring car which has just run out of meter time, but which has not been ticketed, in the hope that your ticket will be paid. Another is to swipe a citation from another vehicle and slip it under one's own wiper to impress a policeman that you have already been ticketed for your overtime parking. Whether this works or not—and it rarely does, since a policeman can often tell by the placement of a citation on a windshield whether he put it there or not—the owner of the first vehicle will be charged double bail.

on the declaration of nonownership—is filed, and returned to the municipal traffic bureau, which reissues an illegal parking notice to the new owner.

The two remaining possible results require the issuance of warrants of arrest. In 5 per cent of the cases, the letter containing the notice of illegal parking is returned to the municipal traffic bureau marked "address unknown." When this happens, the returned letter and attached forms are filed. The names and addresses of the remaining 30 per cent who ignored their notice are placed on a "reserve" calendar. This list, containing the names of the violators, the citation numbers, and the case numbers of the violations, forms the basis for issuing arrest warrants. With the issuance of the warrant, bail is raised to fifteen dollars and the defendant is notified that "For your convenience this warrant will be held in the Traffic Warrant Detail Room . . . for forty-eight hours to afford you opportunity to post bail."

In addition to the information entered on the notice, the warrant also contains the violator's date of birth, business address, occupation, race, sex, operator's license number, height, weight, and age. Since the police officer, whose serial number is also included on the warrant, is "commanded forthwith to arrest the above named defendant and bring him forthwith before Department 3 of the above named court," he may require the identificatory information to carry out his command. Although the command has been signed by a judge with the seal of the court, the signature and seal have been produced by a rubber stamp in the traffic bureau. This is done with the authority of the court under a blanket weekly order stating that a warrant is to be issued for *all* those who did not post bail in compliance with the notice of illegal parking. Thus, each case can be automatically processed. "Efficiency" is clearly the governing principle.

TRAFFIC WARRANT ENFORCEMENT

Approximately 25 per cent of traffic warrants are answered by mail. Those remaining unanswered become the responsibility of the traffic warrant detail. This detail, serving warrants for all parking and moving violations, comprises six officers and is headed by a sergeant. Each officer is normally responsible for one of six "districts" within the city. These districts are designed to achieve a roughly even work load. Traffic warrant officers usually serve about two hundred and fifty warrants per month, averaging three or four inquiries for each warrant served.[6]

[6] The officer to whom the warrant has been entrusted will usually attempt to visit the defendant at his home or place of business during daylight hours—a standard

The warrant police move throughout the community's color and class structure. They deal with the businessman who ignores a warrant because, he claims, the press of business prevented timely payment, and with the welfare recipient who ignored her warrant because she could not afford to post bail. Justice as meted out by the warrant officer is based partly on efficiency—note is taken of how many warrants he "clears"—but also on a principle that seems to combine the idea of rough justice with good public relations. When a warrant policeman tracks down an offender, the man may not have the funds to post bail. The warrant policeman has the authority to arrest such a man, and an arrest is the most *efficient* means of clearing warrants. But warrant policemen are not *required* to arrest in such a situation. Depending on their "judgment," they are administratively authorized to postpone arrest and give the offender time to make bail. The department regards automatic arrest as unduly harsh—such an inflexible policy would be both unjust and result in poor public relations. The able warrant policeman, therefore, is one who clears warrants, but judiciously. For the sociologist, then, the warrant policeman offers an uncommonly good opportunity to observe the process by which police exercise *delegated* authority.

The warrant policeman often deals with what may appear trivial—a citation for overtime parking. By the time it comes to his attention, however, it no longer seems trivial, although it may still be minor. The offender has by this time violated at least two notices to post bail. If several warrants for his arrest are outstanding, he has violated a number of court orders. Therefore, even though he is not yet known to have done anything dangerous to the community, the policeman tends to interpret his disregard for the legal process as *potentially* dangerous. By this process of reasoning, the nonpayment of a traffic warrant and especially of several comes to be regarded by the warrant policeman as a fairly serious indication of unlawful character. Moreover, the traffic warrant policeman is legally empowered to make an arrest. Not only does he have authority, but this is his job. He is both a bill collector and a law enforcement officer. That he has official authority to carry out his job enhances its importance; in turn, its importance is projected on the defendant's character.

It often happens that citizens on whom warrants are to be served do

warrant shift is from 7:30 A.M. to 4:00 P.M. One of the fringe benefits of the traffic warrant detail is linked to the difficulty of finding defendants at home during these daylight hours. The police department permits warrant officers to drive to and from work in their unmarked cars to be able to make inquiries early in the morning or after dinner.

not wish to receive them, and live in neighborhoods whose occupants are on less than friendly terms with the police. The largest Negro neighborhood in the city is considered a "tough" one to work because citizen cooperation with a policeman is apt to be minimal. In this district, the warrant policeman is sometimes unable to locate any suspects for several days, in spite of sixty or seventy stops a day. It is not uncommon, for instance, for a man to use one place—the home of a sister or a cousin—as an official residence and another as the place he lives. Such an arrangement facilitates the avoidance of bill collectors and police. This pattern of living also disposes the policeman, whether by conscious offense or unconscious sexual rivalry, to refer to such a man as a "stud." As one policeman explained when I asked him what the word meant: "Well, that's all they're good for—screwing around and making kids that other people have to take care of. They don't work, they just screw."

The warrant officer has his own ploys to deal with situations presenting obstacles to straightforward answers. Often, he will check the mail to see whether the offender is using the place as some kind of residence. Since identificatory information on the warrant itself is meager, the policeman may resort to deception. If the warrant is for John Smith, the policeman might ring the bell of the residence listed in the warrant and ask for Richard Roe.

"Richard Roe doesn't live here," will be the reply.

"Well, who does?" asks the policeman.

"I do," says the resident.

"Who are you?" asks the policeman.

"John Smith."

"Well, I happen to have a warrant for your arrest."

At this point, the policeman is not required to arrest.[7] He may take

---

[7] Despite these countermeasures, at the time this study was done, the City of Westville had more than thirty thousand traffic warrants outstanding, with bail totaling more than half a million dollars. Almost all were for cars with in-state licenses. It is difficult and costly to enforce out-of-state citations. After a few weeks, the latter are normally discarded.

Unpaid traffic warrants are not a total loss, however. When somebody is picked up under suspicious circumstances for which there is no probable cause for arrest, a routine check will be made to determine whether he has a traffic warrant. It is not uncommon for a prowler to have one or more traffic warrants outstanding.

While the study was in progress, a "warrant book" system developed. Each officer was periodically issued a multilithed pamphlet listing the names of all persons with warrants outstanding. Thus, if a car was stopped on the street, its occupant could be checked to determine whether he had a traffic warrant outstanding. Narcotics detectives especially regarded this as a useful innovation, since, if a suspect had a traffic the amount of bail outstanding from the defendant, or, if the man does not have it, make an arrangement for him to pay later.

THE RACIAL BIAS OF POLICE

In principle, the Westville and Eastville Police Departments, like most in America, are racially unbiased. That is, one would not find in a training manual the idea that Blacks should be treated differently in the criminal process than whites, nor even that Blacks are apt to exhibit greater criminality than whites. The explicit principle is racial equality. Yet from the point of view of the Black, or the white who is generally sympathetic to the plight of the Black in America, most policemen—Westville and Eastville alike—would be regarded as highly racially biased. Before going into the standards the warrant policeman uses, and the reasons for these, we should therefore consider at some length the issue of race bias among police. To what extent does racial prejudice influence the policeman's discretionary judgment? This is an important general question, in part because these attitudes help to form the personal morality and judgment of police in all specialties, and also because such a large percentage of criminal suspects are Black.[8] As will be discussed, however, racial prejudice affects some specialties more than others.

When one observes police in the routine performance of their duties, one hears all the usual derisive terms referring to Blacks and a few others besides. As this volume was going to press, the chief of this "professional" department issued the following directive:

As a matter of policy, the following words and any other similar derogatory words shall not be used by members and employees in the course of their official duties or at any other time as to bring the Westville Police Department into disrepute. These words are:

Boy, spade, jig, nigger, blue, smoke, coon, spook, headhunter, jungle-bunny, boogie, stud, burrhead, cat, black boy, black, shine, ape, spick, mau-mau.

The most common display of a lack of courtesy or objectivity is the use by an officer of unsuitable or offensive language or mannerisms.

There is a particular need to refrain from language which has a derogatory

warrant outstanding, they were legally "covered" in making a search of his person for narcotics (immediately after placing him under arrest for having failed to post bail for a parking or a moving violation).

[8] An excellent discussion of racial differentials in criminal patterns is presented in Marvin E. Wolfgang, *Crime and Race* (New York: Institute of Human Relations Press, 1964).

connotation with reference to race, color, religion, or nationality. Such usage by the police causes deep resentment and antagonism against them.

A negative attitude toward Blacks was a norm among the police studied, as recognized by the chief himself. If a policeman did not subscribe to it, unless Black himself, he would be somewhat resented by his fellows. For example, one Westville policeman, disclaiming negative feelings toward Blacks, commented:

> When I came on this job, I don't think I was prejudiced. I used to play with colored kids when I grew up, ball and things like that, and there were no problems. But when somebody hates you, you get to hate them. I used to work the Bowes Theater on my patrol beat. The colored kids made a lot of trouble. First, I didn't mind too much—I thought they were just kids cutting up. Then after a while I began to see they hated me, just because I was a cop. It didn't matter what kind of cop I was or what I did—they hated me.
>
> Still, I don't think I'm prejudiced—not the way some guys here are. Sure, I call them niggers around the department—everybody does it, so I do it too. But I don't let my kids say nigger at home.

William Westley, who studied police in a midwestern city near Chicago, commented in a similar vein in 1951:

> For the police the Negro epitomizes the slum dweller and, in addition, he is culturally and biologically inherently criminal. Individual policemen sometimes deviate sharply from this general definition, but no white policeman with whom the author has had contact failed to mock the Negro, to use some type of stereotyped categorization, and to refer to interaction with the Negro in an exaggerated dialect, when the subject arose.[9]

Nevertheless, from the point of view of most policemen, such a term as "racial bias" does not constitute an accurate description of his attitude toward Blacks. The average policeman does not like Blacks; and since most policemen are straightforward and outspoken, few would deny such a generalization, at least among themselves. Indeed, in private conversation many white policemen will strongly assert negative feelings toward Blacks. Still, even a policeman who admits to hating Blacks and who openly characterizes Blacks in the most pejorative terms will usually not admit to being racially biased or prejudiced. Why not?

To say of somebody that he is *biased* against another is to make an *accusation* rather than a descriptive report of feelings. The policeman knows what it means to hate or fear or merely dislike. But he finds it difficult to accept a term which transforms an explicit emotion—hatred

[9] William A. Westley, *The Police: A Sociological Study of Law, Custom and Morality,* unpublished Ph.D. dissertation, University of Chicago, Department of Sociology, 1951, p. 168.

—into a fuzzy and condemnatory abstraction. To say of somebody that he *hates* another is a statement of fact—there may be good reason for hating. However, to accuse somebody of bias is to put him clearly in the wrong, since there is never a justification for bias.

Moreover, the term racial bias implies something exceptional about the policeman's attitude; it distinguishes the policeman's antipathy from the run-of-the-mill community attitude. From the policeman's point of view, an accusation of racial bias tends to make a scapegoat of him, when as a rule he is probably no more prejudiced than his fellow citizens who lead lives isolated from Blacks. Unlike most whites, the policeman has some sort of social contact with lower-class Blacks. He has learned that in the Black community the term "nigger" is not necessarily taboo, and that it refers to impoverished and illiterate Blacks, usually of southern origin. While use of the term "nigger" by Blacks expresses the inevitable self-hatred of the oppressed,[10] the policeman is not a student of culture and personality. He thinks of himself as a white policeman and the Black man he is called upon to control as a "nigger."

Indeed, the policeman is directly antagonistic toward euphemisms. Unlike the peacetime soldier, the policeman is *always* in "combat," out on the streets, doing his job. Like the dogface, he is irritated by most manifestations of what he terms "chicken shit"—an inclusive abstraction encompassing minor organizational rules, legal technicalities, and embellished descriptions. The policeman's culture is that of the masculine workingman. It is of the docks, the barracks, the ballfield—Joe DiMaggio was a helluva good "wop" centerfielder, not an athlete of "Italian extraction," and similarly, the Black man is a "nigger," not a member of an "underprivileged minority."

This is not to suggest that policemen are not predisposed to attribute negative characteristics to Blacks and are not "racially prejudiced." They are both more so and less so than this vague term connotes. They are more "prejudiced," in that their feelings against Black men are less repressed than is usual in polite white society. They are less "prejudiced," in that their social world tends to be constructed along ethnic lines, as exemplified by the "kidding around" among the men—"If us Swedes hadn't invaded Ireland, you guys would still be up there in the trees with the monkeys." Thus, although hostile feelings toward the Black are characteristic of white policemen in general, these dispositions are also linked to a broader pattern of racial and ethnic stereotyping.

[10] See Irving Sarnoff, "Identification With the Aggressor: Some Personality Correlates of Anti-Semitism Among Jews," *Journal of Personality*, **20** (1952), 199–218.

It should also be understood that this disposition to stereotype is an integral part of the policeman's world. We described in the previous chapter how policemen are trained to view departures from the "normal." They are called on in many aspects of their work to make "hunch" judgments, based on loose correlations. For example, the concept of *modus operandi* is nothing more than a technique for drawing defeasible analogies between one criminal pattern and another. In effect, it is a stereotype, probably right more often than wrong, which may not be claiming much. Similarly, ethnic stereotypes, like the *modus operandi* of criminals, become part of the armory of investigation.

Furthermore, it is likely that the attitudes of policemen toward Blacks are not significantly different from those of most comparable whites such as skilled workingmen and white-collar workers. Those California citizens who voted "Yes" in 1964 on a proposition to repeal the state law against discrimination in housing illustrate the general prejudice of the white community. Many of these same people would protest being labeled "racially prejudiced," on the grounds they were merely trying to protect property values.[11] The policeman similarly claims freedom from racial prejudice. He is, according to his own standards, not "biased," but merely truthful. Thus, the policeman would object (none ever actually has—this is my analysis, based on numerous conversations, conducted and overheard) to the term racial bias as a portrayal of his attitude on two grounds: it is not descriptive, but accusatory; and it singles out the policeman when in fact he represents a wider body of opinion. His most important objection, however, would be to the ambiguity of the term when applied to the issue of how he does his job. Whatever his personal preferences, and, indeed, their influence upon his work, the policeman sees himself as a man who extends justice evenhandedly, a factor which in itself exerts some control over his behavior.

RACIAL PREJUDICE AND THE WARRANT POLICEMAN

A discussion of the racial prejudices of police is needed as a background to understanding how criteria of police discretion develop within

[11] Another indication of general prejudice is found in the 1962 Grand Jury Report for the county being studied. It states, in its section on law enforcement: "Often the people who represent minorities teach only the rights and not the responsibilities of citizenship." Furthermore, they recommend that a course of study be given by the courts "in the obedience to law and responsibilities of citizenship," although no recommendations were made for courses to the general public on the rights of minority groups.

selected police assignments. It might be thought, for example, that the warrant policeman, given his delegated and therefore greater administrative discretion, will more likely discriminate against Blacks on the basis of prejudices against them. In the discussion that follows, however, I shall indicate how the fact of his delegated authority, plus other factors in his occupational situation, tend to dilute the warrant policeman's racial prejudice in action. That is, I shall endeavor to show how it is possible for him to be accorded wide decisional latitude; to be racially prejudiced; and to carry out his work relatively evenhandedly. I shall also analyze how he may appear to be discriminating against Blacks, when, in fact, whether he is or not depends largely on one's definition of racial discrimination. Later on, I shall indicate how certain tasks required of police—especially ordinary patrolmen—tend to create conditions under which prejudice is more likely to influence occupational conduct. The issue of how police prejudice affects law enforcement cannot, I propose, be adequately discussed without reference to the policeman's assignment.

A traffic warrant policeman's ability is measured in good part according to the number of warrants he "clears" per unit of time. Therefore, the disappearance of a defendant already "in hand" is not regarded lightly by him. As indicated, however, the police department does not require that warrants be cleared by arrest when the defendant cannot post bail.[12] The department permits, to a degree encourages, the individual warrant officer to construct what in effect amounts to a system of "credit." Such a system requires the officer to create a set of criteria on which to base his judgment of whether or not the individual defendant's assurance that he will post bail at a later date is trustworthy. What are the criteria, how are they usually constructed, and how does the race of the defendant influence the decision reached by the policeman?

First of all, if the defendant has a number of warrants outstanding over a period of time—four or five in several years—the wagon will almost certainly be called, unless of course the man can post bail. The largest "package" payment of bail I saw posted was for eighty-four dollars. This included warrants totaling fifty-four dollars for three moving violations, plus two overtime parking warrants totaling thirty dollars. The defendant borrowed the cash from his employer, the proprietor of an auto body repair shop, who did not want to have his employee carted off to the city jail. In this case, the policeman waited forty-five minutes for the defendant to raise bail. The policeman was of the opinion that he was being exceptionally lenient, and that his fellow traffic warrant

[12] This posture illustrates the most propitious conditions for administrative discretion, that is, unspecified and unrecorded procedure.

officers would likely have "called the wagon." Two things saved this defendant from going to jail. He was obviously working and consequently satisfied an important criterion for "credit." Secondly, the officer knew the defendant's boss personally and did not want to inconvenience him by taking one of his workingmen off a job. Incidentally, the defendant happened to be white in this case, and the boss, Black. In the ordinary case, however, the policeman would reason that a man with several outstanding warrants has no intention of posting bail, and that, if let go, he will simply vanish.

In the simple case where the defendant has one warrant for fifteen dollars outstanding, the policeman's primary consideration is the apparent stability of the defendant's residence, because the policeman does not want to lose control over his physical presence. If the defendant owns his own home, or if he owns furniture, he cannot afford to move in order to escape the payment of fifteen dollars. Since Blacks tend to be less stable residentially, the police are less likely to give Blacks time to raise bail. Similarly, if a man, white or Black, convinces the warrant policeman that he is working, and needs until payday to raise his bail, the policeman will likely be sympathetic. Will he be more sympathetic to a white man than to a Black man? My observations say "No," but perhaps police behavior was altered by my presence. There was, however, notable tendency for traffic warrant police to respond favorably to Blacks appearing to possess the middle-class virtues of occupational and residential stability.

By contrast, if a man is receiving welfare funds and must use this money to feed his family, the policeman is likely to consider him a poor risk. Since Blacks are more likely to be on welfare than whites, it may again appear that Blacks receive less consideration. Thus, the race of the defendant may turn out to be a relatively spurious variable, too easily giving the impression that traffic warrant policemen discriminate against Blacks. Accordingly, a traffic warrant policeman may operate according to general standards—which Blacks find more difficult to meet than whites—and still appear to be biased in his work as a warrant officer.

My limited observations found traffic warrant policemen employing special standards only in arresting women (except prostitutes) and irrespective of color. It is degrading for a man to exert coercion upon a woman, especially in public view. A woman who resists arrest by shouting or screaming is inevitably an embarrassment to a police officer, and the problem of controlling her through physical force could become awkward. In addition, a woman who is a mother is especially likely to receive extra consideration from a traffic warrant policeman. The policeman is responsible for seeing to it that provisions are made for the care and maintenance of her children which requires the assistance of other agencies, and as a rule the policeman will make decisions requiring less effort, especially paperwork. Besides, as one officer remarked, "It's not only a helluva lot of trouble to put away a whole family, but you feel like hell locking up a bunch of kids because their mother couldn't post twenty-two dollars bail."

By contrast, the policeman acts entirely differently toward the "stud." He may sometimes sympathize with the Black mother's lack of funds, especially if she is on welfare, but he maintains a fundamental hostility toward the young male. In the policeman's moral world, if a young man is out of work and owes a debt to society which he lacks the money to pay off, he should go to jail for a few days to repair his obligations.

Thus, the exercise of discretion by the traffic warrant policeman takes on certain specific patterns, partly as a result of the requirements placed upon him by the department itself, and partly as a result of his private moral conceptions, which in turn are influenced by his occupational role. He may also appear to be discriminating against the Black, when in fact he may be mainly implementing departmental goals by deciding against the poor, the unemployed, and the residentially unstable, many of whom are Black.[13] Indeed, as a result of the civil rights movement, white policemen sometimes seem *more* color conscious in an interesting fashion. They perhaps used to unconcernedly push a black man around —the suspect was just another "nigger." Now, the policeman may think twice—a Black suspect may appear to him not only as a man with rights, but one with exceptional political power as well.

DISCRETION AND OCCUPATIONAL ENVIRONMENT

The across-the-board standards of the traffic warrant policeman— traceable to a relatively benign occupational environment—do not necessarily characterize all other policemen. Thus, the behavior of the policeman toward Blacks is likely to vary with his assignment within the department, always based on a foundation of strong racial bias. Hostility toward Blacks is apt to be revealed on the street, especially in situations inviting stereotyping. If police are looking for a robbery assailant, and have "nothing to go on" but a vague description of a Black male, innocent Black males will easily be assimilated to the policeman's

---

[13] This analysis suggests that, as in so many other sectors, especially employment and housing, the problem of "bias" is not merely racial, but has broader social and economic implications. At the same time, a cool and objective analysis provides little comfort to those non-whites who face the existential problem of being poor, unemployed, and residentially unstable.

stereotype of the suspect. The more ambiguous the information the police may have about the suspect, the more likely is it that large numbers of people will be treated as potential suspects. Along these lines, Kephart presents the interesting finding that white patrolmen tend grossly to overestimate the percentage of Negro arrests (in Philadelphia, circa 1955).[14]

The policeman whose main job is to maintain the appearance of public order on the street has in several respects a more difficult task than the warrant policeman or the plainclothesman. A uniformed policeman is a conspicuous and visible target for subtle but unmistakable forms of insult such as sidelong glances, pursed lips, or loud sniffs. The problem of the uniform attracting hostility is difficult to measure. One would not know how to interpret answers to a questionnaire, since overt denial of the problem could hardly be interpreted at face value. It is worth noting, however, that the Westville Police Department is troubled by an internal recruitment problem—the refusal of a number of qualified detectives to become lieutenants, even though the salary is higher (by about forty dollars per month). Although there may be several reasons for this unwillingness including added responsibility, irregular shifts, and easier transferability, an additional reason mentioned by several detectives is reluctance to go back into uniform.[15]

The uniformed officer, in addition to being an object of hostility, has a further related problem. He is sometimes asked to move people from one place on the street to another. For this task he requires the cooperation and respect of the citizenry. Sanctions are the only backing with which the patrolman can command the respect of a hostile citizenry. Unlike the traffic warrant policeman, who has the power to make an arrest in his pocket, the uniformed officer has mainly the weapon of violence to prod reluctant citizens (although lately the police have developed more subtle weapons, such as "field contact" reports. When a policeman sees a "suspicious" looking individual he may stop and ask his name, birthdate, place of residence, and note identifying characteristics—height, weight, color, and clothing. He will also, likely, ask the man questions regarding his purpose for being where he is. As hap-

---

[14] "The higher the actual Negro arrest rate in a district, the higher will be the degree of overestimation of that rate by the white policeman of that district." From William M. Kephart, *Racial Factors and Urban Law Enforcement* (Philadelphia: University of Pennsylvania, 1957), pp. 94–95.

[15] We have reported instances in Chapter 3 of the policeman preferring to maintain the secret of his identity. For a more general discussion of management of stigmatic qualities, see Erving Goffman's *Stigma: Notes on the Management of Spoiled Identity* (Englewood Cliffs: Prentice-Hall, 1963), especially Chapter 2.

pens not infrequently, the policeman introduces such an interaction with a statement like "hey, boy, "burrhead," (or any of the other derogatory terms now forbidden by the chief of police). His assertion of authority is usually less than fully appreciated by those so approached.

The Black population is no longer so cowed as it once was, unfortunately for the patrol police. As one patrolman commented:

> It's harder to work in these neighborhoods now than it used to be because we send the kids to school and teach them about rights and then put them back in the neighborhood. I think we ought to either get rid of these neighborhoods or stop teaching these kids about their rights.

When a policeman pushes a man who knows his rights, he receives an understandably hostile response. In an early period (but less than twenty years ago) the police used outright violence to maintain respect.[16] It is now more difficult for them (at least in Westville and doubtless in most other northern urban areas) to maintain control through these techniques because of the operation of civil rights groups, and the increased knowledgeability of the citizens most likely to talk back—the younger males. But it is not color that is necessarily the determining factor. The "uncooperative" white delinquent will be treated just as roughly as the Black. And woe to the white demonstrator who goes "limp" with others during a protest demonstration. For the policeman, this form of protest generates physical labor, hard and, in his view, unnecessary. When a citizen *makes* a policeman sweat to take him into custody, he has created the situation most apt to lead to police indignation and anger.

CONCLUSION

This chapter began the examination of the relation between the occupational environment of law enforcement and the character of police discretion in the simplest offense category—violation of parking meter rules. The only completely clear example of "mechanical" justice is precisely that—the automated processing of citations after they have been submitted to the department by the policeman. Only under these conditions do we find pure "impersonality." At this stage the law enforcement process does not deal with people, but with IBM cards, and is therefore completely without discretion. For the most part, the work of the meter policemen is also similarly impersonal. He typically does not encounter a human being, but an automobile. When a person enters

[16] See William A. Westley, "Violence and the Police," *American Journal of Sociology*, **59** (1953), 34.

the scene of his work, however, the policeman may be required to make a discretionary judgment.

The traffic warrant officer, in contrast to the meter policeman, always deals with people, and also is delegated almost absolute administrative discretion to arrest when the offender cannot produce bail. Given these goals, it is asked, what are the criteria developed by the policeman to extend credit? How does race enter the picture? Hypothetically, a most obvious possibility is for the policeman simply to act out his prejudices, especially those he holds toward Blacks. One could believe that the more discretion offered the policeman, the more his personal biases will be injected into the discretionary decision. Examining the work of the traffic policeman, however, the contrary appears to be true. Followed on his rounds, the warrant policeman seems to use relatively objective criteria. Thus, under conditions of clearly delegated discretion, the warrant policeman appears to develop fairly evenhanded standards for the administration of criminal justice. Assuming that the warrant policeman is not, by nature, more generously endowed with judicial disinterestedness than other officers of the law, how do we account for his relatively judicious disposition?

Examining his occupational environment, we find it especially conducive to developing an evenhanded discretionary stance. First, since the warrant policeman is not required to direct the activities of citizens acting within the law, he does not tend to generate hostilities and counter-hostilities inflaming prejudice. Second, the offense he deals with is relatively minor, not the sort promoting strong feelings of danger to the community or to the policeman himself. Third, when he encounters repeated offenders, a relatively rare occurrence, he may be on friendly terms with them, since they are neither dangerous violators of the law nor organized criminals. Finally, as an officer lawfully warranted to make an arrest which is virtually certain to be followed by a conviction, he does not anticipate the offender will meet with less punishment than he "deserves," according to the warrant policeman's standards. He is confident that his conception of justice will ultimately be served. Thus, the warrant policeman does not find it necessary to exceed his delegated discretion, nor to be especially punitive within its terms. There are of course some warrant officers who are more punitive than others, but the pattern described seems to hold as a rule.

Enforcement specialties presenting other social conditions may arouse the policeman to take personal action increasing or decreasing sanctions against the offender, that is, to exercise discretionary authority where the claim of authority is at least questionable. The street patrolman is especially prone to asserting authority when facing outright hostility without the formal capacity to impose legal sanctions. Thus, when he encounters a situation where he perceives arrogance or hostility on the part of the citizenry, he may be tempted to make strong claims of authority, for which he may have few, if any, lawful grounds. If the uniform sets him up as an object of hatred, it should also, from the policeman's point of view, represent authoritative power and command obedience.

The mere delegation of authority does not appear to determine arbitrary police conduct. On the contrary, when the policeman is actually "boss" of the social situation, his conduct may be tempered. By contrast, when he faces potential danger, as the street patrolman feels he frequently does, he is more inclined to resort to the use of his authority to reduce the perception of danger. Whether or not he has actually been delegated such authority may be open to question, but it is not an important consideration for the street policeman. For him, the uniform constitutes authority, and he is usually willing to back up a challenge with all the force he can command. His job, as he sees it, is to maintain public order, and restraints upon his initiative will only, from his point of view, reduce his capacity to fulfill his assigned task.

Chapter 5

The Confrontation of the Suspect

THE work of the traffic warrant policeman is uncomplicated by the legal requirements for conviction found in other areas of law enforcement. The structure of prosecution is so simple that the prosecutor's office is not required to do any work. For such minor offenses as overtime meter parking, there is in reality no presumption of innocence —in fact, there is an overwhelming presumption of the defendant's guilt. Although the defendant is sometimes acquitted, the burden rests heavily upon him to prove his innocence. Furthermore, the presumption of guilt is strengthened when the defendant ignores a citation and allows it to run to the traffic warrant stage. In such a case, prosecution is unnecessary. Unless there is a mistake of identity, which almost never happens, the defendant is clearly guilty, and the sentencing judge will take extenuating circumstances into account.

This chapter begins to discuss how the policeman develops a stake in the outcome of more usual and more complex cases, those where a conviction is required. Concentrating upon the initial confrontation of a suspected offender by an officer of the law, the principal issue raised is how the nature of prior relations between the policeman and the suspect comes to shape the claiming and exercising of police authority. The first part of the chapter describes the routine processing of traffic violations and the circumstances under which police come to care about how such cases are decided. The second half examines enforcement of prostitution laws. It discusses patterns of prostitution, their effect upon the policeman's understanding of and activities about legal requirements for conviction, the effect of such interpretation on police-prostitute relations, and the influence of these relations on legal outcomes.

MOVING VIOLATIONS: PROSECUTORIAL ROUTINE

In the vast majority of minor traffic offenses, there is no arrest, and the Westville district attorney does not even see a complaint. The matter is presented entirely on the basis of the citation(s) issued by the officer. Complaints are verified by a deputy district attorney only for the more serious traffic violations, such as drunken driving, hit-and-run, reckless driving, and driving on a suspended license. Typically, representatives of the traffic division bring in a number of complaints to be verified by a deputy district attorney. In these cases, the prosecutor theoretically exercises a magisterial function, but in practice the deputy cornered by the traffic police will sign complaints quickly and with only a cursory glance at what he is signing. Routinely, then, deputy district attorneys accept the judgment of the police as to whether charges should be brought.[1]

The overwhelming majority of such charges are settled by the accused's plea of guilty. The prosecutor has a policy of charging all traffic offenses arising out of the same behavioral transaction. Thus, if a citizen fails to signal and passes a red light, all while driving on a suspended license, he will be charged with three separate violations of the vehicle code. It is common knowledge among defense attorneys that this practice facilitates pleas of guilty by defendants.

"Dealing out" a traffic violation typically occurs as follows: at approximately 8:45 A.M. the deputy district attorney for the jury trial department will pick up a copy of the "calendar," the list of the cases scheduled to be adjudicated that morning, from the office of the municipal court clerk. He will take the calendar with him into the courtroom, seat himself at the table set aside for the district attorney, and list the names of the defendants in alphabetical order on three-by-five cards. He will also include the charges against the defendant and the name of his attorney.

While he is so engaged, he will be approached by a number of attorneys, some seeking a "date certain" for trial, others requesting consent to a postponement. Depending in part on his conception of his role, the deputy district attorney will be more or less obliging. Most legal studies of prosecutor discretion refer to the prosecutor as if he were one man. He is usually, of course, multiple men. Thus, the Westville office alone had thirteen attorneys. Their behavior, especially that of the younger ones, could to some extent be distinguished by whether or not they saw themselves as "committed" to a law enforcement career. Those who were seemed less solicitous of defense attorney's feelings than those who were "working for the experience"—which includes the opportunity to meet practicing attorneys in the county.

The majority of the attorneys who approach the deputy district attorney will be either initiating a plea bargain or confirming an earlier agree-

---

[1] This practice suggests that police judgment is generally correct. If the prosecutor were to lose many cases as a result of improper complaints, his staff would soon begin to pay more attention to these.

ment (made usually over the telephone or casually in the hallway). The deputy district attorney will routinely "offer" to drop other charges arising out of the same behavioral transaction in return for a plea of guilty. If an agreement is reached, it will be accepted by the judge as a matter of administrative regularity. The charge, however, is often less important to the defendant and his attorney than its consequences. Therefore, the judge will often be consulted in chambers by the defense attorney, usually in the presence of the deputy district attorney, for further negotiation on the case's actual disposition—fine, time in jail, probation, loss of license.

Traffic cases are, on the whole, processed routinely, partly because the statutes governing traffic offenses limit the judge's discretion in sentencing, but also, from the point of view of law enforcement, because the relationship between the police and the offender is minimal and nonrecurring. The police will be consulted only in the rare case where the defendant claims innocence. Usually the defendant is satisfied to have "gotten off" on one of the counts with which he was charged.[2] Thus, the routine reduction of charges provides conditions enabling the district attorney's office to establish a fairly standardized policy for determining the outcome of traffic violations.

THE MODIFICATION OF ROUTINE: POLICE INVOLVEMENT

In order to demonstrate how police involvement alters the processing of a case by the prosecutor, it is useful to raise the issue of how interactional conditions between the policeman and the suspect may modify the usual "dealing out" procedure. The typical traffic offenses does not allow the policeman much in the way of interaction with the violator: the brief confrontation involves the issuance of a citation (a "ticket") by the officer and allows the offender to continue on his way. There are, however, three sets of circumstances under which the traffic policeman may become personally involved.

[2] A representative of the district attorney's office has written, in response to an early draft of this chapter, that the multiple charge in most of these cases is strictly a legal fiction. As he said:

> Under Sec. 654 of the Penal Code, a defendant may be punished only once for a transaction even though multiple offenses occur within that transaction. This concept has recently been incredibly expanded by our currently pro-defense appellate courts and it is probable that under present law a defendant could not legally be punished for a lesser driving offense within a central serious transaction. Thus, a defendant could not be punished for both drunk driving and the speeding offense which made the officer stop him in the first place, but only for the drunk driving.

First, there are instances where the person charged with a traffic offense abuses the policeman in some way. A motorist who, for example, calls a policeman "a dirty bastard" may earn himself a citation for speeding rather than a reprimand; a citation for a speed contest rather than simple speeding: and finally, multiple citations, such as speeding plus improperly changing lanes, following too closely, improperly displaying registration, faulty muffler, no driver's license in possession and any others that may occur to the officer.

Driver abuse is often associated with a "misunderstanding." There is a legal requirement that a person charged with a violation sign the citation. The citation process is a method of giving the court jurisdiction over the offender. It is, in effect, a release on his own recognizance, without bail. The offender who refuses to promise to appear by giving a written promise (of record) must be brought within the jurisdiction of the court by the usual process (arrest, formal charge, and arraignment). In these circumstances, some citizens believe that the officer is "tricking them into something." When the violator refuses to sign, the officer will detain him and call for a police sergeant. The sergeant will typically explain the signature requirement and the additional ruling that in the event a motorist refuses to sign, orders are to lock him up.[3] Most motorists will sign at this point, but a few stubborn ones have gone to jail.

Secondly, there are violators who are exceptionally prone to using automobiles in an illegal fashion—people who have been picked up by the police several times for a speeding offense, for example.[4] When under such circumstances a motorist has been issued several citations, he may decide to plead not guilty and demand a trial. At this point, if the policeman insists that no counts be dropped, his demand will be considered by the deputy district attorney, whose decision usually depends upon his estimate of the validity of the policeman's grievance.

For traffic police there is, however, sustained personal interaction with only one type of violator, the gang motorcyclist. Usually these people— they may be juveniles, but in the city studied were mostly over twenty-one—are a source of irritation to state as well as local police since they are apt in their wanderings to roam from city to city as well as from county to county. In part, they annoy traffic policemen because of their appearance—which sometimes serves as a source of humor for the po-

[3] The traffic officer about to give a citation is required by statute to lock up the motorist who refuses to sign. See Vehicle Code Sec. 40500 *et seq.*, and Sec. 40300 *et seq.*, particularly 40302.

[4] In a city the size of Westville, it is unusual for a violator to run into the same policeman several times or to become a police "problem," although in some of the smaller municipalities this pattern of events occurs more frequently.

liceman (although it should also be noted that on the road they are occasionally mistaken for policemen). In addition to their appearance,
type of vehicle, general rebelliousness, and reputation as "hoodlums,"
motorcycle gangs engage in specific practices to irritate police. In the
area studied, for example, one motorcycle gang was accused of releasing
oil on the highway, thus endangering the lives of pursuing traffic patrolmen.[5] This practice not only irritates the police—it infuriates them.

In addition, these gangs abuse canons of individual justice, of which
they are well aware, to frustrate law enforcement. Because they wear
similar, colored jackets and ride multicolored motorcycles, they are often
able to avoid being individually identified as violators, unless one of
them is actually caught in the act of speeding. If the officer is in a car, it
may be difficult for him to overtake a speeding cyclist. Furthermore, to
prove speeding, the officer must follow the speeder for a definite period
of time in order to "clock" his speed, and he must also be able to identify the individual speeder. If the entire group were speeding, the problem of individual identification would not be posed. The Flying Devils,
however, will string out with only two or three of fifteen cyclists actually
speeding. If the police should lose sight of the speeders on the highway,
the speeders will have reformed into a group traveling within the legal
limit by the time the police have caught up with them. The officer may
guess as to which one actually was speeding, but even if he is correct,
the speeder will claim that one of his friends may have been speeding.
In addition, a friend is typically available to testify that he and the accused were traveling alongside one another within the speed limit.

One can therefore imagine that when charges are finally leveled at
these cyclists, the police are in no mood to have them reduced. The
eagerness of the police to cooperate in the prosecution makes them willing to testify, even on their own time. A prosecutor who reduced
charges arising out of the same behavioral transaction in a Flying Devil
case would be considered at best "uncooperative," even if his reason for
doing so was that he thought he would lose the action. The Flying
Devils thus present a dramatic illustration of how the routine processing
of speeding cases may be altered as a result of prior hostile relations between the police and the offenders. The behavior of the rebellious
motorcycle gang suggests that the greater the degree to which an
offender or group of offenders irritates the police, the more likely are the
police to demand that their opinions strongly influence decision-making
processes legally accorded to the district attorney's office, and that every

---

[5] This gang, the Flying Devils, is composed of white youths. Police hostility is
directed not at their color but at their patterns of behavior.

effort be made by the district attorney's office to prosecute and convict.

Although the police, in such cases as described, in no way exceed their authority, they do make an atypical assertion of it. It does not follow, however, that whenever the policeman asserts influence over the prosecutor his request is always to heighten the sanction. The type of demand the policeman makes, whether for harsher or more lenient treatment, depends upon the historic character of the relations between the policeman and the defendant. The dynamics of this process are further illustrated by comparing police relations to the gang cyclist with police relations to the prostitute.

THE POLICEMAN AND THE PROSTITUTE

The relation between policeman and prostitute is both similar to and different from his relation to the gang motorcyclist. Although he perceives each in a context of criminality, his relations with the gang motorcyclist are vague and potentially explosive, while those with the prostitute are patterned and more predictable. By describing the behavior patterns of the prostitutes in the context of police administration, her symbolic criminality, her ability to frustrate conviction, and her role in the operation of the vice control squad, it should be possible to demonstrate further how interactional patterns between police and suspect affect the police conception of a criminal case and its outcome.

Before proceeding, some description should be given of the organization and functions of the Westville vice control squad. The squad is headed by a lieutenant, has three sergeants and sixteen patrolmen. Promotions in Westville are made on the basis of civil service examinations emphasizing general verbal ability and formal knowledge of police methods and procedures. Practical ability, or "efficiency," as it is called on the examination, counts for only 5 per cent. During his first three years on the force a patrolman's pay increases automatically until it reaches a maximum beyond which it cannot rise except by promotion. The purpose of such a system is to prevent a chief from giving pay raises and promotions on the basis of friendship rather than objective qualifications. Vice control plainclothesmen hold the same rank and are not paid more than ordinary patrolmen. Their chief reward is the privilege of being plainclothes investigators on the vice control squad itself.

As a member of "the squad," a patrolman works either a 10 A.M. to 6 P.M. shift or, more likely, a 6 P.M. to 2 A.M. shift. There are five details corresponding to crimes in the squad's jurisdiction: gambling (including card games, dice games, and numbers); prostitution; narcotics and dangerous drugs; and bookmaking. There is also a one-man bar detail enforcing licensing laws. Homosexuality is investigated by the vice squad only when male prostitutes are involved. Otherwise this activity falls under the jurisdiction of the morals squad, a special detail for processing statutory rape and sexual psychopathy complaints.[6]

Shifts and assignments to details are frequently based on availability, although there are specialists, especially among the sergeants. Practically everybody on duty (and some who are off) might participate, however, in a large or important gambling or narcotics raid. Furthermore, the jurisdiction of all policemen extends to all crimes. Thus, if a call comes over the radio reporting a robbery, a vice squad narcotics detail might follow up the call if it is not at the moment on some other case. Members of the "squad" take pride in a record of more felony arrests per man than any other division of the police department, although this is largely accounted for by a predominance of arrests for the illegal use or sale of narcotics or marihuana.

BEHAVIOR PATTERNS OF PROSTITUTES [7]

Several prostitution patterns are roughly distinguishable in the city of Westville, according to the color of the girl. White prostitutes typically do not walk the streets, as Black ones do, but instead operate mainly by telephone as "call girls." Although solitary white prostitutes may be found, the white prostitutes of Westville are generally well organized. Thus, one recently arrested madam maintained, in apartments separate from hers, two girls over whom she had absolute control. The girls were forbidden to "turn their own tricks" or to receive telephone calls. The madam had carefully built up a clientele over a period of years, and had a description and pertinent identificatory information about any man

[6] See by J. Richard Woodworth, *The Administration of Statutory Rape Complaints: A Sociological Study,* unpublished master's thesis, Berkeley: University of California, 1964.

[7] Prostitutes are prosecuted under the disorderly conduct provision of the penal code, specifically section 647b, which states that "every person . . . who solicits or engages in any act of prostitution . . . shall be guilty of disorderly conduct, a misdemeanor." A prostitute is one who engages in sexual intercourse for hire. *People* v. *Head*, 146 Cal. App. 2d 744, 304 p. 2d 761 (1956).

Several European countries have "red light districts" where prostitutes stand outside of doorways or in windows and do not accost passersby. In England, prostitutes used to be permitted to stop men on the street. This became such a problem, however, that they are no longer able to do so, even though the act of prostitution is still not unlawful. See the famous *Wolfenden Report* (Report of the Committee on Homosexual Offense and Prostitution, CMD 247, 1957).

who might phone—with much the same intent as banks that ask for the maiden name of depositors' mothers, to have on hand an effective identificatory device. Call girls will also sometimes ask a prospect where he works and what his number is to check whether he is a policeman. If police know the name and number of a customer, and call from his place of business with the cooperation of his employer, they may not fool the call girl either. A caller identifying himself as "Fred Jones" may also be asked questions regarding occupation, place of employment, height, weight, and suit size. Consequently, even when the police obtain the number of an efficiently run call girl operation, it is difficult for them to gain admission without the assistance of a regular customer. Another white prostitute managed to avoid the police by restricting her clientele to men of Chinese extraction, because she knew there was no one of this description on the Westville police force. She was finally caught when a Chinese policeman from another police force was brought in to pose as a customer.

TABLE 1   *White, Nonwhite Women*
Arrested for Solicitation or Prostitution in
Westville during 1962, by Race of Men
Involved (from Westville Vice Control
Squad Records)

Men	Women			
	Nonwhite *		White	
	N	%	N	%
White	121	77	17	85
Nonwhite	36 †	23	3 ‡	15
Total	157	100	20	100

* On police records, one hundred and fifty-two were identified as Negro, five as Mexican.
† Twenty-nine were identified as Negro, five as Oriental, two as Mexican.
‡ Two were Negro, one Oriental.

Unlike the white prostitutes, nonwhite prostitutes of Westville "work" the streets and the bars, but the police find it nearly as difficult to apprehend them as white prostitutes. Black prostitutes typically locate themselves in the bars and on the sidewalks of the main ghetto street, depending upon the warmth of the evening. They also "work" other bars nearer to downtown, some within one hundred yards of the police department. On a warm night, the Market Street bars and sidewalks are crowded with Black people, as are the eating counters, which do a thriving business after the bars close at 2:30 A.M. Roughly between midnight and 4 A.M., white servicemen or "respectable" married men, who are the black girls' chief customers, drive slowly around the block. This manner of driving communicates to the prostitute that the driver is seeking to purchase a "date" or "trick." The police call this manner of driving "trolling," as an analogy to the fisherman who tosses a line over the end of his boat, and proceeds just fast enough to give the impression that the bait is moving. The purpose of customer "trolling" is to permit the girls to avoid the appearance of soliciting. Thus, the girls have educated their customers how to behave to protect them from arrest. The customers, in turn, have informed acquaintances.

Ordinarily, vice control police do not see themselves as patrolmen whose job it is to maintain public order. However, they usually will not hesitate to stop a white man who is engaged in "trolling" and advise him to leave the area. This is a delicate interaction and frequently comes out badly for the policeman, since the "troller" ordinarily resents police interference. The policeman will explain to the "troller" in a brotherly, man-to-man way that he may be "mugged," robbed, or infected. Typically, the policeman's advice is interpreted as an expression of moral and experiential superiority. To a certain extent it is, and therefore is apt to be resented. The policeman also believes what he says and he may, in fact, be correct, at least on a probability basis. He therefore finds the "troller's" resentful response irrational and confusing. As one vice control man put it, with an air of resignation: "I don't know why we should catch hell from these guys for trying to protect them, but we do."

When a prostitute observes a white man trolling, she or her pimp will check to see whether the "heat" (police) are around. Uniformed patrolmen are easily detected and veteran plainclothesmen are almost equally visible to prostitutes. For one thing, all of the members of the vice control squad are white. Even if they were not, the one or two Blacks who might be employed would be quickly identified and word passed around among the prostitutes as to their whereabouts on the street.

In order to deal with the problem of their high identifiability, the vice control police occasionally stop near a vacant lot from which they are able to observe actions on the street through field glasses. In turn, however, the police may be observed by prostitutes and pimps, who drive by so that they can get a closer look at the car parked by the vacant lot. Since the vice control squad's four unmarked cars are all chromeless and practical, they tend to be almost as identifiable to prostitutes and pimps as if the words "VICE CONTROL SQUAD" were printed on their sides. Given the high visibility of the policemen, how do they "score"?

POLICE ENFORCEMENT PATTERNS

To accomplish an arrest leading to conviction with the field-glass technique, the policeman must first observe a prostitute make contact with a customer. If she enters the "trick's" car, the policeman will follow the car and try to make an arrest while the couple are engaging in an act of intercourse. It is difficult for a prostitute to detect an approaching policeman while she is complying with her "date's" desires in an automobile. Although it is impossible to know exactly how many acts of

TABLE 2 *White, Nonwhite Women Arrested for Solicitation or Prostitution in Westville during 1962, by Enforcement Pattern*

	Women					
Enforcement Pattern	Nonwhite *		White		Total	
	N	%	N	%	N	%
Surveillance	59	38	10	50	69	39
Solicitation (plainclothesman)	51	32	2	10	53	30
Solicitation (decoy)	44	28	3	15	47	26
Informer call	3	2	5	25	8	4
Total arrests	157	100	20	100	177	99 †

* On police records, one hundred and fifty-two were identified as Negro, five as Mexican.
† Rounding error.

intercourse a prostitute engages in as against the number of times she is caught, it is probable that with this technique, the ratio of apprehension to commission is low. Nevertheless, the majority of arrests, according to the vice control men interviewed, are made with the "surveillance" method. Even though the apprehension rate is low, however, the method aids in deterring prostitutes from plying their trade. That the police are observing is often so quickly communicated among pimps and prostitutes that arrests are difficult to achieve; on the other hand, the police feel there is some point, as a matter of public order, to keeping streetwalkers prudent in their acts of solicitation.

The informer method is probably more effective than the field-glass technique in the ratio between attempts to arrest and arrests completed, since the police are so easily detected when they survey. In 1962, however, informer calls accounted for only 4 per cent of arrests. This technique typically works as follows: an informer will phone in and say that so-and-so has a man or is bringing a man to Room 6 of, say, the Hotel MacBeth, one of several rundown hotels that permit prostitutes to use their rooms for business purposes. Usually, these hotels are owned by whites who live out of the area, and come around once a month to collect rent. Typically, the man who works with the prostitute is the night desk clerk. He makes his money by "turning over" the rooms several times a night to prostitutes. Occasionally the police find it necessary to kick in a door because the clerk refuses to give them a key (since he is working with the prostitute).

The essence of the decoy method is placement of a man in a position to be solicited. Sometimes the police themselves fill this position; at other times, the police provide their own lures. For "trolling," the ideal is to have a "special employee" use his own car (since even the private cars of vice control men may be recognizable to experienced prostitutes). The use of "special employees" as lures may still require the vice control policeman's participation in the process. The writer recalls standing hidden with two vice control men on an especially cold night for more than an hour, while we observed a "special employee" in an amusement center attempting (without success) to attract a solicitation.

When a vice control man or a "special employee" becomes known, he is said to be "burned up." Experienced men will sometimes be hit upon by inexperienced girls, but obviously not by girls who know the vice control officers. And these men do become known, since there is relatively little movement from vice control back to other departments. As one man put it, "It takes three or four years to learn this business well enough to be really effective." Thus, when a policeman is approached, he is usually new on the vice control squad, or a police trainee entirely unknown to prostitutes.

Some of the private special employees, who receive five dollars for each girl caught, are considered to be highly skilled by the vice control men. One policeman had a favorite lure who was responsible for the arrest of numerous girls. A Black, he was described by the vice control officers as "Joe Trick himself."

He was so good, they never caught on to him. We'd bust the two of them, and he'd go back the next night and bawl out the broad for getting him into trouble. In those cases we'd let the broad cop out with a fine so as not to burn the s.e. [special employee].

Beyond the more practical problem of identifiability, there are several serious issues associated with the decoy method. In using special employees, the police, in effect, transfer police power to citizens who have been given neither a background check into character nor police training in law. As law professor Richard C. Donnelly writes:

The police officer who, in an undercover role, acts as a spy or a stool pigeon should be distinguished from the casual, temporary and non-professional employee. At least mimimum standards of character, intelligence and trustworthiness are appropriately applied to him. He will usually hold his job whether or not a conviction is obtained in the pending case, although it must be recognized that efficiency ratings and promotions may be affected. The temptation of the officer to exculpate himself by fixing responsibility upon others is not great.[8]

On the other hand, if the police act as lures, they expose themselves to the suspicions of ordinary private citizens who would regard the policeman's pretended interest in the prostitute as a form of "entrapment," although legally it may be quite difficult to decide whether a specific set of facts constitutes "entrapment." Even if the policeman were to directly solicit the prostitute by offering her a sum of money for an act of prostitution, such an act might not in itself constitute "entrapment," but rather a failure to prove the offense of solicitation. Policemen are much aware of the public's negative response to arrests in which police (or their special employees) are solicited. One officer expressed concern over the gathering of data on how police arrests of prostitutes are made, fearing that such data would show the police "sometimes" engaging in activities the public might not understand. But then he added: "Hell, go ahead. Anybody with any sense knows that a cop doesn't make a whore out of a girl by putting himself in a position to be solicited. If she wasn't a whore to begin with, she wouldn't have any trouble."

Whatever the "legal technicalities" associated with the decoy method, the police recognize the element of bad faith and trickery involved in such deceptive interactions. In part, their recognition of this element takes a subtle form when, in describing their enforcement activities regarding prostitution, they emphasize the less successful enforcement technique of surveillance. Thus, although all of the policemen interviewed maintained that surveillance accounted for by far the highest proportion of arrests, in fact, solicitations accounted for 56 per cent during 1962. In addition, policemen in conversation indicated a certain uneasiness regarding solicitation arrests, varying of course from individual to individual. One patrolman asked to be transferred from the prostitution detail because of his dislike of these arrests. Even among those, however, who did not experience these qualms, there was a growing feel-

[8] Richard C. Donnelly, "Judicial Control of Informants, Spies, Stool Pigeons, and Agent Provocateurs," *Yale Law Journal*, **60** (1951), 1119–1120.

ing that the use of policemen as "bait" was becoming less effective as a technique for "scoring." As one put it:

> The broads are wisening up, getting real hanky. One of them told me she can always spot a cop because we never say, "Hey, baby, how would you like to turn a trick for ten bucks?" which is what a lot of these trollers say when one of these broads looks good to them. We got to wait for them to set the price, otherwise we don't stand a chance in court. It doesn't matter how many times a broad's been convicted for prostitution. If we set the price, we got no case. The law says we entrapped her.
>
> I was trolling one night and a broad walked over to the car and said, "Mister, I'm in trouble, I could use a little money."
>
> I said, "Well, I might be able to help you out, provided I get something for my money."
>
> She said, "You'll get something, but how much you givin'?"
>
> I said, "How much you asking?"
>
> She said, "How much you offerin' to pay?"
>
> "Well," I said, "How's about a dollar?"
>
> "Oh, mister," she said, "You must be a policeman"— and walked off.
>
> You see, Jerry, we got to get them to set the price and for what, straight date, half-and-half, French or Greek.[9] Otherwise we're doing the soliciting.

These observations suggest that the dialogue between the prostitute and her customer takes on predictable forms according to the prostitute's need to discover whether the potential "date" is a policeman and the policeman's need to keep the dialogue within the limits imposed by legal requirements for a conviction.[10] In addition to conversational devices, another method prostitutes use for determining whether a customer is a policeman is to attempt to kiss him. According to the police, they never permit a prostitute to touch them, and certainly the district attorney's office [11] would frown upon sexual play between a policeman and a prostitute, regardless of who initiated it.

[9] "Straight date" refers to genital intercourse. "Half-and-half" means half "French," half "straight," that is, fellatio followed by genital intercourse. "Greek" refers to anal intercourse. Other sexual acts may be purchased as well, but these are the standard products.

[10] A similar point is made in light literature on police. See *Vice-Squad Cop* (New York: Avon, 1957), 14–16.

[11] J. Richard Woodworth, who was a participant-observer (as a check on my own observations) for six weeks in another municipality in the same county, reports a related problem about the degree to which police behavior toward homosexuals is determined by legal requirements as interpreted by the district attorney's office:

> There has arisen a source of tension between the deputies and one officer on the Ocean Park detail. He alone manages to wait to make his arrest until the offender has his hand, or in one case his mouth, on the officer's penis. The officer argues that this makes a stronger case and, in fact, that the D.D.A.

ENFORCEMENT, POLICE STATISTICS, AND PROSTITUTION
PATTERNS

Police statistics on vice control strategies for "scoring" on prostitutes
are subject to variations depending upon the interactional situation existing at any given time between the prostitutes and the police. Since
these relations are responsive to arrest and evasion tactics which fluctuate with time, statistics on arrest techniques can be regarded as accurate
only for a relatively brief historical period, that is, one where there are
no major changes in the legal or the social structure. A split-half reliability check was made between the first and second half of 1962, and the
patterns were found to be almost identical, with surveillance arrests accounting for 39 per cent during both halves of the year. This finding
suggests stability within a given legal context. By contrast, before 1961,
police were able to pick up "known" prostitutes under a broadly drawn
local ordinance. Under this law, a much larger number of arrests was
possible. During the Second World War, however, Westville and the
surrounding area had a boom-town character, and the police were more
tolerant of prostitutes. However interpreted, the figures do indicate the
frequency with which various arrest techniques are employed, and also
serve as a check on police estimates. Although statistics on race of prostitutes reflect an apparently stable, albeit recent, social situation, these
methods necessarily will fluctuate with the social situation of the Negro.
Whatever techniques the police use for making prostitution arrests, the
overwhelming majority of suspects will be colored, until the racial situation itself changes in Westville.

It is also obvious that police statistics do not necessarily reflect prostitution patterns. According to the prostitutes themselves, girls who are
arrested are usually inexperienced or make a "mistake" when high on
alcohol or drugs, so that they are able to be "conned" by "finks" or
"dogs." The girls also claim they are actually solicited by police or their
special employees and that the police lie on the witness stand. Finally,
the girls claim there is much more prostitution than police arrests would
indicate, but that it is done in a way which usually avoids police detection. Direct solicitation is often made unnecessary by an understanding
between men who patronize prostitutes and the girls. If a man spends

should charge these offenders with the stronger felony violation instead of the
misdemeanor offense that they have been charging. Delmore, the D.D.A. hearing
him say this, told him that in a felony case, the defense attorney could make
him look minuscule and stupid by asking: "And what were you doing while the
defendant was putting his mouth on . . . ?" Privately, Delmore wondered if
the officer might not be enjoying his work too much.

money on a girl in a bar, if they "have a good time together" and he "tosses her a few bills," she also goes to bed with him if that is what he prefers. But she would prefer that he become so drunk as to lose consciousness. If he does, the prostitute has an opportunity to "peel off some of his "roll"—ideally thirty or forty dollars from a roll of one hundred and fifty dollars—both to prevent the "date" from feeling resentful at having been "rolled," and to keep the theft a legally petty one in case the customer does report it to the police. It is in the prostitute's interest to maintain a friendly interactional situation, avoiding the appearance of a commercial transaction. Her most important skills are (1) the ability to size up a man who will be free with his money; (2) the ability to take it away from him, that is, to be attractive enough to be solicited, and skillful enough to separate the money from the man; and (3) the ability to accomplish all this without generating his hostility.

THE PROSTITUTE AS A SYMBOLIC ASSAILANT

If a key to the policeman's perceptual apparatus is his response to symbols of danger, then much of his behavior will be oriented to reducing in his own mind the threat posed by those who exhibit such symbols. One way the policeman does this is to elicit responses from the "symbolic assailant" which the policeman may interpret as diminishing the latter's inclination to criminality. Thus, a policeman may approach such a person with an air of authority and inquire brusquely of him his name and address. If the response is given in a manner which indicates acceptance of the policeman's authority, for instance, by a subdued look or a softly spoken "Yes, sir," the policeman is reassured. The same identification can be given much more aggressively and the "Yes, sir," if it comes, can sound like a sneer. Organized symbolic criminals, such as the Flying Devils, are more likely to challenge the authority of the policeman; this is what a policeman means when he says that so-and-so is a "wise-guy."

Prostitutes usually represent the threat of only minor physical harm to police, although they sometimes show insolence and other signs of hostility such as kicking and scratching. One of the now more experienced vice control officers reported that on his first night with the squad he used his own station wagon to pick up a girl, while an experienced vice control man was hidden in a large cardboard carton in the rear seat. He said that this was probably his most difficult arrest. As he put it:

I took the car to a vacant lot that she picked out. After I stopped the car, I paid her the ten dollars that we'd agreed on for a straight fuck. She took the money and stashed it in her bra, and then pulled her Capri pants way the hell off. Just then Rogers stuck his head out of the cardboard box. Rogers was smiling and when she saw him she flipped. She began screaming and biting and scratching. She tore my shirt and she tore my jacket . . . we practically had to carry her into the station.

This description of what was essentially an initiation ritual for the vice control officer drew smiles of reminiscence and recognition from a few of the other officers in the squadroom. Even though the policeman is always prepared to "use force sufficient to accomplish an arrest," there is a degree of humor associated with another man's inability to control someone who could be, if properly treated, harmless. The prostitute may be a potential assailant. She may carry a knife or a razor—often for self-protection against her customers. A prostitute is not in a position to call the police if her customer should assault her "just for kicks" or to get his money back. This necessary protection, incidentally, is an important service the pimp performs for the prostitute. In addition to this threat which she presents because of her need for self-defense, the prostitute also tends to be perceived as part of an underworld which may be prone to violence.

Nevertheless, the vice control officer has much control over how a prostitute acts when arrested. Whether she is brought in handcuffed, screaming, and kicking, or whether she' is fairly docile and even joking, depends largely on how the policeman treats the woman. Nearly all the vice control officers realize this, but some apparently prefer to exacerbate the interactional situation by degrading prostitutes. Degradation is accomplished by treating the woman as an object of contempt or derision rather than as a "working girl," which is the way she prefers to view herself. The prostitute neutralizes the immorality of her illegal activity by emphasizing those aspects of her work that are tiresome, inconvenient, and dangerous, with the labor involved representing a moral justification for her fee. If the policeman challenges this conception by calling her a "dirty nigger" or by emphasizing that she is a whore (as the rookie did when he needlessly had her expose herself), he will have "trouble on his hands." By contrast, if the policeman treats the arrest as a competition or a game he has won rather than as a moral victory or a harsh joke, the woman will be more disposed to being arrested.

There are three "postures" that the policeman may assume toward the prostitute, each successively less likely to turn her into a fighting, troublesome suspect. As indicated above, if the policeman morally condemns the prostitute by personal insult, he is most likely to arouse her hostility. However, he may also treat her with the impersonality that

Weber has described as the classical characteristic of the bureaucrat.[12] In this type of interaction, the policeman assumes a deadpan expression and issues monotonic commands. When he does so he may be indicating boredom with the job which both he and she know needs to be done. By emphasizing his instrumental status as societal agent, the policeman tends to displace hostility from himself to the more general moral and legal order. Finally, the policeman may treat the arrest situation with the air of mild solicitude somewhat akin to that assumed by the medical doctor with his patients. Here he makes some sort of gesture or remark that indicates concern for the suspect's well-being. For instance, he may offer her a cigarette or simply tell her that she may smoke. By showing this concern, the policeman segregates her specific dereliction from the general moral character of the woman, and thus enables her to maintain belief that she is a "working girl" whose product the "squares" have made unlawful. Thus, by not challenging her basic moral worth, the policeman reduces the hostility of the prostitute toward him.[13]

If a girl comes in kicking and screaming, the police have developed an effective immediate sanction "to slap on her." A city ordinance permits a police officer to quarantine persons suspected of venereal disease. The stated policy of the district attorney's office is to hold every woman arrested for prostitution for a venereal disease check by the local health officers, the evidence available to charge a person with prostitution being sufficient to warrant quarantine (for a period of up to eight days

[12] Bureaucratic impersonality, according to Weber, is "the abstract regularity of the execution of authority, which is a result of the demand for 'equality before the law' in the personal and functional sense." Max Weber, *From Max Weber: Essays in Sociology*, translator H. H. Gerth; editor C. W. Mills (New York: Oxford University Press, 1946), p. 224.

[13] Defense attorneys use similar tactics to gain rapport with a criminal client. In order to gain his client's trust, the defense attorney must segregate his client's illegal behavior from the rest of his moral character, just as a medical doctor might communicate a sense of acceptance of the "whole patient" while rejecting his specific disease entity. The police may utilize interactional tactics similar to those employed by the defense attorney to elicit incriminating information from the suspect. Parsons points out that in medical practice, ". . . segregation operated not only to maintain functional specificity, but also affective neutrality by defining situations which might potentially arouse various emotional reactions as 'professional' reactions. The importance of functional specificity is to define, in situations where potential illegitimate involvements might develop, the limit of the 'privileges' in the 'dangerous' area which the physician might claim. The pattern of affective neutrality then defines his expected attitudes within those limits." T. Parsons, *The Social System* (Glencoe, Ill.: The Free Press, 1951), p. 458. In the legal context, as distinguished from the medical, the problem for the professional is segregation of the client's statuses as well as his own.

in the Westville jail).[14] In fact, only 38 per cent of those arrested are held.[15]

Since every girl arrested on a prostitution charge is supposed to be held, how may we interpret the reality that only two out of five are? One explanation might be that vice control police are notably sympathetic gentlemen who feel uncomfortable when subjecting prostitutes to the unpleasantness of a brief stay in jail. Indeed, one officer, when presented with this evidence, explained it as follows:

> To tell you the truth, Jerry, sure, if a girl gives us a hard time, especially if she hides the money or throws it away—some of them would rather eat the money than let us get it—we'll put a hold on her. I guess we're actually supposed to put a hold on everybody, so there's nothing wrong in putting a hold on her . . . but you know how it is, you get to know some of the girls, and you don't want to give them extra trouble.

Still, this explanation does not account for the fact that the police interpret a straightforward rule in such a way as to make it a matter of administrative discretion, when it specifically is not. Another explanation is to view the police as people unconcerned with authoritative requirements, who violate rules as their impulses or sympathies move them. Such an interpretation, however, is not supported by other observations. Any interpretation of rule violation by the police should first of all consider such transgressions in light of the policeman's need for additional resources to fulfill his major responsibilities as defined by himself and his superiors. Holding a prostitute for quarantine is not considered a "credit" to the policeman's record. Neither the policeman nor the prosecutor is primarily interested in anything but the central "product" of law enforcement: felony convictions. To achieve these (as will be discussed in detail in Chapter 7) may require resources that the prostitute

[14] A general order of the police department issued April 1, 1963, "Venereal Disease Quarantine Procedure" reads:

> Any person arrested for the following offenses may be recommended for quarantine at the time of arrest, or thereafter, if there is reasonable cause to believe that the prisoner may have an infectious venereal disease. Reasonable cause shall be based on available information of circumstances obvious to the officer recommending quarantine.
> 1. Prostitution or assignation.
> 2. Keeper, inmate, employee or frequenter of a house of ill fame.
> 3. Any violation of Penal Code Section 6472 or 7476.
> 4. Any lewd or lascivious conduct.

[15] Most of the officers seemed to believe that one man on the prostitution detail is responsible "for 95 per cent of the holds." Upon checking, it was found that in the period studied (1962) his arrests resulted in quarantine holds 48 per cent of the time, while other officers put holds on 25 per cent of the time.

can provide. For her, "cooperation" with the police may mean more than a simple absence of aggression. It also may include her agreement, if "requested," to act as an informant or a special employee, especially in the enforcement of narcotics laws. The threat of a quarantine hold doubtless exerts some anticipatory pressure on the prostitute to "cooperate" with police. The quarantine hold, however, can serve as a threat only if it is not uniformly administered. Conformity to the rule of uniform administration would, therefore, result in the loss of a valuable item of exchange. Such an interpretation suggests not that the policeman is simply a "nice guy" or an impulsive rule breaker, but that there are systemic pressures upon police to break certain kinds of rules in the interest of conforming to other standards.

CONCLUSION

This chapter has attempted to identify the importance of police-suspect relations in determining the quality and extent of police involvement in prosecutorial decision-making. Its major thesis has been that the nature of these relations may have a significant bearing on the district attorney's conception of criminal cases and, therefore, on the ultimate outcome of these cases.

The first section dealt with the enforcement of traffic laws and the regularities of informal police participation in the prosecution of certain kinds of cases. While most traffic violations are routinely processed by the district attorney's office (owing to legal limitations on judicial discretion and to the nonrecurrent nature of police-offender relations), there are three separate circumstances under which the police are likely to seek to bring about modifications of the routine "deals" handed out by the prosecutor in traffic cases: (1) when the violator has abused the policeman in some way; (2) when an habitual violator has refused to "cop out" and insists on being tried; and (3) when the policeman has come into sustained and frustrating contact with offenders such as the gang motorcyclist. Each of these situations increases the likelihood that the police will demand access to the resources of the prosecutor's office. Thus, under certain conditions, the policeman prefers to implicate the offender more seriously in the criminal process.

Dealing with police-prostitute relations, the second section described how patterns of prostitution, coupled with police strategies for meeting the organized behavior of prostitutes, affect the policeman's personal stake in the outcome of the case. Here we see complications arising. The interest of the policeman has only partly to do with how he feels personally about the suspect. The prostitute may "buy her way out of" the criminal process when it is to the policeman's advantage to make the sale. In cases where the prostitute herself represents an important product to the policeman—for instance, as a defendant on a felony charge—she would require substantial commodities for the exchange. In the more usual case, however, the prostitute may offer to serve as an informant in the apprehension of her pimp or perhaps a narcotics peddler. Most generally, the more valuable a "product" the offender represents to the policeman, the higher the "price" he or she must offer by way of "cooperation."

To gain this cooperation the policeman engages in strategies to create the commodities of exchange. In this chapter we saw how he transforms the "quarantine hold" into such a commodity. By withholding a routine procedure regarded as punishment by the prostitute, he in effect creates a set of punitive sanctions which by law does not exist. These are used both to control the behavior of prostitutes during arrest, thus making the policeman's job easier, and to provide resources for apprehending more serious criminals.

The demand for police "efficiency" creates a type of "professional" police practice in which the concern for legality is minimal. Police are naturally committed to orderly behavior by those arrested, or even brought into custody, regardless of the legality of the confinement. By not enforcing the quarantine hold, the policeman raises the hopes of nonconfinement and introduces a previously nonexistent sanction into the situation. He now has something to give away which he otherwise would not have had. Thus, the nonenforcement of the quarantine hold requirement constitutes a dramatic example of the policeman creating for himself a discretionary structure, previously nonexistent, in order to manage relations with a class of repeated offenders who may be obstreperous.

It should also be noted, however, that the mere fact of arbitrary creation of a sanction does not necessarily lead to enforcement using irrelevant criteria. As with the warrant policeman, one might imagine that greater discretion—in this instance created by the policeman himself—would result in racial discrimination. The evidence, somewhat meager because of the relatively few white women arrested as prostitutes, indicates otherwise. Of the one hundred and fifty-seven nonwhite women arrested in 1962, 38 per cent were held with venereal disease checks. Of twenty whites, eight (about 40 per cent) were held. If one's immediate goal is to achieve complaint behavior, the race of a prostitute is not salient, while her demeanor is. Thus, even when police create conditions where they may act arbitrarily, they do not seem to do so, when seen in the context of immediate police goals.

In sum, neither philosophical principle nor personal prejudices should be taken as the most significant factors for understanding police conduct on the job. Their actual behavior seems to be influenced more than anything else by an overwhelming concern to show themselves as competent craftsman. An obstreperous prostitute symbolizes an affront to a policeman's competence. Measures are therefore taken to create instruments for punishing those who interfere with the policeman's goals— ultimately, survival; mediately, appearance of ability—and for rewarding those who contribute to their achievement. The relationship of these measures to implanting or undermining the rule of law does not seem to be a matter of great concern.

Chapter 6

The Informer System

THIS chapter examines the informer system, mainly in Westville, but with some attempt to describe the general features of informer systems. Analysis of these systems illustrates the importance of "production pressures" for understanding police conduct, by pointing out the stake of the policeman in organized methods for catching criminals. A good portion of the preceding chapter emphasized the personal feelings and attitudes of the policeman as the source of police discretion. The feelings of police are an aspect of the social structure which the prosecutor cannot lightly ignore, simply because he and the policeman are joined together in recurrent interactions. If, however, the personal feelings of the policeman must be given prosecutorial courtesy, the policeman's working apparatus must be accorded even greater deference by both the policeman and the prosecutor. The sheer existence of organized methods suggests that what is at stake is more than a matter of courtesy. The existence of an organized structure invites, indeed suggests, the interpretation that the structure serves a higher goal. For example, university education is able to proceed via a tutorial system or through a system of classes. The existence of a system of classes indicates that the specific university, as a matter of principle, is committed to educating large numbers of students. Such a commitment is neither disregarded nor disavowed lightly. Similarly, while the prosecutor's attention to the policeman's personal feelings toward defendants tends to be largely a matter of convenience and indulgence, the nature of the claim which the policeman makes upon the prosecutor about informants is more persuasive. Because this claim is seen as directly aiding the maintenance of the system, it receives a more generous and sympathetic concern from the prosecutor.

The discussion in this chapter gives special attention to narcotics cases because, as one Westville attorney put it, ". . . that's the area where the real wheeling and dealing takes place." What he meant was that the disposition of narcotics offenses generally occurs through informal bargaining arrangements between defense attorneys and the prosecutor and that these cases are commonly settled outside of the court through guilty pleas. If one looks, however, at the statistics of guilty pleas, one finds that narcotics violations are relatively low in this regard (see Table 1).

There are two related reasons for the discrepancy between attorneys' perceptions of narcotics violations as "dealing offenses" and guilty plea statistics. First, many defendants in narcotics cases do not plead guilty because they have prior convictions and a prior conviction on a narcotics charge is heavily penalized. Thus, defendants will fight seemingly hopeless cases. If a man is on parole and violates it by being in possession of

TABLE 1 *The Relation between Guilty Plea and Offense, Three-Year Totals, 1959–1961, California*

	Per Cent Total Dispositions by Guilty Plea		Per Cent Convictions by Guilty Plea	
Total	65.0%	(87,465)	75.1%	(75,182)
Murder	32.0	(675)	45.0	(480)
Manslaughter	52.6	(544)	57.5	(497)
Manslaughter, veh.	44.2	(448)	51.3	(386)
Robbery	67.0	(5577.)	78.0	(4793)
Assault	49.5	(5103)	69.0	(3662)
Burglary	75.3	(15,141)	84.0	(13,576)
Theft, except auto	65.9	(7546)	74.4	(6682)
Auto theft	74.1	(5490)	81.9	(4967)
Receiving stolen property	62.0	(1467)	74.4	(1221)
Forgery and checks	84.4	(15,275)	90.7	(14,210)
Rape	66.0	(3217)	80.6	(2633)
Lewd and lascivious conduct	55.0	(2382)	71.8	(1822)
Other sex offenses	59.3	(2398)	64.8	(2193)
Narcotics	41.7	(10.872)	53.7	(8439)
Deadly weapons	59.8	(969)	71.5	(811)
Drunk driving	50.7	(1304)	56.4	(1172)
Failure to render aid	48.1	(630)	56.2	(539)
Escape	88.8	(1945)	92.6	(1865)
Bookmaking	38.6	(2751)	51.8	(2049)
Contributing	66.8	(754)	66.8	(754)
All others	47.4	(2977)	58.0	(2431)

Source: Bureau of Criminal Statistics, State of California, Department of Justice, Division of Criminal Law and Enforcement.

heroin, neither he nor the police are likely to want a deal, since any sort of conviction will "put him away" for a considerable time period. Secondly, since defendants do frequently have criminal records, they tend either to go to trial or to negotiate immediately. Thus, narcotics deals frequently take place earlier in the process than, for instance, homicide deals. They are often made with informants before the complaint is drawn and with the consent of the complaining witness, the policeman. Unless the defendant "cooperates" by, say, giving the policeman additional information, the latter is usually reluctant to drop charges. A measure suggesting the extent to which an offense may be dealt out early in the process is the ratio of felony complaints filed to felony arrests on that charge (see Table 2).

TABLE 2　*Police Dispositions of Adult Felony Arrests, 1962, California, by Type of Disposition and Offense*

Offense	Total	Felony Complt. Filed	Misd. Complt. Filed	Released	Other Juris-diction
Total	98813	44%	20%	27%	8%
Homicide	1151	62	7	26	6
Robbery	10411	34	17	40	8
Aggravated assault	12136	27	34	32	7
Burglary	24062	40	21	31	8
Grand theft, except auto	7548	50	16	28	6
Auto theft	8223	43	14	29	14
Forgery and checks	10272	67	14	10	9
Sex offenses	6189	61	14	20	4
Narcotics	10395	40	30	26	7
All other	8426	54	16	19	10

Source: Crime in California, California Bureau of Criminal Statistics, 1962, p. 76.

This measure indicates the degree of "erosion" of complaints but does not tell why the erosion occurred. For instance, more than 40 per cent of adults arrested in robbery investigations are released, the main reason probably being lack of identificatory evidence. The reasons for the release of narcotics arrestees are quite different, as will be explained.

Each of these reasons for the relatively low frequency of guilty pleas in narcotics cases—the early effectuation of "deals" and the strong reluctance of persons with prior narcotics convictions to "cop out"—suggests the importance of the informant system for the outcomes of these cases. An examination of the informer system in Westville, therefore, is a necessary step toward identifying the conditions associated with the policeman's response to principles of legality.

A brief scanning of the informer system reveals the following outline: Since crimes of vice typically do not arise from citizen complaints, the police must have informers to lead them to the criminals. Informers are used to solve other crimes as well, notably burglary, where the police require a source of underworld information. To maintain an informant network, police must pay off each informer, usually by arranging for reduction of charge or sentence, or by not acting as a complainant; and must in addition protect the individual informer's identity. The latter requirement influences arresting strategies of the police, especially about the exclusionary rule; it also affects the plea bargain, since the law enforcement official may be willing to settle for a lesser plea to protect the identity of the informer.

THE POLICEMAN AS COMPLAINANT

Ordinarily, when we think of crime and the criminal, we visualize a unilateral interaction containing an element of assault. "The criminal" is an assailant who makes an unexpected appearance, strikes or threatens a victim, and takes off with ill-gotten gains. Accordingly, a survey asking respondents to rate the seriousness of thirteen crimes showed the two with the clearest implication of assault—child beating, and assault with a deadly weapon—to rank highest in "seriousness" of offense.[1] The prototypical criminal is a robber, a man who violates persons and property. Crimes of assault are prototypical in another important way. These crimes correspond to the usual conception of complaint, apprehension, and conviction. Somebody is robbed or assaulted, and identifies his assailant. In defense, the testimony of the victim is cross-examined, the victim's capacity to see and hear is challenged, and the accused employs various defenses to establish that he was not the one who committed the forbidden act. There is thus a discernible pattern of assault, accusation, identification, and defense. This is the standard crime, popularly portrayed in movies and books, and its structure is both clear and different from the crimes handled by vice control police.

The vice squad is not concerned with those criminal activities where

[1] Arnold M. Rose and Arthur E. Prell, "Does the Punishment Fit the Crime? A Study in Social Valuation," *American Journal of Sociology*, **61** (1955), 247–259.

the malefactor is an assailant. Indeed, the crimes which it seeks to control or redress typically have no "victim," [2] or, more precisely and neutrally, no citizen complainant. Thus, when a policeman investigates a strong-arm robbery, a rape, or a forgery, he ordinarily does so at the request of an aggrieved citizen. By contrast, when a vice control officer arrests a bookmaker, a prostitute, or a seller of narcotics, the gambler, the "trick," or the user are typically not interested in having an arrest made. Since the vice control squad deals with crimes for which there are usually no complaining witnesses, vice control men must, as it were, drum up their own business. [3]

Occasionally, a neighbor of a prostitute or a gambling house operator will complain to the police department and ask for an investigation of what he believes to be illegal activities. When he does, however, he will merely be providing the police with information that he thinks such and such an activity is going on at such and such an address. It rarely, if ever, happens that he is in a position to act as a complaining witness. Moreover, the citizen who is troubled by noise or "peculiar goings-on" is most likely to give information about crimes that, in the policeman's scale of values, are least important. If he phones in at all, he will most likely complain that somebody is running a noisy poker or dice game, simply because such activities *are* noisy. The police will check out such information and are grateful to have it, even if only to confirm their own suspicions and channel their activities. But the citizen is not so likely to be aware of dealings in narcotics (although apartment house managers and hotel managers are sophisticated about these matters and, if they are on good terms with the police, may act as informers). Thus, the vice control police cannot depend solely on citizen complaints for making arrests, but instead must themselves locate the criminals it is their responsibility to apprehend. In other words, the work of the vice control policeman frequently requires his serving as witness and complainant.

---

[2] See Edwin M. Schur, *Crimes Without Victims* (Englewood Cliffs, N.J.: Prentice-Hall, 1965); and Herbert L. Packer, "Two Models of the Criminal Process," *University of Pennsylvania Law Review*, 113 (November, 1964), 1–68.

[3] It may be noted that police operate similarly in vice crimes and other crimes in which the polity rather than an individual is complainant. In order to police any crimes that threaten the state (espionage, counterfeiting) or its morality, informants, spies, stool pigeons, or *agent provocateurs* must be used. Thus, part of the observations made for this study included a counterfeiting investigation and arrests by the U. S. Secret Service. This was a side operation for the writer, who at the time was "working" as a member of the Westville vice control squad. The squad was asked to assist the Secret Service, since it was experienced in processing crimes involving secrecy, the use of informants, and the apprehension of offenders whose criminality is proved by the possession for sale of a forbidden object.

THE POLICEMAN'S VIEW OF THE NARCOTICS CRIMINAL

The vice control squad prizes most highly the capture of narcotics salesmen in part because heavy penalties are involved, but also because the apprehension of such persons is perceived as requiring exceptionally skilled and efficient detective work—as it often does. The job requirements for the narcotics detective tend to fit most closely with the personality characteristics of the ideal investigator described by O. W. Wilson:

The good investigator usually has initiative, perseverance, and a tremendous physical and nervous vitality; he is alert, observant, and inquisitive. He has an unusually retentive memory and the ability to detect fallacious reasoning. He has a practical knowledge of human beings that enables him to get along well with people. He is persuasive and convincing and is able to win the confidence and friendship of those with whom he deals. He has a wide range of acquaintances and sources of information.[4]

The work of the narcotics officer requires that he be an initiator of police activity, rather than a man who performs a service for an aggrieved citizen, as a street patrolman might be called upon to do. It is this *initiative* character of his work which brings a high correspondence to the narcotics officer's job requirements and Wilson's description of the ideal personality demanded by detective work.

What this suggests is that narcotics work is especially symbolic of an efficient professionalism to which trained and intelligent police aspire. As a result, the very nature of the narcotics policeman's work may partly help to explain the tenacity of law enforcement's constant demand for higher penalties against the addict. The existence of severely penalizing narcotics laws provides the police with a category of crimes and therefore with a category of jobs. In addition, narcotics work gives the policeman an especially interesting, gamelike kind of job. Thus, the existence of a narcotics law provides police with an outlet for aggressive intelligence—one that would be closed if serious reforms were to be made in these laws.

Moreover, the penalties associated with narcotics offenses are taken by the police as an indication of how seriously the community views the offense, even though, since the police are legislative lobbyists demanding higher penalties, they are themselves instrumental in establishing the community's views. There is nothing uniquely illogical about this. In a democratic society, legislation is often the outcome of an almost ad-

‘ O. W. Wilson, *Police Planning* (Springfield: Charles C Thomas, 1958), p. 111.

versarial proceeding, with those for and against presenting their own sides. Nothing more need be suggested by the police seeing narcotics arrests as important (in accord with the high penalties attached to them) than that the police believe their own expressed viewpoint. Narcotics police are perfectly aware of organized resistance to high penalties for narcotics offenses, but in general tend to disbelieve the arguments presented by opponents [5] as being impractical and unrealistic (although some of the narcotics officers observed have privately expressed misgivings about the high penalties associated with marihuana use).

By and large the policeman does not view the addict as primarily a sick man or an object of pity, and he has almost no difficulty in perceiving a narcotics arrest as a "good pinch." The "good pinch" is a common term in law enforcement, signifying, first of all, a felony arrest.[6] It follows, therefore, that the policeman will have few qualms about trading the arrest of a common prostitute for the pinch of a marihuana seller. A good pinch, in addition, points to moral culpability on the part of the suspect. Although possession of narcotics and possession for sale are both felonies, the latter is a better pinch than the former, partly because a higher penalty is attached, but also because a "pusher" is more clearly morally culpable than a user.

Actually, the term "pusher" is a popular misnomer, since most addicts will sell narcotics or dangerous drugs if they have the opportunity to do so. The typical legal distinction results from an outsider's understanding of the addict's world. Westville police use a generic term, "hype," to designate, and derogate, persons who take drugs intravenously with the aid of an "outfit" or "fit"—an eyedropper, spoon, and hypodermic needle—rather than orally. Oral drug users are ordinarily legitimate citizens who may be habituated, in the technical sense in which that term is used, but who purchase drugs on a doctor's prescription. Some hypes use "dangerous drugs" or "pills" such as methedrine or percodan, synthetic chemicals which act something like cocaine and morphine, respectively. Accordingly, methedrine tends to hop people up, while percodan slows

---

[5] See, for example, Edwin M. Schur, *Narcotic Addiction in Britain and America* (London: Tavistock Publications Ltd., 1963); Alfred R. Lindesmith, *The Addict and the Law* (Bloomington: Indiana University Press, 1965); and "Our Immoral Drug Laws," *The Nation*, June 21, 1958, 558–562; and Isidor Chein, Donald L. Gerard, Robert S. Lee, and Eva Rosenfeld, *The Road to H* (New York: Basic Books, Inc., 1964).

[6] William Westley defines a good pinch as ". . . an arrest which (a) is politically clear and (b) likely to bring them esteem. Generally, it refers to felonies, but in the case of a 'real' vice drive it may include the arrest and *conviction* of an important bookie." From "Violence and the Police," *American Journal of Sociology*, 59 (July, 1953), 36.

them down. The familiar term "junky" refers to a heroin addict. Thus all "junkies" are "hypes," but not all "hypes" are "junkies," although most are. Moreover, in the absence of genuine narcotics, most "hypes" will use any drugs they can obtain, often substituting dangerous drugs, sometimes in combination, for heroin, which itself may be "cut" so that it produces only a mild effect.[7]

An additional reason for the policeman's lack of sympathy for addicts is their *potentially* dangerous criminality. Thus, a pamphlet by the Westville Police Department states:

It may be that the problem of narcotics addiction has been subject to some exaggeration in recent years, but the police administrator and the prosecutor alike must recognize that in narcotics traffic lies the most serious single threat to the safety and welfare of the community. One addict with a very moderate "habit" will require roughly twenty dollars worth of illicit heroin every day. Since relatively few addicts have the financial means to support such a habit, they must usually resort to some sort of theft. The sale of stolen property on a "forced market" brings about a 20% return, so the addict must steal and dispose of approximately $100 worth of property each day. . . .

During the past several years, crime has increased throughout the nation. Addicts commit crimes of gain, offenses which enable them to obtain funds for the maintenance of their habits; these include robbery, auto-burglary (theft from locked cars), auto-clout (theft from unlocked cars), prostitution and tilltapping (thefts from cash registers).

In addition, law enforcement brochures are likely to emphasize the traffic in narcotics and to suggest that narcotics addiction is associated with *organized* criminality. This reference has two implications, one suggesting organized crime such as rackets and gambling, and the other

[7] According to a story in the Western edition of the *New York Times* (March 11, 1963), methedrine has been partially supplanting opiate derivatives among narcotic addicts in the San Francisco Bay Area. The story quotes Mr. Vincent Chasten, a California state narcotics agent, as saying that in recent months more narcotics addicts seem to be switching to methedrine or some other form of deoxyephedrine and relying less on heroin or some other opium derivative.

"In the first place, there has been a great law enforcement pressure on the opium drugs," he explained. "There are stiff penalties required just for possession, and second offenders are really rapped." Mr. Chasten is additionally quoted as saying "I've had old time addicts tell me frankly that they just had to stay away from the stuff unless they can get it from a doctor. A fellow with a prior conviction just can't stand the risk. So they turn to this stuff."

(By contrast, during field work in Eastville in December, 1963, the writer heard no mention of methedrine use there, and when questioned, the narcotics officers had never heard of it. Heroin was evidently in ample supple on the East Coast, and in purer form—25 to 30 per cent pure—than on the West Coast, where chemical analysis revealed samples to average around 5 to 7 per cent.)

referring to the sort of organization associated with such criminal activities as burglary and "boosting." [8] Moreover, narcotics use is frequently linked with more stereotypical crimes of violence to persons and property. For instance, during one night of observation (with a homicide detective), a Westville bartender was murdered during a holdup. The victim had been shot by a nervous addict who had accidentally (there was no motive) pulled the trigger.[9] Such incidents reinforce the policeman's perception of the addict as a harbinger of violence, even though it is possible that the robber might have been a robber without his addiction.[10]

Finally, it takes all the general training of a policeman to be a narcotics man, plus special training and ability. The narcotics specialist must have a network of informers and know how to stay on good terms with them, while at the same time maintaining the strength of his bargaining position. At times, he must be able to pretend convincingly to be an addict. He must be inventive in circumventing search-and-seizure restrictions. He should have some knowledge of the various drugs in use and the legal consequences of their illegal use. Finally, he must be a skilled interrogator. Thus, those qualities which policemen have come to admire as constituting "real" police work are to be found in the work of the narcotics officer.

THE INFORMER IN NARCOTICS CONTROL

The major organizational requirement of narcotics policing is the presence of an informational system. Without a network of informers —usually civilians, sometimes police—narcotics police cannot operate.[11] It is possible to capture addicts by cruising in an unmarked car in certain neighborhoods and looking for what the police call "furtive" movements [12]—a shuffling that indicates to the eye of the skilled nar-

---

[8] See Mary Owen Cameron, *The Booster and the Snitch* (New York: The Free Press of Glencoe, 1964).

[9] This case provides an additional illustration of the high status position of vice control within the police department. The suspect would talk only to his contact on the vice control squad, and eventually gave him a complete statement of confession.

[10] Harold Finestone, "Narcotics and Criminality," *Law and Contemporary Problems,* 32 (Winter, 1957), 69–85.

[11] In Westville alone, the head of the narcotics detail has at times had a list of about one hundred informants.

[12] For California law on "furtive actions," see the following cases: *People v. Jiminez,* 143 Cal. App. 2d 671; *People v. Bladgett,* 46 Cal. 2d 114; *People v. Amado,* 167 Cal. App. 2d 345; *People v. Anders,* 167 Cal. App. 2d 65; *People v. Brajevich,* 174 A.C.A. 469; *People v. Tahtinen,* 50 Cal. 2d 127; *People v. Augustine,*

cotics policeman that his suspect is trying to dispose of a "joint of weed" (marihuana cigarette) or a "dime paper" (ten-dollar package of heroin). Even if, however, the policeman succeeded in catching such a man, he would ordinarily attempt to use the exculpation of incriminating evidence as "payment" for the suspect's cooperation as an informant. In narcotics work, the apprehension of a man with one joint or one dime paper simply does not constitute a "good pinch." The narcotics policeman is primarily interested in uncovering a large cache, and for this to happen, informants must be employed.

Lately, law enforcement leaders have become increasingly candid about the use of informants. The most direct evidence of this growing openness is a book on the subject written by two leading policemen in the field of narcotics control.[13] The volume is both a teaching manual and a justification for the use of informants. Several justificatory themes are evident. First, it is argued that the citizen owes a duty, legally if not morally, to inform authorities when a crime is committed. As such, this assertion cannot be supported empirically but it is rather a theoretical or ethical statement from the realm of social philosophy. The second theme emphasizes practicality—law enforcement requires the informer's services. A former detective superintendent of Scotland Yard has explained this need as follows:

> . . . if every policeman "worked to rule"—and a great many of them do— I reckon that less than ten per cent of the crimes committed in Great Britain would remain unsolved. That's the dilemma. That's why policemen are so vulnerable. We *must* use informers—and that means you have to play fair with them. You mustn't give them away either to other criminals or to other policemen. You may have to let him go free after he's committed a crime be-

152 Cal. App. 2d 264, 265, 266. In these and other cases, the courts have ruled as probable cause to arrest any of the following kinds of "furtive actions" (under the condition that the individual being observed was suspected of possession of narcotics) : leaning toward or reaching toward the seat of a car or withdrawing the hand from behind the seat of a car; putting something in one's mouth or moving one's hand to one's mouth; throwing object from car window; making throwing motion with one's hand; retrieving object from the base of a tree after having driven a car around the immediate area for over a half-hour; looking over one's shoulder and carefully watching passing cars after having left a dwelling where known narcotics dealers resided. (From Bonnie Lee Martin, *Probable Cause to Arrest and Admissibility of Evidence*, Printing Division, Documents Section, Sacramento, 1960, pp. 53–54.)

[13] Malachi L. Harney and John C. Cross, *The Informer in Law Enforcement* (Springfield: Charles C Thomas, 1960). Cf. also Carroll S. Price, "Sources of Information," *Police* (March–April, 1960), 47–51. Alfred R. Lindesmith has also pointed to open acknowledgment by other law enforcement officials of the use of legal commodities in narcotics enforcement, *op. cit.*, pp. 35–62.

cause then you can "put the squeeze" on him afterwards. Nearly always you have to act on his information so fast that there is no time to apply for search warrants. Even when you have the time you may not have the inclination because a certain amount of publicity is inevitable during the process of application. There are always "layabouts"—out-of-works—hanging around court buildings and if the word gets out it goes through the underworld— which is no bigger than a village to the men and women in it—like a fire through a forest after a drought. In short, the detective moves in a half-world, a sort of legal no man's land strewn with mines which may be touched off by either the legal or the illegal.[14]

The third justificatory theme advanced by the authors has to do with the consequences of informing. The informer is portrayed as an enemy of the underworld and, as such, is seen as meritorious. Thus, the authors, Harney and Cross, quote the following passage by J. Edgar Hoover as a classic expression of the law enforcement position on the use of informers:

. . . Experience demonstrates that the cooperation of individuals who can readily furnish accurate information is essential if law enforcement is to discharge its obligations.

The objective of the investigator must be to ferret out the truth. It is fundamental that the search include the most logical source of information— those persons with immediate access to necessary facts who are willing to cooperate in the interest of a common good. Their services contribute greatly to the ultimate goal of justice—convicting the guilty and clearing the innocent. Necessarily unheralded in their daily efforts, they not only uncover crimes but also furnish the intelligence data so vital in preventing serious violations of law and national security.

There can be no doubt that the use of informants in law enforcement is justified. The public interest and the personal safety of these helpful citizens demand the zealous protection of their confidence. Unlike the totalitarian practice, the informant in America serves of his own free will, fulfilling one of the citizenship obligations of our democratic form of government.[15]

There can be no doubt that informants are "essential" for law enforcement, especially for narcotics control. Thus, it is no accident that a volume about informers should have been written by two highly experienced narcotics officers. It is questionable, however, on the basis of both my own observations and later material in the Harney and Cross volume, that "the informant in America serves of his own free will," in the

---

[14] Cited in John Gosling, *The Ghost Squad* (Garden City, N.Y.: Doubleday, 1959), p. 19.

[15] J. Edgar Hoover, *Law Enforcement Bulletin*, Federal Bureau of Investigation (June, 1955). Quoted in Harney and Cross, p. 9.

sense in which that term is commonly understood. Harney and Cross list seven motives that induce people to give information to the police.[16] The first and most important is fear, primarily of the law and its consequences, but not necessarily so. The fearful informer may be one who for some reason is afraid of criminal associates and looks to law enforcement for protection. A second motive is revenge. A third motive is called "perverse" by the authors: it involves the utilization of law enforcement for one's own illegal purposes, for example, informing on the illegal activities of your competitor. Some people also inform simply because, as one category, they "take pleasure in spreading news to interested listeners," or, as another, they are "demented, eccentric or nuisance type individuals." In addition, there are people who inform for mercenary motives. Finally, there are those who are repentant and desire to reform. As the authors say, "This informer is infrequently seen, but he may be valuable."

From my own observations, narcotics informers include primarily two types of people: those who are not addicts themselves, but who work in or around places addicts frequent; and known addicts. Non-addicts cooperate because they want to avoid difficulties with the police or, more importantly, with "official" agencies that inspect and license. If the police were to report that their places were "hangouts" for undesirable characters, they might be closed down. Furthermore, addicts are not a preferred clientele. Most proprietors prefer to "keep their noses clean" and run places as "respectably" as possible. In addition, it is not uncommon for bartenders to be fences for stolen merchandise and for police to overlook this activity in exchange for information leading to the arrest of addicts. Consequently, hotel owners and bartenders are a regular source of information for police. Generally, however, the kind of information they are able (or perhaps willing) to give is identificatory. They will say they have seen so-and-so around town and "he looked like he was dirty" (on narcotics); or they will tell the name of the occupant in room number 8; or they will reveal the address where so-and-so is staying. Finally, hotel managers will give keys to policemen that permit them to make searches while the occupant is out of the room, and some hotel owners will permit the vice control squad to tap into their switchboards.

Sometimes policemen themselves will act as informants, or, more precisely, as *agent provocateurs*. This generally happens under two sets of conditions: either the legal restrictions regarding disclosure of an informant's identity make it difficult to utilize civilians, or the case is large

---

[16] See Harney and Cross, *op. cit.*, pp. 33–39.

and important enough so that an addict cannot be trusted to carry out the assignment. In such cases, several fairly large purchases of narcotics are required before an arrest will be made; in addition, the purchaser may be required to be a witness. On the whole, however, the police depend upon addicts themselves to obtain information leading to narcotics arrests. Indeed, as Westley says, ". . . the informant is the life blood of the good detective. . . ."[17]

THE INFORMER'S PAYOFF

The informer-informed relationship is a matter of exchange in which each party seeks to gain something from the other in return for certain desired commodities. From the informer, the policeman receives information that assists him in the enforcement of the law. Addicts typically cooperate with police because they have been caught doing something illegal and want a reduction in charges or some sort of "break" in the criminal process. As Harney and Cross say:

It is almost the universal practice of the police, prosecutors and courts to recognize the valuable assistance to law enforcement in this attitude of the informer. This recognition is usually translated into a practical manner as a recommendation for a lesser sentence, a more favorable consideration for parole or probation, the acceptance of a plea to a lesser count in the indictment or through some other favorable action within the discretion of the prosecution.[18]

How does this description square with contrary reports that informants are permitted to commit crimes, that informants are paid off with sizable amounts of money, and so forth? My observations suggest that such reports are exaggerated but not entirely untrue. In the next few pages, I shall analyze elements of truth and fiction in these generalizations by looking at the conditions leading to differing types of informant payoff.

There is a simple reason why the informer does not have the freedom to operate illegally, for example, to be a prostitute or a narcotics peddler, that is sometimes assumed by writers on criminal procedure: police relations with informers are in the pattern of a bargain. Whenever two persons make a bargain it is in the interests of each to hold the strongest position possible; police maximize their position by using the authority given to them by the State. Thus, the Westville narcotics detective will

[17] Westley, *op. cit.*, 1951, p. 70.
[18] Harney and Cross, *op. cit.*, p. 33.

usually arrest a prostitute or addict informer on whom he can be certain to obtain evidence. This arrest then becomes an added value to the policeman's bargaining position. He might offer to recommend a fine in return for the prostitute's cooperation in making a narcotics purchase. The good arrest, however, provides the policeman with a commodity to exchange for this type of service. To assert that the policeman ignores the infractions of persons who have acted as informers in order to maintain their "good will" is to overlook that informers have no specific affection for police and are themselves often coercively persuaded to play their roles by threat of legal sanction. It is true that the policeman needs the informer, but it is equally true that he can often control the informer only by invoking the law. Thus, the narcotics detective cannot disregard "dealing" by an addict because when the addict becomes a dealer, he constitutes a "good pinch." The policeman may disregard "chippying" (occasional use) on the part of an addict, but he will not hesitate to employ his knowledge of the addict's occasional use to his own advantage.

The "balance of advantage" is not so heavily in the policeman's favor that he can "get the goods" on an informer at will. "Hard" evidence is as valuable as it is difficult to produce. While money can buy some information, its amount and worth is often correlated with the relatively insubstantial funds available to the vice control squad for such purposes. The reduction of time in jail or prison can usually purchase more and better information than can available moneys. Although one cannot measure the monetary equivalent of a year's imprisonment, it seems reasonable to suppose that its value is high. This analysis should not suggest, however, that a vice control squad does not require the services of informants at liberty. It simply means that the coin of the informer's realm is primarily not money, but rather is to be found in the discretion residing in the office of policeman and in the office of district attorney. Thus, the main payment is legal authority, and it is handed out at a later stage in the process than is usually assumed.

Having suggested that charge reduction is the primary coin of the informant world, we may analyze why reports persist that informers are permitted to commit crimes and are paid off in sizable amounts of money. The informant is a betrayer. To betray, however, one must first gain the confidence of others. It is useful to contrast the policeman's role with the informer's. If he, like the informer, is disliked, it is not because the policeman is a betrayer, but rather because he is an authority who makes clear he is an enforcer of norms. The informant is exactly the opposite, which is why he is needed by police. When a person knows he will be punished for a particular act, he does not commit it in front of the potentially punitive observer. Thus, a narcotics peddler does not sell to a man he knows to be a policeman. He sells to a companion or to a friend. To act as an informant, however, is to be more than an ordinary companion. An informant is pressed to exhibit extraordinary signs of affection. The nature of his role demands that he *ingratiate* himself with the illegal actor. If a man sells out another, the man who has been sold out may well feel that the rewards given to his betrayer were higher than they actually were.[19] Typically, the betrayed cannot bring themselves to believe how little they have been sold out for. Thus, the warmer and more seemingly trusting the relations between betrayer and betrayed, the greater will be the tendency of the betrayed person to perceive the betrayer's reward as high. Since a competent informant does ingratiate himself, it would not be surprising to find that rewards of informants tend to be exaggerated.

THE PAYOFF ACCORDING TO TYPE OF CRIME

The tendency of the betrayed to exaggerate the rewards of the betrayer accounts only partly for the persistence of reports that informants are permitted to commit crimes and are well paid. In Westville (and in other places as well), informants are sometimes well paid and are sometimes permitted to commit crimes. This situation comes about as follows.

Narcotics police need informants because the detective needs to know where the crime is being committed, if at all. But narcotics police are not the only ones who use informants as an integral part of their enforcement pattern. Burglary detectives, to cite the most relevant example, rely upon informants almost as much as do narcotics detectives. Even though the crime of burglary involves a victim, its enforcement follows a pattern similar to narcotics rather than crimes with victims such as robbery. There are two important differences in the pattern of events associated with a robbery and a burglary. First, although each crime involves a victim, the burglary victim almost never sees the perpetrator of the crime. Thus, like the narcotics detective, the burglary de-

---

[19] There is here a dynamic akin to "cognitive dissonance," a "sweet lemon" theory of postdecisional behavior. It asserts that once a decision has been made, its maker will tend to emphasize positive qualities of the choice taken and negative qualities of the discarded alternative. It also asserts that the less the discrepancy between alternatives, the greater the commitment to the one chosen. See Leon Festinger, *A Theory of Cognitive Dissonance* (Evanston, Illinois: Row-Peterson, 1957). A clear explanation of his theory is reprinted in Edward E. Sampson (ed.), *Approaches, Contexts, and Problems of Social Psychology* (Englewood Cliffs, N.J.: Prentice-Hall, 1964), pp. 9–15.

tective must put out informers into the community to learn who is behaving in a manner suggestive of the commission of a burglary—who, for instance, is looking for a "drop" for "hot goods," furs, T.V. sets, and so forth. Second, burglary is typically a crime of possession. Unless the burglar is caught in the act—which is rare, but which sometimes happens with the aid of an informant—the only way to link the burglar with the crime is to find stolen goods in his possession. This strategy also requires an informant's services and is followed by the same procedure as in narcotics arrests: forced entry, search of the premises, and, in burglary, seizure of the stolen articles.

Unlike narcotics informants, burglary informants are sometimes paid substantial sums of money. One of the main jobs of the burglary detective is to recover stolen property. Typically, if the goods are insured, there is a reward for their recovery, amounting to about 10 per cent of the recovered value. Burglary detectives in Westville are not allowed to keep any of the reward; if there is one, it is usually given to an informant. In addition, the insurance companies will sometimes supply a detective with money for an informant, as will the department itself. This sort of money—to keep an informant "going"—is usually relatively small, involving such sums as five, ten, or twenty dollars. Nevertheless, that substantial sums of money are available and sometimes paid out probably accounts for that notion that informers are well paid. Some are, but rarely.

Furthermore, in informal relations with suspects, police themselves contribute to this notion by dropping remarks that tend to make the role of informer seem more inviting. Thus, in the course of being interviewed, two burglars in police custody brought up the idea that they could make a good living as "special employees." The point is that the police, in their need for informants, typically build up an anticipation of reward that, in return, characterizes them as having "money to burn" on informants. Thus, police strategies for overcoming the restrictions imposed by short funds tend to create a portrait of the police as well-heeled operators. The currency of this idea is useful to the police given their informant requirements, but is disruptive of relations with those segments of the general public offended by police use of informers.

"ASSETS" OF NARCOTICS AND BURGLARY DETECTIVES

Informants generally would rather work for burglary than for narcotics detectives. This preference is not best explained either by the possibility of greater profits in burglary informing or by personality differences of detectives; rather, it is explained by structural conditions associated with burglary enforcement that help to satisfy fundamental concerns of informants. First, the burglary detective is better able than the narcotics detective to protect the criminal status of informants. The informant is concerned lest his identity be revealed, and revelation typically occurs through some discernible link between the informant and the act of arrest. Since narcotics detectives are often required to move quickly, the time span between the act of informing and the act of apprehension is usually small. Burglary detectives, on the other hand, have time to wait and can therefore more easily "keep from putting the S.E. out in front of the deal." If stolen goods are thought to be in Joe's house, and Tom is sent in to check, the burglary detective can obtain a warrant but not act on it for a few days—sometimes a week or more—thus making it almost impossible for Joe to remember who entered his house the day the warrant was issued. In narcotics enforcement, however, it often happens that detectives feel an immediate arrest must be made.

Second, many burglary informants (as well as narcotics informants) are addicts, and it is generally understood by the burglary detective that the money given to the informant will be used to purchase drugs. Of course, this does not mean that the detective gives the informant the money and tells him to go out and buy a "ten dollar paper." Indeed, the detective may even tell the informant to get himself a good meal or to buy some food for his family. Nevertheless, there is often an implicit understanding between detective and informant that the latter is an addict and may use his payoff to buy drugs.

The burglary policeman typically takes a fatalistic attitude toward the services of the addict-burglar-informant. He certainly does not condone the informant's lawbreaking, especially his addiction, and is likely to deplore it, especially when he knows the informant's family. Indeed, the policeman may be genuinely concerned for the welfare of the informant and prefer that he be transformed into an upright, responsible, law-abiding citizen, rather than an addict-burglar-informant. The policeman, however, also perceives the informant's criminal tendencies as inevitable and therefore looks upon the possibility of his transformation as miraculous. Thus, he does not generally see his own use of a man as an informant as contributing to the man's criminality.

The addict may steal to get drugs, but he does not use drugs to steal. Obtaining drugs is his goal—stealing is instrumental (although addicts might have been thieves even if they had not become drug users). Since the business of the narcotics detective is to arrest drug users, he is less tolerant of addiction than the burglary detective. A narcotics detective will routinely arrest a "dirty" informant. A burglary detective would also arrest an informant if he knew he was a burglar. But the commission of a burglary does not alter an individual's appearance and demeanor, while drug use frequently does. An informant may be obviously under the influence of narcotics while he is being interviewed by a burglary detective. Thus, I have several times seen the following situation: an informant walks into the burglary section and is taken into an interrogation room. The detective, for the record, asks the man whether he is "dirty." The reply typically is, "No, man, I told ya, I'm not usin'." The detective nods and asks the man questions about suspects. Afterwards, the detective remarks, "Man, he was dirty." The burglary detective, however, does not perceive this as his primary concern.

As the situation is organized between narcotics detectives and their informants, and burglary detectives and their informants, it has the effect both of permitting the informant to commit crimes, and of permitting the detective to rest easy about their commission. The pattern of the situation may be described in summary fashion as follows. Most informants—both burglars and narcotics offenders—are addicts. In general, *burglary detectives permit informants to commit narcotics offenses, while narcotics detectives allow informants to steal.* Now, this summary is not entirely correct or always true, but it does accurately state a strong tendency. Doubtless, if a narcotics detective happened to catch one of his informants leaving a locked building through a window with a furpiece under his arm, and bracelets dangling from his pockets, he would arrest the informant as a burglar. Similarly, if a burglary detective spotted an informant taking or selling drugs, he would arrest his informant. But usually neither the narcotics detective nor the burglary detective seriously attempts to learn about his informant's involvement in the other detective's field of interest. Not especially caring to learn of such involvement, in talking with the informant, detectives typically steer the conversation elsewhere. A burglary detective was heard to say, for example, "Don't tell me what Joe is shooting. I want to hear about TV sets." Similarly, a narcotics detective was heard to say, "I want to know where he's stashing his stuff, man, not about his hot suits." When experienced informants give such "irrelevant" information, detectives become irritated. They are more tolerant, however, of inexperienced informants, smiling as they "teach" the informant what is relevant and what is not. Like the inexperienced detective, the inexperienced informant must be "broken into" the enforcement specialty. "Detecting," for police and informers alike, is principally the art of making relevant distinctions concerning information. If the detective has lost confidence in the informer, he may turn him over to the other specialist for information pertinent to that man's concern. Usually, however, each detective overlooks criminality in another's primary area of jurisdiction, as a means of gaining relevant information for his own assigned specialty.

INTERPERSONAL REWARDS

A stigmatized identity characterizes most informants.[20] Thus, in our culture, as is evidenced by the children's terms "tattletale" and "snitch" as well as by the underworld's "fink" and "stoolie," informants are objects of contempt and derision. If an informant is also an addict, he is additionally stigmatized. Only an exceptionally strong personality would enable one to ignore this general social evaluation. Since the typical informant is usually not so splendidly self-contained, he is likely to be a man of low self-esteem. As one student of addiction writes:

. . . as the addict's habit grows and almost all his thoughts and efforts are directed toward supplying himself with drugs, he becomes careless about his personal appearance and cleanliness. Consequently, non-addicts think of him as a "bum" and, because he persists in his use of drugs, conclude that he lacks "will power," is perhaps "degenerate," and is likely to contaminate others.

The addict is aware that he is judged in terms of these various secondary social definitions, and while he may attempt to reject them, it is difficult if not impossible to do so when much of his interpersonal and institutional experience serves to ratify these definitions.[21]

Consequently, if the policeman is able to dignify the character of the informant, he will have rendered a valuable personal service. One way professionalized police attempt to bolster the addict's definition of self is to utilize a respectable vocabulary. Thus, informants are officially referred to in Westville as "special employees," although the police privately call them "snitches," a term of less opprobrium than "fink." Far more important, however, so far as status elevation of the informant is concerned, is the quality of the encounter between the police officer and the informant. Obviously, no police officer degrades his informant, because if he did he would probably lose him. Nor can he be overly solicitous. Here the policeman faces a problem that is fairly common in a

---

[20] This conception has been developed by Erving Goffman. See his *Stigma: Notes on the Management of Spoiled Identity* (Englewood Cliffs, N.J.: Prentice-Hall, 1963).

[21] Marsh Ray, "The Cycle of Abstinence and Relapse Among Heroin Addicts," *Social Problems*, 9 (Fall, 1961), p. 134.

society where status distinctions exist, but where acknowledgment of these by the higher status party can be interpreted by the other as a sign of disrespect.

The vice control officer in Westville who was generally acknowledged to "have more snitches than any other officer on the force" seemed able to raise the self-esteem of his informants because of his effective use of several "techniques." (His use of these "techniques" was not a matter of explicit method, from a textbook. From his point of view, such "techniques" were merely good common sense, as indeed they were.) First, he utilized egalitarian symbols: to them, he was "Tom," never "Sergeant" or "Sir." (The use of first names may appear obvious, but it must be remembered that the police are a paramilitary organization; the use of a first name indirectly implicates all other officers in an egalitarianism of which they might not approve.) Secondly, he tended to be nonjudgmental, almost in the manner of a psychotherapist. Accordingly, he acted as if addiction were a sickness, for which the addict was not personally responsible. For instance, he might inquire into an addict's health, and knowledgeably discuss the effects of addiction. This type of discussion, thirdly, indicated to the addict that he and the policeman were both of the same world, that although Tom was a "cop," he was not "square." Thus, by being informed about the nature of addiction, the policeman indicated that both he and the addict-informant were in the police business together as a way of coping with a difficult environment.

In fact, detectives sometimes take a *genuine* interest in their informants, although this concern is inevitably linked to a certain extent with their own needs as detectives. Thus, the English detective Gosling comments:

> I learned—early in my career and accidentally—the value of sympathy for a crook. A small gesture of kindliness . . . brought me a good deal of kudos and set my career on the upward path. After that I began to cultivate thieves. I made friends with them, listened to their troubles, and shut my eyes to their minor misdeeds.[22]

Similar observations can be made in both Eastville and Westville. Indeed, informants not uncommonly build up a dependent relationship with police that in turn aids police in their own work. On the one hand, a detective might spend considerable time trying to get employment for an addict who wanted to work. Indeed, policemen are likely to be most helpful to any criminal who sincerely wants to "clean himself up." On

[22] Gosling, *op. cit.*, p. 17.

the other hand, policemen also tend to be realistic, but surprisingly hopeful, recognizing the typical informant-addict's propensity to fall.[23]

PROTECTION OF THE INFORMANT'S CRIMINAL STATUS

Above all, there is an implied understanding between the policeman and the informant that the policeman will protect the informant's criminal status. Even though addicts in any community come to realize that their best friends may be informants and frequently take precautions against this possibility, none would want it known that he had descended to such depths. Thus, the revelation of an informant's identity ("burning the informant") can have serious consequences for the status of a criminal.

The policeman does not care about the informant's reputation among his fellows, except as it effects the work of the policeman. If the policeman allows the informant's identity to be known, then the policeman's reputation for being trustworthy is harmed. In turn, any action by the policeman which jeopardized *his* reputation for being trustworthy will interfere with his ability to maintain his required network of informants. In this context, trustworthiness does not refer, as it conventionally does, to honesty. The informant would have no objection if the policeman were to take a bribe, perjure himself in the courtroom, or be less than forthright about his sources of information. The trustworthiness of the policeman refers solely to the fulfillment of his obligations to the informant primarily the concealment of the informant's identity. Even if it sometimes means losing a "good pinch," every effort must be made not to "burn" the informant.

This discussion should not be construed as suggesting that the informer may not be arrested outside of the context of his "special employee" activities for other law violations. As discussed above, such an arrest may increase the bargaining position of the policeman. But once the policeman has requested the informant to perform a certain task, such as making an illegal purchase of narcotics, he is also required to make every effort to protect the informant's criminal status.

It should be noted that the informant's role can be dangerous. I learned of at least two cases, one in narcotics and one in another area, where the district attorney dropped charges to protect informants from potential physical harm. In one case, he did so when a responsible police official presented the opinion that the informant would surely be badly

---

[23] Observations also suggested that there was little difference in treatment between white and Black informants. If anything, policemen may have been more solicitous of Black informants, since, in their view, "good ones are hard to find."

beaten, if not killed, were his identity to be disclosed. Furthermore, the job of protecting informants who are sent to prison may cause special problems for correctional authorities if their identity has been disclosed.

CRIMINAL DISCOVERY AND THE INFORMER SYSTEM

The State's rules of criminal discovery are interpreted in Westville as obliging the prosecution to permit the defense to examine police arrest reports.[24] Consequently, the police do not report as the significant events leading to arrest what an unbiased observer viewing the situation would report. Instead they compose a description that satisfies legal requirements without interfering with their organizational requirements. For example, the police will not say in an arrest report that they cajoled, or, in rare instances, threatened a suspect to get information. More importantly, they will not, if possible, reveal that an informant was utilized at all. Indeed, this concealment is a major task of the police. As described earlier, it almost never happens that an informant is not used somewhere along the line in crimes involving "vice," and also in such other secret crimes as subversion, espionage, and counterfeiting. The police themselves testify to this pattern, and it was also observed. Nevertheless, of the five hundred and eight cases in the narcotics files of the Westville police during the period December 1961 to March 1963, less than 9 per cent mentioned the use of an informant. Thus, a chief strategy the policeman uses to maintain his "trustworthiness" with the world of addict informants is to tell less than the whole truth on the arrest report.

Vice cases in general, and narcotics cases especially, differ from the typical crime involving an assailant in that the identity of the culprit is frequently at issue in assailant cases, while it is not in a "possession" or a "possession for sale" case. At most there may be a question of whether the narcotics found on the street after the defendant was seen making a furtive movement were actually his, or just happened to be lying there, or whether the defendant was responsible for the narcotics found in the brassière of his girl friend. Usually, however, the defendant is caught with the narcotics in his possession and the query is whether the police used legal procedures to apprehend the defendant. Generally, this reduces to whether the police had reasonable cause to make a search incident to an arrest.

[24] I am grateful to Professor Edward Barrett for pointing out to me that the rules of criminal discovery—like many other "laws"—are not necessarily as inflexible as they may appear in a single jurisdiction, where a local interpretation prevails.

Since reasonable cause is ordinarily established by the information of an informant, the problems for the police are: what are the conditions under which the name of an informant must be revealed? and, more importantly, how may these conditions be avoided? Since this area of law has been known to change, it is safest to say that, during the period of study, the police found it necessary to disclose the name of an informant where (1) the informant participated in the crime charged; (2) he did not participate but was an eyewitness; (3) the informant's communication was the only justification for the action of the police even though the informant did nothing more than furnish information; (4) in view of the evidence, the informant would be a material witness on the issue of guilt and nondisclosure would deprive the defendant of a fair trial.[25]

At the time of the study, the police had a number of additional stratagems for establishing probable cause while utilizing informants and not disclosing their names. If the police obtained a search warrant based upon the testimony of a reliable informant, the name of the informant need not be disclosed to the defense, provided the validity of the warrant was not challenged,[26] or if challenged, upheld. As the California Supreme Court said in the then controlling case, *People* v. *Keener:* [27]

If a search is made pursuant to a warrant valid on its face and the only objection is that it was based on information given to the police officer by an unnamed informant, there is substantial protection against unlawful search and the necessity of applying the exclusionary rule in order to remove the incentive to engage in unlawful searches is not present. The warrant, of course, is issued by a magistrate, not by a police officer, and will be issued only when the magistrate is satisfied by the supporting affidavit that there is probable cause. He may, if he sees fit, require disclosure of the identity of the informant before issuing the warrant or require that the informant be brought to him. The requirement that an affidavit be presented to the magistrate and his control over the issuance of the warrant diminish the danger of illegal action, and it does not appear that there has been frequent abuse of the warrant procedure. One of the purposes of the adoption of the exclusionary rule was to further the use of warrants, and it obviously

---

[25] Bonnie Lee Martin, *op. cit.*, p. 123.

[26] Under Secs. 1539, 869, Penal Code. It is extremely rare for a warrant to be challenged. The division chief of the Westville district attorney's office could remember no challenge since *People* v. *Keener*, and the public defender could recall only one in his experience in the public defender's office. This was at the insistence of a defendant and the warrant was upheld. As he explained, "Once the police obtain a warrant that's valid on its face (the warrant calls for searching a certain address and that was the one searched) the defense generally folds on the issue of probable cause."

[27] 55 C. 2d 714; 361 P. 2d 587.

is not desirable to place unnecessary burdens upon their use . . . It follows from what we have said that where a search is made pursuant to a warrant valid on its face, the prosecution is not required to reveal the identity of the informer in order to establish the legality of the search and the admissibility of the evidence obtained as a result of it.[28]

While the search warrant is the most expeditious way for the police to overcome the problem of not disclosing an informant's identity, there are other tactics used as well, based mainly upon the general point made in *People* v. *Hicks*:

The identity of an informant need not be revealed when the information merely provides the basis or starting point of an independent investigation by the officers, or merely points the finger of suspicion at the defendant, and where the officers do not rely solely on the information to provide probable cause but arrest or search on the basis of independent observations or investigations.[29]

Typically, as the head of the Westville narcotics detail stated:

If someone is holding on the street, and you get a tip that he's holding, when he spots you coming at him, he's going to do one of three things— either he's going to try to drop the stuff, or try to swallow it, or run. All of these are furtive movements, and you can search on the basis of them without disclosing the name of the informant.

Accordingly, if possible, the police attempt to use the informant as a *tipster* about the location of criminal activities rather than as a *witness* or as a *participant* in the crime. Thus, if an informant succeeds in "making a buy," it may be in the interest of the police not to charge the primary suspect with the crime of selling narcotics but to find another offense with which to charge him, not requiring the informant's testimony. Sometimes it is difficult to find another such crime, or, at least, to find one that carries a heavy penalty. For instance, suppose the police want to trap a dealer who does not himself use heroin, but whom they believe to be selling large amounts. They may in such a predicament make use of a tipster, or, if the case is big enough, create a police informant whose identity they are willing to disclose in return for a conviction for possession for sale.

It does happen, although reportedly with low frequency, that the police are faced with the dilemma of either losing the case or burning the informant. If he is a man who has "turned" a number of cases for them in the past, he will be given much consideration; the police will

[28] *Ibid.*, 722–723.
[29] 165 Cal. App. 2d 548, 552.

make a strong argument to the prosecutor to drop the case or to "deal it out for much less than it is worth." Usually, the prosecutor is more likely to deal out a case than to drop it entirely.

Constitutional interpretation and statutory law in Eastville differ in two salient respects. There is no statute in Eastville prohibiting "use" of narcotics, or prohibiting being "under the influence" of narcotics, as there is in Westville. Consequently, needle marks cannot be used to establish probable cause for an arrest. This interpretation reduces the policeman's chances of "creating" an informant. Secondly, police believe the courts require that the name of an informant always be disclosed. The requirement is singularly important, since it modifies the structure of narcotics enforcement. In contrast to Westville police, those in Eastville cannot use informants to establish probable cause. This does not mean the Eastville police make no use of informants, but that they rely on them less heavily.

In Eastville, the informant is used *primarily* as a tipster rather than as a State's witness to establish the case against the defendant, in conformity with the disclosure requirement. Policemen themselves do the work of informers in Eastville and as a consequence, the Eastville informant is not normally paid with a reduction in charges. The Eastville police have no moral reservations about reducing charges; if anything, they would prefer the Westville situation where charges are reduced and the informant performs the valuable service of providing evidence sufficient to justify search and seizure. Eastville police do not reduce charges because this form of payment is too large for the services the informant is *able* to perform under prevailing constitutional interpretation.

Between the prosecutor and the defense attorney there exists a relationship similar to that between good poker players. For the prosecutor, the name of the informant, in those cases in which it must be revealed to press his case, is like the hole card in a poker game. He sometimes must burn an informant to show he is not bluffing when he presses for a deal. Every hand need not be "seen" in order to keep the adversary honest, but every once in a while each side must go to trial to show the other that he has "the ace in the hole" when he says he does. Thus, because of other pressures on the prosecutor, he is sometimes unable to "cooperate" with the police in their efforts to protect the informant's criminal status.

SUMMARY AND CONCLUSIONS

This chapter has introduced the reader to the structure and workings of the informer system, especially in the work of the narcotics detective, and to some of the consequences of this system for the broader system of justice without trial. It has emphasized, first, that narcotics crimes are typically without citizen complainants and therefore require the development of an information system for the apprehension of narcotics offenders. Second, it has suggested that the vice control squad's access to an information system places it in a key position within the police department. Third, partly as a result of this position, and also because the maintenance of the information system is perceived by the prosecutor as necessary to law enforcement, the needs of this system tend to be given extra consideration by the prosecutor. The interesting issue is the conditions under which it is possible to have reciprocal relations with informants and also the strategies police engage in to create these conditions. That is, what commodities are exchanged by informer and informed, and under what conditions are such commodities created?

The most important and valuable of these commodities, from the informer's point of view, is some sort of "break" in the criminal process. This can be achieved by withholding arrest of an informer when he has committed a crime, bringing about a reduction of charge, making a recommendation for lesser sentence, and the like. But this "leverage" does not necessarily constitute a "license" to engage in illegal activities. On the contrary, it is when the policeman is in a position to exchange an anticipated legal penalty that he is able to obtain the most valuable information. The detective generally turns his back on criminality only when the crime occurs in another detective's area of organizational jurisdiction. Thus, narcotics police typically ignore burglaries when questioning their informants. Likewise, burglary detectives overlook the use of narcotics by their informants and pay their informants money which, they realistically assume, will be used to purchase narcotics.

The policeman may also reward the informant with the commodity of status elevation. That the informant is usually an object of social disdain is indicated by such appellations as "fink" and "stoolie," that are contemptuously hurled at him in popular literature and discourse. A competent detective minimizes the stigma of the informer's position in society (and thus maximizes the value which the informant has for him) by listening to the man's troubles or meanderings, by dealing with him in an egalitarian manner, and occasionally by making an active attempt to improve his condition. Policemen can be, albeit inadvertently, good social workers.

Finally, as the elemental obligation without which even the most careful attention to the other requisites of the informant system is futile, the policeman must protect the informer's identity. Obviously, this is especially true when those informed upon are dangerous; however, even if no danger of physical harm threatens the informant, the loss of esteem associated with the informer's role is so considerable that revelation, except rarely, of the informer's identity would inevitably result in a breakdown of this system of obtaining information.

Since a functional prerequisite of an informant system is to reward the informer, any increase in penalty necessarily gives the narcotics policeman more to work with as anticipated rewards. Penalties thus are the capital assets of the informer system. High penalties for such relatively minor violations as possession of narcotics equipment, or a marihuana cigarette, increase the capital assets of the policeman and create conditions under which the information system will work most efficiently. Policemen rarely make this point, preferring instead to support high penalties on the general grounds of deterrence; but a perfectly evident consequence of a punitive narcotics policy is its contribution to the smooth functioning of the narcotics information system by providing that system with requisite inputs.[30]

From the point of view of understanding the police as a social organization, the informer system highlights the substantial commitment that the police, Eastville, Westville, British, and American, have made to the enforcement of substantive criminal law, irrespective of the constraints embodied in principles of due process. Crimes without citizen complainants result in a structure demanding independent action on the policeman's part, and therefore emphasize the craftsmanlike possibilities of policework. The "professional" narcotics policeman is not one who has internalized, as he might, the purposes of the legal controls of judicial authorities. On the contrary, the "professional" narcotics policeman is a man who has learned to reduce his accountability to the courts, to outwit, often successfully, the spirit and the letter of the rule of law.

---

[30] See George C. Homans, "Social Behavior as Exchange," *American Journal of Sociology*, **63** (May, 1958), 597–606; see also Alvin W. Gouldner, "The Norm of Reciprocity: A Preliminary Statement," *American Sociological Review*, **25** (April, 1960), 161–178; and Peter M. Blau, *Exchange and Power in Social Life* (New York: John Wiley and Sons, Inc., 1964).

These approaches see everyday interaction in the context of an exchange of commodities. The position taken here, however, need not go even so far. Here there is usually an explicit awareness of what is being exchanged. As in all contracts, however, there may be a history of past exchanges as well as anticipation of future bargains which enter into "agreement" in the present settlement.

Chapter 7

The Narcotics Enforcement Pattern

To be understood in its complexity, the informer-informed relation should be analyzed as part of a detailed description of the actual work of the narcotics policeman. This chapter provides such a description at three levels: the routine work of the narcotics officer, the good but routine "pinch," and the apprehension of a so-called "dope ring." Since a major factor in narcotics enforcement is the effect of legal rules, the working norms and conduct of narcotics detectives will be interpreted against a background of such regulations. Especially significant are the differences in response in the ordinary and the "big" case, the latter seemingly providing the conditions that fit with the more common—and judicial—concept of what narcotics enforcement is all about. Finally, we analyze the importance of the existence of an occasional big case as a way to obtaining the necessary commodities needed for the enforcement of the more typical cases.

First, an evening with the narcotics detail of the Westville vice squad is described to illustrate the routine activity of the narcotics policeman and the making of a "good pinch." The night described is typical in that it presents the salient features of the active work of the narcotics officer as well as his supporting organization, while the case that arose that night was middle-sized. On the other hand, the night is unrepresentative to the extent that there was so much activity. For each "caper" that "comes off," other good pinches are planned and fail; it is impossible to say how many, since any investigation resulting from an informant's tip could be regarded as a planned "caper."

ROUTINE ACTIVITY AND THE PETTY INFORMANT

In a municipal police department, vice control officers, like all plainclothesmen, spend a portion of their working hours on surveillance, simply riding in unmarked cars on street patrol. But vice control men spend much less time in this fashion than patrol division detectives, since they frequently are able to "create" crimes through the leads of informants, while patrol division detectives must await the report of a felony before they can take action. Thus, the patrol detective—who rides alone, while vice control men team up in pairs—may find boredom a major enemy. Entire evenings may pass when patrolling detectives do nothing other than drive a car slowly around a city for eight hours. After a while, the detective may feel gratitude for the felon who provides him with activity.

Much of the generative activity in enforcing narcotics crimes takes place within the police station. This is not because narcotics police are lazy but because the nature of narcotics crime requires that invocation of activity be based upon receipt of messages.[1] Thus, all detectives, but especially narcotics detectives, do a lot of work on the telephone. Many of the informants (some of whom are transients) do not have telephones of their own, and others prefer not to be called at home by a policeman. As a result, the narcotics policeman is continually being called to the telephone.

Not all informing, however, takes place over the telephone. Petty informants seem to enjoy wandering into the separate quarters of the vice control squad, and narcotics officers must be available to greet and chat with them. Indeed, due to their constant need for information, narcotics officers encourage informants to "drop in." To this end, the Westville vice control squad is not only quartered separately from the rest of the police department but it even has a special entrance through which informants can pass unobserved by other policemen.

During the evening being described, Sergeant Harris was visited by a long-time addict and regular informant for the vice control squad, who was a mercenary, paid for his information. Members of the vice control squad suspected him of "dealing a little methedrine" himself and had another addict-informant keeping an eye on him. Actually, each addict-informant accused the other of dealing methedrine, but the vice control squad had been unable to convict either.

The informant, especially one who seems odd or eccentric, is in an advantageous position, since he can gain a fairly accurate idea of the physical location of members of the narcotics detail by the simple expedient of telephoning them. Narcotics officers, however, are alert to deceptive techniques used by informants and take care to counteract

---

[1] If the idea that policemen are slow to arrive at the scene of a crime is true, the cause is typically overwork rather than laziness. Policemen seem inclined toward physical activity, provided it occurs in an authoritative context. They do not care to be sent on errands and above all dislike paper work. They seem to enjoy most of all, the processes of investigation: talking, telephoning, going "out on the street." These activities are of course the ones where their authority is most evident and exercised.

these whenever possible. From the officers' point of view, the least serious is the petty informant dealer who, for instance, drops around to the police station to impress the officers that he is "working" in their interest. There are evidently two reasons for the policeman's indulgent response to the maneuvers of an informant of this type. First, although the policeman sees through his artifices, such an informant may sometimes produce useful information and is consequently tolerated. Indeed, the policeman may feel genuinely sorry for such a man. In my experience, most policemen can empathize somewhat with the petty addict-informant. I have several times heard various vice squad detectives express the notion that such-and-such an informant "could have been somebody if he hadn't gotten hooked on that stuff. It's terrible what it does to you." In addition, the petty informant is typically not a symbolic assailant but is perceived as something of a pitiful figure, rather like a punch-drunk prizefighter.

Perhaps the more important reason, however, is instrumental. An informant would at most risk using "only" a so-called dangerous drug when visiting the narcotics detail, since such use constitutes a misdemeanor rather than a felony. Consequently, in the narcotics officer's scale of values, the user simply does not constitute a "good pinch." In practice, therefore, although such an informant does not have a "license" to operate, neither do the narcotics police strive to bring about his apprehension. Of course, if he were to be caught selling drugs illegally, he would surely be arrested (even if only to be released again in return for information).

Police take most seriously deceptive techniques whereby informants attempt to use their working relations with law enforcement officers for positive personal gain. This situation poses the gravest dilemma for detectives by suspending them between the ideals of morality and the demands of efficiency. For example, when informant A says that B is in possession of an illegal object, there is often reason to suspect A's motives. Within the system, the morally acceptable motive is to extricate oneself from a difficult situation. It is not that such motivation is positively countenanced either by the police or by the informants themselves. But if the situation of the informant is perceived as an equilibrium with a set of minuses on one side and pluses on the other, it is seen as understandable for a man in a minus situation to bring himself back to normal. Thus, when the petty informant gives information in exchange for money to purchase drugs, or to avoid a penal sanction, his motives are acceptable, and the police feel no hesitancy in engaging his services.

However, the police do not consider it morally acceptable for a man to inform to gain positive benefits. Policemen may not personally like the idea, but they sometimes find themselves in a position of having to use information given by people who are vengeful, or worse yet, who will gain some unlawful benefit from the arrest of another, such as freedom to take over another seller's clientele if he is sent to jail or the opportunity to strip clean of resalable articles the premises of a man who has been arrested. What troubles police most is the "set-up," the "planting," for instance, of a good supply of narcotics in addict A's house by B to take A "out of the scene." Suspicious of being deceived, police usually check carefully an informant's story if the context makes it appear the informant is somehow being positively rewarded. Policemen have few, if any, moral reservations about setting a trap for a suspected felon on their own initiative. What hurts both pride and morality is to permit a false trap to be set by one "criminal" for another.

SETTING UP A "GOOD PINCH"

In what follows, the events of the "good pinch" evening are described. They are also interpreted in light of how organizational commitments of the police influence their capacity to observe the rule of law.

Shortly after the petty informant left, a telephone call came in from another addict-informant, Charlie, who was scheduled for preliminary hearing on a charge of possession for sale with one prior conviction. Charlie reported that a couple of addicts had stolen a large supply of drugs from a warehouse or drugstore, and had "split up the loot" in his "pad." He could not provide the address of the thieves, although he had visited one of them and thought he might be able to find his way there again. (According to the police, "hypes" find it difficult to remember addresses. Thus, an uninformed narcotics officer might believe an addict to be lying when he claimed to be unable to remember a friend's address.)

Charlie also reported a rumor that one of the thieves, Dave, had been robbed by another addict, Bill. Charlie didn't know where Bill lived either, but he knew a close friend of Bill's who was living in Cedarville. Charlie reasoned that if Bill had any "stuff," it would be likely that Bill's friend, Archie, would also have gotten some.

On the strength of Charlie's tip, Sergeant Harris decided it would be worthwhile to try to locate Archie, since he was well known to the police as an addict. Archie's address was on file, and some checking revealed Archie to be living in the Bismarck Hotel in Cedarville. Before we left, the Sergeant called the Cedarville vice control squad (consisting of two men), explaining that this was his way of maintaining good relations wth adjacent police departments. In addition, the Sergeant notified the State of California narcotics agents, who are invited by the Westville police department to make use of the office space and equipment of the Westville vice control.

The Westville Police Department, especially the vice control squad, is proud of its relations with other law enforcement agencies. This working relationship is important for the efficient enforcement of the narcotics laws, since state agents and the local police provide each other with complementary services. The Westville vice control squad has three resources that state agents lack: they possess greater knowledge of local conditions, have the services of a well-developed network of local informants, and are allowed to arrest for "marks" alone—tiny red bruises that indicate recent use of narcotics. (Using narcotics or "being under the influence" is itself a misdemeanor under Section 11721 of the penal code.) [2] State agents typically do not arrest for "marks," since their chief interest is to uncover large sources of illegal narcotics. The arrest for "marks," however, is an added value in the vice control officer's resources in bargaining for information and thus enables the Westville vice control squad to initiate cases more effectively than can state police. Finally, the Westville squad can call for the services of the local patrol police when "extra bodies" are required.

The state agents are better equipped than the local vice control squad to follow through on cases, especially those involving large quantities of narcotics. Since they have statewide jurisdiction, state police can take a plane from, for instance, San Francisco to Los Angeles to investigate a lead on a supplier in the other city. Furthermore, large amounts of money are sometimes required to make incriminating purchases of opiates or heroin, especially in transactions coming over the border from Mexico. Westville police have neither the funds nor the jurisdiction to handle this type of law enforcement operation. Therefore, local and state police complement each other, the local police by initiating small arrests and the state police by having the resources to track down the bigger "pinches." As will be shown, narcotics arrests are seen as a series of increasingly larger steps up a ladder, at the top of which is the narcotics officer's prize: the "source."

CREATING AN INFORMANT

We left Westville in two cars—four state agents in a flashy-looking hard top convertible, and the Sergeant, and another state agent and I in the 1963 blue Plymouth sedan well known to addicts in the area. As we drove up to

---

[2] Until 1962, one could be arrested in Westville for *being* an addict. However, that was declared unconstitutional in *Robinson v. California*, 370 U. S. 660 (1962).

the hotel in Cedarville, we spotted the two local vice control men, looking like two professional football players on their way to a Friday night movie. One of the state agents recognized a car that seemed to be Archie's, which of course suggested that Archie was either in his room or nearby. Three state agents stayed outside while two of the state agents, the Cedarville vice control man, Sergeant Harris and I entered the hotel.

Inside the hotel, the chief state agent approached the desk clerk and asked whether Archie was in the hotel. The clerk said he thought he was, but that he might well be in another (Dominick's) room. Three policemen and I went to Dominick's room on the third floor, and two went to Archie's second-floor room with a key they obtained from the clerk. Approaching Dominick's room on tiptoe, we heard several men's voices. One policeman suggested that somebody ought to go upstairs and tell the other policemen that Dominick's room was occupied. I volunteered, because I wanted to see what the other policemen were doing in the meantime.

When I arrived they were searching Archie's room. (I relayed the message to the policemen upstairs.) The room served as a painting studio for Archie, and most of the space was crammed with paints, bottles, and canvasses at different stages of completion in an apparently haphazard disarray. The officers, who by my observation were skilled at searching without changing the appearance of the room, had been looking mainly through drawers. They rearranged the little they had upset and the three of us went downstairs.

Legally, the police are not permitted to enter a room and make a search without a warrant, except "incident" to an arrest of some person in the room. Thus, they cannot search an empty room without a warrant, even if they see marihuana on the table through a window. In California, unless a search has some reasonable relationship to an arrest, it becomes an unlawful exploratory search.[3] The practice of making an unlawful exploratory search of the room of a suspected criminal is, so far as I could tell on several occasions, accepted by both the Westville police and the state police. As one policeman commented:

> "Of course, it's not exactly legal to take a peek beforehand. It's not one of the things you usually talk about as a police technique. But if you find something, you back off and figure out how you can do it legal. And if you don't find anything, you don't have to waste a lot of time."

The policeman does not feel legally constrained in conducting an exploratory examination of suspicious premises. Even less does he feel *morally* at fault in conducting a prior search of a known addict's room for narcotics.

[3] See Rex Collings, Jr., "Toward Workable Rules of Search and Seizure—an Amicus Curiae Brief," *California Law Review*, 50 (1962), 443 [citing *People v. Molarius*, 146 Cal. App. 2d 129, 303 P. 2d 350 (1956)].

The process by which the policeman justifies his unlawful exploratory search is similar to that by which many criminals justify theirs. Thus, the policeman distinguishes between *legality* and *morality*, just as the criminal does, and as we all do to a certain extent. The prostitute, for example, justifies her activity by asserting that she engages in an enterprise her "trick" desires. The confidence man rationalizes his deceptions with the belief that "there is a bit of larceny in the soul of every man" and that his motives are no different from his victims'. The civil-rights "sit-in" justifies his "trespass" on grounds of a higher morality. Similarly, the policeman countenances *his* unlawful exploration by pointing to the difficulties of his job and asserting that his activity has no adverse effect upon the person whose property is unlawfully searched, *provided* that person is not a criminal. Thus, the policeman typically alleges that unless he conducts unlawful searches, for example, dangerous addicts might escape capture; furthermore, he maintains that innocent persons have no cause for complaint.

When the group reassembled, it was decided to break into Dominick's room, but without kicking the door in. The following strategy was used: one of the Cedarville vice control men knocked on Dominick's door, and said, "Phone," imitating the Spanish accent of the desk clerk. From inside the door, Dominick said, "What?" and the officer repeated, "Phone." Dominick opened the door slightly, and as he did, several policemen pushed inside.

At this point, it was important for the narcotics officer to keep talking in a friendly, calm tone. "Well, hello, Archie," Sergeant Harris said, "just relax and everybody stay where they are and everything is going to be okay." Archie and Dominick began to protest that they hadn't done anything wrong, and it wasn't nice of the police to "just come busting into" the room this way.

The denial of guilt in this case was important for the police because it implied that the suspect would not mind having his arms examined. Had the suspect refused to answer, and ordered the police out in the absence of a warrant, the police would again have been on shaky legal ground. So far, their suspicion of Archie was based on a reliable informant's word that Archie probably had some "stuff," since he was a friend of an addict who, the informant had heard, was "dealing." This vague, hearsay information was also insufficient legally to establish probable cause for a frisk and an examination of his body.[4] What the police required was a tactic to circumvent the legal restrictions.

[4] See Frank J. Remington, "The Law Relating to 'On the Street' Detention, Questioning, and Frisking," *Journal of Criminal Law, Criminology and Police Science*, **51** (December, 1960), 386–394.

By denying his guilt, the suspect gives the policeman an opening wedge. He can say, as Sergeant Harris did, "Okay, Archie, you know it's my job to check you out," simultaneously grabbing Archie's arm and pulling up the shirtsleeve. Before Archie had an opportunity to emit the words suggested by the look of protest on his face, the Sergeant had his fingers on a pair of tiny red "marks" in the crook of the elbow. By finding the marks in the way he had, the Sergeant had introduced new elements into the legal situation. First, he could reasonably claim that Archie had "volunteered" to show his arms and that no physical coercion was used. More important, from the Sergeant's point of view, by finding marks, he had established reasonable cause for arresting Archie as a man "under the influence" of narcotics. In addition, the legality of the arrest further established a basis for a thorough search, after the exploratory "peek," although it is arguable whether the means of entry would be upheld by an appellate court.

We might ask why the suspect did not assert his legal rights and demand a search warrant as soon as the door was opened. There were several reasons. First, he was physically coerced (albeit by indirection, since no actual violence was used). Five physically well-constituted, armed men (plus one middle-sized unarmed professor) broke in unexpectedly and stood around with no-nonsense looks on their faces. At that moment, it would have taken an act of heroism to order them out.

Second, these men did represent authority. To a certain extent, the suspect must interpret the policeman's behavior as being proper, for the policeman represents the state. His very being conveys an impression of legitimacy to this type of addict, an occupant of a cheap hotel room, a user of narcotics, a struggling painter. In addition to being surprised and upset, the suspect may not be entirely aware of his legal rights, and the police in this situation did not advise him of his rights.

Furthermore, Archie was, after all, a known addict and had previous experiences with the police. Consequently, there was on his part an anticipation of future encounters. If he acted like a "wise-guy" this time (by ordering the police to leave), he could have "the book thrown at him" the next. One narcotics detective reported that no known addict had ever refused him permission to make an examination for "marks," even though there was no legal justification for a search. I have seen a detective pull to the curb and ask a man how things are going, adding, "You wouldn't happen to be dirty, would you?" The detective may look, or just wish the man well and leave.

Finally, there is for the suspect in a room, as for the man stopped by the police on the street, the genuine possibility of innocence combined with the mildness of the request. The police are, after all, making a seemingly innocuous request, permission to glance at the crook of an elbow. Objectively, its fulfillment demands no more exertion than the common courtesy of giving a match or the correct time to a stranger. In a nonlegal context, it might almost be insulting to refuse. In the situation, however, we might think the insulted party would be the suspect; it is far more degrading to be suspected of being an addict than to be asked for a match. But for the already convicted user, most of the stigma has already been manifested. Having once been proved culpable, the suspect can hardly claim to be shocked by the suspicion of use. All of these factors combine to impede assertion of legal rights. Furthermore, if the addict is innocent, the police leave, with the suspect disturbed but not substantially harmed.

The failure to consider such facts by appellate courts and civil liberties lawyers puzzles and annoys the policeman. He claims that he would never do this sort of thing to a respectable citizen, and that the law should somehow recognize the difference in its search-and-seizure rules between respectable citizens and known criminals. Since the search-and-seizure rules are based on concepts of probability, a degree of irrationality in ignoring probabilities associated with an individual's past *status* as an addict cannot be denied. The policeman is far less interested in questions of constitutionality than in the reasonableness of a *working* system.

The criminal law, however, largely because it is so heavily influenced by constitutional requirements, is not necessarily administratively rational. Indeed the principle of legality often stands in opposition to the principle of administrative rationality. Like the policeman, the addict typically does not perceive interactions against a background of higher legal requirements. He operates according to the normative assumptions of everyday life, emphasizing the factual. He knows he is an addict, that he will sometimes be in possession of narcotics and, fearing that he will be discovered, he is not going to unduly antagonize the police. Of all types of "criminality," addiction is undoubtedly the most difficult, because the addict must anticipate continual and relatively uncontrolled participation in the forbidden activity, and, therefore, repeated contact with police.

Moreover, the experienced addict knows much about how police operate and what they are after. He knows they are not interested in a "vag" addict who possesses only a supply of drugs sufficient for immediate personal use. On the other side, the policeman is confident that his behavior is not going to be the subject of an appellate court decision. If no incriminating evidence has been found, it is hardly likely the addict will sue in tort, or even lodge a complaint with the police department, partly because of the practical ineffectiveness of such remedies, but mainly because the addict has an expectation of continuing relations with the police.

The policeman's encounter with the addict is a game with a twist. Each playing is influenced by the anticipation of future games. As a result, it is difficult to describe, in any single instance, the values held by the competing parties, since these are modified by each party's subjective assessment of what his opponent's strength will be in future encounters. Thus, the addict would not sue in tort, nor would he complain to the police department about a narcotics officer's behavior, because this would be taken as an affront by the policeman. Such aggressive behavior on the part of the addict toward the policeman would doubtless lead to another sort of game situation in the future where the addict would be defined as an enemy. Outcomes of games played between superordinates and subordinates are going to vary greatly depending on the conception the authority has of his antagonist. Typically, when no incriminating evidence is discovered, the addict is happy to forget the affair. By the same token, when incriminating evidence is discovered, the policeman expects the addict to "cop out" (confess) sometime during the adjudicative process. In the present case, the copping out occurred early, exactly as anticipated.

The sergeant, the supervising state agent, and the suspect went back upstairs to the suspect's room for interrogation. The purpose was to convince Archie to purchase narcotics from Bill under surveillance. When we reached his room, the state agent opened the conversation by saying, "Look, Archie, you know the score. Tell us how much stuff you've got—and you know you'd better tell us the truth, because we're going to search anyway." Archie showed the agent a "fit" (eyedropper and hypodermic needle) and some pills in the bathroom. The agent found other pills that Archie claimed were vitamins. Additional questions revealed that Archie had been purchasing his drugs from Bill. Archie also said that Bill had quite a lot and that he understood Bill had gotten his supply by "burning" (stealing from) a third person whom Archie didn't know.

Since Archie's story was consistent with the one the police had gotten from the original informant, Charlie, they offered Archie a deal. In return for his "cooperation" (calling Bill and making a "connection" with him that night), they would overlook his "marks" (thus saving him a probable period of ninety days in the county jail). Archie hesitated and tried to argue his way out, but it was perfectly evident that he understood the futility of his argument, especially since he had informed for them in the past. Within a span of ten minutes, Archie agreed to "cooperate." He said, however, that he owed Bill fourteen dollars and couldn't "make a buy from him" unless he could say he would pay him the "bread." The police offered to provide the money, and Archie called Bill, who, according to Archie, had agreed to a sale.

TRIAL BY POLICE

At this point, any lingering doubt the police might have had as to Bill's guilt was erased. They had been only slightly uncertain after the original informant, Charlie, had called and told them that he had personally seen Dave and another addict divide up the spoils of a theft of narcotics and dangerous drugs and that Dave had in turn been robbed by Bill. Now that Archie had "testified" to the effect that Bill was dealing narcotics, any remaining residue of "reasonable doubt" was obliterated.

The use of legal terminology emphasizes the similarity between the reasoning processes of the policeman and those employed by the formal evidentiary standards governing determinations of guilt or innocence. An eyewitness had established that a crime had been committed, and knew the identity of one of the culprits. In addition, he had given hearsay testimony (not admissible in a courtroom) that one of the original culprits had been robbed by a third party, Bill. Although no eyewitness observed this robbery, another witness testified to its effects: Archie not only gave hearsay testimony that Bill "had plenty of stuff," but in addition said that he, Archie, had personally purchased narcotics from Bill. The evidence in this "case" was circumstantial, but strong (depending on the weight conferred on the testimony of the chief witnesses). Moreover, the testimony was given against a background of police experience with the typical behavior patterns of addicts. The stories told by the informants not only fit together, thereby reinforcing the validity of each, but conformed generally to the policeman's conception of usual addict behavior. Therefore, so far as the police were concerned, reliable witnesses had provided circumstantial evidence and eyewitness testimony sufficient to convict Bill.

The standards used by the police to assess Bill's guilt were not unlike those employed by the trial court. (Of course, only one side of the case was stated, since Bill had been given no opportunity to testify or bring witnesses on his own behalf; but for the police this omission was irrelevant.) The evidentiary standards employed by the police in this case are obvious and are those to which reasonable men seem naturally to gravitate. For instance, African tribal judges, as described by Gluckman, employed reasoning similar to that the policeman uses to assess the addict's guilt and to that English and American jurists would likely employ if placed in the social situation of the policeman. Gluckman says:

Judges work not only with standards of reasonable behaviour for upright incumbents of particular social positions, but also with standards of behaviour which are reasonably interpreted as those of particular kinds of wrongdoers. There are social stereotypes of how thieves, adulterers, and other malefactors act. If the witnessed actions of a defendant assemble into one of these stereotypes, he is found guilty, though the judges prefer direct evidence to convict.[5]

In effect, the behavior reported about Bill fit the stereotype of the guilty addict-seller, although guilt had by no means been judicially established. Consequently, for the police, the job now was not to convince themselves of the suspect's guilt, but to demonstrate it in a fashion that would satisfy two closely related requirements: the maintenance of the informer system, and the standard of evidence sufficient to convict in court.

It is instructive to consider the probable legal outcome if at this time the police had decided to arrest Bill on the strength of the evidence presented. In court, Charlie's testimony about Bill's activities would be objected to and upheld as irrelevant, immaterial, and hearsay. Charlie did not see Bill rob Dave of narcotics but had merely heard of this through the addict grapevine. Although Archie's testimony would be admissible, he would be the sole prosecution witness, and any competent defense attorney could destroy Archie's credibility by bringing out that he was a narcotics addict who had been offered a deal in return for testimony. Thus, the case would turn on the testimony of a single vulnerable prosecution witness. By practical courtroom standards, the State at this point had no case against Bill, although by police standards Bill was guilty beyond a reasonable doubt.

Therefore, the police needed Archie's agreement to purchase narcotics from Bill to satisfy judicial criteria for conviction. The primary reason for requiring Archie to "make a buy," however, was not to establish probable cause, but to determine the location of the narcotics and establish that the suspect possessed narcotics, either on his person or "constructively" in his home, or his car or even on the person of a female companion.[6] Because Bill was a user-dealer and therefore likely to have

[5] Max Gluckman, *The Judicial Process Among the Barotse of Northern Rhodesia* (Glencoe, New York: The Free Press, 1955), p. 359.

[6] A person is in possession of a narcotic when it is under his dominion and control, and, to his knowledge, either is carried on his person or in his presence, the possession thereof is immediate, accessible, and exclusive to him, provided, however, that two or more persons may have joint possession and the possession may be individual, through an agent or joint with another. *People* v. *Bigelow*, 104 Cal. App. 2d 380, 388. Cited by Fricke, *California Criminal Law*, 8th ed., 1961, p. 395.

his supply close at hand, his apprehension would be relatively easy. By contrast, if he had been a nonuser-dealer, it would have been much more difficult for the police to capture him successfully, since nonuser-dealers do not generally care whether the narcotics are close at hand. Indeed, from his familiarity with the law about possession, the nonaddict-dealer is likely to have a "stash" or a "stash pad" somewhere removed from his own residence, perhaps at the home of a girl friend, or even in any of the numerous places in the public domain that can serve as "stashes," [7] such as trees, directional signs, the undersides of benches and so forth.

There is an important law enforcement distinction to be drawn between popularly reported *transport stashes*—false heels, false bottomed suitcases, diaphragms—and *storage stashes*. Although it is difficult to deceive police in a search of one's self and immediate effects, it is equally difficult for the police to prove a legal connection between an individual and a stash of narcotics stuffed behind the stairway carpeting of an open apartment house. Thus a "buy" is often required to ascertain the location of the narcotics. In the present case, for example, Bill might have had a "stash" half a block away, in a neighbor's backyard. Archie's job was to trigger Bill into getting his supply, not so much for the police to see where it was, as where it was not.

The police conducted an extended interrogation of Archie about how much "stuff" Bill had, how long he had it, how much he had on hand, and where he kept it. Archie said he thought Bill had gotten the "stuff" about two weeks earlier and had been "shooting and dealing" during this period, but that he wasn't sure exactly how much Bill had on hand, and he certainly didn't know where Bill kept it. Consequently, the police drove to Bill's place in Westville, after Archie had called Bill and told him he had the "bread" he owed him. The police watched Archie enter. He came out more quickly than expected and drove to an appointed spot for a rendezvous. There Archie explained that Bill said he wasn't dressed and didn't want to sell anything tonight, but that he'd give him something in the morning.

The question the police had to resolve was whether they should break into Bill's that night, or wait until morning for Archie to make a buy. After some discussion, it was decided for two reasons to break in immediately. First, it was felt that the longer the wait before breaking in on the suspect, the less likely he would be caught with a sizable amount (large enough to warrant a charge of possession for sale rather than mere possession) or, worst of all, from the policeman's view, they would merely be able to charge him with being "under the influence." When

[7] For a discussion of stashes in an institutional setting, see Erving Goffman, *Asylums* (Garden City, New York: Anchor Books, 1961), pp. 248 ff.

an addict has a large supply over a period of time, he is likely to have built up his habit with the free access. This, coupled with the knowledge that Bill had already sold a portion of his original holdings, made the police reluctant to wait longer.

Second, Bill was on parole, and was required to take the Nalline test weekly. In 1957 the California legislature authorized the court to require the Nalline test as a condition of probation, if the court has reason to believe that the probationer is a narcotics user.[8] The easily administered test involves reading the size of the subject's pupil, followed by an injection of the drug. According to the developers, prior use of an opiate will cause the diameter of the pupil to enlarge, the size of the increase being related to the amount used. Occasional use results in practically no change in pupillary diameter, while absence of narcotics is revealed by reduction of the diameter of the pupil.[9]

If the addict is taking the Nalline test, he will therefore usually be a probationer or a parolee. Even though the test is technically "voluntary" in that the addict signs an "Authorization and Waiver" form, addicts do not generally like it, and submit only as an alternative to jail or State prison. For example, a petty user (a so-called "vag" addict)[10] may receive a sentence of ninety days in the county jail with judgment suspended for as long as three years, provided he takes and passes the Nalline test during this time. He is thus liable for the entire period of

[8] The use of Nalline (a Merck & Co., Inc., trademark for the narcotic, N-allynormorphine) for the diagnosis of addiction was first explored by Dr. Harris Isbell and his associates at the United States Public Health Service Hospital in Lexington, Kentucky, and was further developed by Dr. James Terry, Medical Officer on the Sheriff's staff of the Alameda County, California, Rehabilitation Center. It is now used as a means of controlling addiction in several California counties.

[9] For additional information on the technical, administrative, medical, and legal aspects of the Nalline test, see the following: Harris Isbell, "Nalline—A Specific Narcotic Antagonist: Clinical and Pharmocologic Observations," *The Merck Report*, 62 (April, 1953), 23–26; J. G. Terry, "Nalline: An Aid to Detecting Narcotics Users," *California Medicine*, 85 (November, 1956), 299–301; A. Wikler, H. F. Fraser, and Harris Isbell, "N-allynormorphine: Effects of Single Doses and Precipitation of Acute Abstinence Syndromes During Addiction to Morphine, Methadone, or Heroin in Man (post addicts)," *Journal of Pharmacology and Experimental Therapy*, 109 (September, 1953), 8–20; Stewart Weinberg, "Nalline as an Aid in the Detection and Control of Users of Narcotics," *California Law Review*, 48 (1960), 282–294; Thorvald T. Brown, Chapter IX, "The Nalline Test," in *The Enigma of Drug Addiction* (Springfield, Illinois: Charles C Thomas, 1961), pp. 287–334; and Ernest B. Smith, *Nalline Examinations of Narcotic Addicts: Analysis of Deterrent Effects*, unpublished M.A. thesis, Department of Criminology, University of California, Berkeley, 1960.

[10] The term stems from the days when police used to arrest users under the vagrancy laws. Presently, Sec. 11721 of the Penal Code serves the same purpose.

suspended judgment to examination for use of narcotics [11] by his probation or parole officer, who often delegates his authority to the police.

Relations between probation officers and police are apt to be difficult,
especially when the probationer is a narcotics addict. In this situation, it
is mainly the probation officer who is placed in an ambiguous position
between therapist and policeman.[12] The policeman's goal is, by contrast, much more clearly defined. His immediate task is to make narcotics arrests using every resource at his command. One of his prime resources is the addict. To the extent, however, that policemen make use
of addict-probationers, probation officers fear that the addict will be re-
introduced into the world of criminality from which he has so recently
emerged, interfering with his potential rehabilitation.

The relations between probation officers and police vary from jurisdiction to jurisdiction. In some, they may be hostile. Westville vice control
officers were proud of their cordial relations with the probation department and with parole officers. In general, the police have led the probation officers to believe that whenever a probationer-addict is used as an
informant, the probation officer will routinely be informed. Indeed, the
police department has one man assigned to the Nalline testing program,
who also acts as liaison to the probation department. Meetings between
the two departments are held weekly and telephone conversations may
occur many times each day. Actually, the police do not routinely disclose
the names of their informants to the probation officers but do supply
them with information about their probationers' behavior, especially
when the behavior seems to be illegal. In return for this information,
probation officers (and parole officers) will cooperate with police by giving information, and more importantly by authorizing police to make
an arrest as a violation of probation or parole when the police require
such authorization.

The police were already apprised of Bill's failure to present himself
for the Nalline test the preceding week, and as a result suspected he had
been using narcotics. The Sergeant was on friendly terms with Bill's
parole officer, and counted on him for support in an arrest of Bill for
parole violation. That is, although the parole officer had not specifically
requested that Bill be arrested, the Sergeant depended upon the parole
officer's willingness to affirm he had so requested should the issue arise.
As in many systems of so-called rational procedure, the actual practice

[11] It has happened, but rarely, that a vag addict chooses ninety days in jail over
three years of Nalline.

[12] Lloyd E. Ohlin, Herman Piven, and Donnell M. Pappenfort, "Major Dilemmas
of the Social Worker in Probation and Parole," *National Probation and Parole Association Journal,* **2** (July, 1956), 211–225.

depends on independently created strategies for avoiding the sanctions of regulation, rather than on formal delegation of authority.

The problem for the police then became how to break into Bill's apartment. Especially in vice control, police frequently must kick doors in sharply and quickly, without giving advance notice of their intentions to the suspect. The purpose of such violent entries is evident: to counteract the speed with which the suspect may destroy or hide incriminating evidence. Thus, a floating crap game can take on the appearance of a discussion group in seconds. Similarly, narcotics are easily flushed down a toilet, and most addicts will stash their supply near one. Even the word "supply," however, is misleading because it connotes a substantial amount of matter, when actually large quantities of narcotics are measured in ounces. As a result, the policeman must be able to control the suspect's behavior before a brush of his hand destroys his cache.

In this case, the police questioned Archie on the layout of Bill's apartment. Archie thought it would be difficult for the police to find incriminating evidence on Bill. He explained the house had a front and rear door, with a heavy chain and bolt on the front door, and creaky stairs in the rear. It would be, the police figured, a "tough pad to crack." Finally, Sergeant Harris constructed what turned out to be an effective plan. He called for a "beat car" with flashing red light and uniformed patrolmen to pull up in the street in front of the house, and instructed the patrolmen to make a lot of noise. They were to pound on the front door, demand admission, and if not admitted immediately, kick the door in. In the meantime, he detailed three men up the back stairs while the beat car was driving up front, correctly anticipating that Bill's attention would be riveted on the front of the house when he saw the flashing red light and the beat car outside. This gave the three plainclothesmen sufficient time to station themselves outside the rear door, without being heard going upstairs.

As assumed, Bill panicked when he saw the patrolmen heading for the front door and ran across the length of the apartment to the kitchen in the rear. The top half of the rear door was made of glass and the plainclothesmen stationed outside could see Bill run in and attempt to hide a package of white powder under the refrigerator. Whether they kicked the door in before, after, or simultaneously with Bill's attempt to dispose of the heroin, I cannot say, since I was at the front door behind the uniformed policemen. The fact is, however, that Bill was caught in the act.

The case described above was a "good pinch." It resulted in a charge and conviction of possession for sale upon the defendant's plea of guilty. Because of his youth, the seller was given a relatively light six-month term in the county jail, and his wife was given thirty days. Some time later, I interviewed the wife in the county jail, quite by accident, in connection with part of the study concerning defendants' perceptions of the criminal process. It was clear she did not recall this "Dr. Skolnick" who was interviewing her as one of the "policeman" involved in her arrest. (I was visible throughout the arrest proceedings and the subsequent interrogation, but this new context offered a new identity.) She was pleased with the way her case had gone and felt that both she and her husband had "gotten off" lightly. They each felt, she reported, that they had committed a serious crime, the police had treated them well, the judge had been understanding and the defense attorney, a public defender, competent. Whatever resentment she held was toward the unknown "fink" who had "ratted" on them to the police. The police, however, were perceived as men doing their jobs, an impression they convey well.

THE BIG CASE

Cases like the one now discussed occur so rarely that no special term, other than "big case" or "big one," develops to describe them. This case yielded the largest amount of narcotics confiscated in three years by the Westville department. Since there was much secrecy, it was fortunate that the apprehension took place after rapport had been established with the Westville vice control squad. A member of this squad informed me of developments and invited me (via an unexpected telephone call to my home one evening) to observe the proceedings when "the caper was scheduled to go down."

A major difference between the ordinary "good pinch" and the big narcotics case is whether the ultimate source has been tapped. In the typical "good pinch," narcotics officers make every effort to apprehend a larger dealer. Since Bill had stolen his narcotics from a drugstore, he was himself the ultimate source, and the police could make no further arrests. Most of the time, narcotics officers are not able to arrest important men in the dealership hierarchy, nor are they able to confiscate more than a small proportion of the annual narcotics traffic. In the State of California, a man offering to sell a pound of heroin was regarded by narcotics agents at the federal, state and local levels whom I interviewed as being about "as big as they come." Such a man, of course, purchases his narcotics from another dealer who usually is foreign and therefore may be outside the jurisdiction of federal agents. Since the flow of narcotics is part of an international traffic, even federal agents are usually unable to reach high into ultimate sources of supply.[13]

[13] Official Treasury Department figures indicate that in 1961, 40.26 kilograms of heroin and 20.25 kilograms of other narcotics drugs were seized or purchased by

The analysis of this "big case" illustrates two principles: first, how its enforcement pattern affords the police more leeway in complying with legal rules; and second, how such cases aid the police to acquire the commodities they need to carry out the enforcement of middle-sized cases. In this case, the Westville narcotics detail apprehended a nonuser-dealer whose activities they had been following for almost two years. The nonuser-dealer, the straight businessman in narcotics, is more diffi-cult to apprehend than the man who sells and also takes narcotics. When the "heat is on," or when he perceives it to be "on," the nonuser-dealer can keep away from his source of supply more easily than the addict-dealer. As long as the narcotics are hidden in a neutral stash, the dealer need not be concerned about police apprehension. All involved —the police, the addict, the dealer—are well aware of the implications attached to possession, and perhaps more importantly, to nonpossession of narcotics. Thus, the police always fear that when they set up a "buy," the seller will not show up with the "stuff" on his person.[14]

The apprehension of the nonuser-dealer involved the use of several petty informants, plus diligent and patient police work. The police finally took a room where they were able to keep him under constant surveillance and caught him selling several "balloons" of heroin. When apprehended, nonuser-dealers do not usually agree to serve as inform-ants, since they are themselves exceptionally "good pinches," and are more "reliable businessmen" than addicts. In this case, however, partly because of the persuasive abilities of the police, but largely because there was bigger game in the offing, it was possible, through the cooperation of the district attorney's office, to offer a substantial reduction in charges.

federal authorities; in 1962, 87.80 kilograms of heroin and 21.55 kilograms of other narcotics were seized or purchased by federal agents. The Treasury Department Bureau of Narcotics makes no official estimate of the amount of heroin used annually in the United States, but agents interviewed agreed that the amount confiscated is a small percentage of the amount used. (The figures cited above are given in the Bureau of Narcotics report *Traffic in Opium and Other Dangerous Drugs*, Washing-ton, D.C.: Government Printing Office, 1963, p. 66.)

[14] A shrewd nonuser-dealer had the Westville narcotics police completely stymied at the time of this writing. His mode of operation was based on a skillful combina-tion of use of assistants and of negotiation to take advantage of protections afforded the defendant in the criminal process. He personally handled neither cash nor heroin, and never associated himself with a direct exchange of one for the other. He would have the buyer give his assistant the money for the heroin and would telephone the buyer the next day giving the location of the stash. Furthermore, he had devel-oped a reputation for trustworthiness among his customers; so much so that the head of the Westville narcotics detail ruefully acknowledged, "He gives good quantity and good quality. The only way we'll ever get him is through a conspiracy charge."

Cooperation here meant more and was more dangerous than the cooperation demanded of Archie. Archie merely had to "make a buy." In this case, however, the strategy was to have a state agent make a series of purchases. Where nonuser-dealers are involved, speed of apprehension is not as important as is patience. Unlike the user-dealer, the nonuser is unlikely to consume his supply. The aim is not to catch him quickly but to bring him to the point where he purchases quantities as large as the abundance of his source will permit him to offer. To bring him to this point, he must come to trust his purchaser. Accordingly, the strategy of the narcotics police required the local dealer to make several purchases and to introduce another "buyer" provided by the state police.

The advantage of this strategy is that it allows the purchaser to risk exposure through public testimony. The informant who performs the introduction is still under suspicion, but he can always claim that the state agent was introduced to him by a third party, just as he introduced the agent to the source. In the Pirandello-like setting of a narcotics investigation, it is difficult for an accused party to sort out the actual identities and loyalties of those with whom he has been involved. If the accused chooses to go to trial, however, the true identity of the man who testifies that he purchased narcotics from the accused is revealed. Where the State's witness is a narcotics officer, law enforcement need not be concerned about disclosing identity and, furthermore, can rely on him to testify persuasively. (Police, in my experience, make excellent witnesses.) The only drawback for the police arises from a concern for police resources; each time a policeman participates in such a maneuver he too is partly "burned" and loses some of his value as an undercover agent. Given budgetary limitations, the police can afford to use narcotics agents only in the bigger cases. It is also true that the speed of apprehension typically required in smaller cases normally does not permit police to be used as *agent provocateurs*. Thus, in the "good pinch" described above, a police agent could not have been substituted for Archie since by the time the necessary introductions and purchases could have been made, the *corpus delecti* would have been consumed.

In that "good pinch" only one purchase was made. Here there were four, each large. The state agent was introduced to the sellers, the Gomez brothers, by the informant who represented the agent as a friend "dealing" in the northwestern United States, and able to dispose of large amounts of heroin. The agent was first introduced to the dealer's younger brother, Arthur, who was a partner, but evidently did not personally have the "connections." The agent was especially skillful in using his knowledge of narcotics and his demeanor to impress the younger Gomez that he was an "old-time Mexican dealer" rather than a flashy newcomer. The younger Gomez agreed to let the agent have three ounces of heroin in exchange for cash, and also two ounces on "consignment."

About two weeks later, after payment had been made for the consignment purchase, several recorded telephone calls were made over a four-day period to the older brother Charles. He continued to promise delivery of heroin to the agent, but on each day "backed off," claiming to be unable to locate his "connection." The agent also made a recorded telephone call to the dealer's girl friend during which she told him that Charles was trying to contact the "connection." A week later the agent recorded two telephone calls to Charles arranging for the delivery of heroin to Westville. It was agreed that Charles and Arthur would fly to the local airport, to be met by the agent. On the appointed day, the agent purchased five ounces of heroin [15] from the brothers for close to twenty-one hundred dollars. There was no recording of the actual transaction, but several state agents and members of the Westville narcotics detail observed it from a distance.

At this point, the police saw their next move as luring the defendants to a place where a transaction could be "bugged" by a concealed microphone. Accordingly, the state agent telephoned Charles Gomez and told him he was fearful of the "heat" at the airport, and had arranged for the next deal to take place in a Westville motel room. Two days later, the dealer and his girl friend appeared at the motel, where the agent purchased approximately ten ounces of heroin for twenty-eight hundred dollars. Several other narcotics police were observing near the motel and a hidden camera took a photograph of the dealer entering the motel room. The purchase went off smoothly, however, and any suspicions Gomez might have held were evidently allayed.

A week later the agent called the brothers and made arrangements to purchase as much as twenty-two ounces of narcotics later in the week, in the same Westville motel room. This was to be the setting for the "big pinch," the exchange of five thousand dollars for at least a pound of heroin, with, presumably, the remainder on consignment. The younger Gomez agreed to come and the events leading to arrest were initiated. It was decided that the agent would give the money to the younger Gomez, who was scheduled to arrive with the heroin at eight in the evening. Following the transfer, the younger Gomez was expected to call his older brother and tell him that everything "had come off okay" and that he would arrive home in the morning. After this phone call, the

---

[15] An ounce of heroin is not necessarily an ounce of pure heroin. Usually what is purchased has already been "cut." Most of the heroin sold by the Gomez brothers was about 6 per cent pure.

police planned for the agent to call the elder Gomez and to indicate that there was a "panic" [16] on, and that if the brother could come up that night with another dozen or so ounces of heroin, the agent could pay for it.

Anticipation of a "big case" arouses much anxiety in the police. With each successful purchase, the stakes become higher. There already was enough evidence to arrest and, in all likelihood, to convict the Gomez brothers. But the aim of the police was, at this point, to implicate the brothers as fully and as clearly as possible. Indeed, at a certain point the big case becomes almost an aesthetic matter, and style, defined by the personal satisfactions of the narcotics policeman, counts for almost as much as results. Unfortunately, from the policeman's viewpoint, the expectation of a "big case" not only arouses personal anxiety, but also requires unusual cooperation among law enforcement organizations. This increases the number of men involved, the personal tensions of each, and thus the possibility that the charade will be revealed to the offender.

In the present case these factors resulted in several mishaps that destroyed the aesthetic of this night's work, but which also, against the background of prior incriminating encounters with the offenders, made little legal difference. First, the younger Gomez failed to arrive on schedule. When he did arrive somewhat unexpectedly, the state agent was in conversation with three Westville police officers. Gomez, the state agent later reported, had asked him what was going on, and the agent replied that he was asking directions from these strangers about where to meet the helicopter. (One of the police commented, "This guy Gomez must really be stupid. Any one of our nickel-and-dime dealers here in Westville would have smelled the heat a mile away.") At the time, however, the state agent did not know whether the dealer had caught on to the trap. He could not be certain at how to interpret the dealer's lateness. It might have been, as Gomez explained, that he had difficulty getting the heroin from his connection. But the agent also was concerned that Gomez had become suspicious, arrived early, had hidden the heroin, then returned to the airport. Without the heroin, the evening's plan would be a failure. Nor could the agent be sure that Gomez was not armed; a report that he might be had been received from police in another part of the state.

Under these circumstances, it is not surprising that the usually cool state agent missed the highway turnoff to the motel and arrived twenty minutes late. In the meantime, the police at the motel were becoming increasingly fidgety. Two policemen (and the writer) were stationed in

[16] When an area runs dry of narcotics, addicts in that area, because of their pressing need, will be enormously anxious to the point of panic, and hence the term.

the room next to where the "buy" was to take place, to record the conversation and to be available for assistance should the dealer be armed. Five policemen were in the motel manager's office with equipment for recording the expected telephone conversation with Charles Gomez, and another policeman (along with a newspaperman) was stationed across the courtyard as an additional check on Gomez's movements.

Gomez and the state agent arrived in the room at about 10:30 P.M. In the adjoining room the recording equipment had failed, which not only meant the loss of a recorded conversation of the narcotics purchase, but also heightened concern for the agent's safety and caused partial inability to keep track of Gomez. Presumably, if he left the room, the agent across the courtyard would see him and notify the police in the manager's office via the walkie-talkies with which each of the three police locations were equipped. About fifteen minutes after Gomez arrived, we in the adjoining room were informed by walkie-talkie that Gomez had telephoned his brother to say that everything was okay. We were also told that the detectives in the office had evidently recorded this conversation, but that they were going to listen to the record to make sure. So far everything was proceeding as planned. Fifteen minutes later we were told that Gomez was in custody in the manager's office.

This is what had happened. Gomez decided after his telephone call to go to the lobby to buy a soft drink. When he left, the walkie-talkie in the surveillance room did not respond. The agent became so flustered he forgot to use the telephone to warn the other officers of Gomez's impending arrival. Gomez entered the lobby from a side entrance, because it was a shorter distance from the room, and literally walked into a bevy of policemen listening intently to the recording of Arthur Gomez speaking to Charles. Whether the policemen or the dealer was more surprised, I cannot say. At that point, however, it was incumbent that the police arrest Arthur.

Shortly after Arthur was taken into custody, he was brought out into the courtyard and photographed by the newsmen. The problem for the police at this point was to convince Arthur Gomez to call his brother Charles and to persuade him to come to Westville with additional narcotics. Arthur finally complied about two hours later when, in my opinion, he believed his brother would know that something had gone wrong. In any event, Charles did not arrive the next morning, but was arrested at his home by the state and local police of his area. Both men finally pleaded guilty to two counts of possession for sale and were sentenced to three years in San Quentin prison. The sentence of the younger Gomez was suspended (partly on the recommendation of the police for his "cooperation" in making the telephone call), but he was required to serve the first year of his suspended sentence in the county jail.

The following day a story appeared in the local Westville newspaper with an eight-column headline and front-page pictures reporting that a one-and-a-half-million dollar "dope ring" had been "smashed." The size of the dope ring was reported in the newspaper headline according to the ultimate possible price of the narcotics on the illicit retail market. Actually, the "pound" of narcotics confiscated contained only 6 per cent pure heroin. Such a quantity does go a long way on the retail market, but not nearly as far as the newspaper story suggested.

Such stories serve several functions for the narcotics police. This sort of report gives the policeman public recognition as a reward for his services. In this case, however, the police did not personally feel that they deserved as much recognition as they received. Although the case had yielded an acceptable outcome, it did not "come off" with the smoothness which they regard as the fundamental satisfaction of narcotics work. This is not to say that the police were dissatisfied; rather events had spoiled an unusual opportunity for a masterful arrest and transformed it into a less than craftsmanlike occasion.

Another purpose served by exaggerated newspaper treatment of narcotics cases is to indicate to the public that "dope rings" are in common operation, but that the police are able to "smash" them. To a certain extent, however, the "dope ring" referred to in the newspaper article was itself "created" by the narcotics police. This is not to say that Charles Gomez was not a criminal purveyor of narcotics; but when law enforcement agencies themselves become major purchasers of narcotics, they make someone like Gomez a much more important-appearing dealer than he would have been had not close to twelve thousand dollars worth of narcotics been purchased from him by the State. In this sense, then, in the "big case," narcotics police inevitably are part of the "dope rings" they themselves help to create.

Finally, newspaper stories of this kind serve the more important function of giving the narcotics police support in their campaign for increasingly severe penalties against those trafficking in narcotics. These penalties, as we indicated, provide the police with greater commodities to maintain the information system enabling "good pinches."

SUMMARY AND CONCLUSION

This chapter has described the work of the narcotics officer at three levels: his routine activities, especially with petty informants; the "good pinch"; and "the big case." These levels were shown to be interrelated, since narcotics enforcement typically involves the apprehension of a hierarchy of offenders. Therefore, for that reason, because the ordinary addict is a criminal, actually and symbolically, and also in conformity to a belief that the way to destroy the narcotics traffic is to rid the community of customers, the police pursue the petty user.[17]

In those instances where a petty user has enough narcotics in his possession to lay the basis for a felony charge, his arrest is considered a "good pinch." The apprehension of a petty user affords a degree of satisfaction to the police, but not nearly so much as participation in a "big case," especially when a nonuser-dealer is caught. The latter is considered part of the organized narcotics traffic; bringing about his conviction is therefore regarded as especially meritorious.

Beyond these reasons for the policeman's preference of the "big case" arrest over the "good pinch" is another important consideration. The "big case" provides the policeman with the conditions under which conventional and constitutional standards of legality may best be met. Thus, a typical difference in conditions underlying the two types of arrests is the amount of time the police have: little in the "good pinch," much in the "big case." Greater time permits the police to obtain warrants, allows the offender to make several observed infractions of the law, and enables the police to make more adequate records of infractions.

The main reason the police are able to keep more adequate records in the "big case" revolves around the most important condition distinguishing these two types of arrests. In the "good pinch," the informant is typically an addict, while in the "big case," the informant is typically a narcotics officer. This difference is also related to the amount of time available; since the police must move quickly in the "good pinch," they usually have insufficient time to establish a new identity for the policeman, whereas the addict comes equipped with his own.

Not only is the policeman a better record keeper than the addict-informant but he is also a more persuasive witness during the trial. Even if the informant were able to give convincing testimony, he would be asked to take the stand only in rare instances, since the policeman is usually obliged to protect the informer's criminal status. It is therefore ironic that the cases in which the policeman least prefers to participate arise as test cases to restrict the limits of his behavior. In the narcotics area, a "big case" is rarely the subject of an appellate judicial decision

[17] See generally the panel on "Law Enforcement and Controls" and especially the statement by John C. Cross in *Proceedings of the White House Conference on Narcotic and Drug Abuse* (Washington, D.C.: Government Printing Office, 1962), pp. 23–65.

for the simple reason that the "big case" provides the policeman with the conditions under which constitutional standards of legality may best be met.[18] From the policeman's point of view, meeting these standards is preferable to not meeting them, but he is not so concerned about the standards in the abstract. The meeting of constitutional requirements is primarily a way to demonstrate his ability to do his job well; that is the principle concern of the detective.

[18] One recent important case—which was indeed a "good pinch"—was the case of *People* v. *Ker,* 374 U. S. 23 (1963). Although this decision in some respects limits the policemen's actions, it also recognizes the special circumstances under which narcotics police perform their duties.

Chapter 8

The Clearance Rate and the
Penalty Structure

Eᴠᴇʀʏ complex organization must control the quality of output. Firms manufacturing light bulbs test to determine the average length of time taken by the typical bulb to burn out. Straightforward endurance tests can be made for other manufactured goods, such as stockings and sparkplugs. Most services also involve putting something back into a former shape. The estimate of a repairman's ability may depend on how far out of shape the thing was when brought in to be renewed, but his goal is clear. The owner of a damaged automobile expects it to come out of repair as good as before. In these examples, there is a tangible reference point: commonly held expectations of what constitutes a satisfactory conclusion. The fact, however, that the institutional character of police is uncertain suggests that the goals of police and the standards by which the policeman's work is to be evaluated are ambiguous. Not only is there widespread disagreement among different groups in society about the proper ends and conduct of police activity, but even within the ranks of police specialists there is no clear understanding of goals.

There is even less clarity in defining the relation between police conduct and the implementation of goals. When a policeman observes a juvenile swiping an apple, is he supposed to arrest the thief, to warn him, or perhaps to speak understandingly to him so as to improve public relations? Police are in the business of enforcing the criminal law, but the meaning of "enforcement" is not so simply interpreted. It could, for example, mean "full enforcement," described by Joseph Goldstein as:

(1) the investigation of every disturbing event which is reported to or observed by them and which they have reason to suspect may be a violation of the criminal law; (2) following a determination that some crime has been committed, an effort to discover its perpetrators; and (3) the presentation of all information collected by them to the prosecutor for his determination of the appropriateness of further invoking the criminal process.[1]

[1] Joseph Goldstein, "Police Discretion Not to Invoke the Criminal Process: Low-Visibility Decisions in the Administration of Justice," *Yale Law Journal*, **69** (March, 1960), 559–560.

Goldstein adds, however, that full enforcement is not a realistic expectation. He points to ambiguities in the definitions of both substantive offenses and due process boundaries, limitations of time, personnel, investigative devices, and pressures from within and without the department, as forces which generate selective enforcement.

Similarly, LaFave has systematically examined various types of situations which by their nature preclude processing beyond the office of the policeman himself. One major category of "discretionary situation" mentioned by LaFave includes those cases where limited enforcement resources must be allocated to other conduct thought more deserving of police attention (for example, cases where the violation is trivial or it is thought to be acceptable to the subcommunity involved, or where the victim is unwilling or does not desire to prosecute). Another category of cases where discretionary nonenforcement of the law typically occurs are those for which the legislature may not desire enforcement for a variety of reasons (for example, obscenity laws, vagrancy statutes, morals codes, blue laws, and so on). A third category of cases where nonenforcement is the usual outcome—despite the existence of sufficient police resources —is miscellaneous: here, the criminal process fails to be invoked because of inappropriateness or likely ineffectiveness, or to assist in the maintenance of some other part of the law enforcement system (for example, the narcotics informant network), or because it is thought that enforcement might endanger or cause unnecessary hardship for the offender or the victim (for example, in domestic cases).[2]

Such ambiguities and limitations create difficulties enough about police relations with the outside community. They also, however, create problems for internal administration. If the goals of police work are not clear, how is the effectiveness of the individual "professional" policeman to be measured? To be sure, graft and corruption cannot be countenanced. But what more is required of the policeman as a measure of his achievement? For these purposes, a general statement of the responsibilities of the police chief—"the prevention of criminality and the repression of criminal activity, the protection of life and property, the preservation of peace, and public compliance with countless laws"[3] —is not sufficient. There must also be standards for making such routine decisions as who is a better and who a poorer policeman. Like all formal human organizations, the police, require the development of internal standards of competence and efficiency.

Furthermore, every organization faces the problem of reducing the

[2] Wayne R. LaFave, "The Police and Nonenforcement of the Law—Part II," *Wisconsin Law Review*, (March, 1962), 179–239.

[3] O. W. Wilson, *Police Planning* (Springfield: Charles C Thomas, 1962), p. 3.

resentment of persons who have been negatively evaluated. A common means of establishing satisfaction in the unrewarded is to indicate an objective basis for the decision, that is, the standards used to judge the failure are used to judge everybody else in a position similar to his. To the degree that internal standards do not appear to be objective, a formal organization will arouse the antagonism of persons involved. As a corollary, those who have been promoted or rewarded prefer to feel that rewards have been arrived at objectively.[4]

In police work, however, the development of standards is not simply a problem of internal control, as it might be in a family-owned business. As a governmental organization, the police must also take into account the opinion of the community at large. Indeed, the political community serves as the primary reference group of the police. Sensitive to the force of political opinion, most major police departments assign personnel specifically to the task of improving relations with such political superiors as mayors, city managers, and city councils, as well as with the general public. Whether police are unusually sensitive to demands for efficiency, or whether they are actually required to demonstrate efficiency by means of "hard" criteria, in the absence of clear goals or specific criteria of competence, police in fact collect enormous quantities of data. Primarily, these data serve as a point of reference, the equivalent of a "set of books," permitting outsiders to rate the department. Thus, John I. Griffin, in his text on police statistics, comments:

The activities of a police department necessitate the keeping of records, not only criminal records but records of all the essential activities of the department. . . . These activities might be regarded as comparable to production or sales reports in a business organization in the sense that they tell what the department has done in a given period of time. Both internal and external data possess significance as a purely historical record but, of much greater significance, can be used by the administrative heads of the department in the measurement of accomplishment and efficiency. These data also keep the public informed of police activity and may do much to create a favorable climate of public opinion.[5]

[4] Throughout his *Social Behavior: Its Elementary Forms*, and particularly in Chapter 12, George C. Homans speaks of "the rules of justice implicit in much social behavior" (p. 232). His discussion of this general issue, which he frames in terms of social pressures toward "proportionality" in "costs," "rewards," "investments," and "profits," places the problem of universalistic criteria and resentment at their lack in an interesting theoretical context. (New York: Harcourt, Brace & World, Inc., 1961.)

[5] John Griffin, *Statistics Essential for Police Efficiency* (Springfield: Charles C Thomas, 1958), p. 31.

THE "CLEARANCE RATE"

For detectives, the most important measure of accomplishment has come to be the "clearance rate." [6] Indeed, Griffin states that the clearance rate is the most important indication of the efficiency of the police force as a whole.[7] The clearance rate is also strongly endorsed as a control measure by the leading authority on police management and professionalization, O. W. Wilson. Wilson does not see detectives as dedicated plyers of their trade, much less as heroes; instead, his basic assumption is that investigators, unless checked on, drift into inactivity. At the same time, he is not unduly concerned by this problem, because the control mechanisms are, in his opinion, clear and effective. He says:

> In no branch of police service may the accomplishment of the unit and of its individual members be so accurately evaluated as in the detective division. Rates of clearances by arrest, of property recovered, and of convictions, serve as measures of the level of performance. Current accomplishments in the same class of crime may reveal significant variations between the accomplishment of the incumbent and his predecessor, or between the present and past performance of the same detective. Similar comparisons may be made between local accomplishments and the accomplishments in comparable communities. Chance may cause an unfavorable comparison during a short period, but when the failure in performance extends over six months or a year, a conclusion of diminished effectiveness seems justified.
> A detective division built of members retained on this selective basis is most likely to contain the best investigators on the force.[8]

Wilson and Griffin are by no means isolated spokesmen in their high estimation of clearance rates as a measure of police efficiency. The Federal Bureau of Investigation also compiles national statistics of clearance

---

[6] Among educators, for instance, there are similar questions of what the goals of the profession are. Some emphasize the development of measurable skills, while others maintain a broader conception of the aims of education. One sociologist of education has suggested that the popularity of such devices as teaching machines may in part be attributed to the facilitation of evaluative and control functions. (See Martin Trow, "American Education and the New Modes of Instruction," mimeographed paper.) Thus, whatever may be said for or against "programmed" teaching and its ultimate effect not only upon knowledge and skill, but also upon creativity, it does permit the administrator to rate attainment more easily.

[7] Griffin, *op. cit.*, p. 69.

[8] Wilson, *op. cit.*, p. 112. The Chicago Crime Commission recently lauded Wilson's work as head of the Chicago police force by stating that the improvement in police efficiency measured by the percentage of offenses cleared by arrest was "tremendous." (*New York Times*, July 19, 1964).

rates, published in an *Annual Bulletin* for the year following the date of clearance. These data are collected from 3,441 cities (population, 101, 285,000) in the United States. Thus, the clearance rate has evidently been adopted by most police departments in the United States as a primary means to evaluate detectives.

What is the clearance rate? This is a simple question demanding a complicated answer. Briefly stated, it is the percentage of crimes known to the police which the police believe have been "solved." It is important to note that the clearance rate is based upon *offenses known to the police*. Thus, there can be no clearance rate for crimes without citizen complainants. Although there are difficulties in counting such crimes as homicide, robbery, and burglary, they can be counted. It is impossible, however, to count crimes without complainants. As a result, such offenses as bookmaking, the illegal use of narcotics, and prostitution cannot be analyzed by clearance rates.

In the materials that follow, I should like, mainly from observations of burglary enforcement, to illustrate two processes: (1) how the employment of these quantitative criteria—clearance rates—leads to practices that in turn attenuate the validity of the criteria themselves as measures of quality control; and (2) how emphasis on these criteria has consequences for the administration of justice that may interfere with the legality and the stated aims of law enforcement. It should be emphasized that these analytically distinct processes are closely related to each other empirically. What the policeman does in order to amplify clearance rates may have the consequence of both weakening the validity of clearance rates and interfering with legality and aims of law enforcement. Empirically, however, these processes are not separated.

CATEGORIES OF "CLEARANCE"

An examination of Table 1 shows the designation "cleared" to be a police organizational term bearing no *direct* relation to the administration of criminal law. That is, no set of statistics describing the processes of criminal law—statistics on arrest and prosecution—gives rise to a similar or even a consistently related set of clearance figures. For example, of the 29 per cent of burglaries "cleared" by the Westville police, less than one-quarter (6 per cent) were "cleared" by arrest and prosecution for that offense, while almost two-fifths (11 per cent) were "cleared" through prosecution for another offense. Furthermore, the percentage for any category will vary from year to year. Thus, the designation "cleared" merely means that the police believe they know who committed the offense, *if* they believe an offense has been committed. It does not indicate, however, *how* the crime was cleared.

Two important categories do not appear in the classifications in Table 1. One is the category "unfounded"; the other is called "suspicious circumstance." It will be noted that of the 3,719 burglary offenses *reported* to the Westville police, 3,578 were considered *actual* offenses. The

TABLE 1   *Westville Police Department Crime Statistics on Burglary, Robbery—1962*

	Burglary	Robbery
Reported offenses	3719	613
Actual offenses	2578	566
Cleared offenses	1071	208
Manner cleared:	*Per Cent*	*Per Cent*
Arrest and prosecution	6	20
Occurred in another jurisdiction	0	0
C/w refuses to prosecute	1	1
Pros. another offense	11	4
Complaint refused by DA	1	1
Death of offender	0	0
Pros. by outside department	1	3
Turned over to military	0	0
Reprimanded and released	0	0
Turned over to juvenile authority	8	6
DA citation	0	0
Property returned to owner	0	0
Located or returned home	0	0
Juvenile court citation	1	0
Cleared otherwise	0	0
Total cleared (%)	29	35
Total not cleared (%)	70	66
	99	101
	(3578)	(620)

Source: Westville Police Department Files.

"actual offense" figure, which provides the denominator for computing the clearance rate, is derived by subtracting the "unfounded" reports from the reported offenses and adding the "suspicious circumstances— changed to burglary" figure to the difference.[9]

The possibility of "unfounding" (to coin an inelegant verb) suggests the first move of the detective—to determine whether in fact an offense has been committed. This procedure requires the detective to assess the motives of the complainant. In investigating a robbery, for instance, there are certain situations which indicate quite clearly to the detective that the complainant is not a victim. For instance, if a man reports that he was robbed at 11P.M. on 7th and State, and a policeman says he saw him in another part of town at the same hour, the suspicion is that the man did something with his paycheck which he would rather his wife did not know about, and has reported a crime to police to "take off the heat from his old lady."

Seen the other way round, the complainant must be able to justify himself or herself as a victim. The situation here is a familiar one, existing in any context where a claim of victimization is made to a higher authority. To do this, the victim must be able to produce symbols of victimization to the higher authority, symbols appropriate to the victimization context. In a tennis game, for instance, chalk marks on a ball would be appropriate to show that a player's baseline shot had fallen in bounds. Thus, when called out, the player would be "victimized." In other social situations, the rules of the game are not quite so clear—the jilted suitor may consequently have more or less difficulty sustaining an impression of himself as a victim, depending on whose sympathy he is trying to get. In the criminal law context, the rules of the game are less clear than tennis rules, more clear than those between lovers.

An incident may also be recorded as a "suspicious circumstance" in Westville. The more or less official definition of a suspicious circumstance is that a crime appears to have been committed, but that one of its elements is missing. For example, the major element of the crime of burglary is "the burglarious intent, the intent to commit either grand or petit theft or any felony after the entry has been effected. This requisite intent must exist at the time of the entry." [10] There must also be entry into a building (or one of the other places listed in the statute). If some men happened to be shooting craps in the rear of a store, and entered

---

[9] It is highly difficult to track down the number of instances in which a complaint was first recorded as a suspected crime other than burglary and then changed to burglary. Generally, the Westville police consider the difference between "offenses reported" and "actual offenses" to be "unfounded" reports.

[10] Fricke, *California Criminal Law* (Los Angeles, Legal Book Store, 1956), p. 310.

ostensibly for that purpose, there was no burglary. The patrolman, how-ever, may suspect that the real reason for the entry was to steal, not merely to throw dice. If so, his offense report would list a suspected bur-glary. Or perhaps a householder reports the theft of a watch, but the patrolman cannot find a point of entry. In such an instance, the patrol-man will report a "suspicious circumstance," and an investigation will follow. Thus, complaints are typically screened by patrolmen before being presented to the detectives for further investigation.

In addition to deciding whether an offense has been committed, the patrolman must decide what the offense was, if any. The citizen often makes a general noise—which is partly why citizen complaints are re-ferred to in many police departments as "squeals." A woman may call the police and complain that she has been raped, when in fact she has also been robbed. Because the robbery may appear easier to prove than the rape—for example, if corroborating evidence has been found on the person of the defendant—the patrolman reports a robbery and includes the surrounding circumstances.

Even when it is clear that an offense has occurred, the patrolman (usually with the advice of his sergeant, if the offense appears serious) may decide not to write up an offense report. The following notes illus-trate:

It was a very quiet evening for crime. Only one interesting happening—a call that an assault had been committed. After some time trying to find the house—in one of the courtyards of a city project—Sergeant L. and I arrived on the scene after one of the "beat" patrolmen. (The Sergeant is in charge, by the way, of about nine men who cover six beats, and when-ever any one of them has a special problem the Sergeant will likely arrive.) We walked into a poorly furnished house. A large, rather handsome Black man was seated on a couch daubing at his ear with a towel and being aided by a five- or six-year-old boy.

The man looked dazed and the Sergeant inquired brusquely as to what had happened. (He knew already; before we entered the patrolman told us the man had been cut in the ear by his wife, and also that the man didn't want to file a complaint.)

"She cut me," the man mumbled.

The Sergeant flashed his light on the man's ear. It had been slashed a good half inch through right above the lobe. The beam of the flashlight revealed fingernail marks on the man's neck.

The Sergeant continued to ask the man what had happened. Answers were mumbled and incoherent. In essence, they amounted to: "Nothing really happened, she just came at me with the knife; I was drinking, she came at me with the knife."

There was discussion of whether the man wanted an ambulance. Arrangements were made with a neighboring relative to drive the man to the county hospital.

Before leaving, the Sergeant made sure the man didn't want to file a complaint. We left the house with the Sergeant admonishing him to have the ear taken care of. The patrolman remarked, "As they say, she done stuck."

No offense report is made out for such an incident. It is a family squabble with no complainant. (That the man is Black is also relevant. If the family were white, the police would take the offense more seriously. A stabbing by a white woman of her husband suggests a potential homicide to police, while a similar Black cutting can be written off as a "North Westville battery." [11]) Instead, an *assignment report* recording the incident suffices. Incidents described on assignment reports are not tabulated and are not sent for further investigation to the detective division. An incident may be unfounded only when reported as an offense or as a suspected offense.

In Westville, a large proportion (20 to 25 per cent) of burglary complaints processed by patrolmen are recorded as suspected offenses ("suspicious circumstances") for follow-up investigation by a detective. The detective is allowed wide discretion in the filing of burglary complaints as "suspicious circumstances." Not only does he record a complaint as a suspected offense when one or more of the elements of the alleged crime appears to be missing, but he also may list a complaint as a suspected offense when he believes—even in the absence of hard evidence to support his suspicion—that the complaint is unfounded. For instance, a Black delivery boy claims to have been robbed of the money he was supposed to deposit for his employer. He shows a lump on his head and holds to his story, but the detective does not believe him. Such a complaint is filed as a suspicious circumstance, and as such does not fall into the category of "offenses reported." When a complaint is filed as a "suspicious circumstance," it is "cleared" for practical purposes. Usually the detective concentrates on "actual" offenses and ignores further investigation of "suspicious circumstances." In effect, therefore, every time a complaint is filed as a "suspicious circumstance" instead of as a reported offense, the clearance rate rises (since it is based on the ratio of "cleared" to "actual" offenses).[12]

[11] For a similar illustration, see LaFave, *op. cit.*, pp. 207–210.

[12] Eight hundred and five suspicious-circumstance burglaries were reported by patrolmen in Westville in 1962. Of these, two hundred and eighty-six remained as such after detective investigation and never found their way into the crime reports. Of the remaining five hundred and seventeen, an unknown number were called actual of-

In Eastville, on the other hand, virtually every complaint is recorded as an actual offense. This reporting system was introduced in Eastville as a strong means of control. As form follows function, so may tight controls follow corruption. For example, during the period of my observations in Eastville, a known prostitute reported she had been assaulted and raped. A desk sergeant recorded her complaint as rape, and Eastville's crime rate was thereby heightened. In Westville, a similar complaint would have been recorded as "suspicious circumstance—rape" on grounds that a person practicing criminality is not a reliable complainant. The complaint would therefore not appear in Westville's crime statistics as an offense known to the police.

Many of the Eastville detectives resent the requirement that every complaint be recorded as an actual offense. They feel that, as several noted to me, "It makes us look bad." I questioned one of the supervisory policemen regarding the practice of recording, and he said:

Well, we're an honest police department. All these other departments that have these fancy clearance rates—we know damned well they're stacking the cards. It's easy to show a low crime rate when you have a category like suspicious circumstance to use as a wastebasket. Here, at least we know what's going on—everything is reported. Sure the prostitute could have been lying, and probably was. But the fact is that a prostitute can be raped, and prostitutes sometimes are. After all, a prostitute has a right not to go to bed with somebody if she doesn't want to.

It is certainly possible that the number of reported offenses in many police departments may be manipulated in order to exaggerate the efficiency of the burglary division. Since approximately 20 per cent of the original reports never find their way into the crime statistics and assignment reports are not included in crime reports (thereby greatly reducing the visibility of police discretion), any small statistical changes—on the order of say, 2 or 3 per cent per year—should be given little significance in the evaluation of a department's performance. Yet this is the order of magnitude frequently suggested—in staff meetings, conferences, to outsiders—as evidence of a department's competence. Thus, in general, 22 per cent is regarded as a low burglary clearance rate, 35 per cent is seen as a high one (the national average for 1962 was 28 per cent). A burglary clearance rate which has risen from 27 to 31 per cent, for example is presented as an indicator of significant change.

fenses and became part of the crime report; the remainder were unfounded and never entered the crime report.

CLEARANCE RATES AND THE ADMINISTRATION OF JUSTICE

From the above analysis, it is evident that clearance rates are a somewhat suspect method of judging the competence of an individual policeman, a division of a department, or a department as a whole, assuming for the moment that the qualities clearance rates purport to measure are appropriate indicators of police proficiency. If statistical manipulation were the only unanticipated consequence of this control mechanism, the problems created might be relatively inconsequential. To be sure, the clearance rate might not mirror "real" differences in individual ability from one year to the next, as it purports to, nor might it accurately reflect differences in the proficiency of police departments when these are compared. The implications of these errors might appear serious to individual policemen or to individual police departments when invidious conclusions are drawn about their competence. When it can be shown that under certain conditions the attention paid by working detectives to clearance rates may *reverse the hierarchy of penalties* associated with substantive criminal law, the resulting issues are of greater theoretical and practical importance.

To understand the process of reversal, it is useful to ask how the burglary detective goes about obtaining clearances. The simplest answer is that he persuades a burglar to admit having committed several prior offenses. That is, the exchange principle again operates: in order to gain such admissions, the police must provide the burglar with either rewards or penalties to motivate self-incrimination. In the "professional" Westville Police Department, one sees relatively little evidence of the "stick" and much of the "carrot." In what follows, I should like to describe two cases from Westville, one a routine case, the other a "big" case, to illustrate the strategies and rewards used by burglary detectives to obtain clearances, and to analyze how these strategies may undermine legislative and judicial aims regarding law enforcement.

The first case is the routine "good pinch." Arthur C. was arrested as an auto thief and cooperated with the police by confessing to the commission of two additional thefts of autos and five "classy" burglaries. In return for this cooperation, Arthur received several assets. First, the police agreed to drop the two counts of auto theft and to charge Arthur with only one count of burglary. Secondly, Arthur's formal confession as given to the court showed that he had committed only one burglary. As the sergeant handling his case said:

> We had him cop out to only one charge because we don't really want it made public that he committed the other burglaries. If it were made

public, then the question might be raised as to why we didn't charge him with the other burglaries, and the public doesn't understand these things.

What the sergeant intended to indicate is that the public typically does not understand that the sentence would not be different if the defendant had confessed to one burglary or to five—and the severity of the sentence is the most important consideration to all of the active participants in the system, the judge and the attorneys as well as the defendant and the police. None is especially impressed by the "rehabilitative" capacities of the penal system. Thus, the sergeant added, when asked by the writer if the court did not realize that perhaps other offenses had been committed:

Of course the courts know. In fact we tell the judge that the defendant committed other burglaries, but we don't want it put on the record. So we take the confession in such a way as to implicate the guy with only one burglary, and then that's what he gets sentenced for.

Of course, from the parole board's point of view, it might be of some significance that the defendant had actually committed five burglaries instead of one. Since an extensive burglary record could conceivably reduce the convicted defendant's chances for parole, a confession showing him to have committed only one burglary is to his advantage.

In addition to possibly receiving a reduction of charges and counts, and a recorded minimization of his appearance of criminality, the defendant who "cops out" and clears burglaries is also said to "clean" himself. The term "cleaning" in this context means that the defendant is afforded virtual immunity for future arrests on past burglaries. Thus, if the police have cleared ten burglaries with the defendant's help, he is no longer liable to be arrested for having committed them (even though the statute of limitations might permit prosecution). As a result, when the defendant completes his sentence, he need not fear apprehension for any of the crimes he committed before.

These, then, are the three basic "commodities" which the detective exchanges in return for the defendant's cooperation in admitting to prior offenses: reduction of charges and counts, concealment of actual criminality, and freedom from further investigation of prior offenses. Since it is in the interest of both the defendant and the policeman that the defendant "clear" crimes, the defendant typically cooperates with the policeman once a deal has been set in motion. Indeed, the defendant may occasionally become "too" cooperative by confessing to crimes he never committed, since liability does not increase as a result of admissions made for the purpose of clearing crimes.

It is impossible to know how often defendants claim to have committed the crimes of others. When such claims occur, however, they necessarily undermine the aims of law enforcement by presenting the police with "false positives"—"solved cases" for which synthetic solutions are reached. On the other hand, the policeman's ability to determine the truth of defendants' assertions might minimize error of this sort. Nevertheless, the pressures in the situation are clearly in the direction of overlooking or not inquiring too carefully into the defendant's representations.

CRIMINALITY AS COMMODITY FOR EXCHANGE

There is a more serious problem about clearance rates as a control mechanism. If clearances are valued, then criminality becomes a commodity for exchange. Thus, it is possible that in some cases defendants who confess to large numbers of crimes will tend to be shown more leniency in prosecution than those who are in fact less culpable. This is not to suggest that an inverse correlation actually exists between the number of offenses which a person admits having committed and the severity of the penalty which he receives. (To test the truth of any such generalization would be difficult since it would be necessary to have an accurate accounting of the crimes for which defendants actually were responsible. Because the maintenance of such records would in itself threaten to upset the operation of the system for maximizing clearance rates, an observer would need at least to see the processing of the cases themselves.) Rather, the situation in which detectives are expected to demonstrate proficiency is structured so as to invite the policeman to undermine the hierarchy of penalties found in substantive criminal law. The following case is presented to illustrate more fully the process of undermining. This case, a "big one," is not statistically "representative," but does, I believe, fairly represent pressures inherent in the situation. It was not especially selected, but simply occurred during the period of observation.

Essentially, the undermining process in the "big" case is more conspicuous because the police "get" more and have to "give" more in exchange. The process by which the police obtain clearance in a "big" case is therefore merely an exaggerated instance of the process in the routine case. In this case (the Moore case), approximately thirty-five thousand dollars worth of jewels, furs, and other valuable objects had been stolen from a leading citizen. Partly as a result of the citizen's status, and partly because of the value of the stolen goods, the police looked upon the case as an unusually important one to "break." "Breaking it" would and did lead to praise from the general community, including the press and television. I was able to work on the case with the sergeant to whom it had been assigned, and followed him on the laborious and time-consuming round of checking out false leads, questioning neighbors and witnesses, and interviewing informants and potential informants. The description of the development of such a case would make interesting popular nonfiction. I intend to describe only that part of it relating to the analytical point of how emphasis on clearance rates as a measure of the competence of detectives can interfere with stated aims of law enforcement by creating an informal hierarchy of penalties. That part of the case follows:

After considerable investigation, two of the four suspects were "picked up on a roust," that is, they were arrested on minor charges in order to give the police an opportunity to interrogate them. After they had been placed in custody in Jonesville, an all-points bulletin was sent out which came to the attention of the Westville detectives assigned to the Moore case. The Westville detectives were given permission to interrogate the suspects by the Jonesville Police Department and especially, as a matter of courtesy, through the Jonesville detective who arranged the "roust."

In the meantime, the Westville detectives had independently gathered information which, added to the considerable information held by the Jonesville detective, pointed to the culpability of these suspects in the Moore case. The information regarding the recent activities of one of the suspects, who will be called Jerome, was especially comprehensive. As the sergeant put it in describing the interrogation to me:

We know enough to make him feel that we got him by the balls. We have enough information so that we can almost tell him where he took a piss twenty-four hours a day for the last few days. Actually, we don't know what is what so far as real evidence is concerned, but we know so much about his general activities, that he thinks we know a lot more than we actually do.[13]

After six hours he finally says he wants to make a deal. It turns out that he's got a charge hanging over him in another state and says he'll make a deal if we don't send him back. Then he copped out and told us how he did the Moore job and who he did it with.

He agreed to work for us and so we turned him loose and told him we wanted the fence. The first thing he did was to set up Rich [another member of the burglary team; the third was James, and there was also a fence]. Then James, who's in jail in Smithville, calls us up and says he wants to help us out, and with his help and Jerome's help we got the fence all wired up

---

[13] This is a typical ploy detectives use during interrogation. By indicating to the suspect that they know more than they actually do, they frequently are able to bluff the suspect into believing that they have "hard" evidence.

tight. [There was an additional reason for "helping" here. Jerome and James both mistrusted—indeed hated—the fence, since in their opinion he had cheated them by pretending to have gotten less for the stolen articles than he actually had.]

Over a period of about ten days after the arrest, burglary police from neighboring cities frequently visited the Westville jail, since, between the two of them, Jerome and James could account for more than five hundred burglaries. James himself provided the police with more than four hundred clearances. I witnessed several interrogations of James regarding burglaries he had presumably committed and, in my opinion, it was relatively simple for him to "fake" clearances. One need not have been exceptionally shrewd—and James was—to sense the detectives' pleasure at writing off old cases. This is not to say that the detectives who interviewed him were easily deceived. But from the detail with which he recalled burglaries he had committed in the past year, the policemen could tell that James had committed numerous burglaries. When he expressed vagueness of memory as to those two or three years old, he thereby created a situation in which the police would have either to be extremely scrupulous, and thus forego potential clearances, or "feed" him information to refresh his recollection (which, to this observer, appeared to be rather easily renewed).

Rich and the fence each received substantial prison sentences. Jerome and James were charged as misdemeanants. Jerome spent four months in custody, while James was permitted to finish out sentence on another charge, for which he was already serving time, and was released after thirty days. In part, Jerome and James were given a liberal reduction in charges because they had served as informants and also because they had agreed to appear as State's witnesses. These services were an important aspect of their "cooperation" with law enforcement.

At the same time, however, the two burglars had also given the police numerous clearances. While it would be virtually impossible to separate out the effect of their "cooperation" as informants and State's witnesses as against their "cooperation" in giving clearances, it would be unrealistic to discount the importance of their providing "clearances" in accounting for their lenient treatment. James, who had certainly committed numerous burglaries and had admitted having participated in more than four hundred, received what he regarded as no sentence at all. Jerome, James, the sergeant, and I spent almost five hours reconstructing the events of the case, the backgrounds of Jerome and James, and the morality of the outcome. All agreed that "it wasn't right" that the penalties should have been distributed as they were, although the defendants felt that rough justice had been served since they claimed to have been mistreated by law enforcement authorities in the past. The sergeant, also a shrewd observer, sensed that there was something decidedly wrong with the process. From his point of view, which was largely shared by other detectives interviewed, the society would be better served

. . . if we didn't have this clearance business hanging over our heads. We get guys like this and they hand us clearance after clearance and on FBI books we look terrific. But the fact is that large numbers of burglaries are committed by a relatively small group and when we get one of them we have to give him a good break in order to make ourselves look good. It's a ridiculous system, but that's the way they run things upstairs.

The reader may raise the question as to how the police arranged these low charges with the district attorneys of several jurisdictions. It was not always easy. In one jurisdiction, the district attorney insisted upon heavy prosecution despite the fact that a promise of leniency had already been made to one of the suspects. Eventually, the police view prevailed, on the grounds that unless the district attorney agreed to "back up" the discretionary actions of the police, they would, in future burglary investigations, be seriously impaired. It is unlikely that police discretion can, as one writer has suggested,[14] be exercised without the cooperation of the district attorney. Since the district attorney depends largely upon the policeman for evidence, the policeman has a good deal of influence over the district attorney's exercise of discretionary authority. It is not that the policeman interferes with the work of the district attorney when his work is in the traditional legal domain; rather, the policeman, by gaining the cooperation of the district attorney, usurps the prerogatives of the prosecutor to control the policeman's activities.

SUMMARY AND CONCLUSIONS

This chapter has described and analyzed the processes by which clearance rates are constructed, as part of the broader issue of how the ambiguous institutional character of police influences the actual administration of criminal law. Thus, the chapter concentrated on the issue of how clearance rates—so important to internal control processes—may affect the penalty structure associated with substantive criminal law.

The behavior of the detectives involved should not be seen as an instance of corruption or even of inefficiency. On the contrary, their actions are to be interpreted as an unanticipated consequence of their superiors' development of a method for controlling their efficiency. The

[14] Goldstein, *op. cit.*, especially pp. 568–569.

response of the detective to the clearance rate is easily understandable. It stems from a sociological tendency manifesting itself in all work organizations: the worker always tries to perform *according to his most concrete and specific understanding of the control system.* That is, in general, workers try to please those supervising *routine* activities. Thus, in prisons (or at least in the one studied by Sykes), the guard is judged according to how successfully he maintains a smoothly running cell block. Prison authorities overlook infractions in minor rules and judge the guard's competence by the composure of his cell block. As a consequence, guards permit minor rules to be broken in order to comply with their immediate superiors' over-all aim of keeping the prison under physical control.[15] (How such arrangements react upon the still more general aims of incarceration, such as building up respect for law, is a question beyond the scope of the present study, but surely significant for sanctioning policy.)

Actually, police practices about clearance rates are more strictly comparable to the practices of foremen and production line workers rather than to those of prison guards and inmates. There are numerous examples and allusions in sociological literature of "positive deviance" on the production line—of reshaping, reinterpreting, or ignoring formal rules in order to make the best possible appearance in terms of the most current and pressing demands.[16] A most dramatic recent one is contained in Bensman and Gerver's [17] description of the use of the "tap" in a wartime airplane plant. The tap is a hard steel screw used to bring nuts and bolts into a new but not true alignment on airplane wings, and its use is described as being both "the most serious crime of workmanship conceivable" and "imperative to the functioning of the production organization." The pressure, for these workers, is to show a high production rate. The *ultimate* goal may be ignored under the more immediate pressures to produce. When means are found to raise production, rules are circumvented—not with impunity, however, but only under the strain of production quotas.

Similarly, the detective is inclined to engage in those activities improving *his* appearance as a competent worker. One cannot say that the detective is unconcerned about his work, but rather that he typically engages in practices—such as, for instance, "saving" clearances from

[15] Gresham M. Sykes, "The Corruption of Authority and Rehabilitation," *Social Forces*, 34 (March, 1956), 257–267.

[16] Probably the best-known illustration is found in George C. Homans' *The Human Group* (New York: Harcourt, Brace and Company, 1950), pp. 48–80.

[17] Joseph Bensman and Israel Gerver, "Crime and Punishment in the Factory: The Function of Deviancy in Maintaining the Social System," *American Sociological Review*, 28 (1963), 588–598.

month to month—that put the best possible light on his competence and dependability when his record is examined by superiors. Thus, the perceived necessity of measures of departmental efficiency results in the development of techniques by detectives to enlarge the magnitude of the criteria for measuring their performance. One of these techniques is to exchange the prerogative of charging crime for "clearances," with the result that in major cases criminality may inadvertently be rewarded. Thus, the statistical control system, intended to prevent detectives from drifting into inactivity, may tend to reverse the hierarchy of criminal penalties established by the legislature.[18]

These consequences do not, however, stem from the personal deficiencies either of working policemen or those men who might be termed police "efficiency experts"—men like O. W. Wilson or the personally dedicated and honest head of the Westville Police Department, who are attempting to develop methods for running a "modern and efficient" police department. Instead, the problem stems from the well-motivated attempts of such experts to develop measurable standards of efficiency. Unfortunately, meeting these standards tends to become an end in itself, a transformation found in many organizations. In this process, Blau and Scott interpret the organization's relation to its environment as a crucial factor. They write, "As long as its very survival is threatened by a hostile environment, its officers will seek to strengthen the organization by building up its administrative machinery and searching for external sources of support."[19] As an organization, the police provide a clear example of this development. Requiring a "set of books" to demonstrate competence of performance, the "clearance rate" has been developed as a measure of the effectiveness of the police department, especially the detective branch. This concern with efficiency, however, may also have the unanticipated consequence of developing detective initiative to the point of reversing the hierarchy of penalties associated with the substantive criminal law. Thus, the standard of efficiency employed in police departments may not only undermine due process of law, but also the basic standard of justice—that those equally culpable shall be given equal punishment.[20]

---

[18] On the problems created by statistical records in a similar setting, see Peter M. Blau, *The Dynamics of Bureaucracy* (Chicago: University of Chicago Press, 1955), pp. 36–67.

[19] Peter M. Blau and W. Richard Scott, *Formal Organizations: A Comparative Approach* (San Francisco: Chandler Publishing Company, 1962), p. 231.

[20] It is worth noting that the findings of this chapter also strongly support the idea that rates of deviant behavior are as dependent on the actions of officials, as on the conduct of so-called deviants. For a brief and cogent development of this position see John I. Kitsuse and Aaron V. Cicourel, "A Note on the Uses of Official Statistics," *Social Problems*, 11 (Fall, 1963), 131–139.

Chapter 9

Police Attitudes
Toward Criminal Law

A PROFESSOR of law recently concluded that there are two prevalent models of the criminal process in the United States, the "due process model" and the "crime control model." [1] The due process model views the criminal process as conforming to the rule of law. It is a model stressing the possibilities of human error, especially the frailty of authority under pressure. Above all, it is a model emphasizing *legal* guilt over *factual* guilt. Thus, an accused is to be held guilty if, and only if, the factual determinations made against him have been presented in a procedurally regular fashion by lawfully constituted authorities acting within duly allocated competences.

For example, the convicting tribunal must have jurisdiction and venue, the power to deal with this kind of case in an appropriate locality and the case must have been brought within a limited time. Lest there be "double jeopardy," the accused must not have been previously convicted or acquitted of the same or a substantially similar offense. He must also fall into the category of persons who can be considered criminally responsible, thus excluding children and the insane. Such requirements for legal guilt, and there are others running through the criminal law process, have nothing to do with whether the State can prove that the accused committed the act that is charged as the offense against him. If these procedural criteria are not met, the accused is *legally* innocent.

The crime control model, by contrast, emphasizes *factual* guilt. Its chief principle is efficiency through rational administration or "the system's capacity to apprehend, try, convict, and dispose of a high proportion of criminal offenders whose offenses become known." [2] This model stresses social control over individual justice. Its operative norms are those of a productive enterprise; its success is gauged by a high rate of apprehension and conviction in the context of mass administration of criminal law.

Previous chapters have discussed features of law enforcement drawing

[1] Herbert L. Packer, "Two Models of the Criminal Process," *University of Pennsylvania Law Review*, 113 (November, 1964), 1–68.

[2] *Ibid.*, p. 10.

the policeman toward the crime-control model. The ability of known "criminals" to frustrate and harass law enforcement, the commitment of the police department to structures for apprehending criminals, and the perceived demands of political superiors for evidence of the policeman's ability and initiative, all combine, in the context of nontotalitarian norms about the initiative of workers, to bring policemen to interpret procedural requirements as frustrating the efficient administration of criminal justice.

This chapter further examines factors contributing to this process. It might be thought, for example, that instances of factual guilt not meeting legal criteria in dramatic crimes—homicide, rape—are what impels the policeman toward the crime control model. That is doubtless true, but I believe its force is overrated, even by policemen themselves in their own propaganda. From my observations, I would suggest that equally, if not more important, is the presence of procedural requirements in routine cases, especially those where the character of the defendant is clear. This chapter analyzes the legal processing of prostitution cases from this viewpoint and shows how the policeman's self-conception as a "craftsman" contributes to the seeming irrationality of procedural requirements based upon the rule of law.

PROBLEMS OF OBTAINING EVIDENCE

The detective sees himself as a craftsman charged with carrying out assignments that, when stated generally, seem simple. In their complex particulars, however, these tasks may demand considerable skill. One such general task is finding facts; another is finding them in such a way as to allow them to be introduced as evidence; and finally, the facts must be strong enough to meet legal standards of proof and inference. That is, it is not enough that the policeman personally concludes, with complete confidence in his experienced judgment, that the defendant is guilty. He must also meet legal criteria to transform personal knowledge and feelings into a conviction.

The Westville district attorney's office, for example, requires eyewitness testimony to a solicitation before it will press the charges. If a prostitute has solicited a policeman or a special employee, the police have no problem in producing such evidence. Suppose, however, the police were to arrest a man and woman in a hotel room after following them because the man was white, the woman black, and the neighborhood colored. To achieve a conviction under these circumstances, the police must obtain a story from one of the parties incriminating the other. Take the following observed situation:

After half an hour of "detecting," by listening in at closed doors of a cheap hotel, two vice control policemen decide the couple they are after is behind the door of room 14. They knock on the door; the girl answers. They identify themselves as policemen and immediately "split the pair" in order to determine whether the man's story and the woman's jibe. Among other things each says, the man claims he has known this girl for a while, the girl that she met him tonight. The policemen decide to take the pair to the squadroom for further interrogation. One policeman drives while the other sits between the pair and allows no talking in the patrol car.

At this juncture, the police see their task clearly. They must obtain a story from the man which incriminates the woman. The man, however, may actually be as guilty as the woman—guiltier if, as is often the case, he solicited her. The police justify their tactic on grounds of expediency; without testimony of the man they would be unable to secure a conviction against the woman. Recognizing that the women may not be deterred by the shame, inconvenience, and expense of arrest and conviction, since professional prostitutes regard arrest as a predictable part of a precarious career, while their customers might be, law enforcement officials interviewed nevertheless doubted that it would be more effective to have a policy of arresting men.[3] The case described below exemplifies the department's prostitution policy in practice:

The man was a white serviceman, thirty-two years old, the woman a twenty-one-year-old Negro. When they were brought into the vice control squadroom, the woman was placed in a holding cell, a concrete windowless structure, approximately the size of a "walk-in" closet. The lights were not turned on. The man was brought into an interrogation room, about the same size as a holding cell, but brightly lit and containing a small table and three chairs, one for the interviewee, one for the interrogator, and one for a witness (usually another policeman—in my role as participant-observer I continued to identify myself as a policeman by the simple expedient of not identifying myself otherwise).

The first thing the man was told was that he could walk out the door if only he would tell the truth—"All we want to know is when she set the price, how much, and for what. We know already because we were listening at the door, but we want to hear the truth from you." (Actually, we did not know; we could not hear very well through the door.) The man told a long rambling story which did not incriminate the woman, and he was placed in a holding cell while she was being interrogated. Like him, she denied solicitation had occurred, although she admitted that she had never

---

[3] The rationale of the prosecutor bears a close resemblance to the "functional" explanation offered by Kingsley Davis. See his article, "Prostitution," in Robert K. Merton and Robert A. Nisbet (ed.), *Contemporary Social Problems* (New York: Harcourt, Brace and World, 1961); pp. 273–274.

seen the man before and that she was living with a "boy friend" in the room where she was found with the serviceman.

She was taken out of the interrogation room, and the man was brought back in. This time the man admitted that the woman had been sitting on his lap, had gotten up after he had unbuttoned her blouse and said, "Let's get down to business."

In this second interview the man recalled that he had replied, "How much?"

When the interrogator asked the man what the woman's response had been, the serviceman said, "She didn't say anything."

The interrogator pointed out to the serviceman how improbable his story was, had him tell it again, told him to try and remember a little bit more, used flattery, sarcasm, threatening glances, pleaded for understanding, and finally, after about an hour of grilling, gave up. Obviously frustrated and annoyed, he called me outside and said, "See what we're up against. If we can't get this guy's cooperation we haven't got anything to book her on. We've got to let them both go, even though we're damned sure there was a solicitation here. But unless that guy says she set a price, our case won't stand up in court. But I'm going to tell the S.O.B. off before I let him go."

We returned to the interrogation room, handed the serviceman back his ID card, and the policeman "told the man off," which included advice to the effect that if he didn't like what he was being told, the serviceman could see him on the street anytime and settle the matter. The serviceman was very deferential, claimed he had told all he could remember, only the truth, and thanked the policeman. My impression was that the serviceman was an old hand at this game and knew just which parts of the story to leave out, although it is also possible that the woman did not respond to his "How much?" thinking the serviceman was a special employee of the police department or a policeman.

It never occurred to the policeman to arrest the serviceman (who had admitted soliciting the woman), mostly because men as a rule are freed, but also because the Westville police have a standing arrangement to turn over all servicemen arrested on vice activities to the service police. They feel that if they were to prosecute a serviceman, he would be placed in "double jeopardy" since he would be subject to sanctions by the service as well as by the civil government. Besides, most policemen are former servicemen themselves, and are inclined to give a soldier or sailor a break whenever possible. What bothered the policeman about this serviceman was not that he "was out looking for a piece of tail"— policemen expect no less of servicemen—but that he had refused to incriminate the girl. "After all," the policeman explained to the serviceman, "we do cooperate with the service police and try to give you guys a break."

When the man left, we opened the door to the holding cell and found the girl sobbing quietly. The officer told her how he was going to "give her a break" and let her go "this time" (when in fact he simply had insufficient evidence to convict). Then he told her that since he had done her a favor, he would like one in return. There followed a detailed explanation of a purchase of marihuana that he wanted her to make as a "special employee."

She agreed, under the circumstances, for what probably were a number of reasons. First, she was likely participating in various petty illegal activities. Thus, in the course of the interrogation it developed that she was living in Westville with a "boy friend" and at the same time was married to a serviceman stationed fifteen hundred miles away. Secondly, to a Black girl from the South, the power of the police must appear awesome. She had already been locked up in a dark cell for more than an hour, and was not so secure in her position that she could refuse a policeman a favor. Finally, "to sweeten the deal" she was offered a small sum to act as a "special employee." To the girl, however, the most important consideration was probably the good will of the police, whom she might expect to encounter in the future.

To the policeman, such an evening's work is largely a frustrating failure, even though it is all part of his job and even though he has enlisted an informant. He has uncovered a solicitation, but because of the "technicalities" of criminal law is unable to "score," to obtain evidence sufficient to convict. Even if he is able to secure such evidence on the night of the arrest, however, it often happens that policemen are further frustrated by certain constitutional aspects of criminal procedure, such as the defendant's right to be freed on bail. In the administrative context of the processing of a criminal case, constitutional protections for the defendant come to be regarded primarily as administrative obstacles.

THE POLICEMAN'S VIEW OF CRIMINAL JUSTICE

Although the policeman may have enough evidence to book a woman for solicitation or prostitution, unless she is held for a venereal disease check it is possible for the defendant to bail out immediately after being booked. The bail for a prostitution charge is always five hundred and twenty-five dollars (in Westville), no matter how many prior arrests and convictions the woman may have incurred. Bail bondsmen charge 10 per cent of the bail, which means that a prostitute must raise fifty-two and a half dollars to gain her immediate release. The defendant is given the right to have the sergeant at the jail make two phone calls to raise bail. Some prostitutes will have the sergeant call their pimp or a "steady trick." Others, who have been on the street for a long time, have an informal "credit" arrangement with a bail bondsman. Thus, it is rare for a well-organized, working prostitute to be unable to make bail, although a young, inexperienced girl without "connections" may remain in jail until her trial (or plea of guilty, after which she may be given probation). Under these circumstances, an experienced prostitute can be back on the street within several hours after arrest. If it is early enough in the evening, she may continue to ply her trade.[4]

The ease with which a prostitute is able to return to illegal activity is frustrating to the policeman. In his opinion, if the community wants to keep prostitutes off the streets, a system permitting them to return within a couple of hours after arrest is irrational. Thus, to the policeman, pretrial release is basically an irrational right given to the defendant by a state already tendering defendants an unreasonable measure of solicitude at every stage of the process.

Furthermore, and even more important, the policeman does not feel that he will have "his day in court." As one vice control man put it, "Our worst problem with whores is the plea of not guilty." When the suspect is booked, she is given a date in court, the date itself varying depending upon whether she makes bail or not. If she does not make bail and is booked before 2 A.M., she is placed on the same day's calendar (provided she has not been arrested on a Friday or Saturday night, in which event she will be placed on Monday morning's calendar). After 2 A.M. she is placed on the calendar for the following day. Appearing before the judge the following morning, she is charged, reminded of her rights to an attorney, and of the availability of the public defender for indigent defendants. (Usually there will be a deputy public defender present in the courtroom.) Sometimes the defendant will elect to plead guilty immediately, but most of the time she will request the services of a private attorney or of the public defender. In turn, the public defender will routinely request, and will be routinely granted, a day's continuance in order to interview his client.

The next day the public defender may plead his client guilty, or he may request a date for trail. On a misdemeanor, the defendant must be tried within thirty days, but the situation of the defendant who makes bail and the one who does not is enormously different, since the defendant who cannot make bail must spend the time between being charged and the trial date in the county jail. This period of time, which may be less than thirty days, is known in the system as "dead time," since the judge need not take it into account in sentencing, although he may. Accordingly, it is generally in the interest of the defendant who

[4] Unless she has been held for a venereal disease check. See Chapter 5, p. 108.

cannot make bail to have guilt or innocence decided as quickly as possible in order to minimize "dead time." This period of pretrial detention may also serve as an incentive for a defendant to plead guilty when the chances for acquittal are regarded by her attorney as problematic.

When the policeman complains of the "problem . . . of the plea of not guilty" he is referring to the woman who makes bail, not to the defendant serving "dead time" in the county jail.[5] In contrast to the defendant who cannot make bail, it is generally in the interest of the bonded defendant to prolong the trial date. She has a sense of freedom which she does not wish to lose by undergoing the hazards of a trial and a possible finding of guilt.[6] In addition to a psychologically founded impetus to remove oneself from the adjudicatory process, there are legal and social reasons for so doing. In order to convict, the prosecution must present a witness who will testify that the woman solicited him. If the witness is a serviceman, he may be shipped out of the area in the meantime, thus destroying the prosecutor's case. Or he may die, or even change his mind about testifying. As one deputy district attorney put it, "A postponement may not hurt us, but it cannot do us any good. Our cases never get better as they get older."

Furthermore, if a woman is a professional prostitute, she may be rearrested one or several times while the initial case is pending. With several counts against her (and a crowded court calendar), there is some implicit pressure on the district attorney to settle for a plea of guilty on one of the counts, since the judge is unlikely to impose a heavier sentence for several counts than for only one. Thus, the pretrial period for the prostitute out on bail is one of "freedom" in a double sense: she not only maintains her normal citizenship rights but she also enjoys a degree of immunity from prosecution for illegal activities during this period. Finally, if the judge does fine her, the woman will have had additional time to earn some money to pay off the fine and her attorney's fees.

[5] On the importance of bail in the administration of criminal justice see Caleb Foote, "The Bail System and Equal Justice," *Federal Probation*, 19 (1955), 43; C. E. Ares, A. Rankin, and H. J. Sturz, "The Manhattan Bail Project: An Interim Report," *New York University Law Review*, 38 (1963) 67 ff; Patricia Wald, "Pretrial Detention and Ultimate Freedom: A Statistical Study—Foreward," *New York University Law Review*, 39 (1964) 631–640; and Anne Rankin, "The Effect of Pretrial Detention," *ibid.*, 641–655. For a bibliography and general discussion of bail reform see Daniel J. Freed and Patricia M. Wald, *Bail in the United States* (New York: The Vera Foundation. 1964).

[6] I have encountered only one defendant who *wanted* to go to prison, and this was a lower class Negro male who had spent eight years in state prison and wanted to go back to his "home." Indeed, he had committed a harmless petty theft to effect his return.

The postponement of cases is consequently a source of irritation to the police, who feel that it interferes with the purpose and outcome of their duties. In addition, a postponement may involve some personal inconvenience for the vice control man. Whatever his stated shift may be, an officer always tries to complete a specific assignment. The work of a prostitution detail necessarily includes the handling of discontinuous and relatively short assignments, usually running a few hours. These assignments are, however, unpredictable enough to insure that actual hours may run into overtime. It is not uncommon for a vice control policeman to work into the early hours of morning and still be required to make a court appearance at 9 or 10 A.M. In addition, it may happen that a court appearance scheduled for 10 A.M. does not end until noon, and may drag on until afternoon. Since most vice control men work a 6 P.M. to 2 A.M. shift, it simply may not "pay" to return home at either end of a shift because of a court assignment, especially if the officer commutes. Consequently, a postponed case may result in notable inconvenience for the policeman.

The district attorney's office attempts to remedy this possibility by sending out subpoenas two weeks in advance of trial to police officers. Defense attorneys are called a day before a case is ready "to go" to guarantee that the defense attorney will not request a postponement at the last minute. Even with such precautions, however, it occasionally happens that policemen fail to be notified of postponements.

Moreover, police feel that judges are too lenient with defense attorneys who request postponements. The police perceive postponements as defense "tactics" (as indeed they are) and regard these as unfair and unethical. Furthermore, the police feel that judges, as a rule, give them less consideration than they give to defense attorneys. The policemen see attorneys as demanding and receiving a degree of "consideration" irrelevant to their role in the legal process. Thus, the police claim, a defense attorney may privately request and receive a postponement from a judge, with the implicit (if not explicit) understanding that the reason for the postponement is the client's inability to pay the attorney.

Although police charges may tend to be overstated, in fact there are built-in pressures upon the judge to cooperate with defense attorneys (aside from identification as fellow professionals), while the police have relatively little informal access to the judge and no direct means of interfering with his work. Their pressures usually must be filtered through the office of the district attorney, except in some instances where a judge is a former district attorney, friendly to police. By contrast, the defense attorney has more than conversational influence. He may refuse to "be reasonable" and insist upon his client's legal right to trial by jury within the thirty days trial deadline period in cases which normally could be settled by the accused's plea of guilty. If this were to happen with any frequency, the calendar could become clogged, and the State would lose some cases simply because these could not be adjudicated within the legally prescribed time period. Furthermore, if this were to happen, the

TABLE 1   *Disposition of Persons Charged with Prostitution and related Sex Offenses by the Westville Prosecuting Attorney, August 1962–February 1963 **

	Charge			
Disposition	Solicitation or Prostitution (647b PC)	Pandering (266 PC)	Female Impersonation (3408 PC)	Total
Dismissed	21	1	4	26
Probation	2	—	—	2
Not guilty	4	—	—	4
Fine	29	—	1	30
Judgment suspended	18	—	2	20
Jail	12	1	6	19
Continued	14	—	—	14
Total	100	2	13	115

* This period of time happened, by chance, to be the period covered in the prosecuting attorney's "vice book" when the attempt was made to secure disposition data. Thus, data for this period of time were used because of accessibility, which was related to currency. It is doubtful that any systematic bias was thereby introduced.

judge who handles the jury trial calendar would be called to task by the presiding judge of the municipal court.[7] That is, administratively speaking, the most important task of the judge is to keep his calendar moving. In order to accomplish this, he must keep the prosecuting attorney and the defense attorney operating "within bounds." A judge who permits either side to become excessively balky impedes the achievement of this goal. A judge can exercise the full limit of his authority with a specific defense attorney or two, perhaps one considered a "nut" by the community of defense attorneys. He cannot, however, lightly disregard the ordinary defense attorney's "reasonable" request that he be afforded an

[7] Each month a record is kept, and distributed to all municipal court judges, of the disposition of jury trials for that month. At the bottom, in capital letters and distinctly set apart, is a sentence which reads "CASES DISMISSED UNDER SEC. 1382 P.C.," the thirty-day trial provision requirement. It should be, according to the administrative standards of the court, followed by the word "NONE."

opportunity to be paid for his services. Neither can the district attorney, since the defense attorney can also interfere with the work of the district attorney. Thus, on the basis of the potential sanctions built into the structure of the judicial system, the judge unavoidably tends to inconvenience the policeman rather than the defense attorney.

Statistics reflect the analysis of the social structure. Only a small proportion of persons charged in Westville with solicitation or prostitution receive jail sentences. Of the eighty-six closed cases appearing in the files of the district attorney's office between August 1962 and February 1963 (an additional fourteen were being continued), only 14 per cent received jail sentences. Five per cent of those charged with solicitation or prostitution were found not guilty at trial; 24 per cent were dismissed outright by the judge; and 34 per cent received fines. These, however, are regarded by prostitutes, by defense attorneys, and by police as the equivalent of "license fees" for continuing prostitution activities.

The remaining 21 per cent were given sentences of from thirty to one hundred and eighty days in the county jail, with judgment suspended. The consequences of such a sentence are ambiguous. Technically, if a woman under a suspended sentence for prostitution is arrested once again during the period under which judgment has been suspended (usually a year or two), she may at the discretion of a judge be required to serve her earlier jail sentence plus any new one imposed. In practice, however, Westville judges take earlier suspended sentences into account only after conviction, and some judges will, after a period of a year or so, ignore the earlier suspended sentence and "merely" fine the prostitute for her most recent conviction. When this happens, both police and prosecuting attorney feel that justice has been thwarted.

"PLEADING OUT" PROSTITUTION CASES

When the police do bring prostitution cases to court, they will typically put pressure upon the district attorney not to accept a plea of guilty in exchange for a fine. Since police have recurring relations with prostitutes, they have a considerable stake in influencing outcome. If interactions between police and prostitutes were minimal and nonrecurring, the policeman's authority would not be challenged by the possibility of a defendant escaping conviction. But policemen need prostitutes —as informers, for instance—and are also regularly called upon to control them. Consequently, an arrest which does not lead to conviction and a jail sentence undermines the policeman's ability to constitute an authoritative threat to the prostitute.

It may happen, however, that the district attorney has little choice in whether to accept a plea of guilty. In chambers, the bargaining is largely between judge and defense attorney over sentence. The district attorney can do little more than represent the police position to the judge in chambers. He obviously cannot refuse to accept a plea of guilty, because if the issue were to go to trial the defendant might be acquitted by a jury. Even if she were found guilty, the judge might still impose a fine rather than a jail sentence. In a prostitution case, consequently, the significant representation by counsel takes place in the judge's chambers before trial, and the outcome will tend to vary with the private moral conceptions of the judge.

This is not, however, to assert, as many attorneys would, that it is impossible to generalize about the outcome of such an interaction because it "all depends upon the personalities of the people involved." What an attorney means by such a statement is that the interaction is not entirely predictable, since its outcome depends on who the parties are and what their prior relations have been. This assertion is true, of course, but it still appears that the variations in "role" explain far more than variations in the "personality" of those occupying such roles. For example, during the study, a vigorous defense attorney became a judge. While he maintains privately the position that it is senseless to jail prostitutes, as a judge he does so if the woman has been convicted with some frequency, about twice in a year's time. Furthermore, he still talks privately like a defense attorney, but acts publicly like a judge. He feels that in his role as a judge he must adjudicate between parties, not simply uphold the defense attorney's point of view as presented in the context of a negotiation. Finally, he realizes that the defense attorney may not privately agree with the position he takes in a negotiation but also takes it in line with role obligations.

The following is a description of negotiations in another judge's chambers of five prostitution cases. It is typical in the sense that it expresses how the differing role obligations of judge, defense attorney, and district attorney shape the interaction and its outcome.

Present were the judge, the defense attorney, the district attorney, and the writer. The vice control officers were not permitted to participate directly in the bargaining. While the group was being assembled, the district attorney whispered to me: "While I'm supposed to be abstractly responsible to the community for anything I do, actually I'm directly responsible to the officer who makes the arrest. He's the person that I have to explain any of my actions to."

When everybody was seated, negotiations were opened by the defense attorney, one of the most experienced and respected in the county, and Black himself, who was defending five Black women accused of prostitution.

"Judge," he said, "these girls don't want any time so I know I'm going to have a lot of difficulty making a deal, but I want to say that I don't really think that these girls are so responsible. I think the police created the whole thing. All the girls were trying to do was make a little Christmas money." Everybody smiled at this remark, including the defense attorney.

It is important to note that the defense attorney began bargaining with the judge, not with the district attorney. All concerned understood that what was being bargained over was sentence, not charge. Among some defense attorneys this ploy is known as "wiring the judge" before "copping out."

The defense attorney continued, "Do you think it will do any good to go through with these cases individually? I sort of want to know how you feel about them, Judge, because if you feel you are going to have to give them time, then it doesn't even pay to waste any of our time talking further."

It was clear that, faced with the prospect of five jury trials, and the criterion of efficiency, the judge was not going offhandedly to declare the impossibility of a fine, even though there was no timewaiver problem in these cases. Thus, the opening move by the defense attorney was a strong one.

The judge responded by explaining his attitude toward prostitutes. He said that a long and checkered history of prostitution showed that there wasn't much that could be done to help these girls. . . . "I would like somehow in some way to rehabilitate the girls, to change their life pattern, and if they are new at the game I am willing to give them a break. But if they have spent a great deal of time as prostitutes, I feel that the only thing I can honestly do as a judge is to give them punishment so as to deter them from committing the same kind of acts in the future."

The defense attorney replied, "Judge, privately I agree with you, but as an attorney I have to see what I can do for my clients."

The judge indicated that he understood the defense attorney's position and was not holding him to account personally, but that as a judge he also had to do his job. The judge suggested that they take the cases one at a time and see what they could do with them. The defense attorney was agreeable: "Why don't you look at Jane Darrow's record, Judge, and see what you would give her, without any comment from me."

The judge began to look at Jane's record and as he was doing so, the defense attorney, instead of holding back comments as he had promised, kept making side remarks which emphasized the general "social problem" nature of prostitution as against the individual culpability of his clients. "If only they'd tear down these shack-up hotels and put up some street lights there wouldn't be so much of a problem."

Actually, the defense attorney was expressing his conception of the kinds of broad "sociological" reasons which would impress a "liberal" white judge. The attorney was acting on behalf of his clients in saying these things, because what he said did not reflect accurately his own private moral conceptions. These are rather complex because, as a Black attorney in what, from where he sits, is at best a "liberal" white community, he sometimes expresses apparently contradictory moral sentiments. However, on the subject of prostitution, he will privately express the idea that prostitutes earn their living in the best way that they know how; that they provide a service for which men are willing to pay; and that unless they create a public health problem they should not be harassed by the community. Furthermore, that within the Black community, with opportunities for earning a living limited as they are, prostitution is often tolerated, if not accepted, morally.

Apparently Jane was the worst offender of the lot, with the worst record, because the defense attorney said, "Judge, she's had the gamut, the record, but I'll tell you, she just won't plead, knowing she's going to jail. In fact," said the defense attorney, "if I gave them Jane, they'd give up all the others."

One couldn't quite tell who the "them" was, whether it was the district attorney or the vice control squad, but it seemed to be the vice control squad, and the defense attorney appeared cognizant of the pressures from this source on the district attorney.

The judge asked the defense attorney what his defense would be. He replied, "Well, Judge, you know the man that went into that house and they caught coming in and out, he was simply—he was an old friend of the family. He'd known this girl for years, and her mother and his father were old family friends, and he just went in there because he was a friend of the family. When he came out these vice squad officers said to him, 'Do you know what kind of a woman she is?' and he said, 'I don't care what kind of a woman she is, she's an old friend of mine.' He'll testify to that, Judge."

The defense attorney added that the arresting officer was Rogers. The defense attorney contended that if Rogers took the stand he'd "wipe up the courtroom with him" because Rogers, he said, made the worst impression possible.

The judge didn't commit himself on Jane Darrow, but went on to a couple of the other cases and looked over the records of the girls. He commented along the way that he'd probably have to give some of them "time," although maybe some of them could get away without any "time," because he felt that some of the cases contained an element of entrapment. The district attorney agreed there probably was an element of entrapment in some of the cases.

The defense attorney said, however, he wasn't going to argue entrapment, because when you argue entrapment you admit that the solicitation had been made and this doesn't always turn out too well for your client in a jury trial.

The judge asked rhetorically—since he already knew the answer—"I don't suppose most of them want probation?" The defense attorney agreed with the judge, who responded by saying, "All these are old-timers, isn't that right?"

The defense attorney said, "All but one, Diane Smith. She doesn't want probation, though, because she doesn't want any probation officer coming around to her house on this charge. She's got a daughter graduating from Cedarville High."

The defense attorney then repeated that these girls didn't want any time and presented to the judge the technique of moral rationalization used by the prostitute. He said that these girls felt that they weren't doing anything that was very wrong; that they weren't doing anything that was very different from what other women do, except that they slept with a number of men, instead of one; that they earned their money fair and square, in an exchange of sex for money; and that it was a private exchange that they felt wasn't wrong to make. He further argued that a sentence of time wasn't going to change the behavior of any of these girls.

The judge said in reply that none of these girls had ever gotten one hundred and eighty days and the defense attorney shot back that one of them had and was still out on the streets. The judge looked at her record and agreed that one of them had.

The judge said that he felt that perhaps the time spent in jail might not in fact do these girls any good, but he wasn't going to agree beforehand not to give any of them any "time." The defense attorney said he felt that he could beat some of these cases, but that he would not like to have to.

The defense attorney brought up once again, as he had throughout the interview, the fact that these trials would be so time-consuming on everybody's part, and it would be a good idea to not have to go through the business of trial. He tried to show that he was sort of on the judge's side, that he did not really think too much of these girls. He placed himself in the position of a poor guy representing clients who are making large demands upon him, and there was nothing he could do but hold to a fast, hard bargain. It was the ancient "I'd like to, but my partner won't let me" bargaining routine—"My client is the one who insists that there be no time."

The judge said, "Well, I guess then we'd better have some jury trials. I just won't agree to tie my hands in advance as to sentencing." The defense attorney said, "Okay, I guess we'd better. We'll just have to write them up on the calendar." As he left, the defense attorney thanked the judge and the the judge said, "What are you thanking me for? I haven't done anything for you." The defense attorney smiled and said, "Oh, that's all right, Judge, I understand your position in this."

We all left the judge's chambers and went out into the courtroom. The district attorney immediately went over to the members of the vice control squad who were present and told them that no deals had been made. They were very happy, almost jubilant. They said that they didn't want any deals to be made, that even if they had to lose some of the cases, they wanted to go through with court trials.

They left the courtroom and were interviewed in the corridor. Asked why they were so happy that no deals had been made, since it would require a lot of court time for them, one said,

"We don't care about that. We don't even mind working overtime and not getting paid for it. What we don't like is being dealt out in the judge's chambers." He continued, "We ride around all night and, when we make an arrest, we feel that the arrest ought to stick. If we set up a case, then we want to see it go through. When we write one up, we want to see it move. We don't want it dealt out. . . . We don't even care if we lose some of the cases. We want to indicate how many arrests we've made, and we want to show that we went to trial with them. Many of these cases are dismissed out of hand, and if they're dismissed, the judge that they are coming before now doesn't know why a girl had a case dismissed earlier. What often happens is that a girl will come before the judge and he'll try to give her a break so he will dismiss the case. But the next time she's arrested, she may not come before the same judge, and that judge will look at the dismissal and think that she was brought up on a wrong beef, when it's just that the other judge was feeling sorry for her."

ADMINISTRATIVE BIAS OF THE CRAFTSMAN

The hostility the policeman expresses toward the prostitute is not, however, unconditional. The policeman does not express the same antagonism toward the prostitute who does not "play the system for all it's worth," or the prostitute who is "cooperative with law enforcement." His objection to the prostitute is best understood in light of his stance toward principles of criminal procedure.

The policeman views criminal procedure with the *administrative bias of the craftsman,* a prejudice contradictory to due process of law. That is, the policeman tends to emphasize his own expertness and specialized abilities to make judgments about the measures to be applied to apprehend "criminals," as well as the ability to estimate accurately the guilt or innocence of suspects. He sees himself as a craftsman, at his best, a master of his trade. As such, he feels he ought to be free to employ the techniques of his trade, and that the *system* ought to provide regulations contributing to his freedom to improvise, rather than constricting it. There is in his attitude toward judges, for instance, a sentiment akin to

that of Shaw's epigram, "Those who can, do; those who cannot, teach."
Like other doers, he tends to be resentful of critics who measure his
value by abstract principles rather than the "reality" of the world he
knows and lives and sees.

To further understand the consequence of his craftsman's bias, it
must be understood that the policeman draws a moral distinction between criminal law and criminal procedure. (I have never heard a policeman actually articulate, argue, and defend the distinction, but it is
implicit in his general outlook.) The distinction is drawn somewhat as
follows: The substantive law of crimes is intended to control the behavior of people who willfully injure persons or property, or who engage in
behaviors eventually having such a consequence, as the use of narcotics.
Criminal procedure, by contrast, is intended to control authorities, not
criminals. As such, it does not fall into the same *moral* class of constraints as substantive criminal law. If a policeman were himself to use
narcotics, or to steal, or to assault, *outside the line of duty*, much the
same standards would be applied to him by other policemen as to the
ordinary citizen. When, however, the issue concerns the policeman's
freedom to carry out his *duties*, another *moral* realm is entered.

Statements are often made, typically by civil libertarians, to the effect
that "policemen ought not to break the law in carrying it out." From
sociological vantage, the important point is the different meaning of the
word "law" as used by the policeman and by his critics. Unlike the policeman, civil libertarians do not in this context draw a moral distinction
between the law of crimes and criminal procedure. This is not, for the
moment, to suggest that civil libertarians are wrong in the demands they
make upon police. No policy judgment need be implied here. Rather,
it is important to make a conceptual distinction which will help to understand the policeman's attitude toward legal constraints.

In contrast to the criminal law presumption that a man is innocent
until proven guilty, the policeman tends to maintain an administrative
presumption of regularity, in effect, a presumption of guilt. When he
makes an arrest and decides to book a suspect, the officer feels that the
suspect has committed the crime as charged. He believes that as a specialist in crime, he has the *ability to distinguish between guilt and innocence*. If pressed, and in public, most police would not advocate that
criminal trials are generally unnecessary. If one talks to policemen for a
period of time in private, however, the impression is gained that the
policeman feels that most trials are a waste of taxpayers' money since, as
one law enforcement spokesman put it, "We do not charge innocent
men." Indeed, the policeman sees himself as a merciful administrator of
justice as well. Vice control men feel, for example, that any "breaks" a

particular defendant deserves have already been meted out according to personal discretionary standards of police, appropriate in their operational environment.

The administrative presumption of regularity may well prevail among all persons in the system, defense lawyers, judges and juries, although in differing degree. Arthur Train states the regularity presumption nicely when he says:

People as a rule don't go rushing around charging each other with being crooks unless they have some reason for it. Thus, at the very beginning the law flies in the face of probabilities when it tells us that a man accused of crime must be presumed to be innocent. In point of fact, whatever presumption there is (and this varies with the circumstances) is all the other way, greater or less depending upon the particular attitude of mind and experience of the individual.[8]

Placed in the routine context of criminal law administration, the presumption of regularity is the most obvious and commonplace assumption that can be made. That is, it *is* reasonable to assume that trained people do their jobs properly. To understand the force of this assumption, one need only observe several *voir dire* examinations of jurors in criminal cases, and notice the stress placed by the defense attorney on communicating to the jury the right of the defendant as to a presumption of innocence, and the burden of proof of the prosecution to prove its case beyond a reasonable doubt. Prosecutors, at least in Westville, prefer to try cases before experienced jurors, and defense attorneys before a "greener" panel because each perceives that the greater the experience of a juror, the more likely is he to attribute a presumption of regularity to law enforcement, rather than a presumption of innocence to the defendant.

Among criminal lawyers, this is the fundamental distinction between those who are regarded as "prosecution-minded" and those who are termed "defense-minded." The "prosecution-minded" lawyer envisions the adjudication of criminality as a "rational" administrative task, placing much confidence in "specialists" whose job it is to deal with criminals. The "defense-minded" lawyer, on the other hand, emphasizes the peril of interfering with the liberty of a human being. He sees the sanctions as being so high that it is dangerous not to presume the innocence of the defendant. Furthermore, he is troubled that the police will behave in an arbitrary fashion, with greater concern for their own stake in the outcome than for the society's interest in justice. The consequence

---

[8] Arthur Train, *Courts and Criminals* (New York: Scribner's, 1921), p. 15.

(and a deep and inevitable source of tension under the circumstances) is that the policeman must feel his work is being "interfered with" well beyond what a "rational" system would demand.

Accordingly, the policeman feels that criminal procedure has been unfairly weighted against him. In the policeman's administrative eyes, any "balance of advantage" lies not with the State but with the defendant. The policeman finds it difficult to fathom and to justify a system which, on the one hand, requires that he be increasingly knowledgeable and competent in general areas as well as those relating specifically to police work, and, on the other, sometimes nullifies his best efforts by interposing seemingly irrational requirements and procedural delays.

THE QUASI-MAGISTERIAL ROLE OF THE PROSECUTOR

One channel for tempering police resentment toward criminal law is the office of the prosecutor. By representing the law as an authoritative symbol, the prosecutor tends to curb police hostilities toward legal strictures. The prosecutor thus plays a quasi-magisterial role, somewhere between policeman and judge, a role he eases out of as the case progresses. In the early stages, the prosecutor acts most like the magistrate; in the later stages, he necessarily comes to represent law enforcement.

The initial contact of policeman with prosecutor occurs when the former brings a complaint to be charged. This encounter may be critical, because it is an important point for making decisions about the conception of the case—whether the complaint should be dismissed, whether the charge should be reduced to a lesser offense or to a misdemeanor. On most occasions, police do not attempt to influence the deputy district attorney one way or the other. During the study, forty-eight attempts were observed in which police tried to influence a municipal district attorney's decision.[9] In forty, the police argued for a heavier charge, and in eight, for a lighter one. The deputy accepted the policeman's argument in slightly more than one-quarter of the cases. The deputy, however, rarely made an outright refusal. Instead, he usually made one of two explanations: (1) that the defendant would not likely receive a more severe sentence as a result of a heavier charge; or (2) that if the officer were to obtain additional evidence, the deputy would charge as requested.

In most felony cases, if the defendant is "held to answer" to the su-

[9] The figures were gathered in two municipal prosecutors' offices in the county studied. They should be interpreted with caution as they represent no sample of a known population. There was, however, a high degree of inter-interpreter reliability for the two offices observed.

perior court, his file containing his rap sheet, arrest report, preliminary hearing, and an assessment by the municipal deputy is sent to the "screening deputy" in the county prosecutor's office for the purpose of filing an "information." [10] The assessment by the municipal deputy is supposed to alert the "screening" deputy to particular problems or items of information. For instance, it may be noted that the prosecution witness "makes a lousy impression on the stand" or that, despite such a fact, the complaining witness does not want to drop charges.[11]

In deciding the charge or charges upon which to file an information, the "screening" deputy will again frequently talk to the policeman. It should be understood, in terms of the status hierarchy of the prosecutor's office, that deputies on the county level are of higher status than those at the municipal level (except for those holding positions of rank in the municipal offices, especially Westville's). Thus, only after a deputy gains experience on the municipal level, will he be sent up to the county office (unless he has compensatory outside experience). In this respect, the municipal offices serve as "farm teams" for the county office.

As a result, the "screening deputy" in the county office will view more critically the work of the municipal deputy, and will also understand that the municipal deputy may be subject to some greater degree of police influence. The "screening deputy" may interview the policeman and the complainant himself, depending upon whether he has questions as to the charge, or perceives discrepancies between the charge and the evidence brought out at the preliminary hearing. (The screening deputy is empowered to change the charge, provided the offense in the information was encompassed within the same behavioral transaction as the original charge.)

Usually, changes are in the direction of charging the defendant *less* seriously than the deputy did down below. Not only is the municipal deputy subject to greater police pressure but he is also wary of undercharging, since the charge can always be reduced on the information. Overcharging is usually regarded as an "error" by the "screening deputy," but an understandable one. As one "screening deputy" who, like most county deputies, had formerly been in a municipal office said:

[10] Usually, cases of general public concern are presented to a grand jury for "indictment." Functionally, however, the "information" and "indictment" are equivalents. See, Fred M. Henderson and William L. Ritzi, "Grand Jury Proceedings," in *California Criminal Law Practice* (California Continuing Education of the Bar, 1964), pp. 251–273.

[11] In rape cases, such a request will usually be honored.

If I were down there I'd probably do the same thing. If you don't have to try the case, then you can be a lot looser in what you charge, and a lot of the time these guys just get careless. But if they had to take this case into court and try it, they would be a lot more careful. I know that if I had to try a case that I was charging, I'd be a lot more careful.

Of course, the screening deputy's anticipation of courtroom exposure makes him less likely to accept the request of a policeman. While the municipal deputy might be willing to "take the heat" from the "screening deputy" for overcharging (to maintain friendly relations with the police) the "screening deputy" is less interested in these relations than in not losing, which is different from winning. If the case should come to trial "overcharged," the defendant may gain an acquittal, while with a lesser charge, he may be found guilty on the same facts. Deputies are called upon to educate policemen that agreement to a lesser charge does not represent capitulation, so much as reality: a considered judgment that the defendant would probably be convicted of the lesser offense, but not of the greater.

When an information is filed, the case passes on to the "calendar man," the representative of the district attorney in the courtroom on issues pertaining to date of trial. He must be prepared to say whether a case is likely to "go" or not, and therefore must keep in close touch with defense attorneys. He thus functions as the routine "plea bargainer" for the prosecutor. The calendar man's dealings with police are minimal, unless a "problem," such as the wish to protect the identity of an informant, is noted on the assessment sheet coming up from the municipal deputy.

If the case is not "settled" on the day the information is read, it is assigned to a trial deputy (although it may still be, and frequently is, pleaded out before trial). When the trial deputy enters the picture, the case is his to prepare for the courtroom. Frequently, such preparation requires further interviewing of witnesses, especially of police, who are as a practical matter easily available. By my observation, when the trial deputy questions the police, he is not at all reluctant to criticize the policeman's actions in the case. For instance, in one such interaction observed, the policeman was told that his failure to caution the defendant in a recorded statement might prejudice the jury unfavorably. According to several deputies questioned on this matter, it is indeed the policy of the office to "educate" policemen.

Furthermore, the police seem not to resent such "correction," and appear to enjoy their role as "assistants" to these higher-ranking law enforcement personnel. Unlike the municipal district attorney, the county deputy is generally an experienced courtroom operative, and is more likely to be accepted by the police, who tend to weigh experience heavily. He is perceived in a fashion similar to that in which the captain of a team or a higher military officer would be viewed—possibly with some resentment, but with clear acknowledgement of his right (and duty) to correct errors. At the superior court level, the policeman and the district attorney become part of the same team. Thus, although the prosecutor plays a magisterial role in the sense of assessing with a critical eye the validity of complaints and the strength of a case, he ultimately represents law enforcement. In playing this role, however, he not only interprets criminal law to the policeman, but also, in the process of interpretation, *legitimizes its authority* and tempers police resentment toward criminal law.

CONCLUSION

This chapter has described a portion of the working basis for the policeman's conception of criminal law. By examining the processing of prostitution cases, it has shown how the policeman develops the craftsman's administrative bias; he sees the world in probabilistic terms. When he sees a black girl and a white serviceman enter a hotel together, he assumes an act of prostitution is in the offing. To him, these are not constitutionally protected citizens, but predictable actors whose misbehavior he usually judges correctly. Sometimes, to be sure, he may be in error. The probabilities, however, are so strong, he feels, that his judgment is rarely going to be wrong.

Given that assumption, he finds it utterly unjustifiable to have imposed upon him a series of "obstacles" that (1) impede the exercise of his expert opinion, and (2) permit criminals to frustrate the stated aims of the community as expressed in substantive criminal law. For him, due process of law is, therefore, not merely a set of constitutional guarantees for the defendant, but also *a set of working conditions* which, under increasingly liberal opinions by the courts, are likewise becoming increasingly arduous. No comparable worker, he would assert, is given so little consideration. Thus, by presuming the defendant to be innocent as the first in a series of frustrating obstacles, the State requires the policeman to work in a milieu filled with extraneous and, to him, needless restrictions. If these were "rational" he might countenance them. In his world of fact, however, they appear highly irrational, since they do not conform to his experience. One cannot "presume" a defendant to be innocent when the character and actions of the defendant so strongly suggest guilt. The very notion of making a presumption so frequently contrary to fact violates his craftsman-like conception of self, and induces negative attitudes toward due process of law. The policeman, in short, is primarily interested in *factual* guilt. Indeed, the idea of *legal* guilt leaves him cold and hostile.

To a degree, these feelings are tempered through the quasi-magisterial role of the prosecutor. In the latter, the policeman finds a man who is both a sympathetic ally and an interpreter of constitutional legality. The prosecutor need not be successful in making the policeman approve of the strictures of due process of law, which he typically does not admire himself. By accepting their legitimacy, however, he demonstrates to the policeman that it is at once possible to disagree with the rules of the game as they are laid down, and at the same time to carry out the enforcement of substantive criminal law—if one learns skillfully how to interpret these rules into action.

Chapter 10

Conventional Morality, Judicial Control, and Police Conduct

THE issue of law and morals has been heavily debated in legal and political philosophy, as well as in sociology.[1] The philosophical issue is one of legislative choice: should morals be enforced through law? Liberal philosophers, notably Mill, have staunchly defended a separation between law and what might be termed conventional morality. Mill was especially critical of "gross usurpations upon the liberty of private life," citing as the most blatant example the prohibition of the sale of "fermented drinks."[2] On the other side, it is argued that conventional morality holds society together and must be enforced by law. "Immorality, contends Sir Patrick Devlin, ". . . is what every right-minded [Christian] person presumes to be immoral."[3] It must be stamped out, and by the use of "those instruments without which morality cannot be

[1] See H. L. A. Hart, Law, Liberty and Morality (Stanford, California: Stanford University Press, 1963), especially his selected bibliography, pp. 85–86. In sociology, the issue is most thoroughly discussed by Durkheim in his Professional Ethics and Civic Morals (London: Routledge and Kegan Paul, 1957). See also Howard Becker's Outsiders: Studies in the Sociology of Deviance (New York: The Free Press of Glencoe, 1963).

Sellin and Wolfgang, in attempting to measure delinquency, have emphasized the problem of lumping all sorts of acts together as "juvenile delinquency" under broad titles of offenses. For example, they say, "Certainly there are vast differences in the types of offenses that are listed as 'assault with intent to ravish.' The conduct of a 16-year-old boy, who attacks a 30-year-old woman, drags her into a dark alley to assault her sexually but is thwarted by screams and the appearance of a police officer, is surely different from a 9-year-old boy's exploratory sexual curiosity with a neighbor girl aged 8." Thorsten Sellin and Marvin E. Wolfgang, The Measurement of Delinquency (New York: John Wiley and Sons, 1964), p. 84. Although it is difficult to define "hard-core crime," it is significant that Sellin and Wolfgang see this as an important distinction in understanding rises and falls in criminality as reflected in official statistics.

[2] John Stuart Mill, On Liberty (New York: Random House, 1947), Chapter 4, "Of the Limits to the Authority of Society over the Individual."

[3] Sir Patrick Devlin, The Enforcement of Morals (London: Oxford University Press, 1959), p. 16.

maintained. The two instruments are those of teaching, which is doctrine, and of enforcement, which is the law." [4]

It is not my intention to engage in an extensive philosophical review and debate, although this is not to suggest that such a dialogue is trivial or unimportant. For example, the assumption of the need for enforcing conventional morality as a means of maintaining society could be challenged, especially if the society is composed of groups with strong ethnic, relgous, racial, and social class identities. Under such conditions, enforcement of conventional morality may well increase conflict since one group's "immorality" may be another's pleasure. Nor should a lack of extended argument be taken to suggest that the materials of this study are unrelated to the issue of the legal enforcement of morals. On the contrary, I propose that one of the great shortcomings of this debate has been the paucity of data or even hypotheses specifically about the social and legal consequences of the enforcement of conventional morality. This chapter discusses some of the more outstanding consequences on police work, resulting from society's use of criminal law as an instrument for achieving moral conformity. The chapter especially concentrates on the neutralization of judicial controls, by examining the effect of the exclusionary rule on observed police practices in the area of "immoral" offenses. These are the crimes for which the exclusionary rule has practical relevance. The legal enforcement of conventional morality therefore provides the most pertinent setting for analyzing the process through which the effectiveness of judicial controls on police behavior is neutralized.

SOME CONSEQUENCES OF ENFORCING CONVENTIONAL MORALITY

The enforcement of conventional morality typically produces two closely related factual consequences. One is a more threatening environment for the policeman. The other is the development of organizations for purveying forbidden goods and services. In the introductory chapter, we noted that the problem of maintaining order through the use of law is complicated by the fact that the idea of what constitutes social order is itself varible. Conceptions of order may be rigid, as, for example, when order is seen as existing only when people dress alike, think alike, actively participate in programs of self-improvement, and refrain from activities which may be harmful to themselves. Under totalitarian conditions such as these, many "social problems" could be subjected to the

[4] *Ibid.*, p. 25.

remedy of criminal enforcement, including drinking alcoholic beverages, using drugs or marihuana, smoking cigarettes, eating cholesterol or dealing in foreign currency.[5] The question ultimately rests on the extent of the social contract, the point at which individual liberty prevails over societal needs as these are defined by authorities.

In a total society, there is little focus on individuality and much on general social requirements. As a result, the *potential* criminal population rises, and with it, increased contact by the populace with those charged with reducing criminality. By contrast, in nontotalitarian societies most citizens have few contacts with public officials. "Their private lives," writes a student of citizenship, "are mainly outside the ken of government, and ready compliance with laws or rules further minimizes the occasions for legal and administrative actions."[6] If one could assume that we actually live in a society whose citizens subscribe overwhelmingly to the sort of "Christian morality" contemplated by Lord Devlin, the totalitarian implications of his position would be far less manifest. Under such circumstances, *conventional* morality would indeed be, as the term suggests, *customary* morality. The United States is surely not that sort of nation, and England is increasingly less so, if it ever was. It is all too easy to define the morality of the powerful as the morality of custom.

One of the consequences of *legal moralism*[7] is, therefore, to strengthen totalitarian tendencies by "criminalizing" the environment. Moreover, to carry out the analogy of the policeman as craftsman, the extension of criminal sanctions beyond the area of assaults against persons and property into the area of so-called conventional morality increases the "production quotas" for police. Such an increase in the area of the policeman's jurisdiction not only makes him the guardian of public morality but also makes his work appear more dangerous. There are those who are actually assaultive and must be guarded against, but there are also the potentially assaultive—those who will attack others to gain the means for continuing illegal activities. By such a process, the policeman's conception of the environment is altered and necessarily becomes more threatening because there are more people around who are more likely to engage in what are defined as illegal activities. If the policeman's job is to observe deviations from "normality," a more rigid

[5] See Harry V. Ball and Lawrence M. Friedman, "The Use of Criminal Sanctions in the Enforcement of Economic Legislation: A Sociological View," *Stanford Law Review*, 17 (January, 1965), 197–223.

[6] Reinhard Bendix, *Nation-Building and Citizenship* (New York: John Wiley and Sons, 1964), p. 20.

[7] This term was introduced by H. L. A. Hart, *op. cit.*, p. 6.

definition of normality will make him more watchful and suspicious.

A closely related development is the growth of social organizations for satisfying and creating illicit demands. Whenever "immoral" conduct is forbidden and criminal sanctions are used to prevent its occurrence, purveyors of the forbidden—a criminal underworld—typically arises. This has been the American experience following the prohibition of alcohol, opiates, and gambling. Forbidding an activity offers a "protective tariff" to those engaged in the sale of illicit goods and services, thereby increasing the profits of their activities. Herbert Packer has described the operation of this tariff in narcotics as follows:

As we know from current experience . . . people go on buying narcotics even if they have to steal money to pay the price. Economic theory explains this phenomenon by introducing the concept of elasticity of demand. It is only when the demand is quite elastic that increases in price will reduce the amount demanded. People who are willing to pay two thousand dollars for a car will not ordinarily want the same car if its price is suddenly doubled. But when the demand is inelastic, when the commodity is something that people want so badly that they will pay almost any price to get it, if its sale is illegal, the crime tariff goes into operation. Regardless of what we think we are trying to do, if we make it illegal to traffic in commodities for which there is an inelastic demand, the actual effect is to secure a kind of monopoly profit to the entrepreneur who is willing to break the law.[8]

Police response to the presence of organized criminal activity based upon the sale of forbidden goods and services may take two characteristic forms of conduct antagonistic to the rule of law. One response is for the police themselves to become part of the underworld and share in its corruption and profits. This was the situation in one of the communities studied. In Eastville, the attempt to solidify societal morality through proscriptive legislation has resulted in a lawless collaboration between police and segments of the criminal underworld. The most interesting feature of this collaboration was the means the police used to justify it, and at the same time to maintain a conception of themselves as responsible policemen, as craftsmen doing their job. Faced with the general human problem of justifying the morality of personal "misbehavior," the Eastville police did not see themselves as being crooked or especially disreputable but instead distinguished relative degrees of "immorality" among crimes of vice. Bookmakers and numbers operators were seen as "businessmen." One detective interviewed described them as especially reliable and trustworthy, insisting that police named by a bookmaker in

---

[8] Herbert L. Packer, "The Crime Tariff," *The American Scholar*, 33 (1964), 551–557.

a famous case as having been "on the take" were, in fact, men who had refused to cooperate with the gambling operation. The truth of the assertion aside, it suggests a moral rationale for a working relationship between police and illegal gambling operators. Illegality is defined not by law, but by the morality of the prohibited behavior; those who accept the bribes and gratuities of gamblers are not characterized as "crooked" but as "realistic." As was stated to me:

Hell, everybody likes to place a bet once in a while. It's all part of the system. [Are there cops who don't play the game?] Sure there are honest cops on the force, and more power to them. You take Captain———. Why, you can't buy him a cup of coffee. You go out with him and he's always got his dime on the counter. But most of us are realistic.

The same policeman insisted, however, that there was no payoff from prostitutes. He took the view that prostitution was inevitable, and not especially immoral. He asserted, however, that police were not "on the take" from prostitutes, as a rule. The main reason, he felt, for the distinction between prostitution and gambling was the lack of "trustworthiness" of prostitutes, by which he meant that prostitutes, unlike gamblers, could not be counted on to protect police in case of an investigation. Most Eastville police, he felt, regarded prostitutes as people so heavily involved in other criminal activities, especially use of narcotics, that they would quickly "fold" if pressed for information by a state investigator. Being "on the take" from prostitutes was not seen so much as an immoral act, but as involving too great a risk to the continuance of one's career.. In other words, even the police themselves may not subscribe to the standards of "conventional" morality defined by the legislature.

The one area where the conception of morality of Eastville police closely paralled that of the legislature was in the prohibition of the use of marihuana and narcotics. In this realm, several of the Eastville police were vehement, and all interviewed felt that narcotics use posed a serious danger to the community and restrictions upon its use were not nearly severe enough. As one said:

These goddam search-and-seizure rules are our enemy. These sellers get away with murder and we can't do a goddam thing about it. We know guys who are walking around Eastville with the stuff, but we can't bust 'em. [What do you do about it?] Sometimes, the only thing you can do is scare the hell out of the guy. [What do you mean?] Well, we tail them, harass them, give them a hard time. I know a lot of professors think you can handle guys with kid gloves, but they don't know what it's like. I mean, sometimes you've got to do something on your own.

Even if the police do not yield to the temptation to be corrupt, the enforcement of narcotics law and other crimes for which there are no citizen complainants is extremely difficult if enforcement is expected to proceed by the rule of law. The existence of newly created crimes not only produces a larger population of criminals, but also brings about feelings of crisis. Under such conditions, law enforcement officials, who find it hard to enforce such laws, become impatient with the constraining rules of due process of law. By this process, then, the actual substance of criminal law may create conditions of greater or lesser pressure on police to violate procedural rights.

Recognition of the relation between the substance of criminal prohibitions and the manner police will carry out their work is by no means new. Sir Robert Peel was profoundly aware of the relationship, and patiently set about to revise the criminal law of England before introducing his bill to form a metropolitan police force. As Reith describes Peel's work:

> Peel realized what the Criminal Law reformers had never done, that Police reform and Criminal Law reform were wholly interdependent; that a reformed Criminal Code required a reformed police to enable it to function beneficially; and that a reformed police could not function effectively until the criminal and other laws which they were to enforce had been made capable of being respected by the public and administered with simplicity and clarity. He postponed for some years his boldly announced plans for police, and concentrated his energies on reform of the law.[9]

During the 1820s, Peel first took the laws relating to theft, offenses against the person, and forgery, and consolidated them. There had been, for example, one hundred thirty statutes relating to larceny. He condensed all these into one act, a small book of thirteen pages and he also drastically reduced penalties. Under Peel's reform, the death penalty was abolished for more than one hundred offenses, leaving capital punishment for only the more serious felonies; there were similar mitigations in less serious crimes. For example, Peel reduced the penalty for fishing in another person's water from seven years transportation to an obligation to pay three times the value of the fish caught.[10]

In the United States, by contrast, the trend seems to be in the direction of increasing penalties, especially for "victimless" crimes. Penalties for the use and sale of narcotics have generally been upward on both the state and federal levels. The Federal Narcotics Bureau has been espe-

[9] Charles Reith, *The Police Idea: Its History and Evolution in England in the Eighteenth Century and After* (London: Oxford University Press, 1938), p. 236.

[10] A. A. W. Ramsey, *Sir Robert Peel* (New York: Dodd, Mead, and Company, 1938), p. 69.

cially active in promoting this, approving such laws as Michigan's which requires the imposition of a twenty-year sentence as a minimum for a first selling offense.[11] As we indicated above, high penalties come to define the seriousness of the offense itself and encourage the police to be zealous in the enforcement of violations.

The classic illustration of the effect of such an approach on police work was national prohibition. Writing in 1935, Thurman Arnold had some cogent observations on the effects of this law on operative law enforcement:

Before . . . prohibition . . . the problem of search and seizure was a minor one. Thereafter, searches and seizures became the weapon of attack which could be used against prohibition enforcement. For every "dry" speech on the dangers of disobedience, there was a "wet" oration on the dangers of invading the privacy of the home. Reflected in the courts the figures are startling. In six states selected for the purpose of study we find 19 search-and-seizure cases appealed in the 12 years preceding Prohibition and 347 in the 12 years following.

Because the creed of law enforcement has a habit of arising out of laws which are impossible of being enforced, it seems to be more of an influence in this country today than in any other. England seems to have escaped it through a tradition of private prosecution. There, the prosecutor may take the position that it is a matter within his discretion as to what laws he will enforce and what laws he will leave to enforcement at the expense of private individuals who are complainants. This furnishes a logical escape from the demand of any small minority that their preference for any given legislation be turned into governmental action, which is not open to a prosecutor in this country.[12]

Arnold's observations specify yet another consequential feature of so-called unenforceable laws. Not only do the crimes embraced usually involve voluntary participation in the forbidden activity, but also the "victim," an indignant third party offended by the activity, is offered the enforcement machinery of the state to apprehend the offender. The policeman, instead of acting in his traditional role as friend and protector of persons who have been robbed or assaulted, is himself placed in the position of surrogate complainant for an anonymous (and perhaps non-existent) third party. Thus, "victimless" crimes offer the services of thousands of trained men on behalf of remotely offended citizens, and

[11] Alfred R. Lindesmith, *The Addict and the Law* (Bloomington: Indiana University Press, 1965), p. 48.

[12] Thurman W. Arnold, *The Symbols of Government* (New Haven: Yale University Press, 1935), p. 164. Herbert Packer has made a similar point in his article, "Two Models of the Criminal Process," *University of Pennsylvania Law Review*, 113 (November, 1964), 1–68.

in the process modify the character of the administration of criminal law.

THE EXCLUSIONARY RULE

The most celebrated device for enforcing police lawfulness is the "exclusionary rule" of evidence. The rule is simple to present in its broadest form:

Upon appropriate motion by the defendant in a criminal prosecution, evidence obtained from the defendant in violation of his constitutional rights to be free from unreasonable searches and seizures will be suppressed by order of the court.[13]

The rule originated in the federal courts with the cases of *Boyd* v. *United States* [14] and *Weeks* v. *United States*,[15] decided by the Supreme Court of the United States in 1886 and 1914, respectively. In 1955, the California court in *People* v. *Cahan* [16] overturned its long established law and adopted the exclusionary rule. Between 1914, when the Supreme Court of the United States decided *Weeks*, and 1960, when it decided *Mapp* v. *Ohio*,[17] only half of the American states had adopted the exclusionary rule. Of these, twenty appeared to have adopted the rule without substantial qualification. Although these states included many of the most populous jurisdictions, New York State was not among them. As a result of the *Mapp* v. *Ohio* decision, announced on the last day of the 1960 term, all states are now required, by reason of the due process clause of the Fourteenth Amendment, to exclude from state criminal trials evidence illegally seized by state officers.

The assumption behind the rule as a control device was stated in fullest clarity by Judge Traynor in *People* v. *Cahan:*

Granted that the adoption of the exclusionary rule will not prevent all illegal searches and seizures, it will discourage them. Police officers and prosecuting officials are primarily interested in convicting criminals. Given the exclusionary rule and a choice between securing evidence by legal rather than illegal means, officers will be impelled to obey the law themselves since not to do so will jeopardize their objectives.[18]

[13] Francis A. Allen, "The Exclusionary Rule in the American Law of Search and Seizure," in Claude R. Sowle (ed.), *Police Power and Individual Freedom* (Chicago: Aldine Publishing Co., 1962), p. 77.

[14] 116 U.S. 616 (1886).

[15] 232 U.S. 383 (1914).

[16] 44 Cal. 2d 434, 282 P. 2d. 905 (1955).

[17] 81 S. Ct. 1684 (1961).

[18] 44 Cal. 2d 434, 448.

Thus, the adoption of the exclusionary rule in California was based on an assumed relation between judicial sanctions and the behavior of policing authorities. This assumption would be difficult to "test" rigorously. I believe, however, that the following materials, plus some of those already presented, shed light on the issue. These materials are based upon actual observation of the working of the rule, and more precisely, the working under it. While the rule, of course, applies to all classes of crime, it is pertinent in fact mainly to cases involving conventional morality, or "victimless crimes," those cases falling principally under the jurisdiction of the vice control squad, especially the narcotics detail.

Briefly stated, the exclusionary rule rejects illegally seized evidence. The question, then, is, what constitutes "illegal seizure"? If the rules of search and seizure permitted police to do anything they wanted at any time, for example, to kick in a door on pure hunch, then evidence seized as a result of such entry would still be admissible under an exclusionary rule. The rule excludes only *illegally* seized evidence. Consequently, once an exclusionary rule has been adopted nationally, the question becomes one of defining the legality of search-and-seizure practices.[19] To my knowledge, there has not been any actual observation of police behavior under the exclusionary rule, nor any firsthand discussion of the conditions under which this rule has force. The remainder of this chapter will discuss the meaning of the exclusionary rule to the policeman, the perspective of the police about the rule, and arrangements leading to greater or lesser compliance with arrest rules.

THE POLICEMAN'S VIEW OF THE EXCLUSIONARY RULE

Under the exclusionary rule, there are two consecutive problems facing the policeman. Initially, he must consider what behavior constitutes

[19] The *Mapp* case did not affect the State of California, since it had already adopted the rule and was developing case law on the legality of arrest procedures. See Rex A. Collings, "Toward Workable Rules of Search and Seizure—An Amicus Curiae Brief," *California Law Review*, 50 (1962), 421–58. Following the *Mapp* case, however, the issue remained as to whether states should be permitted to develop their own precedents, as California had, or should be required to follow the decisions of the federal courts with respect to the legality of a particular kind of search or seizure. On June 10, 1963, with its decision in *Ker* v. *California* (374 U.S. 23), a California case, the Supreme Court of the United States decided the question in favor of federal standards. At the time, however, it was not clear whether federal standards would afford the police greater or lesser latitude than the line of California cases had contemplated. Certainly, a close reading of the *Ker* decision (affirming the conviction of the petitioner) shows the police as having considerable freedom, especially regarding arrest without warrant and surprise entry in narcotics cases.

a legal search, or more precisely, a legal arrest, since most searches are made "incident" to an arrest without a warrant. Secondly, the police-man must develop a strategy to make his behavior take on the appear-ance of legality, if not the reality. In the "good pinch" of Archie (the addict-informer described in Chapter 7), the question of legal interpre-tation was not paramount. The police understood the need to create "probable cause" for an arrest to be able lawfully to search the suspect's apartment and seize his narcotics. Since the circumstances, however, did not offer sufficient time to locate a magistrate who would affirm a war-rant for the suspect's arrest, the police fell back on another arrangement developed for just such emergencies. The reader will recall a working agreement between the parole officer and the vice control police by which the parole officer informally delegated arresting authority to the police. The police, however, do not prefer such arrangements, even though they are party to them. In their opinion, the law of arrest is im-properly interpreted by the courts and they would much prefer a differ-ent context—one not putting them in the position, as they see it, of being required to find ways to avoid restrictions of arrest laws. From the police point of view, the whole problem could be resolved if the courts were to revise their stand on the legality of arrest.

This issue has been much discussed by legal scholars. At the heart of the controversy is the question of whether the courts should continue to focus upon the legality of the arrest rather than the reasonableness of the search and seizure in determining whether to reject evidence on the basis of the exclusionary rule.[20] To the lay reader, the distinction may appear without substance, but it is crucial in the law of arrests, searches, and seizures. When the courts focus on the legality of the arrest, police actions are more closely constrained, at least legally. By contrast, if the focus were on the reasonableness of the search, the police would have considerably greater latitude.

This point requires further explanation. The present standard for a policeman making an arrest is that he have "reasonable cause" to do so. If the police have "reasonable cause" to make an arrest, they also have the right to search, provided the search relates to (is "incident" to) the arrest. In behavioral terms, the issue is whether the police are required to have enough evidence for an arrest *before* they are permitted to search a man's person or home and seize his property, or whether they can search him first, to seize evidence that can be used *afterward* to justify the arrest.

The issue of precedence is of considerable practical consequence. A

---

[20] Cf. Edward Barrett, "Personal Rights, Property Rights and the Fourth Amend-ment," *Supreme Court Review* (1960), 46–74.

policeman observes an individual behaving "suspiciously," but not enough to constitute "probable cause" for an arrest. The policeman would like to search the suspicious individual to determine whether something of a criminal nature, for example, a marihuana cigarette, is in the man's pocket. In turn, the finding of the marihuana cigarette would provide the policeman with "probable cause" to make an arrest. The commonly voiced objection to delegating the police the right to search before arrest is, of course, that the police would abuse the privilege by searching indiscriminately, until they discovered evidence sufficient to constitute "probable cause." By contrast, the police maintain that they are able craftsmen who can determine with high accuracy whether a suspect "merits" a search.

It is often difficult for police to draw a line between what, on the one hand, constitutes suspicious behavior, and on the other, provides sufficient evidence to infer "reasonable or probable cause" for an arrest—even under present standards allowing search only as incident to an arrest. No simple formula can determine reasonable cause, since many factors must be taken into account. Those discussed in California cases include:

. . . nature of information, character of informant, delay which might enable a guilty person to escape, details of description, time of day, flight, furtive conduct, presence at the scene of the crime, results of consent to search, results of reasonable investigatory search, admissions by the person being questioned, criminal record of the arrested person, criminal record of associates, reputation of the premises, and recent crimes in the neighborhood.[21]

The policeman's problem is therefore shared to a degree by the courts, who are called on in numerous cases, each with a different factual situation, to decide under what conditions police have legal cause for arrest and, therefore, grounds to search and seize. Given the frequency of decision, legal requirements about a novel factual situation may be unclear.

The policeman typically feels that courts have provided insufficiently clear standards for routine decisions. Where the policeman perceives the line between legality and illegality as hazy, he usually handles the situation in the interest justifying a contention of legality, irrespective of the actual circumstances. He therefore operates as one whose aim is to legitimize the evidence pertaining to the case, rather than as a jurist whose goal is to analyze the sufficiency of the evidence based on case law.

Bearing in mind the obligation to fulfill the search-and-seizure requirements, his strategy is to try to locate as many congeries of events as appear to fulfill their mandate. Thus, the policeman perceives his job not simply as requiring that he arrest where he finds probable cause. In ad-

[21] Collings, *op. cit.*, p. 439.

dition, he sees the need to be able to reconstruct a set of complex happenings in such a way that, subsequent to the arrest, probable cause can be found according to appellate court standards. In this way, as one district attorney expressed it, "the policeman fabricates probable cause." By saying this, he did not mean to assert that the policeman is a liar, but rather that he finds it necessary to construct an *ex post facto* description of the preceding events so that these conform to legal arrest requirements, whether in fact the events actually did so or not at the time of the arrest. Thus, the policeman respects the necessity for "complying" with the arrest laws. His "compliance," however, may take the form of *post hoc* manipulation of the facts rather than before-the-fact behavior. Again, this generalization does not apply in all cases. Where the policeman feels capable of literal compliance (as in the conditions provided by the "big case"), he does comply. But when he sees the case law as a hindrance to his primary task of apprehending criminals, he usually attempts to construct the appearance of compliance, rather than allow the offender to escape apprehension.

POLICE WORK UNDER THE EXCLUSIONARY RULE

In practice, it may be equally difficult to characterize the precise nature of specific events upon which the *inference* of probable cause may be based as to define the concept itself. For instance, there is in practice nothing clear about a concept like "furtive conduct," a set of behaviors establishing probable cause for an arrest. An incident observed one evening illustrates this point:

I was accompanying a couple of narcotics policemen (one state, one Westville) in an unmarked car. The driver, a Westville policeman, made a slow but wide right turn, said "oh-oh," and beckoned to a tall Negro man standing on the street, perpendicular to a straight line drawn from the driver's seat.
I saw the man glance left and right, and move slightly, with a jerky motion, less pronounced, but akin to that of the first-base runner trying to bluff a pitcher into making a throw. The driver jumped out of the car, began talking to the man, who backed up against the trunk. A few seconds later, I heard scuffling noises, and the state agent jumped out of the car to assist the driver. I jumped out also. By the time I got to the rear of the car, the man had been pushed down on the trunk by the driver, who had one hand on the man's throat and the other on his arm, pinning him down. In the meantime, the state agent had grabbed the other arm and was trying to extract something from the man's mouth.

What had happened was this: the man had made what the policeman later described as a "furtive" movement. A known addict, he was, to the officer's trained eyes, trying to dispose of an item of incriminating evidence that the policeman thought the suspect had dropped onto the pavement. When approached, however, the suspect turned around and backed off to the police car, with his left hand closed. The officer asked the man to open his fist. Instead, the man quickly brought his hand to his mouth, popped a marihuana cigarette into it, and tried to swallow. The policeman immediately grabbed the man's throat to cut off his air supply, and prevent him from swallowing. Incredibly, the suspect was able to swallow the cigarette despite the choking administered by the policeman.[22]

Even if the suspect had not managed to swallow the "joint," however, it might have been difficult for the policeman to have convinced a magistrate that "reasonable cause" was present for an arrest and incidental search. As the policeman said:

> It's awfully hard to explain to a judge what I mean when I testify that I saw a furtive movement. I'm glad you were along to see this because you can see what we're up against. . . . I can testify as to the character of the neighborhood, my knowledge that the man was an addict and all that stuff, but what I mean is that when I see a hype move the way that guy moved, I *know* he's trying to get rid of something. [Emphasis supplied by the speaker.]

I asked the policeman if he had ever been wrong in this kind of judgment and he replied that he had, but felt that he was right often enough to justify a search, even when lacking evidence to arrest the suspect.

Thus, as a matter of principle, the police would like to have greater freedom to make searches *not* "incident" to an arrest. That is, they would like to be able to search first and then arrest on the basis of incriminating evidence disclosed by the search. Generally, however, constitutional interpretation has not accorded this liberty to the police:

> In the law of arrest and by long constitutional history, "reasonable" has been interpreted as the equivalent of probable cause. An officer acts reason-

---

[22] It is worth noting that the choking of this man was the only instance of so-called police "brutality" I ever witnessed, although it should also be noted that the possible use of physical force by police is an important *structural* factor, one which the suspect must take into account regardless of its low frequency. Had I not been along, the man might have been handled more roughly after the arrest. I cannot say. An important point, however, is that the man's behavior was interpreted as *disrespectful*. As one officer said to him, while he was being questioned at the stationhouse (and complaining of the choking), "Goddammit, you'd better learn that when an officer of the law tells you to open up your mouth and spit out what you've got in there, you'd better open up."

ably if, on the facts before him, it would appear that the suspect has probably committed a specific crime. This is the context in which the word is used in the fourth amendment and in most state arrest laws. Our cases sharply distinguish the reasonableness of an arrest on probable cause from unreasonable apprehension grounded on "mere" suspicion.[23]

Understandably, the police oppose the continuation of such a "strict" interpretation of the Constitution. They claim to have special skills enabling them to detect criminal activity, or its potential, and thus the privilege of prior search would not be abused. In addition, police and their spokesmen typically argue that a judicial standard based on the reasonableness of the search would not only *not* interfere with the rights of the average citizen, but would, on the positive side, protect him against the ravages of criminal behavior. Thus, one leading opponent of the exclusionary rule takes the position that the " ' turn 'em loose' court decisions" placing limitations on the right of police to search and seize have had the effect of "actually facilitating" the activities of "the criminal element" and asserts that these decisions have caused some of the increase in crime over the ten-year period starting in 1950.[24] While admitting that "in any democratic society police efficiency must necessarily incur a considerable measure of sacrifice in deference to the rights and liberties of the individual," this same critic contends that "some sacrifice of individual rights and liberties has to be made in order to achieve and maintain a safe, stable society in which the individual may exercise those rights and liberties."[25]

The validity of the argument that the rights of the average citizen would be enhanced by a judicial standard of reasonableness of search and seizure varies, however, with the type of citizen about whom one is expressing concern. One of the unanticipated consequences of the policeman's standard of "reasonableness" is that it adversely affects many honest citizens living in high-crime areas. To a degree, all persons residing in such areas are "symbolic assailants." A "symbolic assailant," the

[23] Caleb Foote, "The Fourth Amendment: Obstacle or Necessity in the Law of Arrest?" in Sowle (ed.), *op. cit.*, p. 29.

[24] Fred E. Inbau, "Public Safety v. Individual Civil Liberties: The Prosecutor's Stand," *Journal of Criminal Law, Criminology and Police Science*, 53 (March, 1962), 86.

[25] Inbau, "More About Public Safety v. Individual Civil Liberties," *ibid.*, 53 (September, 1962), 329. Other presentations of the law enforcement point of view regarding arrests and the exclusionary rule are made by Rex Collings, *op. cit.*; Frank J. McGarr, "The Exclusionary Rule: An Ill Conceived and Ineffective Remedy," in Sowle (ed.), *op. cit.*, pp. 99–103; O. W. Wilson, "Police Arrest Privileges in a Free Society: A Plea for Modernization," *ibid.*, pp. 21–28; and Chief William Parker, *Parker on Police* (Springfield: Charles C Thomas, 1957), pp. 113–123 *et passim*.

reader will recall, need not in fact be a criminal, but needs merely to conform to the stereotype. By this standard, Negroes who live in black ghettoes are especially prone to being searched according to a "reasonableness of the search" [26] standard. Furthermore, given the cognitive disposition of the police described earlier, they tend to polarize the population between respectable people and criminals—who, in their eyes, may include otherwise respectable citizens not conforming to the policeman's portrait of respectability, as, for instance, bearded college students.

The most serious difficulty with the "reasonableness of the search" standard for police conduct—indeed, with "reasonableness" in general as a justifying norm for official behavior—applies to all judgments made on a probability basis. If an honest citizen resides in a neighborhood heavily populated by criminals, just as the chances are high that he might be one, so too are the chances high that he might be mistaken for one. The probabilities, from the point of view of the individual, are always the same—either he is or is not culpable. Thus, behavior which seems "reasonable" to the police because of the character of the neighborhood is seen by the honest citizen in it as irresponsible and unreasonable. About *him*, more errors will necessarily be made under a "reasonableness" standard. Indeed, the fewer the honest citizens in such an area, the more the police will be perceived by them as "brutal," "offensive," "unreasonable"; and justifiably so, because the chances are in fact greater that the police will treat honest citizens as criminals. It would also seem to follow that, to the extent the police treat honest citizens living in high-crime areas as criminals, the police inadvertently encourage them to take on the behavior patterns of their more criminal neighbors. For them, the inevitable message is the futility of honesty.[27] Whether police behavior is or is not truly "reasonable" depends on who is judging it: the police doing their job in a high-crime zone, or the honest citizen living in such an area.

In a private communication, Professor Edward Barrett commented upon this section of the manuscript as follows:

The central legal notion is that official interference with person or property should be discriminate. . . . Inherent in the notion (and inevitable in any enforcement process) is the fact that innocent persons will from time to

---

[26] Barrett, *op. cit.*, 15.

[27] On the point of "secondary deviance" which this discussion raises, see Edwin Lemert, *Social Pathology* (New York: McGraw-Hill, 1951), pp. 75–76. "When a person begins to employ his deviant behavior or a role based upon it as a means of defense, attack, or adjustment to the overt and covert problems created by the consequent societal reaction to him, his deviation is secondary."

time be subjected to the process. Is the problem significantly different when it is the innocent person in the high crime area and the innocent person in another area who meets a description or who is carrying a bundle late at night? I suppose the difference mainly is, as you point out, the likelihood that the same innocent person will be subjected to frequent police contacts because he is usually in the suspicious area. And he may not be free for a variety of reasons to move out of the area. But still what is the solution? Does not a furtive movement in one part of town constitute probable cause where the same movement would not in another? Would not police reaction in one part of town be discriminate and in another indiscriminate? Can we afford to structure the system to protect persons living in ambiguous situations?

These pointed and practical questions illuminate the difficulties of reform of criminal procedural rules. All too often writers on the subject fail to give sufficient consideration to the simple notion that legal practices must have a differential impact in a stratified and racially constructed society. As we see here, the negative consequences of the norm of reasonableness are intensified in the highest-crime areas, which also tend to be the most highly "ghettoized."

POLICE CULTURE AND LEGAL RULES

Arguments about legal standards are usually unrealistic, whether they come from civil liberties advocates or law enforcement spokesmen. Each group assumes the behavioral efficacy of legally formulated restraints. The civil libertarian typically feels that tighter strictures ought to be placed on police, and that if they were, police would feel obliged to conform. The law enforcement spokesman makes a matching behavioral assumption when he argues that restraints on police behavior are already too severe. My observations suggest, in contrast to both these positions, that norms located within police organization are more powerful than court decisions in shaping police behavior, and that actually the process of interaction between the two accounts ultimately for how police behave.[28] This interpretation does not deny that legal rules have an effect, but it suggests that the language of courts is given meaning through a process mediated by the organizational structure and perspectives of the

---

[28] Arthur L. Stinchcombe, "Institutions of Privacy in the Determination of Police Administrative Practice," *American Journal of Sociology*, **69** (September, 1963), 18. As Stinchcombe puts it, "Presumably there is a long chain of events on a large scale, structuring rewards and constraints in police practice . . . with respect to the norms established and continually enforced in a few court cases."

police. In the following paragraphs, I intend briefly to analyze aspects of the policeman's situation shaping the process by which he develops a set of behaviors and attitudes about the exclusionary rule.

It is instructive to begin this discussion by considering a situation where a narcotics officer observes a known addict make a subtle body movement, indicating to the policeman that the man is carrying some narcotic or drug in violation of a law forbidding the possession of narcotics. The policeman would prefer to have any seizure he makes be accepted as evidence in court under the exclusionary rule. Whether it is or not, however, will not determine his decision to search the suspect. His reasons for selecting arrest criteria are numerous.

Above all, the policeman sees his job as ferreting out crime. The idea that the policeman should be "alert," "vigilant," "on his toes" to the possibility of crime seems the fundamental craft requirement of the policeman. He may try later to figure out what the suspect did which might have justified a search. But the policeman would ordinarily feel embarrassed to report to a superior or to a colleague, for example, that he had hesitated to search an addict on the street because he had first to meditate upon the addict's legal rights, and that, because of his hesitation, the addict had in the meantime escaped, or had disposed of the incriminating evidence. It is part of the policeman's job to locate and confiscate illegal substances. Thus, even if a search revealing possession of an unlawful weapon or an unlawful narcotic was conducted not as "incident" to an arrest, the policeman would have done part of his job simply through the act of retrieval. By failing to make the putatively "unreasonable" search, the policeman would not only have failed to gain a conviction, but would also have missed collecting objects or substances regarded as dangerous. In the policeman's view, only good can come of a search legally defined as "unreasonable," provided the search jibes with the normative assumptions of the police organization about reasonableness.

Arthur Train, writing in an earlier part of the century, implies that police rules have long been conflicting and confusing, and sympathizes with the dilemma faced by the policeman.

It is easy while sitting on the piazza with your cigar to recognize the rights of your fellow-men, you may assert most vigorously the right of the citizen to immunity from arrest without legal cause, but if you saw a seedy character sneaking down a side street at three o'clock in the morning, his pockets bulging with jewelry and silver—! Would you have the policeman on post insist on the fact that a burglary had been committed being established beyond peradventure before arresting the suspect, who in the meantime would undoubtedly escape? Of course, the worthy officer sometimes does this, but his conduct in that case becomes the subject of an investigation on the part of his superiors. In fact, the rules of the New York police department require him to arrest all persons carrying bags in the small hours who cannot give a satisfactory account of themselves. Yet there is no such thing under the laws of the state as a right "to arrest on suspicion." No citizen may be arrested under the statutes unless a crime has actually been committed. Thus, the police regulations deliberately compel every officer either to violate the law or to be made the object of charges for dereliction of duty. A confusing state of things, truly, to a man who wants to do his duty by himself and by his fellow-citizens![29]

Of course, a policeman cannot walk up to a man in broad daylight and demand that he stand facing a wall with hands raised, simply because the policeman has decided that to search every tenth citizen on Main Street would be an effective mode of enforcing criminal law. But if a policeman can give some reason to his *organizational superiors* (including the district attorney) for conducting a search, in practice the worst punishment he can suffer is loss of a conviction. If a search yields no incriminating evidence, those who are illegally searched are usually pleased to drop the matter.

On the other hand, if something is found, the moral burden immediately shifts to the suspect. The illegality of a search is likely to be tempered—even in the eyes of the judiciary—by the discovery of incriminating evidence on the suspect. For example, when a suspect turns out actually to possess narcotics, the perception of surrounding facts and circumstances about the reasonableness of the arrest can shift in only one direction—against the defendant and in favor of the propriety of the search—even if the facts might have appeared differently had no incriminating evidence been discovered.

The case of *Ker* v. *California* [30] offers an interesting illustration of the tendency to affirm what is later found to be correct. In this case, reasonable cause was not at issue, but the affirmative tendency is expressed in a related area. The salient facts are: an informer's tip, plus some police observations, connected Ker with specific illegal activities involving a known marihuana seller named Murphy. Police officers observed Ker and Murphy conversing, but the officers could not tell whether anything had been exchanged between them. As Ker drove away, however, they recorded his license plate numbers. A check with the Department of Motor Vehicles revealed Ker's address. Officers were dispatched to his

[29] Arthur Train, *Courts and Criminals* (New York: Charles Scribner's Sons, 1921), pp. 6–7.
[30] 374 U.S. 23 (1963).

residence. "They then went to the office of the building manager and obtained from him a pass key to the apartment. Officer Berman unlocked and opened the door, proceeding quietly, he testified, in order to prevent the destruction of evidence, and found petitioner George Ker sitting in the living room."

The means of entry was upheld, by a 5-4 decision of the court. The dissenters (Mr. Justice Brennan, the Chief Justice, Mr. Justice Douglas, Mr. Justice Goldberg) argued:

Even if probable cause exists for the arrest of a person within, the Fourth Amendment is violated by an unannounced police intrusion into a private home, with or without an arrest warrant, except (1) where the persons within already know of the officers' authority and purposes or (2) where the officers are justified in the belief that persons within are in imminent peril of bodily harm, or (3) where those within, made aware of the presence of someone outside (because, for example, there has been a knock at the door) are then engaged in activity which justifies the officers in the belief that an escape or the destruction of evidence is being attempted.[31]

The dissenters' objections were answered by Mr. Justice Clark's opinion for the court, as follows:

Here justification for the officer's failure to give notice is uniquely present. In addition to the officer's belief that Ker was in possession of narcotics, which could be quickly and easily destroyed, Ker's further furtive conduct in eluding them shortly before the arrest was ground for belief that he might well have been expecting the police. We therefore hold that in the particular circumstances of this case the officer's method of entry, sanctioned by the law of California, was not unreasonable under the standards of the Fourth Amendment as applied to the States through the Fourteenth Amendment.[32]

If one looks at the world primarily through practical lenses, the exclusionary rule is difficult to defend, since it frequently denies the introduction of what would otherwise constitute perfectly acceptable evidence. In my opinion the *Ker* case may also be read as an illustration of the persuasiveness of factual guilt and administrative efficiency over the principle of excluding illegally obtained evidence. I do not doubt the "principled" intentions or moral character of the majority of the Supreme Court. Nevertheless, the language used may be interpreted as a general tendency to give weight to fact, irrespective of how it has been obtained. Thus, I am suggesting that the court itself might have voted differently in a laboratory situation that held all the preceding circumstances constant, but which showed the marihuana not to be present.

[31] 374 U.S. 23, 40–41.
[32] 374 U.S. 23, 47.

If such tendencies are present in the court, they are even more pronounced early in the case, where the police are involved. Here, the onus typically shifts to the suspect if he is found to have incriminating evidence in his possession. The policeman has an upper hand under such conditions, even when his legal position is questionable. Especially in the "small pinch," the policeman is not usually interested in arresting the man with a "joint" or two of marihuana, but in using him to "turn" his supplier. In that situation, the exclusionary rule may not appear salient to the defendant.

That incriminating evidence is found is a fact not lost on the defense attorney, either. For him, too, operating in a context of "reasonableness," as understood in the administrative sense, the defendant comes to represent a less defensible client. The attorney may decide to fight the case energetically on a search-and-seizure point, and he may even win an acquittal for his client. In the routine minor case, however, evidence may influence the defense attorney to persuade his client to plead guilty. This tendency is pronounced when, as so often happens, the reasonableness of the arrest is a borderline judgment. Under such circumstances, the case will not go to trial, and the exclusionary rule issue will consequently not be invoked.

The worst that can happen to the individual policeman for an illegal search is loss of a conviction as a result of the exclusionary rule. Superiors within the police organization will, however, be in sympathy with an officer, provided the search was administratively reasonable, even if the officer did not have legal "reasonable" cause to make an arrest. The officers who searched Archie's room, for instance, would certainly not have been prosecuted by the Westville district attorney for trespassing, had they been caught. Besides, as discussed above, Archie would never have made a complaint against the police because he is an addict. Moreover, civil suits for false arrest are difficult to prove.[33]

Finally, the case of *Ker v. California* illustrates that the problematic character of legality encourages the police to test the meaning of due process of law. Suppose, for instance, we were to try to construct a model entirely in consonance with the rule of law for the conduct of a police force. Surely, if this were to be a practical model, we would have to take into account the latitude afforded the police by *Ker v. California*. There are presently any number of practices utilized by the police that a dedicated civil libertarian would not regard as conforming to the rule of law. On the other hand, it would not be at all unreasonable for law enforce-

[33] Caleb Foote, "Tort Remedies for Police Violations of Individual Rights," *Minnesota Law Review*, 39 (1955), 493.

ment officials to feel, as regards these same practices, that "justification . . . is uniquely present," to cite the words of Mr. Justice Clark. Thus, every court ruling based upon the practical needs of the police as a working organization tends to reinforce—in the sense of the term as used by experimental psychologists—the tendency to continue every questionable practice that can be justified in the name of expediency, unless expressly forbidden.

Consequently, all these reasons—the norm of police alertness; the requirement that police confiscate illegal substances; the tendency toward a presumption of the legality of the search once the illegal substance is found; the fact that in a "small pinch" the policeman is usually not interested in an arrest but in creating an informant; the fact that the defense will be impressed by the presence of incriminating evidence; the sympathy of police superiors so long as policemen act in conformity with administrative norms of police organization; the difficulty of proving civil suits for false arrest; the denial of fact by the exclusionary rule; and the problematic character of what behavior is permitted when justification may appear to a court to be "uniquely present"—militate against the effectiveness of the exclusionary rule. In short, the norms of the police are fundamentally pragmatic. Since the policeman has everything to gain and little to lose when he uses the "reasonableness of the search and seizure" standard in small cases, he does so, even though this is not the prevailing legal standard.

To make these observations, however, is not to deny the possible effectiveness of sanctions on police behavior as a way of insuring compliance with procedural rules. *I do not wish to be understood as implying that the legal structure under which the police work has no effect, but rather as stating the conditions under which its effects may be perceived.* The policeman is more likely to take seriously the more rigorous standard—"search incident to an arrest"—the better the anticipated pinch. Or, put another way, the exclusionary principle puts pressure on the police to work within the rules in those cases where prosecution is contemplated.

At the beginning of a case, or in general patrolling activities, police are only slightly deterred by the prospect of loss of a conviction, because they are still exploring. Thus, the police thought it "reasonable" to search Archie's room beforehand even though the search was illegal, partly because they really had little to lose at that point. Similarly, they have little hesitancy about "frisking" a suspect against whom they have no reasonable cause to make an arrest. Once their explorations have borne fruit, however, they are apt to pay greater attention to the formalities of the rules of search and seizure. When these explorations indicate that a "big case" is in the making, then conditions have been provided under which court injunctions can be taken most seriously. The big case affords time to establish probable cause, to obtain a warrant, and most important, to use a police-informant rather than an addict-informant whose criminal status needs to be protected. Thus, the rule seems to control police almost in direct relation to the gravity of the crime of the suspect.[34]

POLICE ATTITUDES TOWARD THE JUDICIARY

The practical concerns of police do not enter the thinking of the judiciary on the problem of how policemen should act in carrying out their duties. This is not because the policeman's domain of concerns is wider than that of the judge, but rather because their concerns are different, although somewhat overlapping. The police, for example, perceive such informal arrangements as the informer system as necessities if they are to perform their duties adequately. Judges do not—and cannot without abdicating responsibility to evaluate the policeman's work— take such arrangements into full account. The policeman and the judge consequently measure the quality of the policeman's work against inharmonious standards derived from the different responsibilities of each. Or, stated another way, while the policeman and the judge are part of the same *system*, they are not connected with the same organizations.

One often hears policemen criticizing the "reasonableness" and "intelligence" of judges, sometimes expressing wonderment at how such wrongheaded men could rise to high positions of authority. Implicitly, and sometimes explicitly, there is an invidious contrast drawn between the supervisory policeman, for instance, the captain or chief, and the judge. When the supervisory policeman, however, evaluates the patrolman's behavior toward a suspect, his frame of reference encompasses all the obligations a policeman has. Indeed, the supervisory policeman may be a more severe taskmaster than the judge. The judge may care only whether the policeman complies with the law of arrest and confession, while supervisory law enforcers are likely to be concerned that the po-

[34] It would be interesting to observe the operation of the rule within a police force where corruption prevailed. Against such a background, the exclusionary rule is helpless to improve the performance of police. Indeed, I have heard it alleged that the exclusionary rule has been used as a means of sustaining a corrupt system. In such instances, police arrest their collaborators in ways which violate rules of search and seizure, thereby effectively barring prosecution. At the same time, an appearance of zealous law enforcement can be maintained.

liceman "shape up" in a number of behavioral and attitudinal sectors —his ability to cooperate with his associates, his punctuality, his discipline within the organization, and his physical presentability. Thus, the greater "understanding" that the officer may attribute to the supervisor can be located in the similarity between the supervisory policeman's frame of reference about the arresting process, and the arresting officer's. Consequently, the supervisory policeman is able to temper demands in one area of police behavior with an understanding of the arresting officer's obligations in another, for example, his commitment to the informer system. By contrast, the judge need not find it a necessary part of his job to inquire into the consequences of his ruling for police organization and efficiency.

Pleased by the understanding shown by their superiors, policemen generally find it hard to understand why a judge should have so much "say" over their work, especially as supervisory policemen become increasingly "professional." What law enforcement personnel neglect to take into account, however, is not only the obligations of judges to a wider community of interests than the police; they also fail to analyze further consequences. Suppose supervisory police were to be given greater authority. At least in the police force studied, the principal effect might be reduction of cohesion and morale in the police organization itself.

Supervisory police are already attentive to opinions expressed by the general community. Like administrators of various large organizations, including some universities, their inclination is to mollify the concerns of various interests in the larger community, while turning a relatively deaf ear to the constituency over which they wield authority. A student spokesman at the University of California "free speech" crisis expressed a general problem of large-scale organizations when he said: "They (the administrators) haven't been interested in finding out what we want—they care only about what they can give to keep us quiet." The same sort of problem is heightened in large police departments, where the norms of military-like obedience camouflage resentments which might otherwise be publicly expressed. Thus, if supervisory police were, for instance, to rule on warrants and probable cause, they would be in the position of sometimes having to invoke a wider perspective and rule against the behavior of their own men. At the same time, they would also be in the position of supporting the same behaviors in their role as leaders of the agency. Either they would begin to take on the perspective of the judge, in which case police demands might remain unsatisfied; or they would maintain the police perspective. If so, the police would be a self-regulating agency, there being in the *system* no provision for a position esteeming legality over agency requirements. This presently seems to be the situation desired by police officials.

SUMMARY AND CONCLUSION

This chapter has attempted to indicate how the enforcement of morals through law affects the capacity of the police to operate within the constraints contemplated by the rule of law. By criminalizing the environment, such laws incline the police to a more rigid conception of order which heightens both the perception and presence of danger in the environment. They also are associated with the development of a criminal underworld that may lead to corruption or a tendency toward zealous law enforcement. In such cases an "operational code" develops that is antagonistic to the principles of due process of law. Given the task of enforcing "unenforceable laws," it is not surprising to find police demanding working conditions from the courts to lighten their burden, and if, as is presently the trend, heavier restrictions are placed upon the police, they may well ignore these or grow even more hostile toward due process principles in their attempt to enforce legal morality. Such observations demonstrate some of the difficulties created for the police as a working organization by the attempt to achieve moral consensus in a heterogeneous society through criminal punishment. The ineffectiveness of this means as an instrument for achieving social cohesion is, of course, ultimately belied by the very term, "unenforceable law."

Major attention was concentrated upon analyzing the process by which legal controls—in this case, the exclusionary rule—are neutralized in the context of police work. The impact of the exclusionary rule, as the police view it, has not been to guarantee greater protection of the freedom of "decent citizens" from unreasonable police zeal, but rather to complicate unnecessarily the task of detecting and apprehending criminals. From the pragmatic perspective of the police, the right to conduct exploratory investigations and searches ought largely to be a matter of police-supervisory discretion. Because he is enmeshed in a network of professional responsibilities and values not shared by judges, the policeman fails to respond to judicial interpretations of legality. Instead, his allegiance is to police organization and its evaluative standards. Since police organization interprets its fundamental duty as discovery of criminal activity or its potential, yet finds its endeavors contingent on a secondary obligation to remain within the boundaries of legality, the policeman responds by attempting to infuse the character of legality—perhaps after the fact—into his actions. In this effort, he makes use of his authoritative appearance, the generally inferior—criminal—status of his suspects, his relations with other officials such as probation officers, the wide interpretation he is allowed to give to· legal concepts such as "furtive movement," and the incriminating effect of illegally seized substances and objects his investigations sometimes reveal.

Since in the policeman's hierarchy of values, arrest and subsequent conviction are more important the "bigger" the "pinch," compliance with the exclusionary rule seems contingent upon this factor. Its effectiveness also increases once detection activities have turned up substantial evidence of crime. The effects of the exclusionary rule and, in general, judicial controls over police behavior are, therefore, best understood when examined through the filter of police culture. This culture sees the procedural rule as something to be observed rather than obeyed; it is an unpleasant fact of life, but not a morally persuasive condition. The policeman, as a tactical matter, recognizes an obligation to appear to be obeying the letter of procedural law, while often disregarding its spirit. Thus, the working philosophy of the police has the end justifying the means; according to this philosophy, the demands of apprehension require violation of procedural rules in the name of the "higher" justification of reducing criminality.

When an appellate court rules that police may not in the future engage in certain enforcement activities, since these constitute a violation of the rule of law, the inclination of the police is typically not to feel *shame* but *indignation*. This response may be especially characteristic of "professional" police, who feel a special competence to decide, on their own, how to reduce criminality in the community. The police, for example, recognize the court's power to bar admission of illegally seized evidence if the police are discovered to have violated the constitutional rights of the defendant. They do not, however, feel morally blameworthy at having done so; nor do they even accept such injunctions with good grace and go about their business. On the contrary, the police typically view the court with hostility for having interfered with their capacities to practice their craft. Police tend to rest their *moral* position on the argument that the "independence" and social distance of the appellate judiciary constitutes a type of government—by the courts— without the consent of the governed—the police. Thus, the police see the court's affirmation of principles of due process as, in effect, the creation of harsh "working conditions." From their point of view, the courts are failing to affirm democratic notions of the autonomy and freedom of the "worker." Their political superiors insist on "production" while their judicial superiors impede their capacity to "produce." Under such frustrating conditions, the appellate judiciary inevitably comes to be seen as "traitor" to its responsibility to keep the community free from criminality.

Antagonism between the police and the judiciary is perhaps an inevitable outcome, therefore, of the different interests residing in the police as a specialized agency and the judiciary as a representative of wider community interests. Constitutional guarantees of due process of law do make the working life and conditions of the police more difficult. But if such guarantees did not exist, the police would of course engage in activities promoting self-serving ends, as does any agency when offered such freedom in a situation of conflicting goals. Every administrative agency tends to support policies permitting it to present itself favorably. Regulative bodies restricting such policies are inevitably viewed with hostility by the regulated. Indeed, when some hostility does not exist, the regulators may be assumed to have been "captured" by the regulated. If the police could, in this sense, "capture" the judiciary, the resulting system would truly be suggestive of a "police state."

Chapter 11

The Working Policeman,
Police "Professionalism,"
and the Rule of Law

THE traditional concern of criminology and of writers on "social control" is the maintenance of order in society. This study suggests that such a view is limited both philosophically and sociologically. "Social control" must deal not merely with the maintenance of order, but with the quality of the order that a given system is capable of sustaining and the procedures appropriate to the achievement of such order. Thus, a given set of social and legal conditions may lead to order in a stable democracy but not in a stable totalitarianism. Meaningful sociological analysis of order cannot, therefore, be value-free, because such a posture falsely assumes the equivalence of all types of order.

This research rejects the "value-free" approach, and concentrates instead upon the social foundations of legal procedures designed to protect democratic order. In the workings of democratic society, where the highest stated commitment is to the ideal of legality, a focal point of tension exists between the substance of order and the procedures for its accomplishment. "The basic and anguishing dilemma of form and substance in law can be alleviated, but never resolved, for the structure of legal domination retains its distinguishing features only as long as this dilemma is perpetuated." [1] This dilemma is most clearly manifested in law enforcement organizations, where both sets of demands make forceful normative claims upon police conduct.

In addition to this fundamental dilemma, there are further complications. Neither form nor substance, law nor order, is an entirely clear conception; and what it means for police to use law to enforce order is also somewhat problematic. The empirical portion of this study looked

[1] Reinhard Bendix, *Nation-Building and Citizenship* (New York: John Wiley and Sons, 1964), p. 112.

into the question of how the police themselves conceive the meaning of "law" and "order" to find out how these conceptions develop and are implemented in police practices. Social conditions in the varying assignments of police heightened or diminished the conflict between the obligations of maintaining order and observing the rule of law.

This chapter considers the implications of the research. First we summarize findings about these issues and suggest that the dilemma of the police in democratic society arises out of the conflict between the extent of initiative contemplated by nontotalitarian norms of work and restraints upon police demanded by the rule of law. Second, we consider the meaning of police professionalization, pointing out its limitations according to the idea of managerial efficiency. Finally, we discuss how the policeman's conception of himself as a craftsman is rooted in community expectations, and how the ideology of police professionalization is linked to these expectations. Thus, this chapter focuses upon the relation between the policeman's conception of his work and his capacity to contribute to the development of a society based upon the rule of law as its master ideal.

OCCUPATIONAL ENVIRONMENT AND THE RULE OF LAW

Five features of the policeman's occupational environment weaken the conception of the rule of law as a primary objective of police conduct. One is the social psychology of police work, that is, the relation between occupational environment, working personality, and the rule of law. Second is the policeman's stake in maintaining his position of authority, especially his interest in bolstering accepted patterns of enforcement. Third is police socialization, especially as it influences the policeman's administrative bias. A related factor is the pressure put upon individual policemen to "produce"—to be efficient rather than legal when the two norms are in conflict. Finally, there is the policeman's opportunity to behave inconsistently with the rule of law as a result of the low visibility of much of his conduct.

Although it is difficult to weigh the relative import of these factors, they all seem analytically to be joined to the conception of policeman as *craftsman* rather than as *legal actor*, as a skilled worker rather than as a civil servant obliged to subscribe to the rule of law. The significance of the conception of the policeman as a craftsman derives from the differences in ideology of work and authority in totalitarian and nontotalitarian societies. Reinhard Bendix has contended that the most important difference between totalitarian and nontotalitarian forms of subordination is to be found in the managerial handling of problems of authority and subordination.[2]

Subordinates in totalitarian society are offered little opportunity to introduce new means of achieving the goals of the organization, since subordination implies obedience rather than initiative. As Bendix says, ". . . managerial refusal to accept the tacit evasion of rules and norms or the uncontrolled exercise of judgment is related to a specific type of bureaucratization which constitutes the fundamental principle of totalitarian government." [3] By contrast, in non-totalitarian society, subordinates are encouraged to introduce their own strategies and ideas into the working situation. Bendix does not look upon rule violation or evasion as necessarily subverting the foundations of bureaucratic organization, but rather sees these innovations as "strategies of independence" by which the employees "seek to modify the implementation of the rules as their personal interests and their commitment (or lack of commitment) to the goals of the organization dictate." [4] In brief, the managerial ideology of nontotalitarian society maximizes the exercise of discretion by subordinates, while totalitarian society minimizes innovation by working officials.[5]

This dilemma of democratic theory manifests itself in every aspect of the policeman's work, as evidenced by the findings of this study. In explaining the development of the policeman's "working personality," the dangerous and authoritative elements of police work were emphasized. The combination of these elements undermines attachment to the rule of law in the context of a "constant" pressure to produce. Under such pressure, the variables of danger and authority tend to alienate the policeman from the general public, and at the same time to heighten his perception of symbols portending danger to him and to the community. Under the same pressure to produce, the policeman not only perceives possible criminality according to the symbolic status of the suspect; he also develops a stake in organized patterns of enforcement. To the extent that a suspect is seen as interfering with such arrangements, the

[2] See his *Work and Authority in Industry* (New York: Harper Torchbook, 1963); and *Nation-Building and Citizenship* (New York: John Wiley and Sons, 1964).

[3] *Work and Authority*, p. 446.

[4] *Ibid.*, p. 445.

[5] There is, perhaps, some ambiguity in this posing of the situation of the worker in totalitarian society. Police in a totalitarian society may have the opportunity to exercise a great deal of "initiative." See Simon Wolin and Robert M. Slusser (eds.), *The Soviet Secret Police* (New York: Frederick A. Praeger, 1957), *passim*; and Jacques Delarue, *The Gestapo* (trans. Mervyn Sevill) (New York: William Morrow and Company, 1964), *passim*.

policeman will respond negatively to him. On the other hand, the "cooperative" suspect, that is, one who contributes to the smooth operation of the enforcement pattern, will be rewarded. Accordingly, a detailed investigation was made of exchange relations between police and informers, in part to ascertain how informers are differentially treated according to the. extent to which they support enforcement patterns, and partly to analyze how the policeman creates and uses the resources given to him.

In attempting to enrich his exchange position, the policeman necessarily involves the prosecutor in supporting his enforcement needs. The prosecutor, of course, also has a stake in the policeman's work performance, since the policeman provides him with the raw materials of prosecutorial achievement. Our observations suggested, however, that although he is ultimately the policeman's spokesman, the prosecutor performs a quasi-magisterial function by conveying a conception of legality to the policeman.

Most interesting, of course, is the basis on which the prosecutor's greater attachment to legality rests. We may point here to pertinent differences between policeman and prosecutor. One, of course, has to do with socialization. The prosecutor is a product of a law school, with larger understanding and appreciation of the judiciary and its restraints, especially constitutional ones. The policeman, on the other hand, generally has less formal education, less legal training, and a sense of belonging to a different sort of organization. Such differences in background go far to explain the development of the policeman's conception of self as a craftsman, coupled with a guildlike affirmation of worker autonomy. The policeman views himself as a specialist in criminological investigation, and does not react indifferently either to having his conclusions challenged by a distant judiciary or to having "obstacles" placed in his administrative path. He therefore views the judiciary, especially the appellate courts, as saboteurs of his capacity to satisfy what he sees as the requirements of social order. Each appellate decision limiting police initiative comes to be defined as a "handcuffing" of law enforcement, and may unintentionally sever further the policeman's attachment to the rule of law as an overriding value. In addition, the policeman is offended by judicial assumptions running contrary to probabilistic fact —the notion of due process of law staunchly maintains a rebuttable presumption of innocence in the face of the policeman's everyday experience of an administrative presumption of regularity.

Although the prosecutor is legally accorded a wider area of discretion than the policeman, the setting of the policeman's role offers greater opportunity to behave inconsistently with the rule of law. Police discretion is "hidden" insofar as the policeman often makes decisions in direct interaction with the suspect. The prosecutor typically serves at most as advisor to these dealings. Whether it is a question of writing out a traffic citation, of arresting a spouse on a charge of "assault with a deadly weapon," or of apprehending an addict informer, the policeman has enormous power; he may halt the legal process right there. Such discretionary activity is difficult to observe. By contrast, prosecutorial discretion frequently takes place at a later stage in the system, after the initial charge has been made public. The public character of the charge may restrict the prosecutor's discretion in practice more than the policeman's, even though the scope of the prosecutor's discretion is far wider in theory.

Internal controls over policeman reinforce the importance of administrative and craft values over civil libertarian values. These controls are more likely to emphasize efficiency as a goal rather than legality, or, more precisely, legality as a means to the end of efficiency. Two analyses were made along these lines. One was of the clearance rate as an internal control process. Here it was suggested that the policeman operates according to his most concrete and specific understanding of the control system, and that the clearance rate control system emphasizes measures stressing the detective's ability to "solve" crimes. It was further shown how it is possible for this control system to reverse the penalty structure associated with substantive criminal law by rewarding those evidencing a high degree of criminality. Thus, persons with greater criminal experience are frequently better "equipped" to contribute to the "solution" of crimes, thereby enhancing the policeman's appearance as a competent craftsman. The introduction of this control system into police work was analyzed to illustrate a response to the difficulties experienced by organizations that produce a fundamentally intangible service, or at least where "output" is subject to a variety of interpretations. Such an organization requires internal measures of the competence of employees, plus a set of measures (which may be the same) for assessment by outside evaluators.

The dilemma of democratic society requiring the police to maintain order and at the same time to be accountable to the rule of law is thus further complicated. Not only is the rule of law often incompatible with the maintenance of order but the principles by which police are governed by the rule of law in a democratic society may be antagonistic to the ideology of worker initiative associated with a nontotalitarian philosophy of work. In the same society, the ideal of legality rejects discretionary innovation by police, while the ideal of worker freedom and autonomy encourages such initiative. Bureaucratic rules are seen in a democracy as "enabling" regulations, while the regulations deriving from the rule of law are intended to constrain the conduct of officials.

The conflict between the democratic ideology of work and the legal philosophy of a democracy brings into focus the essential problem of the role of the police. The police are not simply "bad guys" or "good guys," authoritarians or heroes. Nor are they merely "men doing their jobs." They are legal officials whose tendencies to be arbitrary have roots in a conception of the freedom of the worker inhering in the nontotalitarian ideology of the relation between work and authority, a conception carried out in the context of police work. Seeing themselves as craftsmen, the police tend to conduct themselves according to the norms pertaining to a working bureaucracy in democratic society. Therefore, the more police tend to regard themselves as "workers" or "craftsmen," the more they demand a lack of constraint upon initiative. By contrast, *legal actors* are sympathetic toward the necessity for constraint and review.

PROFESSIONALISM AND POLICE CONDUCT

The idea of professionalism is often invoked as the solution to the conflict between the policeman's task of maintaining order and his accountability to the rule of law. The meaning of this idea, however, is by no means clear. In sociology, there have been two main traditions, one emphasizing professional ideals and values, the other stressing technical competence. In Durkheim's view, what is distinctive about the idea of "professional" groups is not merely that such groups have high status, or high skill, or a politically supported monopoly over certain kinds of work, or a distinctive structure of control over work—most important is an infusion of work and collective organization with moral values, plus the use of sanctions to insure that these moral values are upheld. Arguing against the laissez-faire doctrines of the classical economists, for example, Durkheim pleaded for the introduction of morality into economic life:

[W]hen we wish to see the guilds reorganized on a pattern we will presently try to define, it is not simply to have new codes superimposed on those existing; it is mainly so that economic activity should be permeated by ideas and needs other than individual ideas and needs . . . with the aim that the professions should become so many moral *milieu* and that these (comprising always the various organs of industrial and commercial life) should constantly foster the morality of the professions. As to the rules, although necessary and inevitable, they are but the outward expression of these fundamental principles. It is not a matter of co-ordinating any changes outwardly and mechanically, but of bringing men's minds into mutual understanding.[6]

An alternative concept of "professionalism" is associated with a managerial view emphasizing rationality, efficiency, and universalism. This view envisages the professional as a bureaucrat, almost as a machine calculating alternative courses of action by a stated program of rules, and possessing the technical ability to carry out decisions irrespective of personal feelings. As Weber says:

> Above all, bureaucratization offers the optimal possibility for the realization of the principle of division of labor in administration according to purely technical considerations, allocating individual tasks to functionaries who are trained as specialists and who continuously add to their experience by constant practice. "Professional" execution in this case means primarily execution "without regard to person" in accordance with calculable rules.[7]

In the effort to introduce fairness, calculability, and impersonality into an American administration of criminal justice that was often riddled with corruption and political favoritism, most writers who have seriously examined police have also tended to subscribe to reforms based upon the managerial conception of "professional." Reviewing the works of such police reformers as O. W. Wilson or William Parker, we find that the conception of "professional" emphasizes managerial efficiency based upon a body of "expert" knowledge. A recently completed volume by law professor Wayne LaFave contains a similar point of view. In his concluding chapter, LaFave advocates a conception of the police as an administrative agency, with, presumably, the presumptions of regulation associated with such "expertise." He writes:

> The development of police expertness should be encouraged, and its existence should be recognized when appropriate. . . . There is need, and ample precedent in other fields, for the development of methods of communicating the existence of police expertness to trial or appellate courts which are called upon to decide arrest issues. The relationship between the court and the economic regulatory agency might serve as a model in the absence of a more highly developed proposal.[8]

There are, however, costs in developing a professional code based upon the model of administrative efficiency. Such a conception of pro-

---

[6] Emile Durkheim, *Professional Ethics and Civic Morals* (trans. Cornelia Brookfield) (Glencoe: The Free Press, 1958), p. 29.

[7] *Max Weber on Law in Economy and Society* (ed. Max Rheinstein, trans. Max Rheinstein and Edward Shils), (Cambridge: Harvard University Press, 1954), p. 350.

[8] Wayne R. LaFave, Arrest: *The Decision to Take a Suspect into Custody* (Boston: Little, Brown and Company, 1965), pp. 512–513.

fessionalism not only fails to bridge the gap between the maintenance of order and the rule of law; in addition it comes to serve as an ideology undermining the capacity of police to be accountable to the rule of law. The idea of organization based on principles of administrative efficiency is often misunderstood by officials who are themselves responsible for administering such organizations. In practice, standardized rules and procedures are frequently molded to facilitate the tasks of acting officials. The materials of this study have clearly demonstrated that the policeman is an especially "nonmechanical" official. As Bruce Smith says:

> The policeman's art . . . consists in applying and enforcing a multitude of laws and ordinances in such degree or proportion and in such manner that the greatest degree of protection will be secured. The degree of enforcement and the method of application will vary with each neighborhood and community. There are no set rules, nor even general principles, to the policy to be applied. Each policeman must, in a sense, determine the standard to be set in the area for which he is responsible. Immediate superiors may be able to impress upon him some of the lessons of experience, but for the most part such experience must be his own. . . . Thus he is a policy-forming police administrator in miniature, who operates beyond the scope of the usual devices for control. . . .[9]

Smith may be making his point too strongly. Nevertheless, as a system of organization, bureaucracy can hope to achieve efficiency only by allowing officials to initiate their own means for solving specific problems that interfere with their capacity to achieve productive results. Some of these procedures may arise out of personal feelings—for example, relations between police and traffic violators—while others may become a routine part of the organizational structure. Examination of a procedural code, for example, would disclose no reference to the systematic use of informants. Given the task of enforcing crimes without citizen complaints, however, it becomes necessary for police to develop alternative methods to those used to apprehend violators in "standard" or "victimizing" crimes. These techniques of apprehension may demand considerable organization and skill on the part of the individual official, skill not so much in a formal administrative sense as in the sense of knowledge and ability to work within the effective limits of formal organization. As described, for example, the informer system requires so much ability that an aesthetic of execution has come to be associated

---

[9] Bruce Smith, *Police Systems in the United States* (New York: Harper and Brothers, 1960), p. 19.

with its use; it has become such an intrinsic component of police work that the abilities of the "professional" detective have come to be defined in terms of capacity to utilize this system.

As a bureaucratic organization, however, the police and governmental institutions, increasingly and generally, have a distinctive relationship to the development of the rule of law. The rule of law develops in response to the innovations introduced by officials to achieve organizational goals. It is certainly true, as Bendix asserts, that "A belief in legality means first and foremost that certain formal procedures must be obeyed if the enactment or execution of a law is to be considered legal." [10] At the same time, while legality may be seen as comprising a set of unchanging ideals, it may also be seen as a working normative system which develops in response to official conduct. The structure of authoritative regulations is such that legal superiors are not part of the same organization as officials and are expected to be "insensitive" to "productive capacity" as contrasted with legality. Thus, for example, a body of case law has been emerging that attempts to define the conditions and limits of the use of informants. Legality, therefore, develops as the other side of the coin of official innovation. As such, it is both a variable and an achievement. To the extent that police organizations operate mainly on grounds of administrative efficiency, the development of the rule of law is frustrated. Therefore, a conception of professionalism based mainly on satisfying the demands of administrative efficiency also hampers the capacity of the rule of law to develop.

The police are increasingly articulating a conception of professionalism based on a narrow view of managerial efficiency and organizational interest. A sociologist is not surprised at such a development. Under the rule of law it is not up to the agency of enforcement to generate the limitations governing its actions, and bureaucrats typically and understandably try to conceal the knowledge of their operations so that they may regulate themselves unless they are forced to make disclosures. But the police in a democracy are not merely bureaucrats. They are also, or can be conceived of as, legal officials, that is, men belonging to an institution charged with strengthening the rule of law in society. If professionalism is ever to resolve some of the strains between order and legality, it must be a professionalism based upon a deeper set of values than currently prevails in police literature and the "professional" police department studied, whose operations are ordered on this literature.

The needed philosophy of professionalism must rest on a set of values conveying the idea that the police are as much an institution dedicated

---

[10] Bendix, *op. cit.*, p. 112.

to the achievement of legality in society as they are an official social organization designed to control misconduct through the invocation of punitive sanctions. The problem of police in a democratic society is not merely a matter of obtaining newer police cars, a higher order technical equipment or of recruiting men who have to their credit more years of education. What must occur is a significant alteration in the ideology of police, so that police "professionalization" rests on the values of a democratic legal order, rather than on technological proficiency.

No thoughtful person can believe that such a transformation is easily achieved. In an article estimating the prospects for the rule of law in the Soviet Union, Leonard Schapiro has written, "It is perhaps difficult for dictators to get accustomed to the idea that the main purpose of law is, in fact, to make their task more difficult." [11] It is also hard for police officials in a democracy to accept this idea. In the same article, Schapiro reports the case of two professors who were criticized for urging the desirability of adopting certain principles of bourgeois law and criminal procedure, arguing that observance of legal norms must prevail over expediency in government legislation and administration. They were officially criticized for incorrectly understanding "the role of legal science in the solution of the practical tasks of government," [12] a criticism not too different from the sort often leveled by "professional" police administrators in the United States against those who, for example, insist that the police must act legally for their evidence against the accused to be admitted. The argument is always essentially the same: that the efficient administration of criminal law will be hampered by the adoption of procedures designed to protect individual liberties. The police administrators on the whole are correct. They have been given wide and direct responsibility for the existence of crime in the community, and it is intrinsically difficult for them to accustom themselves to the basic idea of the rule of law: "that the main purpose of law is, in fact, to make their task more difficult."

THE COMMUNITY AND POLICE CONDUCT

If the police are ever to develop a conception of *legal* as opposed to *managerial* professionalism, they will do so only if the surrounding community demands compliance with the rule of law by rewarding police for such compliance, instead of looking to the police as an institution

[11] Leonard Schapiro, "Prospects for the Rule of Law," *Problems of Communism*, 14 (March–April, 1965), 2.

[12] *Ibid.*, p. 7.

solely responsible for controlling criminality. In practice, however, the reverse has been true. The police function in a milieu tending to support, normatively and substantively, the idea of administrative efficiency that has become the hallmark of police professionalism. Legality, as expressed by both the criminal courts community with which the police have direct contact, and the political community responsible for the working conditions and prerogatives of police, is a weak ideal. This concluding section will attempt to locate the main sources of support for the managerial concept of police professionalism.

A posthumously published article by Professor Edmond Cahn distinguishes between "the imperial or official perspective" on law and "the consumer perspective." [13] The official perspective, according to the author, is so called "because it has been largely determined by the dominant interests of rulers, governors, and other officials.[14] In contrast, the "consumer" perspective reflects the interests and opinion of those on the receiving end of law. In the "consumer" view, therefore, constraints on the decision-making powers of officials are given more importance than the requirements of the processing system and those who carry out its administration. Cahn adds, in addition, that "A free and open society calls on its official processors to perform their functions according to the perspective of consumers." [15] At the same time that he argues against it, however, Cahn demonstrates in his own article the empirical strength of the presumption of correctness in official conduct. So in large part do the materials in this study.

The "official perspective" is most persuasive because it operates as the "established" mode of law enforcement, in the broadest sense of that term. The administration of criminal justice has become a major industry in modern urban society. FBI data show that during 1963 there were 4,437,786 arrests reported by 3,988 police agencies covering areas totaling 127 million in population. In California alone during 1963 there were 98,535 adult felony arrests and 595,992 adult misdemeanor arrests. There were in addition 244,312 arrests of juveniles.[16] During 1962 to 1963, the District Attorney of Los Angeles County had a staff of 546 (with 180 lawyers) and a budget of just over $4,800,000.[17]

---

[13] "Law in the Consumer Perspective," *University of Pennsylvania Law Review*, 112 (November, 1963), 1–21.

[14] *Ibid.*, p. 4.

[15] *Ibid.*, p. 9.

[16] Edward L. Barrett, "Criminal Justice and the Problem of Mass Production," in Harry W. Jones (ed.), *The Courts, and the Public, and the Law Explosion* (Englewood Cliffs, N.J.: Prentice-Hall, 1965), p. 95.

[17] *Ibid.*, p. 98.

Under these circumstances of mass administration of criminal justice, presumptions necessarily run to regularity and administrative efficiency. The negation of the presumption of innocence permeates the entire system of justice without trial. All involved in the system, the defense attorneys and judges, as well as the prosecutors and policemen, operate according to a working presumption of the guilt of persons accused of crime. As accused after accused is processed through the system, participants are prone to develop a routinized callousness, akin to the absence of emotional involvement characterizing the physician's attitude toward illness and disease. That the accused is entitled to counsel is an accepted part of the system, but this guarantee implies no specific affirmation of "adversariness" in an interactional sense. Indeed, the most respected attorneys, prosecuting and defense alike, are those who can "reasonably" see eye-to-eye in a system where most defendants are guilty of some crime.

The overwhelming presence of the "official" system of justice without trial provides normative support for the policeman's own attachment to principles of administrative regularity in opposition to due process of law. Under such circumstances, it should not be surprising to find the policeman adopting the "official" perspective too, since his role is to make the initial decision as to whether a charge has been warranted. Having made the charge, he of all people can hardly be expected to presume the innocence of the defendant. He has, in practice, listened to the defendant's story and assured himself of the latter's culpability. In his own mind, there are numerous guilty parties whom he has not arrested because he does not feel their cases will hold up in court, even though he is personally convinced of their guilt to a moral certainty. Police may feel most strongly about the "irrationality" of due process, but in fact other role players in the system of criminal justice may also be observed to be more concerned with efficiency than legality. If the policeman is the strongest advocate of a "rational bureaucratic" system emphasizing factual over legal guilt, he may well be simply because it is the definition of his ability as a worker that is most affected by the application of the rule of law.

An "order" perspective based upon managerial efficiency also tends to be supported by the civic community. The so-called power structure of the community, for example, often stresses to the police the importance of "keeping the streets clear of crime." The La Loma County Grand Jury, composed of "prominent" citizens—mainly businessmen and bankers—typically expresses concern not over violations of due process of law, but over a seemingly ever-rising crime rate and the inability of police to cope with it. Similarly, the Westville *Courier*, the city's only newspaper, makes much of crime news, exaggerating criminality and deploring its existence. The police, quite sensitive to press criticism, find little support for the rule of law from that quarter. Indeed, when a newspaper runs an editorial, or a political figure emphasizes the importance of "making the streets safe for decent people," the statements are rarely qualified to warn law enforcement officials that they should proceed according to the rule of law. On the contrary, such injunctions are typically phrased as calls for zealous law enforcement or strict law enforcement. James Q. Wilson has described this as the "problem of the crusade." As he says:

> Even if the force has but one set of consistent ends specified for it by the commissioner or superintendent, and even if adherence to those ends is enforced as far as possible, it is almost inevitable that there will come a time when the commissioner will decide that something must be done "at all costs"—that some civic goal justifies any police means. This might be the case when a commissioner is hard pressed by the newspapers to solve some particularly heinous crime (say, the rape and murder of a little girl). A "crusade" is launched. Policemen who have been trained to act in accord with one set of rules ("Use no violence." "Respect civil liberties." "Avoid becoming involved with criminal informants.") are suddenly told to act in accord with another rule—"catch the murderer"—no matter what it costs in terms of the normal rules.[18]

The emphasis on the maintenance of order is also typically expressed by the political community controlling the significant rewards for the police—money, promotions, vacations. Mayors, city councilmen, city managers draw up police budgets, hire and fire chiefs of police, and call for "shake-ups" within the department. Even the so-called "liberal" politician is inclined to urge police to disregard the rule of law when he perceives circumstances as exceedingly threatening. Thus, Wilson adds:

> When Fiorello La Guardia became mayor of New York City he is said to have instructed his police force to adopt a "muss 'em up" policy toward racketeers, to the considerable consternation of groups interested in protecting civil liberties. The effort to instill one set of procedural rules in the force was at cross-purposes with the effort to attain a certain substantive end.[19]

In contrast to that of political authority, the power of appellate courts over the police is limited. In practice, the greatest authority of judges is to deny the merit of the prosecution. Thus, by comparison to the direct sanctions held by political authority, the judiciary has highly restricted

[18] James Q. Wilson, "The Police and Their Problems: A Theory," *Public Policy*, 12 (1963), p. 199.
[19] *Ibid.*

power to modify police behavior. Not only do appellate courts lack direct sanctions over the police but there are also powerful political forces that, by their open opposition to the judiciary, suggest an alternative frame of reference to the police. By this time, however, the police have themselves become so much a part of this same frame of reference that it is often difficult to determine whether it is the political figure who urges "stricter law enforcement" on the policeman, or the law enforcement spokesman who urges the press and the politician to support his demands against laws "coddling criminals," by which he typically means rulings of appellate courts upholding constitutional guarantees, usually under the Fourth, Fifth, Sixth, and Fourteenth Amendments. Whether the policeman is the "man in the middle," as Wilson portrays him, and as police prefer to present themselves, or whether police have by this time come to be the tail wagging the press and the politician, is the subject for another study. Beyond doubt, however, there are enough forces within the community, perhaps by now including the police themselves, to provide the working policeman with a normative framework praising managerial efficiency and opposing due process of law.

CONCLUSION

This chapter has indicated, how the police respond to the pressures of the dilemma of having two sets of ideals thrust upon them. As workers in a democratic society, the police seek the opportunity to introduce the means necessary to carry out "production demands." The means used to achieve these ends, however, may frequently conflict with the conduct required of them as legal actors. In response to this dilemma, police "experts" have increasingly adopted a philosophy of professionalism based upon managerial efficiency, with the implied hope that advancing technology will somehow resolve their dilemma. As indicated, it has not, and by its very assumptions cannot. First of all, in those areas where violations of the rule of law occur, advanced technology often results in greater violation. Technological advances in the form of wiretaps, polygraphs, stronger binoculars, and so forth only make the police more competent to interfere with individual liberty. Secondly, the model of efficiency based on bureaucracy simply does not work out in practice. Warran Bennis has catalogued the limitations of bureaucracy in general, and such limits are certainly applicable to large urban police forces. The following is a sample:

1. Bureaucracy does not adequately allow for personal growth and development of mature personalities.

2. It develops conformity and "group-think."
3. It does not take into account the "informal organization" and the emergent and unanticipated problems.
4. Its systems of control and authority are hopelessly outdated.
5. It has no adequate juridical process.
6. It does not possess adequate means for resolving differences and conflicts between ranks, and most particularly, between functional groups.
7. Communication (and innovative ideas) are thwarted or distorted due to hierarchical division.[20]

The working policeman is well aware of the limitations of "scientific" advances in police work and organization. He realizes that his work consists mostly of dealing with human beings, and that these skills are his main achievement. The strictures of the rule of law often clash with the policeman's ability to carry out this sort of work, but he is satisfied to have the argument presented in terms of technological achievement rather than human interaction, since he rightly fears that the public "will not understand" the human devices he uses, such as paying off informers, allowing "fences" to operate, and reducing charges, to achieve the enforcement ends demanded of him.

Police are generally under no illusions about the capacity of elected officials and the general public to make contradictory demands upon them. A certain amount of lip service may be paid to the need for lawful enforcement of substantive criminal law, but the police are rarely, if ever, rewarded for complying with or expanding the area of due process of law. On the contrary, they are rewarded primarily for apprehension of so-called "notorious" criminals, for breaking "dope-rings," and the like. As a matter of fact, police are often much more sophisticated about their practices than the politicians who reward them. Police, for example, generally recognize the complexities of the meaning of such a term as "hardened criminal" and of the difficulties involved in carrying out a system of enforcement in line with the strictures of due process of law. The working detective who has used an individual as an informant for years, who has developed a relationship with the man in which each can depend on the word of the other, is not taken in by newspaper exaggerations of the man's "criminal" character.

Finally, the dilemma can never be resolved as it contains a built-in dialectic. Appellate decisions upholding the integrity of procedural requirements may well move large segments of the community to a greater concern for the security of the substantive ends of criminal law. Especially when the police are burdened with the responsibility of enforcing unenforceable laws, thereby raising the spectre of a "crime-ridden" com-

[20] Warren Bennis, "Beyond Bureaucracy," *Trans-action*, 2 (July–August, 1965), 32.

munity,[21] decisions that specifically protect individual liberty may increase pressure from an anxious community to soften these, and thus contain the seeds of a more "order-oriented" redefinition of procedural requirements. During the tenure of the "Warren" Court, the U.S. Supreme Court was increasingly indulgent of the rights of the accused. Whether this trend will continue, or whether the courts will redefine "due process of law" to offer legitimacy to what is presently considered unlawful official behavior may be contingent upon the disposition of the civil community.

If this analysis is correct in placing ultimate responsibility for the quality of "law and order" in American society upon the citizenry, then the prospects for the infusion of the rule of law into the police institution may be bleak indeed. As an institution dependent on rewards from the civic community, police can hardly be expected to be much better or worse than the political context in which they operate. When the political community is itself corrupt, the police will also be corrupt. If the popular notion of justice reaches no greater sophistication than that "the guilty should not go free," then the police will respond to this conception of justice. When prominent members of the community become far more aroused over an apparent rise in criminality than over the fact that Blacks are frequently subjected to unwarranted police interrogation, detention, and invasions of privacy, the police will continue to engage in such practices. Without widespread support for the rule of law, it is hardly to be expected that courts will continue advancing individual rights, or that the police will themselves develop a professional orientation as *legal* actors, rather than as efficient administrators of criminal law.

[21] Police statistics also contribute to this perception. See Gilbert Geis, "Statistics Concerning Race and Crime," *Crime and Delinquency* (April, 1965), 142–150.

Contemporary Law Enforcement in Democratic Society

THE ASPHALT COWBOYS

T HE first full draft of this book was completed in the fall of 1964 just as the Westville police were beginning to confront an emerging new set of problems: the student movement, the antiwar movement, and an increasingly militant civil rights movement, along with a rising crime rate. "Law and order" was to become an increasingly popular demand as well as a political force and slogan. Such developments, which were to involve all American police, catapulted law enforcement into an unprecedented public prominence. By 1966, when the first edition of this book was published, significant numbers of Americans were already challenging the wisdom of government policy and the legitimacy of government action. Following a decade noted for quietism, the younger generation of the sixties experienced tear gas and clubs and guns as a means for resolving political differences. Streets and campuses became battlegrounds, visible through television to the nation and the world. The potential "criminal" population thus embraced large segments of American society, particularly those who were not white or who were college age.

For some, the institution of policing became the first line of defense against domestic threats to security; for others, it became an oppressive force heedless of lawful restraint. Visibility led to popular interest, television shows, movies, and social controversy. The city was to become America's new frontier, and the police were romanticized into asphalt cowboys, riding the range of urban crime and disorder.

Four social developments accompanied the rise of turbulence and the increasing significance of police during the latter half of the 1960's. *The first was militance surrounding the civil position of non-white minorities,* particularly blacks, but also of Native Americans and those of Mexican ancestry. During the 1950s and early 1960s this issue—the civil position of nonwhite Americans—would have been called "civil

246

rights," but by the late 1960s that very conception became subject to challenge through (a) disillusionment with the capacity of the legal system to achieve positive social change; (b) the awakened consciousness of a history of oppression, slavery, and genocide, sparked in particular by rioting in American cities; and (c) a "law and order" backlash that led to the election of public officials who regarded militancy as a threat to established power positions, which indeed it was.

The second dominant development was the Vietnam War. In a few short years, beginning in the spring of 1965, and culminating in an explosive wave of antiwar protest in the spring of 1970 when President Nixon ordered troops into Cambodia, street marches and other forms of protest against American involvement and conduct in Southeast Asia became so familiar a feature of our national life as almost to acquire the status of an institution. The anguish of the period affected all Americans. For protesters it was summed up in Senator Fulbright's declaration that we are a sick society. "Abroad," he told the American Bar Association, "we are engaged in a savage and unsuccessful war against poor people in a small and backward nation. At home—largely because of the neglect resulting from 25 years of preoccupation with foreign involvement—our cities are exploding in violent protest against generations of social injustice." [1]

The combination of nonwhite, especially Black, militancy and anti-Vietnam War protest led to an increasing polarization in American society. The working-class American, from whose ranks the bulk of police personnel in America are drawn, was also anguished. His sons and cousins and brothers were fighting in Vietnam, and he regarded the protests generated on college campuses as a direct threat, not only to the security of the nation but to the security of his closest kin. In addition, Black militancy and ghetto riots led to a perception of an increasing danger of Black criminality among the largely working class, generally ethnic, neighborhoods of American cities. It would be a serious mistake to neglect the real and perceived deprivations associated with life in what might be called the white ghettos of urban America. As then Secretary, Robert Wood, of HUD put it:

The average white working man has no capital, no stocks, no real estate holdings except for his home to leave his children. Despite the gains hammered out by his union, his job security is far from complete. Layoffs, reductions, automation, and plant relocation remain the invisible witches at every christening. He finds his tax burden is heavy; his neighborhood services poor; his national image tarnished; and his political clout diminishing . . .

[1] *San Francisco Chronicle*, August 9, 1967, p. 1.

one comes to understand his tension in the face of the aspiring black minority. He notes his place on the lower rungs of the economic ladder. He sees the movement of black families as a threat to his home values. He reads about rising crime rates in city streets and feels this is a direct challenge to his family. He thinks the busing of his children to unfamiliar and perhaps inferior schools will blight their chance for a sound education. He sees only one destination for the minority movement—his job.[2]

A third development was the introduction of drug use into wider segments of American life. Until the late 1950s, marijuana use had been restricted largely to black communities and to a tiny proportion of whites associated with the world of jazz and popular music. During the early 1960s, marijuana use increasingly spread to college campuses throughout the United States, and to a wider segment of American society. As use spread, perceptions changed. According to the Federal Bureau of Narcotics marijuana was a dangerous drug which led to hallucinations, violence, and criminal tendencies. Young people who used marijuana found none of these results but instead experienced heightened sensual awareness, the deep rhythm of rock music and more intensive sexual pleasures. They came to regard the legitimation of alcohol which dulls the senses and often results in painful aftereffects from heavy use as absurd in contrast to the severe criminal penalties associated with marijuana use.

As mistrust of official interpretations of drug effects became widespread, so too did experimentation with other drugs leading to the development of a drug subculture, mainly around such hallucinogenic drugs as LSD and mescaline, but also the amphetamines, a particularly dangerous form of drug whose seemingly benign early effects often lead to heavier dosages and later deterioration. Equally, if not more serious, was the problem of heroin addiction since it seemed so directly related to street crime.

The drug enforcement apparatus, well developed during the original research period of *Justice without Trial*, was becoming increasingly powerful in the 1960s, reflecting public anxiety over street safety. While the quality of urban life was surely declining during the 1950s and while simplistic punitive remedies did not remedy and may well have contributed to that decline, increasingly punitive drug policies could be attributed to a combination of three factors: (1) the entrenched power and subsequent growth of drug enforcement bureaucracies; (2) public gravitation toward the police as a symbol of social stability; and (3) the increasing politicization and political power of the police during the late 1960s.

[2] Robert Wood, unpublished paper, delivered at The National Consultation on Ethnic America, Fordham University, New York City, June 1968.

The growing tendency of the police during the 1960s to see them-selves as an independent, militant minority asserting themselves in the political arena may be a less extreme problem than overt police law-lessness in the sense that it may not necessarily be in violation of the law or departmental orders. Nevertheless, the issues raised by *the fourth department, the politicization of the police* are, if anything, more com-plex and far-reaching.

The police see themselves, by and large, as a distinct and often de-prived group in our society. As Robert Fogelson comments:

To begin with, the police feel profoundly isolated from a public which, in their view, is at best apathetic and at worst hostile, too solicitous of the criminal and too critical of the patrolman. They also believe that they have been thwarted by the community in the battle against crime, that they have been given a job to do but deprived of the power to do it.[3]

One result of this isolation is a magnified sense of group solidarity. Students of the police are unanimous in stressing the high degree of police solidarity. This solidarity is more than a preference for the com-pany of fellow officers, esprit de corps, or the bonds of fellowship and mutual responsibility formed among persons who share danger and stress. It often includes the protective stance adopted regarding police misconduct. A criticism of one policeman is seen as a criticism of all policemen, and thus police tend to unite against complaining citizens, the courts, and other government agencies. Students of police feel that this explains both the speedy exoneration of police when citizens' com-plaints are lodged, and the paucity of reports of misconduct by fellow officers. It seems clear, for example, that the officers who took part in the famous Algiers Motel incident[4] did not expect to get into trouble and the presence of a state police captain did not deter them.

When police solidarity took political form, police power in the large cities of America became considerable. Police organizations quite con-sciously built this power, continue to do so and its impact is felt through-out the political system. Policemen ran for office as mayors in Minne-apolis and Philadelphia and were elected. Whether or not the police have become a dominant political force in any given city, there is no doubt that in most major American cities the police during the 1960s and into the 1970s became a political force to be reckoned with.

Why shouldn't the police be a political force? After all, police are citizens, and their full participation in public life should be applauded

---

[3] Robert M. Fogelson, "From Resentment to Confrontation: The Police, the Negroes, and the Outbreak of the Nineteen-Sixties Riots," *Political Science Quar-terly*, June 1968, pp. 224–225.

[4] See John R. Hersey, *The Algiers Motel Incident*, (New York: Knopf, 1968).

rather than discouraged. Yet political involvement of the police raises serious problems. First, aside from the military, the police enjoy a practical monopoly on the legal use of force in our society. For just such a reason our country has a tradition of wariness toward politicization of its armed forces, and thus both law and custom restrict the political activities of members of the military. Similar considerations are applicable to police.

In some ways police are an even greater source of potential concern than the armed forces because they are so close to the day-to-day workings of the political process and so frequently interact with the population. These factors make the line between legitimate political advocacy and abuse of the political process difficult to draw and an immediate problem. For example, bumper stickers on squad cars and political buttons on uniforms, impart a potentially coercive political message to the populace being policed.

A second concern that has led to restrictions on members of the armed forces is the fear that unfettered political expression, if adopted as a principle, might in practice lead to political coercion within the military. Control over promotions and disciplinary action could make coercion possible, and pressure might be exerted on lower-ranking members to adopt, contribute to, or work for a particular political cause. Thus, again, regulation (and sometimes prohibition) of certain political activities has been undertaken. For example, superiors are prohibited from soliciting funds from inferiors, and many political activities are prohibited while in uniform or on duty. Such considerations, again, apply to the police.

Even when coercion of the populace (or fellow force members) does not exist in fact, politicization of the police may create the appearance of such abuses. This can affect the political process and create both hostility toward the police and disrespect for the legal and political system.

Moreover, lobbying, campaigning, and the like tend to make the policing function itself appear politically motivated. Since the policing function is for so many people such an important part of our legal mechanisms, the actual or apparent politicization of policing would carry over to perceptions of the entire legal system. So the politicization of the organized police is at once a reality and a dilemma between values of free expression and limitations of political expression by this special class of public officials.

It is in the context of these four main developments that projected police into national prominence since the writing of the original manuscript of this book—the increasing militancy of nonwhite communities during the 1960s, student and antiwar protests, the increasing use of marijuana and perhaps other drugs in American society, and the increasing politicization of the police—that we should locate developments in the Westville and Eastville police departments.

WESTVILLE AND EASTVILLE

One of the dilemmas in undertaking a new edition is whether to continue using the fictitious names for the cities studied. After much consideration, I decided to use the convention adopted in the first edition, for two reasons. First, the fictitious names underscore the intent to discuss general issues as they reveal themselves in a particular department rather than to evaluate the quality of the police department. Accordingly, this work is not an exercise in evaluation research, but an analysis of how events affect an organization, its goals, and the goals of its leadership. Second, although many readers will surely be able to identify "Westville" and "Eastville," others will not. I treasure one review of the first edition that praises the contents of the book but chides the author for employing anonymous names for the cities involved. The reviewer argued it was perfectly evident that Westville was Los Angeles and that Eastville was Boston, and suggested therefore that the fiction was absurd. Of course, the reviewer was wrong.

Eastville

During the past decade the problems of the Eastville Police Department were to center most explicitly on two related issues: (a) explosive black militancy and (b) a decaying inner city with an ineffectual and a corrupt municipal and police administration. During the summer of 1967 Eastville experienced one of the most devastating riots of the whole troubled decade. Twenty-six persons were killed and more than 1000 were injured. A report by a select commission on civil disorders, appointed by the State governor, reported that "Both Negroes and whites sense a pervasive feeling of corruption at City Hall." The commission proposed a special grand jury investigation of the alleged corruption. Four past grand jury presentments had charged political interference with the police department and failure to enforce gambling laws, but no legal action had followed these presentments. Law enforcement officials around the country privately concluded that Eastville was heavily influenced, if not controlled, by organized criminal elements. One authority on organized crime accused the state government of corruption, as well as the City of Eastville. The State governor's special committee, following the riot, cited the police chief and the mayor for (a) their failure to train the police department, both physically and psychologically, for dealing with an outbreak of riot; (b) failing to comprehend the depth of the bitterness of the Eastville black community; and (c) the shabbiness of Municipal Court justice, which they characterized as inefficient, undignified, and confused.

On the basis of the Governor's Commission report—and particularly citing the "pervasive feeling of corruption in the city"—a special grand jury was convened in 1968; it indicted the police chief for "willfully refusing to enforce states' gambling laws." Although considerable evidence was brought out at the trial against the police chief, the judge took the case from the jury, and ordered the chief's acquittal on grounds of insufficient proof but also because "a police director could not be held responsible for violations of law by his subordinates unless there was proof that he participated in or assented to the violations."

Accusations of corruption continued to plague Eastville, its police department, and indeed the whole state administration. In 1969, the mayor was indicted and convicted of corruption in connection with gambling interests. All of this offers further evidence for the contention in the first edition that police corruption involving crimes of vice cannot be the isolated activity of a few "rotten apples" but must be systemwide, a finding substantiated by New York City's Knapp Commission in connection with corruption in that police department. The state government—under a new governor—is now seriously considering legalizing several forms of gambling, including casino gambling.

Westville

It may be appropriate to discuss my relationship to the Westville Police Department since the conclusion of the writing of the first edition. I wrote there that when I studied the Westville Police Department, my connection with the University made little difference, that I was regarded as another state employee. At that time, the proximity of the University of California at Berkeley was of minor concern to the Department and to its personnel. Throughout the 1960s, however, the University of California at Berkeley became a center of the antiwar movement, of Black militancy, of the new counterculture and all its ramifications. Accordingly, it became an important focus of concern for the Westville department. No longer could a researcher associated with the university remain anonymous.

Indeed, just as I was completing the first draft of this book, on a Friday in October 1964, the Westville Police Department was called upon by the Chancellor's Office of the University of California at Berkeley to participate in crowd control efforts. Thousands of people, mostly students, were gathered in Sproul Hall Plaza to listen to a young man named Mario Savio address them on the importance of the rights of students to organize civil rights demonstrations on campus that might result in illegal sit-ins off campus. Mario Savio's platform was the roof of a campus police car that held Jack Weinberg, a young man who had been arrested by campus police for illegal leafletting. Following Weinberg's arrest a number of students surrounded the car and made it impossible for the car to move.

This spectacle, the symbolic defilement of a police vehicle, angered and embittered the several hundred Westville police who were to see it. Moreover, the Westville police were called on a Friday afternoon. This meant that policemen who would otherwise have been preparing for a weekend of relaxation were required to stand in an underground parking lot in full riot gear. In addition, the chief of the department was present. Reportedly a strict disciplinarian, the men could not slouch or break ranks without his noticing, and arousing his disapproval. Finally, the Westville Chief had been promised that if the crowd did not disperse by 6:00 P.M. they were to enter the campus and disperse the crowd. This promise had been made by the Chancellor's Office but was countermanded by the then President of the University of California, Clark Kerr, who negotiated a temporary settlement with the small group of students that were later to become known as the leaders of the Free Speech Movement.

Doubtless, the bitterness later contributed to what could only be most generously described as the rough handling given students who were to occupy Sproul Hall and to be arrested in December of 1964. Following those arrests, Westville and its police department were perceived by many students and faculty at the University as exceptionally harsh and brutal. The university community was in turn perceived by the Westville Police Department and its men as a potentially serious threat to local order and national interest. These hostilities and cross perceptions were to intensify during the spring of 1965 as the University became a headquarters for civil rights marches into Westville, and as the University began to emerge as a major center of anti-Vietnam War activities and organization. To the surprise of some, and the consternation of other Westville police, I participated in civil rights marches and antiwar activities. This began a period of polarization between the Westville police and me—neither I nor my students were any longer welcome to study the department—and the Westville police and the Berkeley campus that was to last into the 1970s. Polarization between police and universities was not solely a Berkeley phenomenon. It spread over the entire nation and shaped an antagonistic relationship between police, students, and many faculty throughout the United States in the late 1960s and early 1970s.

WESTVILLE AND AMERICA: MAJOR DEVELOPMENTS

By 1966 the civil rights movement was steadily shifting away from demands for constitutional guarantees to a broader and more radical conception of necessary changes in the position of minorities, particularly of Blacks. "Negro" organizations were becoming "Black" and increasingly militant as the term "Negro" disappeared from the language. Young Blacks were forming themselves into defense groups to protect against what they interpreted as the oppressiveness of American society. One of the most influential of these groups, if not the most influential, arose in Westville and its particular enemy was the Westville Police Department.

The period of 1965 to 1967 was one of great turbulance for the Westville community and for the police department. In addition to the experience of social upheaval, the department underwent considerable change internally. One chief resigned and he was replaced by another, considered a solid policeman by most of the men in the department, but reportedly a man of little sympathy and understanding for minorities in the city. This chief died unexpectedly and was replaced by a man whom we shall call Chester James, a man who was to prove an increasingly controversial figure from 1967 until his retirement late in 1973.

Legal Professionalism and Community Relations

Of all the issues facing the Westville Police when Chief James took over, relations with the local Black community was most pressing. As indicated, Westville was an ideological center of black militancy. Although other cities may have had greater numbers of militants, the headquarters of an important militant organization was located in Westville, and during the 1960s there were frequent, sometimes bloody, even fatal, clashes between police and leaders of the black militant organization. In part, hostility was attributable to emerging interpretations of the role of Blacks in America, in part to tensions of the period, and in part to long standing irritations between the Black community and the Westville police that were coming to a head during the middle 1960's. As one high police official—not Chief James—stated:

I guess it was about 1969 when we first took a real close look at what we were doing in the police department. During that period of time our police force was apart from the community, existing solely to go out and wage war on crime. We had very little interest in any of the other problems, things that, as a matter of fact, as we later came to determine, the community was clamoring for: such things as alternatives to arrest on the street, as referral, as developing expertise in family crisis intervention, and handling landlord-tenant disputes. With the consistently rising black populaton in the city—conservatively estimated at somewhere around 35% but more likely around 42% and about 58% in the public school system—such problems as landlord-tenant disputes and family disputes and disorganized family situations definitely needed some attention.

According to this official, no community agency was designed to solve real problems of real people. Because police were in the phone book and because they were available, they were constantly called upon to do something. He offered the following example of how police would confront a family dispute between husband and wife:

The first question we would ask, if the wife happened to be the victim of a battery or happened to be pushed around by the husband was "Do you want your husband arrested?"
"Well, no I don't. He's got a hell of a drinking problem."
"Do you want him arrested?"
"No."
"Well, okay, madame your problem is civil, see your attorney."
"What attorney?" "I don't have any money." "I don't want to get a divorce." "I just want this problem solved." "What can I do?"
"It's civil, madame, if you don't want him arrested."

According to this official, the failure of both the police and other public agencies to respond to community problems, as well as the more aggressive posture of police on patrol, created further tensions. "On the whole," he concluded, "I think that we can frankly say that the minority population at that time, particularly Blacks, definitely did not like the police department. Definitely did not like them."

These observations are borne out by other interviews my students and I conducted with Black residents of Westville. A graduate student in political science, who is studying the Westville Police Department in its community relations, has conducted approximately fifty interviews with Black Westville residents about their feelings toward the department. The student, who was himself born and grew up in the Black community of Westville, says that during the middle 1960s the attitude of the average Westville Black was quite hostile toward the police department; but that during the past several years, as a result of innovations introduced by Chief James, attitudes on the part of most Blacks toward the police department are more trusting and positive.

He offered as an illustration a fight he had recently witnessed between two young Black men in a Black neighborhood. The police were called and stopped the fight. A few years earlier, he said, such an event would have precipitated a hostile, glaring crowd. Now, there was no visible anger and residents accepted the presence of the police as a routine necessity.

In my interviews around the police department there seems to be a frank recognition, at least among ranking officers, that Black militants were not unrepresentative in their hostile feelings, although perhaps more expressive and volatile in their methods. The militants were seen by several officers as symbolic representatives of the frustrations of the community, who ultimately had a double-edged impact on police-community relations. On the one side, they dramatized and gave expression to underlying grievances held throughout the community. On the other, they frightened and enraged individual working policemen, who became very wary. Some Westville Black radicals have argued that wariness reduces police misconduct because of fear of retaliation should police behave in a hostile or unlawful manner.

Within the police department, however, changes in police conduct toward minorities was held to be due in part to a better understanding by police of the social situation of minorities, that is, to police education; in part, to a perception of Black political strength, through the election and appointment of city officials; and, in part, to a tough policy of internal investigation of citizen complaints instituted by Chief James, a policy that made him extremely unpopular with rank-and-file police.

As indicated in the body of this book the subculture of police puts heavy emphasis upon police solidarity. When a policeman violates a rule, whether it be a rule of law or a rule handed down by administrative authority, other rank-and-file policemen tend to look away or to back up the rule violator. Thus, if a policeman commits some violation of rules, other policemen are expected to ignore the violation. In many police departments when police lie to cover-up their own misconduct, or that of other policemen, it is tacitly understood that internal affairs investigators will not press too closely. By contrast, under Chief James, internal affairs investigations were carefully investigated, policemen were required to tell the truth, and if they did not, either about themselves or others, they were fired. As a captain put it to me in an interview:

In the past we have had problems with full investigations. Many of the complaints alleged by the community against the police were tough to pinpoint, especially anonymous complaints. We do listen to anonymous complaints if people desire to have us listen. But some years ago we made a complete mailing to everybody in the city and asked them to complete the forms and get them back into the police department about complaints. But tracking down facts about complaints both from police and citizens is difficult.

So far as police are concerned what you need is a strong policy statement that will be followed. Now, we tell our policemen before we talk to them regarding a complaint that if you lie, if you aren't truthful about any aspect of this investigation, you're fired. When you put out a statement like that you've got to back it up with strong action. The first, second, third time somebody came along that lied, they were fired.

Now I think it is just common knowledge that when an internal affairs investigator asks you a question it is understood that either you tell him the truth or you will be fired regardless of whether you are involved in the alleged incident or not. You must be truthful at all times. We're at the stage now where I think there is 100% improvement in this area of the police department.

This interpretation was backed up in part by rank-and-file policemen who were interviewed; in part, it was criticized. There was general agreement that if you lied you were fired. In six years, thirty-eight policemen were discharged by the Chief after investigation by the Internal Affairs Division. Others resigned. Yet there was considerable disagreement within the department on whether that ought to be department policy. Furthermore, there was considerable question as to whether the penalties handed down through internal affairs were fair or overly strong and consistent. For example, a former head cf the Police Officers' Association thought that the Chief was fair in disciplinary matters and would listen but that he was an overly punitive disciplinarian, tougher than he himself would be if he were Chief, and certainly tougher than most of the men of the department would have desired.

Another serious innovation introduced by the police chief was to impose a penalty for the use of racial slurs on the part of any policeman. For example, it was strictly forbidden that any policeman, at any time, under any circumstances, including the telling of a joke, employ the word "nigger" while in uniform or in the confines of the police department. Penalties on the order of five, ten, and fifteen day suspensions were in fact imposed for this sort of violation. Moreover, not only was the Chief publicly sympathetic to the needs of the Black community; he often appeared on public television and in newspaper interviews stating his philosophy of police professionalism that emphasized: (1) the rule of law regardless of who suspects were; and (2) service to all segments of the community.

The Chief's outspokenness and his hard disciplinary attitudes frequently brought him into open and public conflict with the rank and file. At one point during his tenure the Police Officers' Association publicly voted no confidence in his future as Chief of Police. When questioned about this, a former Police Officers' Association official explained:

The policemen have felt, many times, although I don't think there are a half dozen who really know his side of it, that he was more a sociologist than a police chief. But in this community, and I think in any community, you've got to have empathy for the people you're dealing with or you're not doing your job. I think that he had real feeling for the black community. Let's not kid anybody, they've had their problems in Westville with the police department along with the general problems that cause much of their activities with the police. Anyhow, I'll tell you one thing, we were slated to be the city most likely to explode and we never really exploded. We've had small racial conflicts but we've never really had anything big. I think that his keeping the lines of communication open with the black community has to a great extent been what has kept us from blowing up.

In addition to these changes, the Chief brought in a number of innovations. These included a woman legal advisor who had a background in civil rights law, a civilian administrator, a family crisis intervention program, a diversion and referral program, a landlord-tenant investigation program, and emphasis on consumer fraud.

One of the most interesting changes was to tape record actual conflicts between citizens and police as these occurred on the street. In time the department built up a library of such "critical incident" tapes, and used these tapes in a "Conflict Management Section" to teach new recruits how to prevent difficult situations from escalating into violence.

Another innovation was the "peer review panel." Here policemen who experience an unusual amount of conflict with the public sit down with fellow officers, who review his handling of "critical incidents." Even this innovation became controversial within the police department. Some felt it was a fine idea, while others felt it degenerated into a form of "brainwashing."

In police circles, Chief James came to be regarded as a progressive police chief, an innovator, but also as too innovative, even eccentric. Within his own department, opponents criticized his policies and were especially critical of his procedures for carrying them out. From interviews, two sources of resentment seemed closely related. For example, some interviewees were simply opposed to firearms policy, or to his internal affairs policy, or to any of the other innovations he had introduced on grounds that the crime prevention function of the police was undermined during his administration.

Other and more sophisticated critics did not openly disagree with his policies, indeed praised the policy innovations, but directed criticism toward his personality and management style. He was described by several interviewees as a man with a liberal ideology in the community and an authoritarian management style within the department. None doubted his integrity, his devotion to work and duty, and his single-mindedness. But several doubted whether he needed to have been quite so stern and unyielding, and whether his innovations actually worked. In any event, by 1970, the Westville department had acquired a national reputation and was the subject of stories in a variety of prestigious newspapers, magazines and other periodicals. One weekly news magazine wrote that:

The . . . department now has acquired a national reputation as a near paragon of virtue; it has become downright zealous in guarding the constitutional rights of suspects and repairing the battered relations with the city's large population of Blacks.

The Chief himself traces the changes in the department in part to a greater understanding of the role of police in society, achieved through reading, experience, and reflection; and in part to the direct experience of unlawful police conduct in connection with an antiwar demonstration in 1967, shortly after he became Chief. "I knew," he said, "what the problems were in the department and decided then that I would undertake change based on the incidents as they occurred, and that I would institute changes." He describes as most troubling a period early in his tenure when police shootings occurred with regularity. In his words:

Attempted burglary of a laundromat was the typical occurrence. The police would get reasonable cause to believe that we see a perpetrator, chase him on foot, know that we couldn't capture him on foot and we'd discharge fire on him. In this particular one I think the fellow was hit in the back or the back of the head and was killed. That sort of thing was going on during the two or three months period with some frequency. That, in combination with policemen shooting and missing.

At that particular time, 1968, there was a lot of tension. We were ready for a riot in the city. We'd have a policeman go out and make an arrest, and two hundred people would gather around. Well, I knew that what I had to do was to place a restriction on discharging firearms to preclude firing at fleeing burglars and automobile thieves except in defense of life, and the community knew it. I kept getting calls from the community, because I have very close relations with many black people in the community, and many white.

The big problem I had was trying to get an understanding in the police department as to the need for these restrictions, so it would not be an act solely on my part, without some degree of understanding. So I was talking to deputies and talking to captains. Within the police department at that time we really had a black-white thing. Police against the black militants, and police against criminals and criminal equated with black. So I kept talking and talking and talking to a particular deputy chief, who was in charge of uniformed men. Can't you, I asked, do something to bring about understanding that we'll not accomplish anything by using shooting? They're lawful, but human lives are being wasted and we're not accomplishing a damn thing.

Well, it got so, Jerry, that I wasn't sleeping at night. These things occurred with enough frequency, either where they were in fact hitting and shooting and injuring and killing, or shooting and missing, that day by day it just bothered my conscience.

Well, I kept going back to the City Manager. He knew what was going on. It was in the paper, you know, the discharging, and of course at that time we had continuous, literally continuous allegations of police brutality. The whole city was just heated up. I was waiting for the riot any day but particularly I was concerned about the waste of life. I kept talking to the City Manager about my feelings. And he listened, usually on the phone. Whenever we had another shooting, I would fill him in about it. And I would say we have to take action on this, we have to take action. And he would say to let me know what you're going to do.

So finally one day, I think it was the ninth of July, there had been other shootings which had occurred during the past couple of days. I couldn't sleep. I would lay awake until 4 o'clock in the morning, waiting for the next shooting. I came to work and there had been another one. So I talked to the deputy chief again. But I wasn't getting any counsel or support from any of my subordinates, none of them. I was alone with the damn thing and had been with everything else and I was for years after that.

By 2 o'clock in the afternoon I decided I had had it. I was tired and I knew I had to put the restrictions into effect. So I called the City Manager on the telephone and I got him out of a meeting and said to him that we have the next lineup of patrol at 3 o'clock and I'm going to dictate a special order prohibiting shooting of fleeing burglaries and automobile thieves except in defense of life. And he said, okay, but are you going to do it as a matter of simply putting in the prohibitions or are you going to stop it until you review your order? I said well I'm going to stop it but I also filled in the word review. I really didn't know what he meant, but now I realize that guy was remarkable because he was the one who threw in the review idea. What he was doing obviously was to suggest a word to use so that it would not appear to be absolute. It would then be politically acceptable.

He called me back about 3:30 and said Chief, he said, refresh my memory. What did I expect you to do? I said you didn't expect me to do anything. You supported my putting these restrictions into effect. He said, okay you put these restrictions in as Chief of Police and I supported it 100%. We never did talk about it again as a matter of fact. He was a remarkable guy. I could have copped out as Chief of Police and said that he had ordered me to put in these restrictions, but I wasn't about to do that. And he supported me 100%.

Of course, all hell broke loose. The Mayor took exception to it. My policemen went up in arms about the damn thing. The business community went up in arms. Then I got overwhelming support from the black community, which really counted, and from parts of the white community. Without the City Manager's support I could never have made it. He knew the risk he was taking, and he backed me all the way all the time.

By the close of 1968, Chief James had issued orders saying that the Westville Police Department was going to operate absolutely within the law. Unlike other police chiefs who attacked the decisions of the Supreme Court and the Court itself, Chief James repeatedly stressed that the police were to operate through law, whether these were statutes or court decisions governing police conduct.

His hardline "law and order within the police department" view was continually reinforced through the discharge or suspension of police. He says:

Policemen now understand that if they act outside the law, they are going to be held to account. Unfortunately, as it was in 1967 and as it is today, it's a matter of them recognizing that the department will take action if there's a transgression. This is unfortunate because in my experience the Chief is just about alone . . . The feedback I've been getting ever since I became Chief is that a number of policemen fear the community and the Chief. Fortunately, we've had such a great turnover in personnel since I became Chief that the majority of policemen now expect that if there is not adherence to the law and to the policies and procedures of the department, violators will be held to account. This policy works to achieve behavioral conformity; it is difficult to determine whether police attitudes have actually changed.

The department has made a considerable effort to replace those leaving with officers of ethnic minority background. In the fall of 1973 there were 69 Black officers, 19 Mexican-Americans, 7 of Phillipine extraction, 5 Chinese, 3 Japanese, and 3 or 4 others such as Native-Americans or Hawaiian. As an indication of increasing confidence by local Black citizens, especially young men, in the police department, the last two recruit classes numbered approximately 75 per cent Black recruits.

At the same time, residual racism persists in social relations among the officers. Although all belong to the Police Officers' Association, there continues to be a white social organization of police, and a Black one. Even here, socially, one can discern a split between older white officers on the one side, and younger officers and the highest ranking administrators on the other. Obviously, such a categorization is imperfect. Nevertheless, there does seem to have been a continuing tension between supporters and opponents of Chief James. Roughly, opponents can be divided between those who disapprove of Chief James and his policies and those who are careful to distinguish between their disapproval of the Chief's management style and personality—he is regarded by critics as inconsiderate, egotistic, petty, vindictive—and approval of his general philosophy of police operating within the rule of law and emphasizing community service. Among the latter group of critics, however, it is sometimes difficult to judge whether their contemporary liberalism would have existed absent the aggressive leadership of Chief James. Surely, events would have moved some just as they did Chief James. For others, it is simply impossible to tell.

Other critics point out that if you look at the department as a whole —from 1963 to 1973—there has been some desirable change in the behavior of patrolmen, who are now more likely to be considerate of the feelings of citizens they contact, but relatively little change in attitudes or culture; and remarkable continuity in such areas as vice control and criminal investigations. Thus, in the major areas considered in the body of the first edition, there has been little, if any, change.

VICE CONTROL

Since *Justice without Trial* so heavily stresses vice control, it is worthwhile considering how that aspect of law enforcement has fared. One important change has been in the area of citizen behavior—Northern California in particular has experienced increasing use and acceptance of marijuana by young people, including many who were to join police departments and prosecutorial staffs. By now most college and law students have tried marijuana. Although probably less than a majority use it regularly, the use of marijuana simply does not elicit shock. Indeed, a majority of San Francisco voters voted to legalize its use, on a referendum that failed statewide.

A casual attitude to marijuana use was evident in several interviews at all levels. By contrast, in 1963, I observed a superior court case where a young man, without a prior record, middle-class, white, was sentenced to prison for possession of three marijuana cigarettes found after he was stopped for reckless driving. Today, such an outcome is inconceivable. Such a young man would never go to trial, but would instead be "diverted," under a recently passed law, to some social agency. If he "successfully" fulfilled the terms of "diversion," by, for example, attending a course on drug abuse, the charges would ordinarily be dropped by the district attorney. Most patrolmen no longer make marijuana possession arrests, although some still do.

Main emphasis is upon harder drugs, and upon marijuana where larger quantities are involved for sale, or where a marijuana arrest can be used to "turn" an informant.

The Informant System

The informant system remains virtually unchanged in vice control since the early 1960s even though the practical use of informants has been curtailed by recent court decisions. One in particular, (*Theodor* v. *Superior Ct.* (1972) 8 Cal. 3d 77) has been especially significant. It holds that an informant's identity can be kept secret if the purpose of disclosure is merely to aid in showing that the police did not have probable cause to make an arrest; but if the defendant can make a plausible case that the informant may be a material witness on the issue of guilt or innocence, the prosecutor has to disclose the name of the informant, who can then be subpoened as a material witness and cross-examined. If the prosecutor refuses to name the informant, the judge must dismiss the case.

There is still a significant delegation of discretionary power to the individual officer. The officer is still empowered to barter in criminal justice, offering reduced punishment in exchange for information. The informant relationship is still regarded as central to the work of the vice control officer, and information, supposedly leading to the apprehension of a more serious lawbreaker is the goal of the vice control operation.

At the same time, the increasingly widespread use of drugs, plus the high penalties associated with possession and sale of heroin; plus the vice control operation's perceived need to produce felony arrests has led to skepticism within the administration of the department about the utility of the vice control operation and to some frictions between the vice control division and the district attorney's office.

A decade ago, the district attorney's office was likely to be particularly solicitous of the vice control division's interests. Today, with a change in the perception of drugs, particularly of marijuana but other drugs as well; with a rising crime rate and an even more crowded calendar, and with additional restrictions on the maintenance of the secrecy of informant identity, the DA's office is likely to be more skeptical of the whole control enterprise. As one high ranking member of the DA's office stated in an interview:

I think the major change over the last ten years is that you no longer see any big emphasis on our part—that is, the DA's office, in a lot of drug stuff. The police are a little harder to figure out. They still seem to feel, especially the vice cops, that drug busts can control drug use. But I think most thoughtful people believe you're just diverting resources into somebody else's problem, or what ought to be somebody else's problem.

His own disillusionment with drug enforcement was strengthened, he said, when he examined a study his office undertook of 80 heroin users. The study found that prosecution of the small time heroin dealers —the ones in possession of several "balloons," that is, condoms of heroin selling for $5 or $10 (nickel and dime bags) was occupying what he considered an inordinate amount of office effort. The study located the ineffectiveness of such arrests in what he termed, quite appropriately, the "lateral snitch" phenomenon. As he explained:

The vice squad does not seem to get above a certain level of heroin dealer. They get "A" and squeeze "A" and he turns "B"; "B" turns "C" and "C" turns "D" and so forth. The last guy is "Z" who can't turn anybody. All the defendants "A" through "Y" turn out to be guys who are helping the vice squad, and we're supposed to give them a break. But "Z" is no bigger a dealer than "A" or "G" or "Y." Maybe if we could get a "Mister Big" it would be worth it. But it just didn't appear that was happening. You would just get into this basic strata, and go out laterally. It's a waste of time and money.

Obviously, one main reason for the lateral snitch phenomenon is the legal requirement that informants' names be produced when defendants can plausibly argue, as they often can, that the informant is a material witness on the issue of guilt or innocence. Thus, the police can make as many arrests as ever, but it becomes much more difficult for the prosecutor to gain convictions without disclosing the informant's identity. This results in a continuing conflict if the efficiency of the police is measured by the number of arrests and the efficiency of the prosecutor is measured by the number of convictions. The police are likely to blame their troubles on the courts while prosecutors tend to be more accepting of court decisions, even when they disagree with them. They tend to become annoyed with the police to the degree that police fail to see *conviction* as the purpose of *arrest*. "Lateral snitching"—that is, plea bargaining in the same strata—is thus a logical outgrowth of three combined factors: (1) the structural persistence of the informant system in "victimless crime" enforcement; (2) the functional need to keep informant identity secret even in the face of new legal requirements; and (3) the perceived organizational pressure on the vice squad to be productive through arrests. It is difficult to determine how much this perception is delusional and how much it actually results from organizational checks on efficiency. Probably it is a combination.

An Evening With Vice Control in 1973

In the early 1960s, the Westville vice police wore suits and looked like everybody's stereotype of a cop. The 1960s have caught up with the physical appearance of the squad. A Friday evening finds one policeman, dressed for undercover work, appearing hip, presenting a flowing red mustache, scuffed cowboy boots and worn, blue jeans. Others appear casual—their sideburns and mustaches create the appearance of sports car or ski equipment salesmen.

A quick description of activity in the 20 × 20 ft room: On one wall are three desks and on the other two desks directly across. A secretary, bouncy, heavy-set, and talkative, is talking and typing reports. The red-haired officer sits typing his own report, his expression a combination of serious concentration and routine nonchalance. Two other officers, appearing more working class than hip or funky, are on their way to a narcotics assignment to buy. One says he's not going to carry "heat" on this job.

"Oh be careful," says the secretary, "I hope you know what you're doing; this is dangerous."
"Be careful," adds the redhead with genuine concern.
"Thanks," says the other, sounding brave but also just a bit scared.

A man of enormous girth waddles into the room. Later on I learn that he is a "troller," a civilian used by the police to encourage girls to make a solicitation, or entrap, depending on one's point of view.

An older man in his forties, a narcotics sergeant, walks in, and talks about an arrest he made today—a woman who sells yellows and reds to kids and carries a loaded gun in her purse.

"That's the kind of arrest you like to make," says the redhead.
The sergeant nods his head in agreement.
"We're happy about this one."
Somebody outside yells, "Clear!"

When the answer—"all *clear!*"—is returned, two policemen walk in with three handcuffed young women. Their appearance suggests that they are streetwalkers. As the officers write up the report, which requires asking questions of the arrested women, their demeanor combines politeness and social distance. No trouble, routine police work. The girls are told that they will have to spend three days in quarantine in 1973—

this feature of prostitution enforcement has not changed at all in West-ville—before appearing for arraignment and bail setting. They are un-happy. Later on, one of the arresting officers assures me that half the girls arrested in Westville in the past year were found to be venereally diseased.

Pretty soon, the "clear!" call and the rustling sounds are heard again. Again, the affirmative answer. This time Sergeant K. walks in with Officer M. and two people. One is a very tall, heavy-set black man and a curvacious, striking, but fading blonde.

The man and the woman are separated and the booking process commences. He is charged with "inveiglement" and she with "pimping," an unusual charge for a woman. It is discussed for the next 15 or 20 minutes by the vice officers. I am told that she had been arrested on prostitution charges several times. The vice squad has developed a witness who will testify that she tried to induce a sixteen-year-old girl to work for the Black man. Thus, she is alleged legally to be a "pimp." He is said in fact to be her pimp and the "inveiglement" charge, which is a felony, constitutes an allegation that one has attempted to induce a minor into prostitution.

While Sergeant K. goes off to the booking room I talk to Officer M. I tell him that I studied the vice squad ten years ago and that I worked with Sergeant Tom Harris at that time. Officer M., who has been with the department for ten years, has worked vice for the last four. Although a young man in his early thirties, he is an oldline Westville cop in the legalistic style. I asked him how things have changed in the last ten years and he replies that arrests have gone up. In the old days, he explains, you had to arrest people on charges of prostitution and that meant often that whoever was setting a girl up would have to go into a room with her, get the money, get her to take her clothes off. Now, he says, all they have to do is get the girls to solicit. (In fact, what he says isn't true. It used to be that a solicitation sufficed for arrest.) But the important issue is his perception of the course of this police duty. He is not sure.

We sort of have a caucus. We meet with the District Attorney's Office. We talk with each other. We have meetings.

Detective Harris is now with the district attorney's office as an investigator. Officer M. observes that Harris really still runs things from the DA's office. He is still reputed to have more SE's (special employees) than anybody else around. Sergeant K. finishes his booking and we ride to Al's Restaurant. A complaint has been received from Al that too many pimps and whores are hanging around. Sergeant K. tells me about how important prostitution enforcement is.

Many people talk about legalizing prostitution or getting rid of the criminal penalties but they don't really know what they're talking about. If you were to do that you'd have more of these type of people and they're really bad guys. People don't know what it takes, how much work it is to set up an arrest of a good pimp.

I suggest that after ten years of observation I hadn't noticed any reduction of prostitution desipte considerable police activity. Indeed, he had told me that there were 91 arrests in September 1973 of prostitutes and that arrests would exceed a thousand for the year. He answers that prostitution would be even more prevalent without enforcement.

We drove around the neighborhood of Al's for about ten minutes. We spot a young couple, seated, talking, in a parked car. Sergeant K. stops his car, looks at the young man. He returns the glance, apprehensively, and nods. Sergeant K. walks out of the car, to the young man's car, and says, "What are you doing here?"

"Just sitting," says the young man.

"Who's that with you?" says Sergeant K. The young woman says nothing.

"She's my wife," says the young man.

Sergeant K., who is about the same age, in his middle twenties, says, sarcastically, "Did she tell you to say that?"

The young man understands. "Look, she's my wife," he insists.

She begins to say something. The young man hushes her up.

"Get out your driver's license," he says to her. She pulls her license out from her purse. The young man pulls his out of his wallet, takes the woman's and hands the pair of licenses to Sergeant K. Each license shows the same last name and the same address.

Sergeant K. explains hurriedly, "Oh look, this is a dangerous neighborhood; there are a lot of bad guys out here who won't mind taking advantage of a couple sitting in a car so you'd better move it." Then he adds, "And besides you're parked in a red zone."

He walks back to the car, slides behind the wheel, smiles and says to me, "That was some last line, wasn't it? You're parked in a red zone." We both laugh and I say, "Well, they turned out to be married after all, didn't they?"

He replies, "I don't know that, I just know that they have the same last name."

Sergeant K. is a topnotch vice cop, respected by other policemen. He is alert, suspicious, aggressive, puritanical, and judgmental.

We discuss drug enforcement. He acknowledges its limitations, for example, that only about ten per cent of the drugs coming across the border are able to be confiscated. Such facts do not alter his attitude. He believes in hard enforcement against all drugs, including marijuana.

He also believes in prostitution enforcement. Sergeant K. and I, it soon becomes clear, have little chance of persuading one another on desirable legal policies for drugs and prostitution. We can both agree, however, that vice control enforcement has scarcely changed since the early 1960s.

CRIMINAL INVESTIGATIONS

Social organizations change slowly. Police departments, as social organizations, not only support that generalization, but must surely qualify as contributing to the slower end of a hypothetical social organization change scale. One can perhaps suggest a further distinction: within police departments those units most removed from direct public contact are likely to be least amenable to changes in structure, procedure, attitudes, and behavior. Accordingly, we would expect patrol and traffic divisions to be more responsive to innovation, and vice control and criminal investigation to be less.

In 1972, the Westville Police Department received an L.E.A.A. funded grant that was supposed to initiate procedures to help improve the department's response to citizen calls for service by integrating the operations of specialized units within the department. An interdisciplinary research team combining police and outside specialists was formed to study the department's organization and procedures, to make recommendations for change, and to study the effects of innovations. After about a year of work, the research team expressed serious disappointment concerning the capacity of the department to change detective practices. In a report prepared for the Chief, the research team wrote:

We completed this report more than a year after our initial approach to C.I.D. (Criminal Investigation Division). We are struck, in retrospect, with the manner in which change has—and has not—occurred in C.I.D. in the interim. On the surface, a number of changes have occurred—paper flows, job descriptions, and investigative priorities have been somewhat altered. On a more important level, however, little change is presently evident—investigators' understanding of their job appears to have remained roughly the same, and C.I.D. has not substantially improved the quality of service it provides the public.

Perhaps the most striking testimony to the difficulties of introducing change are found in the research team's observations on the clearance rate. The reader will recall how Chapter 8 discusses the process through which "multiple clearances"—that is, the linking of a suspect to crimes other than the ones for which he had been arrested can result in (1) actually rewarding criminal activity by reducing penalties for multiple commissions coupled with admissions; (2) inducing suspects to lie; and (3) reducing the interest of police in determining whether the clearance offering suspect had lied. The researchers found that these observations still applied, and comment almost poignantly about the incapacity of a police department to introduce change, even in the sure knowledge that the traditional practice is a failure. Thus, they write:

> Most of the investigators in C.I.D., most of their supervisors, as well as departmental commanders, were aware of the problems associated with the use of the clearance rate. Most would admit that there were abuses, and that multiple clearances served no useful purpose. Nevertheless, the use of clearances was deeply engrained: Departmental command required that C.I.D. keep records of them to satisfy the F.B.I. and the public; C.I.D. command felt that they would be evaluated according to their production of clearances; investigators believed that they would be evaluated similarly by their superiors; and, while all these feelings were true to some extent, everyone would admit privately that clearance rates were ridiculous measures. Nevertheless, they were a tradition that would not be easily abandoned.

PERSISTENCE AND CHANGE IN AMERICAN POLICING

During the past ten years I have talked to many police, attended numerous conferences, and lectured to police groups and departments. On the national scene, Westville continues to be an innovative and progressive police department, despite internal difficulties and resistances to change. If it is difficult to achieve change in such a police organization as Westville's, it is more difficult in most others'. The police continue to be a solitary group in an occupation marked by danger, authority, and the pressure to produce. Corruption, which grows well in such an environment, has probably not risen in the past decade, but its visibility surely has. Various reports have suggested that police graft in the areas of gambling, prostitution, and drugs are a way of life in many American police departments. At the same time, the American police community is constantly striving to define its occupational prerogatives and to raise something called "standards," although nobody is quite sure what these standards ought to be. Often, one hears or reads in this connection the word "professionalism," but that concept continues to remain open to a variety of interpretations.

Westville continues to exemplify the "professionalism" dilemma. Unlike "Eastville" and other police departments, it has not for many years experienced public charges of corruption. Its ranking officers are committed to higher standards of police training, conduct, and organization. Yet within the department such commitments have engendered sharp debate and sometimes bitter personal conflict. For example, a substantial number—perhaps a majority—of ranking officers and men felt that Chief James' management style had undermined departmental morale because policemen feared to use their authority to investigate potential crime on the street; feared departmental reprisal should they exceed their legal authority.

This is exemplified by the following incident: I was riding patrol one evening with a policeman who pointed out three Black teenagers standing on a streetcorner as we rode by. "That's what I mean, Jerry," he said. "I should get out and question those kids, in a nice way, of course. But departmental policy now forbids that unless I have legal probable cause. Clearly I don't. But I sure would like to talk with them and see whether I get a feeling about whether they're potential burglars."

The politicization of the police during the 1960s also raises questions about the meaning of professionalism. It resulted in important developments shared by the Westville police with departments all around the country—the formation of an independent *de facto* police union, growing out of the old welfare association. Although calling itself an "association," it is an independent union without affiliation. Every person who joins the department must join the association, and dues are automatically deducted. The association does everything a union does—it furnishes insurance and hospitalization and is the legal bargaining agent under state law. In 1972, the community voted for compulsory and binding arbitration on wages and working conditions. Although most unions feel that the threat of a strike is too valuable a weapon to give up, the Westville Police Association feels both that police strikes are inappropriate and that they are, on the whole, financially benefitted by being tied in to a pay formula based on percentage increases given to industrial and craft workers in the surrounding communities. Not so incidentally, such an arrangement unites the financial interests of police with those of industrial workers who can strike for higher wages. Although such an arrangement might appear initially to be incompatible with developing aspirations of police "professionalism," such a judgment is inconsistent with the increasing unionization of public sector professionals, especially those in education and public health. But even when unionization and professionalism can be reconciled, the specific agenda for reconciliation is rarely clear.

The New Regime

Chief James resigned in the fall of 1973. He was given a retirement dinner organized by his successor and attended by more than 800 persons representing every segment of the community. Accolades were most fulsome from representatives of minority groups, and perfunctorily polite from the police association representative, who at least made an appearance, however faint his praise of the outgoing Chief. His successor is a youthful, articulate, and thoughtful man who served as Deputy Chief under Chief James. In a lengthy interview he associated himself with the policy directions of Chief James, while acknowledging that his association with these policies was at first grudging and skeptical. He is personally more acceptable to the rank-and-file policeman than Chief James was, but also repeatedly points out that he was a full participant in both making and carrying out his predecessor's policies.

His own attitudes are best expressed in his interpretation of the example of the three Black teenagers standing on a streetcorner. His interpretation proceeded as follows:

In the old days we would see those kids and go over and jack them up. That's the way we kept the beats clean. The difference now is that if you're driving down that same street and see those same kids standing on the corner, you have to recognize they have every right to be there. But—if that policeman thing snaps in your head that says you should talk to them, by all means you should do so.

With one change. And that change is the fact you may very well be, and probably are, the intruder. You have to accept the fact that if they tell you to "jam it" or to butt out, you may well have no alternative. Some guys think the department doesn't want field interrogations, car stops, drunk arrests. That's wrong. The policy has always been to use good judgment and operate within the rule of law.

The problem, however, continues to be whether the average officer possesses the interpersonal street skills of the new Chief, and the judgment to back off when appropriate; or whether an invitation to conduct field interrogations will, with time, once again increase the hostility of the nonwhite communities of Westville toward the department. Only time will tell.

Whatever happens in the Westville Police Department, it must continue to operate in the social context of America. There has been among scholars and criminal justice personnel alike increasing recognition, over the past decade, of the inadequacy of American institutions of criminal justice from police through courts through corrections. In a decade of rising crime rates it is patently evident that increasing police budgets and major expenditures for research and development have hardly provided for increased public safety. Criminal investigators solve a very small percentage of crimes, smaller than clearance rates suggest, and increased time for criminal investigations seems to yield little in the way of increased productivity of felony convictions. Most recently, a startling study of and by the Kansas City Police Department strongly suggests the ineffectiveness of patrol forces as a crime deterrent.

The courts have become increasingly crowded. In the future, because of recent Supreme Court decisions in *Brady* v. *United States* [5] and *Parker* v. *North Carolina*,[6] trials will probably constitute an ever diminishing proportion of the criminal case load. Justice without trial, with its own unwritten rules and practices, with the "herding" of defendants, and the low visibility decisions of the police, will become increasingly characteristic of the American criminal justice system. As the *Harvard Law Review* commented:

The Decisions in *Brady* and *Parker* are crucial to the present administration of the criminal justice system. Almost any defendant who offers to plead guilty can avoid the risk of receiving a more severe sentence if he were to be convicted at trial. The overwhelming caseloads confronting prosecutors and judges make them willing to reduce or drop charges or to recommend and give lenient sentences in return for guilty pleas. Given the present amount of resources available to handle criminal trials, if approximately seventy percent of the dispositions and ninety percent of the convictions did not end in guilty pleas, the criminal justice system would shift from its present low gear to a halt. *Brady* and *Parker* so plainly accept the practice as to stimulate a collective sigh of relief throughout the country from prosecutors and trial judges who had been troubled by *Jackson's* invalidation of a sentence differential between those persons who went to trial and those persons who pleaded guilty.[7]

The correctional system is widely recognized as a failure. Practical scholars and students of the correctional system are more and more advocating the elimination of incarceration and diversion away from the system on grounds that not only does it not rehabilitate but that it is positively harmful for those who might otherwise conform to conventional notions of rehabilitation. All of these developments raise serious questions about the future of American criminal justice. Specialists in theoretical and applied criminology have in the past decade achieved a remarkable record of debunking the effectiveness of past practices and contemporary innovations, yet government funding seems directed toward sponsoring the latest social control fad.

Eventually, students of criminal justice, including the police, will have to realize that criminal justice institutions are quite limited in

[5] 397 U.S. 742 (1970).
[6] 397 U.S. 790 (1970).
[7] "The Supreme Court, 1969 Term," 84 *Harvard Law Review*, pp. 150–151.

their capacity to influence, much less control, the world around them. Any society that needs increasingly to rely upon law enforcement for its public and private safety is a society in trouble. American society and American police are in a continuing dilemma. No reasonable person wants a police force that is flaccid, inefficient, and untrained. At the same time, an increasing reliance on police for social stability constitutes a pretty good indication of the weakness of bonds of social community. So, as a society, we want both to improve the police while minimizing their significance as a social institution. The horns of that dilemma should keep students of the police and of American society busy for some time. In the meantime, as in the past decade, social change will engender opportunities for innovation in policing, opportunities to alter the values and attitudes governing police conduct.

A Brief Survey of the History, Economy and Population of Westville, California

EARLY HISTORY

IN 1770, a Spanish expedition traveling overland from San Diego visited the Westville region. It was half a century before the arrival of the first colonist, Sergeant Luis Maria Peralta. He was granted sixty-eight square miles, of which the central fifty-three square miles is present-day Westville, by Spain's last governor of Alta, California, Pablo Vicente de Sola. Too old to use the land himself, Peralta placed it in charge of his four sons, finally dividing it among them in 1842. For eight years, the Peraltas were allowed to raise their cattle and crops in a peaceful and lazy *rancho* style of life.

The first American settlers leased one hundred acres of land from the Peraltas in 1850 and became farmers, raising grain crops. The California Gold Rush, already underway, brought the rich Westville land to the attention of more and more Americans. Some of these claimed squatter's rights over part of the land. The Peraltas unsuccessfully attempted to drive them off. In response, the squatters, working with Horace W. Carpentier, a recent graduate in law from Columbia College, forced the Peraltas to grant them a lease for a city. Later, when Peralta was about to sell the leased land to someone else, Carpentier persuaded a friend, a state senator, to make him enrolling clerk of the senate; he was able to have Westville incorporated on May 4, 1852, stopping Peralta's sale. Shortly afterwards, in an election with more votes than voters, Carpentier was elected mayor.

Carpentier continued to increase his power and wealth. By promising the city council a few wharves and a schoolhouse, Carpentier acquired the franchise for a ferry and absolute title to the entire waterfront. During the 1860s the "Big Four"—Stanford, Huntington, Crocker, and

Hopkins—started building the Central Pacific Railroad for which West-ville was the proposed western terminus. When they asked the city council for waterfront land, the council found the land was not theirs to give. Carpentier, however, was able to. He formed a corporation, "West-ville Waterfront Company," with Stanford as an associate and deeded his waterfront holdings to it; the corporation then transferred five hun-dred acres of tideland to the railroad.

The city council, realizing belatedly that it had given Carpentier and the Central Pacific complete control over Westville's most valuable property, began to act. The city brought suit and in 1910, after pro-longed litigation and at an expense of several million dollars, settled with Carpentier's assignees. The city would hold the waterfront in ex-change for long-term leases to the assignees.

Led by a later mayor, a reform movement attempted to wrest some control of transportation from the Central Pacific-Carpentier corpora-tion. The mayor persuaded another railroad to locate in the area. The mayor was aided by Francis ("Borax") Smith of Death Valley fame. Smith invested large profits from his local Borax mines, and a number of advances are to his credit, although he may not have intended them. He tied together the street railway systems of the area, founded other transportation to compete with the monopoly, and, in partnership with Frank Havens, established a realty syndicate as a holding company for their joint real estate properties. Through the syndicate, land in the county was bought, developed, and connected by a rail system. One source estimates that the syndicate came to own one-sixth of the county. In 1910, Smith joined others to form the two hundred million-dollar United Properties Company. This collapsed in 1913 because of some shady practices and the founders were ruined; but their developments remained—to the advantage of the city and county.

ECONOMY

The world wars increased the prominence and size of Westville. Four large shipbuilding concerns located there during World War I, enhanc-ing its industrial base. But it was not until World War II that the full potential of Westville's location was realized. At that time, the army and navy established supply bases there and the shipbuilders imported thousands of workers from the Far East and from the depressed areas of the South. Between the census of 1940 and the special federal census of 1945, Westville's population enlarged from 302,163 to 400,935. From 1940 to 1943 the number of persons engaged in the manufacturing trades grew from 61,000 to 216,000. In other words, most of the new residents were engaged in manufacture—in fact, they probably were brought or attracted to the area by the opportunities.

Today Westville's manufacturing industries are diversified into over eight hundred and fifty plants. Nearly half of the land used for this manufacturing is devoted to heavy industry. Of the new plants and plant expansions in La Loma County, Westville is presently getting about 50 per cent, although it has been receiving a declining proportion of the total since 1947. Among its new plants are fabricated metals, chemicals and allied products, furniture and fixtures, food and kindred products, lumber and wood products, and transportation equipment.

About 36 per cent of the civilian residents of Westville in 1950 were employed in service occupations, 37 per cent in distributive occupations, 27 per cent in conversion occupations, and 6 per cent in extractive occupations. Future growth in employment is predicted mainly in the public and private service occupations and, to a lesser degree, in the distributive and conversion occupations. This prediction is based on the observation that other cities, when they reach a high level of economic development, tend to increase the number of service activities related to manufacturing and business. The increase in nonwhite population, who mainly are employed in service industries, will also raise the portion of the population so employed.

Westville's economic relation to Mountain City has also been changing. In 1912, Westville was primarily a "bedroom city"; four-fifths of the commuters to Mountain City came from Westville and adjacent areas. In 1954, only about one-third of Mountain City's commuters came from the Westville area. Between 1912 and 1954, the daily travel into Mountain City from other nearby counties increased proportionately to their populations; travel from the vicinity of Westville only doubled while its population quadrupled.

Mountain City is often called the "financial center" and Westville the "industrial town." This is true of local businesses but not of resident populations. Westville has only a slightly higher percentage of her residents employed in industrial plants than Mountain City (8.0 per cent compared to 7.3 per cent in the 1950 census). Commuters make the difference greater: commuters to Westville come primarily to industrial jobs while those to Mountain City go to office jobs.

Westville is one in a chain of twelve cities included in two counties which make up a more or less unified metropolitan area with a total population somewhat larger than that of Philadelphia. They are linked by common streets and by public transit facilities; they constitute a single consumer market and a single labor pool; and cultural, recreational, and other community facilities are used without regard to city boundaries. Westville, however, gets slightly over 50 per cent of the total retail trade in the county, although this too is declining, as it is in the central cities of many large metropolitan areas.

The Westville Planning Commission has been fighting the tendencies toward suburbanization and housing decay, which started following World War II. The building of a twenty-eight story, forty-seven million dollar office and shopping center has encouraged others to build in Westville. The city, too, has been building public structures with an eye to the overall improvement of Westville. So far it has built a new state office building, a new courthouse and jail facility, and a large airport. The planners have struggled for a seventy-five-million-dollar redevelopment plan to deal with two hundred and fifty blocks of North Westville and for ten million dollars for the rehabilitation of one of Westville's parks. The success of these attempts remains to be seen.

POPULATION

Westville's population in 1960 was 367,584, a decline of 4.4 per cent from the 1950 population. In 1970, Westville experienced a further decline of around one per cent to 361,561.

Since 1945 there has been a continuous net outmigration of children under fifteen. This will probably continue as approximately nineteen thousand people are displaced by the expected demolition of temporary public housing projects and other housing for proposed freeway construction. The outmigration of the parents of these children has been replaced by the immigration of other adults, especially adults sixty-five years and older.

Westville's physical growth is now stopped on all sides. In the future, the number of persons working in Westville will probably increase faster than the city's population. Along with this suburbanization, noted everywhere, is the development of suburban shopping centers, one of the drains on Westville's retail sales.

MINORITY GROUPS

While the total population of Westville has shown a decline, the nonwhite population has greatly increased. The loss of population has occurred in the white sector. This distribution of the nonwhite population has changed radically in the last twenty years.

Examining only those census tracts in Westville with more than 1 per cent of the city's nonwhite population, we find in 1940 that 17 of the 72 census tracts examined contained 84 per cent of the total nonwhite population. In 1950 the *tripled* nonwhite population was still concentrated in the same area: 16 of the 72 tracts had 89 per cent of the total nonwhite population. During the 1950s, the increasing nonwhite population started to expand from that area and, by 1960, 26 of the 72 census tracts

White and Nonwhite Population of Westville,
1940 to 1960

Year	Per cent of Total Pop. Nonwhite	Per Cent of Total Pop. White	Total Pop.
1940	5	95	302,163
1950	14	86	384,575
1960	26	74	367,548
1970	35	65	361,561

including 86 per cent of the total nonwhite population. At this time the nonwhite population was 26 per cent of the total population.

Picture Westville as a rectangle with the longer sides stretching from northwest to southeast on the map. In 1940 and 1950, the nonwhite population lived almost entirely in a triangular region in the extreme northwestern corner of the rectangle. During the 1950s, they moved from this area along the western and northern sides of the rectangle.

Westville has a sprinkling of other ethnic and racial groups. Asians, brought in to work on the railroad, were at one time a highly visible group with their own section of town and own types of occupation. Gradually Asians have become less distinct in Westville; people no longer identify one part of town in "Chinatown." Races other than Negro constitute only 4 per cent of the population of Westville. People with Spanish surnames make up 7 per cent of the population. Other ethnic groups have increasingly less distinctive identities.

Comparative Data on the Westville Police[1]

WESTVILLE stands well above the average middle-sized city in its budgetary allotment for police services (see Table 1). Its 1962 per

TABLE 1   Per Capita Expenditures on Police Services

	1960	1961	1962	1963
Administrative	$13.97	$14.76	$14.99	$15.19
average *	(36)	(37)	(38)	(37)
Westville	18.65	19.13	19.49	20.06
Eastville	21.95	23.87	24.79	25.75
San Francisco	19.76	21.11	21.41	23.13
Washington, D.C.	31.60	34.36	35.34	36.11
Kansas City, Mo.	14.21	13.96	13.46	13.21

* This is an average based on the number of responding departments as indicated by parentheses.

capita expenditure on police services was 37 per cent greater than the average expenditure by thirty-eight cities and its 1963 allotment was 32 per cent greater. The per capita expenditure on police services by Westville, however, was considerably less than that by Eastville, San Francisco, and Washington, D.C. The latter two jurisdictions are considerably larger (approximately two times larger—see Table 5) than

[1] The data for these comparisons were gathered from the excellent compilation of information by the Police Department of Kansas City, Missouri, in their annual *Survey of Municipal Police Departments*. The Kansas City *Survey*, issued continuously since 1955, gives figures on all responding departments from cities of from 300,000 to 1,000,000 population. For the purposes of determining the short-run stability of these comparisons, the data presented here represent the four years 1960 through 1963, inclusive. Where population figures have been used as the base for computations (specifically, in computations of population density, per capita expenditures on police services, and police-population ratios), the 1960 census data were used for 1960 and population estimates for the years 1961 through 1963.

Westville, and since it is likely that the per capita expense of public administration and public services increases with population in a roughly direct way, this per capita comparison may not be entirely sound. Eastville, on the other hand, is similar to Westville in size and minority group composition, and thus its greater expenditure on police services is striking.

TABLE 2   *Salary Levels by Rank* **

	Admin-istrative Average	Westville	Eastville	San Francisco	Washing-ton, D.C.	Kansas City, Mo.
Captain						
1960	$654	$ 907	$650	$ 930	$842	$583
1961	682	944	717	1000	842	583
1962	717	985	717	1017	842	583
1963	732	1015	717	1056	852	583
Sergeant						
1960	531	677	500	677	673	474
1961	549	705	558	728	673	476
1962	576	735	558	740	673	478
1963	594	758	558	768	771	450
Patrolman ("rookie")						
1960	396	558	375	546	400	383
1961	409	581	425	591	400	383
1962	419	606	425	602	400	383
1963	431	625	425	627	471	383
Detective						
1960	509	693	450	693	645	462
1961	535	721	525	745	645	464
1962	559	752	525	758	645	466
1963	564	775	525	787	733	468

** Where a jurisdiction reported a salary range for a particular rank, the highest salary figure is given here.

It can be seen from Table 2 that Eastville's relatively high expenditure on police services did not filter down to the police department level in the form of high salaries. Almost without exception, the salary levels of the Eastville jurisdiction were below the average salary levels for middle-sized cities for the four-year period at hand. In contrast, the Westville police at all ranks enjoyed considerably better pay than the police of the average department. The Westville rookie in 1962, for example, received better than seven-fifths the salary of the average rookie in 1962 in middle-sized cities. Indeed, it is only at the highest ranks that the salary levels of Westville were greatly and consistently surpassed by the salary schedule of San Francisco, the highest-paying jurisdiction. Eastville, with one of the highest crime rates in the nation, had nearly twice as many police per one thousand inhabitants in 1962 as Westville, and more than twice as many in 1963. Westville's police-population ratio in those two years was well under the average ratio for middle-sized American cities, but since the ratio for Washington, D.C. was consistently greater than that even of Eastville (and Washington's salary schedule much higher than that of Eastville), there is no reason to conclude that the police-population ratio is meaningfully related to salary levels.

TABLE 3   *Per cent of Total Budget for Police*
Services Allocated for Salaries

	1960	1961	1962	1963
Westville	84.5	83.9	88.1	88.4
Eastville	92.8	93.4	92.9	93.1
San Francisco	92.2	89.4	88.2	93.0
Washington, D.C.	74.5	73.9	69.2	72.9
Kansas City, Mo.	84.7	86.4	89.1	90.7

Table 3 shows the interesting fact that the Westville jurisdiction consistently utilized less of its budgetary allotment for police salaries than Eastville, San Francisco, or Kansas City. Only Washington, D.C. had a lower percentage utilization of its budget for police salaries than Westville. It is likely that the remainder of the Westville budget served to provide the Westville department with the purchase and maintenance of more adequate laboratory facilities, criminalistics equipment, and other law enforcement resources, thus enabling the Westville department to compensate for its low police-population ratio. This interpretation would square with the hunch that Eastville, with its high-percentage utilization of resources for salaries and its high police-population ratio, aimed at a more extensive coverage of the community in terms of manpower than did Westville.

According to the FBI's *Uniform Crime Reports* bulletins, the size of the Westville police force has been declining fairly steadily since the

early 1950s. Over the period 1958–1963,[2] the force underwent a net de-
crease of 8 per cent, the magnitude of this drop probably being slightly
greater than the population decline for that period. The Eastville force,
on the other hand, decreased in size by only 1.6 per cent for the same six-

TABLE 4   *Police-Population Ratios* *

	1960	1961	1962	1963
Administrative average	1.93	1.92	1.90	1.89
Westville	1.97	1.93	1.75	1.74
Eastville	3.45	3.42	3.46	3.68
San Francisco	2.43	2.35	2.34	2.32
Washington, D.C.	3.63	3.72	3.72	3.70
Kansas City, Mo.	2.00	2.00	2.00	2.00

* Number of *authorized* police per 1,000 population.

year period, according to the FBI source. Table 4 shows Westville to
have consistently had the smallest police-population ratio of the cities
compared.

It can be seen from Table 5 that perhaps another reason for the low
police-population ratio in Westville is the comparatively low population density of Westville. Conversely, the high population density of
Eastville might account in part for its high police-population ratio.
Whatever correlation exists between population density and police-
population ratios can probably be attributed in large measure to the
association between population density, socio-economic conditions, and
crime rates. Thus, a picture of the Westville jurisdiction emerges in
which a relatively low population density and a comparatively low
crime rate [3] allowed for the provision of a well-paid and relatively thinly
distributed police force. Contrasting conditions would seem to have
prevailed in Eastville.

Another contrast between Eastville and Westville appears in connection with the policies of the respective jurisdictions with regard to re-
muneration for court appearances and overtime work. Westville police
were encouraged to appear in court and thus aid in prosecution by being
granted equal time off. Work beyond the standard number of hours

[2] The choice of this time period is dictated by the fact that in 1958 the FBI
adopted a new enumerative method for its compilation of data on municipal police
forces.

[3] The 1961 *Uniform Crime Reports* bulletin shows Westville's crime rate to have
been well less than half the crime rate of Eastville.

TABLE 5   *Population, Square Mile Area of Jurisdiction, and Population Density*

	1960	1961	1962	1963
Westville				
Population (thousands)	361	367	372	372
Area (square miles)	73.6	73.6	73.6	73.6
Population density (thousands/sq. mile)	4.91	4.99	5.08	5.08
Eastville				
Population	396	402	402	405
Area	23.5	23.5	23.5	23.5
Population density	16.86	17.11	17.11	17.23
San Francisco				
Population	716	743	744	753
Area	93.10	89.10	89.10	129.37
Population density	7.69	8.34	8.35	5.82
Washington, D.C.				
Population	747	764	764	784
Area	68.25	68.25	68.25	68.25
Population density	10.94	11.19	11.19	11.45
Kansas City, Mo.				
Population	468	502	520	530
Area	129.8	167.8	290.3	316.8
Population density	3.61	2.99	1.79	1.67

per week was also similarly compensated for in Westville. In Eastville, on the other hand, while the police were allowed equal time off for overtime work, they were expected to make court appearances at their own time and expense.

In terms of employment and retirement benefits, the Westville department generally outranked the Eastville department. The number of paid vacation days and holidays per year in Westville for the four years 1960 though 1963 was 30 per cent greater than in Eastville. Police retirement benefits in Westville were also considerably better than in Eastville. While the two jurisdictions did not differ in terms of the number of years of service or the minimum age requirements for receipt of the minimum pension, the minimum retirement benefits in Westville were greater than those in Eastville. It is, however, worth noting that minimum retirement benefit provisions in San Francisco and Kansas City were more favorable than those in Westville. What is perhaps most revealing of the contrasting retirement programs of Eastville and Westville is that minimum and maximum benefits equivalent to those in Westville accrued to the Eastville policeman only after five years more service than was required for minimum and maximum benefits in Westville. In addition, it must be kept in mind that the salary basis for computing pensions in Eastville was markedly lower than in Westville.

As might be anticipated, these differences in resources and inducements between Eastville and Westville correspond to internal organizational differences. The most striking superficial difference between professional and old line police is in appearance. Seen as a force, the Westville police are much more military looking, especially in uniform, than their Eastville counterparts. They are as a group younger, taller, straighter, and shinier. The Eastville police, of whom there are nearly twice as many for a population not much larger or differently composed, tend to be older, fatter, and occasionally raggedy-looking—often enough, however, to make the whole force appear sloppy. Furthermore, the environs of the Westville police are similar to and enhance their appearance. They are housed in a modern building, have the latest technical equipment at their disposal, and boast a jail—with a central television room—reminiscent of the latest style in Army barracks.

The most significant social structural difference between the old-line Eastville department and the professional Westville force is in degree of *centralization*. The Westville force is contained within one building, with one strong central authority—the chief—while the Eastville department has a chief and an executive director, one appointed by the civil service and one by the mayor, and five precincts, each headed by a captain. This structural difference has certain functional consequences, all of which are related to degree of *familiarity* with the public.

Each precinct, as one Eastville officer described it to me, is like a feudal domain. The captain who heads the precinct lives within its bounds, and there he reigns somewhat like a lord. He must pay his fealty to the politician who controls the area politically, but in return for this his tenure is protected. Ultimately, more attention is paid to political "clout" than to the requirements of law enforcement, even in terms of efficiency alone. This is not to suggest that most of the routines of police work are not carried out. The property of merchants, for example, is protected, although merchants are also expected to participate in the system by making various contributions. (It was suggested politely to me in Eastville, for instance, that going out with the men a couple of nights before Christmas would cramp their style, since they didn't work Christmas eve, and this was the last night they would be able to receive gifts from merchants.)

A correlate of this type of organization is typically the presence of graft and corruption. Thus, in Eastville, organized illegal gambling is commonly winked at; while it is not in Westville. So much is protection of gambling in Eastville ingrained in the system that Eastville police interviewed refused to believe that there was no numbers racket in Westville (especially since Westville has a comparably-sized Negro population and ghetto) and that if there was bookmaking, it was on a relatively small scale.

History and Organization of the Offices of Public Defender and District Attorney in La Loma County, California

HISTORY OF LEGAL INSTITUTIONS IN LA LOMA COUNTY

PRIOR to California's admission to the union, its government was based on the Mexican Constitution of 1837. This constitution set up a complete system of courts but paid little attention to how prosecution should be carried out. There was a *Tribunal Superior* (supreme court) which was the final court of appeal. The *Fiscal* or attorney general would prosecute all cases before this court. Below the *Tribunal* were courts of second instance and courts of first instance; there is no indication whether or not people were hired to prosecute cases before these courts. At the bottom level were *Alcaldes Courts*. The majority of cases began and ended in these courts. The *Alcalde* was appointed by the governor of the district or, in some cases, elected by the people of the area. He usually wielded the sole legal authority in the area, performing at once the functions of judge, prosecutor, town constable, sheriff, recorder, treasurer, justice of the peace, clerk, and so on. During the trial, the *Alcalde* was both judge and prosecutor.

In 1847, following the war in California between Mexico and the United States, military commanders ruled over California. During this period of time, there was a large migration of gold-seekers to California—men who had little respect for the *Alcaldes* system. In the ensuing chaos, two forms of law enforcement developed. In some areas, the miners elected the local *Alcalde* to office and enforced his decisions. In others, miners' courts (a sort of popular tribunal) were organized to deal with offenders. In neither kind of court were there trained prosecutors. Then came statehood.

The California State Constitution of 1849 provided for a system of courts and for an attorney general but allowed the legislature to create a system of county and town governments. In 1850, the legislature created counties and established the office of county district attorney. This effort to set up new legal machinery again weakened the existing machinery of miners' courts and *Alcaldes*. During the period of transition—partly in response to the weak law enforcement—vigilance committees appeared. The leader of this committee acted as judge, the members as jury, and one of the members as prosecutor. Witnesses were heard. If the defendant was found guilty, the sentence—usually death—was imposed and carried out immediately.

La Loma County was created on March 25, 1853, out of parts of two adjacent counties. San Miguel was chosen as county seat, and the county government began functioning on June 6, 1853. For a number of years after this the county seat moved from place to place, pushed by the whims of the voters. For a time it was Los Robles, then Sherman Township in the South Westville area; then it was shifted to a new location in Westville where it remained until 1936, when it was transferred to its present site in Westville.

Although state law requires that certain offices be established in each county, the counties are allowed discretion to decide whether the office is to be elective or appointive. In La Loma County, the office of district attorney is elective; the public defender is appointed by the board of supervisors. He is thus under the direct control of the board and responsible to it. The district attorney, as an elective officer, is only indirectly subject to the board in matters of administration, budget, and personnel. The deputy public defenders are all under the Civil Service Commission, out of the way of direct political manipulation. The positions in the district attorney's office are unclassified; they do not require examination and are not accorded tenure.

THE PUBLIC DEFENDER

The idea of using a public officer to defend persons charged with crimes goes back as far as sixteenth century Spain. In California, the first public office was created in 1912 in Los Angeles. La Loma County opened its office some fifteen years later. Civil cases are sometimes handled by the public defender, although the development of legal aid societies and the small claims court have curtailed his civil practice in recent years. Mainly, he defends indigent persons accused of crime.

During the first half year of operation, the public defender handled the duties alone. In his report to the board of supervisors for that year he wrote: "While the Charter imposes upon the Public Defender the duties of defending not only felony but misdemeanor and civil cases, it has been necessary for me to decline to handle a number of misdemeanors and civil cases, practically all of my time having been taken up with preliminary examinations and felony cases in the Superior Court." For the fiscal year 1927 through 1928, the public defender had one deputy. At the end of that year, the district attorney of La Loma County wrote

Growth of Activities and Personnel of Public Defender's Office Since Beginning in 1927

Fiscal Year	Court Appearances	Total Cases Handled	Number of Attorneys on Staff
1927–28	883	285	2
29–30	1025	411	3
34–35	2125	632	3
39–40	2208	599	3
44–45	2809	1239	3
49–50	2653	1229	5
54–55	6000 (approx.)	1802	9
59–60	8166	4042	11

Source: Annual Reports of Public Defender.

to him, as follows: "The figures contained therein [in the annual report] confirm my own opinion that you have done splendid work for the County since your appointment under the new Charter. I had no idea, however, that you were handling so many cases, and I hardly see how you can accomplish this amount of work with the limited staff attached to your office."

California as a whole has a dual system of court-appointed attorneys and public defenders. Some thirty-eight counties depend entirely on court-appointed attorneys for defense of impoverished defendants. Twenty counties have an office of public defender and at the same time use court-appointed private attorneys when the public defender for some reason cannot accept a case. In two of the counties having public defenders, the office is elective.

In August, 1963, the La Loma County public defender's office employed thirteen attorneys, five office girls, one part-time office girl, and two investigators. By 1974 the office expanded dramatically to include 81 attorney's and 17 investigators.

THE DISTRICT ATTORNEY

Under the power granted them by the California Constitution of 1849, the 1850 legislature created the various counties and county district attorneys. These district attorneys were to have wide powers, especially in criminal matters. (The legislature also created a county attorney in 1849 who was to have civil powers; the following year the office was dissolved.) An examination of the wording of California laws brings out resemblances to the New York State provisions for district attorneys.

It was not until 1891 that California required that the person occupying the post of district attorney be a member of the bar. Other changes in the office may be noticed across the years. Until the 1920s, the district attorney was primarily an officer of the court. That is, he relied on the sheriff, police, coroner, or grand jury for the evidence to base his prosecution. His job was principally to appear in court. Since that time his role has expanded. He now has an investigative unit attached to his office which can conduct independent inquiries into current cases, although the bulk of the investigation for cases is still handled by municipal police and the sheriff. Also, the bulk of cases are brought through the information route rather than via the grand jury.

The first district attorney of La Loma County was elected in 1853. It is difficult to determine the exact number of persons employed in the district attorney's office or the number of cases handled in any year, between that time and the present. The district attorney does not make an annual report to any other agency, and does not regularly compile formal statistics. Thus, it will be possible only to present material for that office at two points in time.

The earliest report on the district attorney's office the writer was able to uncover is of the California Taxpayers Association in 1933. In that year the office had a staff of forty employees who were deployed in the following way (Chart 1). In 1963, the La Loma district attorney's office employed nearly one hundred people (Chart 2).

CHART 1   *Organization of La Loma District Attorney's Office, 1933*

1 district attorney, 1 assistant district attorney, and an office staff of 10 assigned to general duties.
9 deputy district attorneys assigned to superior court criminal cases.
5 deputy district attorneys and 1 stenographer assigned to police and justice court (3 of these deputy district attorneys in 2 Westville police courts, 1 in Cedarville, and 1 for all the others).

5 deputy district attorneys assigned to civil matters (1 each to board of
  supervisors, sheriff, school districts, city offices, public administrator).
8 investigators to handle criminal cases and a few civil cases.

CHART 2   *Organization of La Loma District Attorney's Office, 1963*

Main Office:
  1. Criminal Branch
     assistant district attorney in charge
     12 deputy district attorneys

  2. Civil Branch
     assistant district attorney in charge
     assistant district attorney dealing with board of supervisors
     assistant district attorney
     10 deputy district attorneys dealing with matters of probate, guardian-
       ship, flood control, condemnation suits, suits against the county, etc.

  3. County Schools Branch
     assistant district attorney in charge
     2 deputy district attorneys, dealing with lawsuits by and against schools,
       acting as counsels in bond and construction matters, etc.

  4. General Duties
     district attorney with private secretary
     10 in stenographic pool
     5 specialized secretaries—law clerk, receptionist, calendar, etc.

  5. Inspectors Branch
     12 inspectors (criminal investigations only)

Branch Offices:
  1. Westville Office
     assistant district attorney in charge of Westville and other branch
       offices
     15 deputy district attorneys
     3 girls in office
  2. Elmville Office
     1 deputy district attorney, part-time
     1 girl (paid by city)
  3. Cedarville Office
     4 deputy district attorneys
     1 full-time girl paid by city
     1 part-time girl paid by county
  4. Pineville Office
     6 deputy district attorneys
     3 girls

There is some specialization of duties among the district attorneys. In the Westville office, one deputy handles all welfare fraud cases. In the civil division, one deputy handles all reciprocal actions, another all guardianship matters, and another probate matters. But considering the large number of attorneys involved, the specialization is limited.

Attached to the district attorney's office is the family support division. This division, headed by a former law enforcement official, investigates cases of nonsupport, decides on the suitability of prosecution as a means of enforcing support, and discovers and prosecutes abuses of welfare aid. The Westville branch employs seven interviewers and six investigators; the Cedarville branch, two interviewers and one investigator; Pineville, three interviewers and one investigator; and Elmville, one investigator. By 1973, the La Loma District Attorney's office had also expanded enormously as Chart 3 indicates.

CHART 3   *Organization of La Loma District Attorney's Office, 1973*

Main Office:
1. Criminal Branch
   assistant district attorney in charge
   22 deputy district attorneys handling felony trials

2. Special Service Division
   assistant district attorney in charge
   12 deputy district attorneys handling grand jury matters, consumer fraud investigations and prosecution, homicide cases, research and training, legislation and other specialized matters

3. General and Administrative
   district attorney and chief assistant
   2 deputy district attorneys handling planning, policy, and procedure
   1 office manager and 20 steno/clerical handling calendars, reception, telephone, and general clerical

4. Inspectors' Division
   Chief of inspectors and 23 inspectors handling criminal investigations

Branch Offices:
1. Westville Office
   assistant district attorney in charge
   22 deputy district attorneys
   11 steno/clerical

2. Elmville Office
   1 deputy district attorney
   1 steno

3. Cedarville Office
   1 assistant district attorney in charge
   5 deputy district attorneys
   3 stenos

4. Pineville Office
   1 assistant district attorney in charge
   10 deputy district attorneys
   5 stenos

5. Ashville Office
   1 assistant district attorney in charge
   5 deputy district attorneys
   2 stenos

6. Oakville Office
   2 deputy district attorneys
   1 steno

7. Family Support Division
   This division headed by an assistant district attorney, investigates cases of nonsupport, decides on the suitability of prosecution as a means of enforcing support, and discovers and prosecutes cases of fraud or abuses of welfare aid.

   The main office of the Family Support Division is located in Westville (separate from the Westville Branch Office). The Westville Family Support Division Office is headed by an assistant district attorney and employs 4 deputy district attorneys, 7 investigators, 8 interviewers, and 19 clerical staff.

   The Cedarville Office employs 3 interviewers; the Pineville Office 1 investigator, 5 interviewers, and 5 steno/clerical; the Elmville Office employs 1 investigator and 1 steno.

Civil cases are no longer handled by the District Attorney's Office. This function is now handled by a separate office of County Counsel.

Appendix D

The Westville Police Questionnaire

DURING the first months of 1964, a questionnaire survey of the policemen in the Westville Police Department was conducted. The department granted time during the preduty briefing so that those working in the patrol and traffic divisions could answer the questions. A special assembly of the detective division was called so that the questionnaire could be administered and seventeen officers answered during their free time.

To encourage honest answers, the questionnaire was jointly sponsored. The official stamp of approval was given by the police chief; the questionnaire was presented to the patrolmen in the official context of their briefing and was discussed by their commanding officer. In order to forestall suspicion that their answers would be used against them in some way, the policemen were promised that their officers would never see the answers except in tabulated form; in addition, the Police Benefit Society announced its "support" of the questionnaire. Nevertheless, there is always reason to believe that police are an unusually "suspicious" group of respondents, a proportion of whom might "cut-up" or falsely answer a survey.

BACKGROUND CHARACTERISTICS

Two hundred and eighty-five policemen answered the questionnaire. At the time of the study there were six hundred and sixteen policemen employed by the department. The chart on page 266 compares the actual number of men at each rank with the number who were given questionnaires to answer. At each rank level, about half of the employed personnel were given questionnaires to answer. These respondents were not randomly selected; they are policemen who were on duty over the several days and shifts during which the questionnaire was administered. No reasons have been uncovered to cause doubt that this sample is representative of Westville policemen.

Seventy-two per cent of those answering had been in the Westville

Police Department for nine years or longer, 48 per cent for longer than fifteen years. Of those remaining, 12 per cent had been members of the department for less than two years, 16 per cent for between three and eight years.

Only 6 per cent had not graduated from high school, while 41 per cent ended their formal education with high school. Forty-five per cent claimed some college training, and 8 per cent had a college degree.

Ninety per cent of the Westville policemen were married. Of those

*Number of Policemen in Department
and in Questionnaire Survey, by Rank*

Rank	Number in Department	Number Surveyed
Chief	1	0
Deputy chief	3	0
Captain	10	7
Lieutenant	26	10
Inspector	45	28
Sergeant	79	38
Patrolmen	452	201
Total	616	284
		(1 of unknown rank)

remaining, 3 per cent were single, the rest separated or divorced. When asked what social class they considered themselves to be in, 66 per cent classified themselves as "middle class"; 32 per cent rated themselves "working class"; and the remaining 2 per cent divided equally between "upper" and "lower" class.

Westville policemen reported that their fathers held a wide variety of occupations. When compared with the labor force distribution of the 1960 census, it appears that policemen's fathers worked as officials, managers, and proprietors, as sales and public service, and as craftsmen, foremen and kindred, more frequently than did the general population. Less commonly than the general population were they engaged in clerical, farm, or cooperative-type jobs.

In religious preference, the proportion of policemen of each faith was nearly identical with the published figures on the American population at large.[1] Catholic was the religious preference of 36 per cent of the policemen, Jewish of 1 per cent, Protestant of 56 per cent, and "none" of 6 per cent. Nearly half (49 per cent) of the policemen reported that

[1] Figures published in *Yearbook of American Churches*, 1960, and reproduced in *Information Please Almanac*, 1963, p. 331.

they seldom or never go to church. Of the rest, 22 per cent attend occasionally, 29 per cent pretty regularly.

Near the end of the questionnaire, the police were asked the following question: "Aside from being an American and a Californian, is there an ethnic or nationality background you identify with or regard yourself as? If so please state—e.g., English, German, Italian, Irish, Jewish, Negro, or none." Thirty policemen did not answer. The largest part of the rest gave the answer that many multiple ethnic-stock Americans would give: "none" (42 per cent). The following list ranks the other replies: Irish (15 per cent), German (10 per cent), English (7 per cent), Italian (5 per cent), Negro (4 per cent), Portuguese (3 per cent), other miscellaneous answers (14 per cent).

JOB PREFERENCES AND DISLIKES

Several open-ended questions asked the policemen which tasks they considered least and most enjoyable. When asked which assignment they would choose if they had free choice, the largest group in each police division, except patrol, chose their present assignment. Patrolmen equally divided their preferences between patrol and detective work. Particularly strong preferences for their present assignment were registered by the detectives (63 per cent) and by the vice squad (75 per cent). Strangely enough, not only did most policemen prefer their present assignment—most (about 50 per cent) believed that their present assignments were the most difficult in the police department. The sole exception was the traffic division, whose members named patrol as the most difficult assignment; the other divisions rated patrol as the second most difficult assignment.

When asked what they considered to be the two most serious police problems, each division gave an answer which reflects to some extent the principal problems which it faced. The traffic and patrol divisions most often mentioned the relations of the police with the general public, i.e., the public's lack of respect for the police, lack of cooperation in the enforcement of the law, etc. The detectives considered racial problems and demonstrations the most serious problem. The chief problems identified by the vice squad were lack of cooperation in enforcing the law from the agents of the legal system—the district attorney, legislature, and, particularly, the courts.

ATTITUDES TOWARD POLICE WORK

Some of the most interesting variations in the survey were uncovered by the question, "All things considered, how do you like police work as an occupation?" Sixty-one per cent of Westville policemen liked police work "very much" as an occupation, 31 per cent liked it fairly well, 5 per cent were indifferent, and 4 per cent disliked it. Enjoyment of police work rises with education; as in other studies, liking police work and having close friends who are policemen went together. Likewise, the better one's wife knew the wives of other policemen, the more liking was expressed for police work. Those who had just become policemen expressed the strongest liking for police work (83 per cent like it very much). Aspiring policemen liked their work more than the nonaspiring. Slightly more than half (58 per cent) of the men said they aspired to a higher rank than the one they then held (80 per cent of the captains aspired to higher rank, 100 per cent of the lieutenants, 12 per cent of the detectives, 83 per cent of the sergeants, and 56 per cent of the patrolmen). Of those who aspired, 69 per cent liked police work very much; among nonaspiring men, 53 per cent liked police work very much.

Liking police work was also related to beliefs about police prestige. Thirty-eight per cent of those who liked police work very much rated the prestige it received from others as excellent or good; among those who were indifferent to or disliked police work only 4 per cent rated its prestige as excellent or good; while on the topic of prestige, nonaspiring policemen more often rated police prestige as poor than did aspiring policemen.

POLICE BELIEFS

As a measure of their attachment to a traditional value of the society, the policemen were asked how important they thought it was that a man own his own home.[2] Fifty-two per cent thought it very important, 32 per cent fairly important, 11 per cent thought it was fairly unimportant, and 5 per cent very unimportant. College graduates in general thought home ownership less important than the rest. Importance of ownership increased with the liking for police work and also with the time on the force. (Of those on the force for five years or less, 46 per cent rated it very important; 69 per cent of those on twenty-one years or longer rated it very important. The latter relation may well be a generational difference.)

The importance attributed to home ownership was also related to several other social characteristics. Those policemen with blue-collar fathers

[2] Originally I had intended to ask more detailed questions about beliefs on political and social issues. These were vetoed by the police officials, who felt it would not be appropriate to ask such questions in a questionnaire with official backing.

rate home-owning very important more often than those with white-collar fathers (57 per cent to 43 per cent). The more regularly the policeman reported attending church, the more value he placed on home ownership. In addition, the rough order of social class among churches which has been established in other studies appears here. The lower the social class of the church attended by the policeman, the higher did he value home ownership.

In the political realm, policemen were asked how interested they were in national politics. Twenty-six per cent indicated extreme interest; 46 per cent said they were quite interested; 24 per cent moderately interested; and 4 per cent were not much interested. This interest in national politics increases with education, with liking for police work, and with the number of best friends who are policemen.

POLICE CHARACTER TRAITS

At the very end of the questionnaire were three questions which sought to identify those character traits which policemen most admired. Each policeman was asked to place eight qualities in the order (1) which best described him now, (2) which will best describe him in ten years, and (3) which best describe what he would like to be. Because these questions came last in the questionnaire and because they are difficult to answer, about 30 per cent of the respondents failed to answer all or part of them. Among those who did answer, there is agreement among the three questions. That is, the three top qualities chosen to describe oneself now are also chosen to describe oneself in ten years and to describe how one would like to be. Also, the qualities which were least preferred (ratings 7 and 8) were consistently least preferred under the three situations (with one exception). The strongest first choice for all three conditions was "Good health and relative freedom from worry" (41 per cent to 62 per cent). The strongest second choice was "Congeniality and the ability to make friends" (34 per cent to 37 per cent). The strongest third choice was "The ability to exercise leadership in the making of important decisions" (22 per cent to 26 per cent). On the fourth, fifth, and sixth choices there was no single strong preference. The seventh choice under all conditions was "Social prestige" (24 per cent to 47 per cent). The strongest choice for eighth place was "Financially well-to-do" (50 per cent to 62 per cent), except when the person was describing himself as he would like to be. The eighth place choice of this desired self was "Social prestige" (41 per cent).

The three character traits which fell in the middle were:

"Usually achieve a high level of skill in every serious undertaking (on the job and elsewhere)"

"A widely informed person"

"A keen sense of social and moral responsibility"

When these rank order selections are cross-tabulated with the social background, participation, and attitude variables mentioned earlier, their order remains the same. For example, the predominant first choice of everyone is "Good health and relative freedom from worry"; those who are more active in police social activities *more* often make that their first choice, but it is still the predominant first choice even of those who are inactive. Thus, it seems fair to say that this ordering of character traits does in fact represent some of the values of Westville police.

CONCLUSION

In attempting to understand police conduct, however, these variations seem relatively unimportant. There are individual differences, and certain tendencies associated with social characteristics of policemen, but behavior is explained much more by the nature of the work of the policeman. If a man holds rank, his work necessarily differs from that of the ordinary patrolman. At the same time, a lieutenant in the vice squad, and a lieutenant in the traffic division will be doing very different things on the job. The most critical variable, therefore, for understanding *law enforcement* is the nature of the policeman's work assignment.

Index